The Question of Europe

The Question of Europe

Edited by
Peter Gowan
and
Perry Anderson

VERSO
London · New York

The Editors and the Publishers gratefully acknowledge
Svetlana Alpers and Michael Baxandall for the use of the cover picture.

First published by Verso 1997
© in the collection Verso 1997
© in individual contributions the contributors 1997
All rights reserved

Reprinted 1997

The right of Peter Gowan and Perry Anderson to be identified as the editors of this work
has been asserted by them in accordance with
the Copyright, Designs and Patents Act 1988

Verso
UK: 6 Meard Street, London W1V 3HR
USA: 180 Varick Street, New York NY 10014-4606

Verso is the imprint of New Left Books

ISBN 1–85984–836–2
ISBN 1–85984–142–2 (pbk)

British Library Cataloguing in Publication Data
A catalogue record for this book is available from the British Library

Library of Congress Cataloging-in-Publication Data
A catalog record for this book is available from the Library of Congress

Typeset by CentraCet Ltd, Cambridge
Printed by Biddles Ltd, Guildford and King's Lynn

Contents

v

Preface

Four decades after the signature of the Treaty of Rome, there is now a vast literature on the European Community. But it cannot be said that its workings are widely understood within any of its member states. The reasons for this are not hard to seek. If the Community remains so opaque to its citizens, this is no doubt because it fuses two forms of complexity, each disconcerting enough in itself. On the one hand, its institutions notoriously give the impression of an impenetrable labyrinth of shifting, formal and informal, networks of decision. On the other, whatever patterns can be traced in this maze appear generically incongruous with the concepts we normally employ to make sense of government, at national or international level. If the first problem brings to mind Palmerston's *boutade* about the issue of Schleswig-Holstein – which only three people understood: one was dead, the other mad and the third had forgotten – the second often suggests Polonius trying to make sense of the shape of his cloud.

At the same time, the objective difficulties in capturing the nature of the Community have been typically compounded by much of the writing about it. In its day-to-day working, the European Union is essentially a body of functionaries working within rules negotiated between governments. The literature on the Community, for the most part focusing on either its institutional mechanisms, or the accommodations between states behind them, reflects the dominance of these two realities. The natural idioms of bureaucracy and diplomacy are technicality and euphemism, and their imprint is all too visible in the blandness or obscurity of the larger part of specialist commentary on the EU.

The design of this volume is intended to break with the standard conventions on the subject. The essays in it are written from sharply

ix

committed, but widely differing political standpoints. Contributors
extend from the Right to the Centre to the Left (where we are situated
ourselves, without necessarily agreeing with each other). The one trait
they have in common is to give short shrift to *bien-pensant* discourse
about the Community, of any kind. They have been selected for clarity
and vigour of argument, and sharpness of polemical contrast. In this
sense, the book can be read as a series of inter-connected debates about
the nature and future of European unity.

A second departure from current norms may seem more paradoxical.
It would be logical to think that of all subjects European integration
would most naturally transcend national barriers to the exchange of
ideas and argument. Little, however, could be further from the case.
The overwhelming bulk of writing about Europe remains sub-European
in context and consequence – that is, untranslated and unfamiliar
beyond its country of origin. This is true even of the most central works
in the field. It is enough to note that what is by any standards the
leading study of the origins of the Common Market – Alan Milward's
Rescue of the European Nation-State – is still, five years after its appearance
in English, unavailable in any other European language; other examples
could be multiplied.

It might even be argued that there has been a certain regression
since the prewar period when, at least in the world of ideas, there was
easier interchange of views about Europe between – say – Ortega, Eliot,
Benda or Curtius than exists for any successors today. The collection
below seeks to overcome some of our ironic current provincialism by
bringing together contributors from at least the four largest countries
of the Community, Britain, France, Germany and Italy, and two of its
smaller ones, Ireland and Sweden. Obviously, this still leaves significant
gaps. Among others, there are no Iberian or Benelux voices, and
Anglophone signatures predominate. But this is still a wider constellation than has been customary for some time.

Finally, the variety of viewpoints represented is not only political or
national, but also intellectual. Contributors are drawn from a full
spectrum of disciplines, which include history, economics, philosophy,
law, political science and sociology. The result is discussion of a broader
range of topics than standard treatments allow. The institutional and
diplomatic machinery of the European Union remains central to any
realistic consideration of it, and is given its due salience at the outset of
the volume. No less important, however, are the economic dynamics of
the project of monetary union – the commanding enterprise of the
1990s. The juridical logic of an 'ever closer union', pledged by the
Treaty of Rome, has by contrast generally received little attention. Here,
however, the arguments for and against a European constitution are

taken as crucial to the future of the Union. These in turn presuppose specific conceptions of civic identity, whose definition poses questions of cultural meaning that are explored in their own right. The collection then ends with reflections on the place of Europe in the world at large, at the close of the millennium.

Such are the principal themes of the book. Its organization is loosely temporal. It begins with the origins of European integration after the war and its subsequent course of development, about which there is an increasingly lively debate among historians. This has been stimulated above all by the pioneering work of Alan Milward, whose central claim is that, far from representing an erosion of the authority of the nation-state in Western Europe, the process of economic integration tended on the contrary to restore it, by furnishing a new basis for popular allegiance to government in the material security it helped bring about. So it is appropriate that the book opens with Milward's critique of earlier 'functionalist' views of European unity, and calls for a more complex programme of research into the sources of democratic support for integration – in effect, a theoretical manifesto.

Engaging with Milward's general position, William Wallace then suggests that while the West European nation-state may indeed have been 'rescued' by the Community in the 1950s and 1960s, nevertheless since then it has been forced into relative 'retreat' by the growth of a dense web of economic and cultural interpenetration across frontiers over which it has lost control – without, however, Brussels gaining any compensatory powers over it. Perry Anderson offers another view of Milward's case. His essay queries its stress on the role of democratic electorates in the build-up of integration, arguing that the strategic calculus of diplomatic establishments in Paris and Bonn, and the remarkable route-march towards federalist goals taken by Monnet and his circle – with dextrous use of support in Washington – counted for more in the final outcome: one that came to disconcert founders and successors alike, in different ways that continue today.

The second part of the book considers the political and economic landscape of the European Union after Maastricht. Conor Cruise O'Brien presents a scathing view of federalist dreams from a classically realist standpoint, that sees the Community as an arena for national political rivalries in which French illusions of hegemony lie shattered by the rise of a swaggering greater Germany, already flexing its muscles in Eastern Europe. John Keegan, less inclined than Milward to treat economic development as a welfare-generating sphere distinct from power-political competition, recalls the spectre of European unity under German leadership at the start of the 1940s – interpreting monetary union as a renewed framework for consolidating German dominance

over the continent, as the economic means to all political ends. In a
reversal of perspectives, Peter Gowan then asks what are the underlying
sources of British Euro-scepticism about Europe, and concludes that
they lie less in the direction taken by the Community over the past
decade – more congenial to Anglo-Conservatism than meets the eye –
than in the domestic insecurities of UK politics.

At the opposite pole to British fears, German hopes for closer
European integration find bold expressions in the document written by
Karl Lamers for the CDU/CSU Bundestag group – a paper that casts
aside diplomatic niceties to advocate the pursuit of federal union by a
Franco-German 'hard core', setting the pace for the rest of the Community, and steering enlargement to meet Germany's security concerns
in the East. The candour of these proposals caused some cultural shock
when they were first published. No one, however, is better placed to
mediate characteristic British and German preoccupations than
Timothy Garton Ash, who writes with informed sympathy for opinion in
both countries. His central theme is the dangers of the project of a
single currency, the fruit of an essentially Franco-German understanding, for European unity in a wider sense. For Garton Ash, the drive to
monetary union in the West risks fatal postponement of the entry of
East European countries into the Community, a task of incomparably
greater significance as the turn of the millennium approaches. In a
synoptic register, Perry Anderson then sets the three leading problems
facing the European Union in the 1990s – the design for monetary
union, the rise of Germany, and competition for entry from the East –
in a common focus, arguing that each contains a radical indeterminacy
that threatens the stability of all existing arrangements.

The next section, on the economics of monetary union, opens with a
second contribution by Alan Milward. Responding in part to Anderson's
review of his work, Milward moves his analytic framework up to
Maastricht, with some striking hypotheses about the social bases for the
deflationary logic of the Treaty – to be found in the decline of industrial
employment and the growth of wide electoral strata living on fixed
incomes, for whom sound money has become more important than job
creation. His essay is followed by a text in a very different key. Tommaso
Padoa-Schioppa, *esprit fort* among central bankers, was the Italian mind
behind the Delors Report that set in motion the drive to European
monetary union. Here he explains how his pioneering ideas on a single
currency evolved, and how the formidable task of designing a practical
transition to monetary union, in which he played a central part, was
unexpectedly achieved. However, no technical *tour de force*, Padoa-
Schioppa stresses, can in the long run substitute for the democratic
political form that true European unity requires. Meanwhile, he notes,

Italy itself remains an anomaly in the run-up to a single currency, the profile of its public finances threatening to compromise the historical balance of the project.

Four assessments of Maastricht and its aftermath follow. Wynne Godley points out the perils of denying member states traditional tools of macroeconomic management without creating any new instruments at a supranational level – warnings now echoed across the political spectrum, and already a source of tension between Paris and Bonn. Sam Aaronovitch and John Grahl discuss ways in which the transition to a single currency might be de-linked from deflationary pressures within member states, and the projected European Central Bank play a more constructive role in supervising growth than generally envisaged. Guy Standing spotlights the deepening social failure of the West European economies to generate employment, and argues that the conventional remedies – tacitly enshrined at Maastricht – of more flexible labour markets can only increase inequality and insecurity: evils for which much more radical solutions, moving towards reconsideration of work and guaranteed minimum incomes, will have to be considered. Finally, from the United States, Edward Luttwak unleashes a blistering attack on the doctrinal rigidity of central banks as tantamount to a new kind of religious superstition, whose epitome – he argues – can be seen in the tablets for 'convergence' handed down from Maastricht, with devastating results for economic growth and social peace alike.

The final part of the book looks at the future both of the Union and of Europe at large. It opens with the fundamental question of the kind of public law under which European citizens will live. The national culture in which this issue has been most deeply debated is – not by accident, in view of a long intellectual tradition – that of Germany. The setting for the exchange published below was the judgment of the German Constitutional Court on the validity of the Treaty of Maastricht. Little noticed in Britain, its decision was not only of immediate consequence for the Treaty itself – which the Court's decision in effect unilaterally amended (it is perhaps indicative of the position of Germany in the Community that no other signatory challenged it, or arrogated the same right to itself) – but has potentially far-reaching implications beyond it. Dieter Grimm, Professor of Public Law at the University of Bielefeld and Justice on the Court, was one of the authors of the decision. Here he explains why, in his view, there can be no democratic constitution for Europe, since a democracy requires a culturally homogeneous population to sustain it, and no such European people – as opposed to the distinct nations of the continent – exists.

In a reply to Grimm, Jürgen Habermas rejects this conclusion, contending that although a common European identity may not exist

today, a European constitution would precisely help to foster one, based
not on traditional cultural bonds but on shared political principles. His
text is followed by a forthright polemic from Joseph Weiler on the
reasoning of the Maastricht decision itself, which, surface citations to
the contrary, he contends, descends essentially from the most suspect
source in prewar German jurisprudence, the doctrines of Carl Schmitt.
In place of ethnic ties, Weiler offers an alternative theory of the
relationship between national identity and democratic community
which he holds to be more in keeping with the multicultural realities of
every European country today.

Questions of identity become a central focus in the next two
contributions. Writing from the horizon of a cast-off fragment of Europe
at the other end of the world, his native New Zealand, J. G. A. Pocock
weaves a richly quizzical set of reflections on current self-definition in
the Old World, as the empires of the past – in every sense – threaten to
dissolve into postmodern flatlands swept only by the surf of market
forces. For Anthony Smith, by contrast, national identities persist
robustly within Europe, and are likely to neutralize all attempts to
construct a – necessarily in large part artificial – European identity
above them, one inevitably lacking the affective bonds of myth and
memory that alone cement a strong sense of collective belonging.

The book concludes with two essays scanning possible trajectories for
Europe into the next century. Jacques Attali, special adviser at the Elysée
under François Mitterrand, and first chief of the European Bank of
Reconstruction and Development, speculates on four possible futures
for the continent: a cohesive federal Union founded on the single
currency; a looser free-trade area stretching to the borders of Russia; a
Euro-Atlantic community under American leadership; and a partnership
between a zone including Russia in the East and a federated group in
the West. Though he regards both monetary union and enlargement to
the East as desirable, Attali doubts whether they are compatible, and
more generally whether European élites have the will to build a
structure genuinely independent of the United States – leaving the third
scenario as perhaps the most likely.

If Attali's optic is characteristically French in its concern with classic
relations of power between blocs, Göran Therborn writes as a Swedish
sociologist on the socio-economic and cultural trajectories that look
most probable for Europe in the next century. In a trenchant survey
that sets the continent firmly in its place within the wider world, he is
sceptical that it will ever again count for much as a politico-military
force, but suggests that – if all went well – it might offer a social model
to others rather like that of Scandinavia within Europe itself: a margin
of relative welfare and equity, a modest source of inspiration rather

than a bearer of power. That, of course, he concludes, is only one possibility: the social and territorial divisions of Europe, many now worsening, could yield much worse outcomes. On this note of cautious realism the collection ends.

Our thanks to Sebastian Budgen for indispensable help in preparing this volume.

February 1997

PAST

History

1

The Springs of Integration

Alan S. Milward

What has come to be called the 'integration of Europe' is a notion whose origins were unpropitious, the offspring of American disillusionment with the dangerous political disunity of the European continent and naive progressivist optimism. But it has become established in historical, economic and political discussion as summing up all those trends – in whatever sphere of activity, business, law, culture, politics, ideology, or the more everyday life of Europeans – which are widely, although by no means universally, thought to have brought European nations into a much closer unity. Since the obvious political expression of these trends is the evolution since 1952 of the successive European Communities into the European Union, the history of that evolution has usually been called the history of European integration. The subject thus has its own unity and has become an area of historical discussion and analysis in its own right.

As so often happens in historical research, this separate historiography of integration was forced into independent existence partly by the conservatism of the historical profession. Early historical research in this area was, for example, typically published in journals whose primary concern was with political science, international relations, or sometimes applied economics. One distinguishing trait of the historiography of European integration has been its close links to political and economic theory, simply because political scientists and economists offered theoretical explanations of the process of European integration before detailed historical research became possible. It followed that much research was centrally concerned with testing the validity of these theoretical propositions.

There is not much left intact of the complex rival theoretical positions

5

on the subject of the political science of the 1960s. Under the weight of historical events since then, and under factual bombardment by historians, political science has retreated to a more pragmatic and less teleological ground. Indeed, for many political scientists the process of European integration is now seen much more as one directed by the greater powers in their own interests – as many diplomatic historians would always have liked to see it – and not as a new and inevitable trend.[1] There is even less left of the economic theories of the same period that linked market expansion in the form of trade liberalization to economic growth as a permanent characteristic of the modern state. The interest is now far more in explaining the continuation of mercantilism and the 'new' protectionism.[2] Having demonstrated in its adolescence that the ideas of its parents were inapplicable to the modern world, the history of European integration is now faced in adult life with the task of replacing them with something better. As it sets about this task, what themes could it pursue?

Functionalism and neo-functionalism have all retreated to the periphery of the territory of political science. In economics the so-called 'new growth theory' puts more weight on the microeconomics of market adjustment and trade regulation than on the assertion that market expansion improves productivity rates and incomes and that European integration was a classic example of this process. The serious historical issues of how far the common market of the European Economic Community did contribute to higher growth rates of national income for its member states than, for example, in the United Kingdom before 1973, and how far the relatively faster growth rate of the United Kingdom than the original member states after that date was due to entry into that common market, are only now beginning to be tackled by historians. Their answers will surely be much more complicated than the simplistic assumptions of early growth theory.[3]

For many political scientists the process of European integration is now seen, rather as traditional historians of diplomacy tend to see it, as a process directed by the interplay of the foreign policy of great and medium-sized powers in search of the traditional objectives of influence and security. There is a solid core of historiography of the period in which long-run cultural, economic and social trends do not appear, presumably because they are not thought to explain much. Casting aside its former theoretical dependence on these long-run trends, political science seems increasingly to accept that any theoretical explanation of European integration should start from and perhaps be confined to those areas of state activity which used to be called 'die grosse Politik'.

The timing by which government archives are opened for inspection

– almost nowhere can they be inspected less than thirty years after the event – has enhanced this trend. The biggest contribution of historical research to European integration in the early 1990s has been made by a cluster of publications dealing with the United Kingdom's first attempt to join the European Economic Community and its failure in 1963.[4] Without exception these publications have depicted the United Kingdom's application and its prehistory of negotiation as the attempt of a declining, but still important, middle-ranking power to retain its worldwide influence by shifting away from its weakening association with the Commonwealth to closer links with Europe. The motivation in this case for European integration has been invariably depicted as an adjustment of the United Kingdom's world strategic position. Similarly, General de Gaulle's veto on the British entry has been portrayed as solely a strategic decision. The major event which currently preoccupies historians in their pursuit of a history of European integration has in fact been analysed as though it were solely a matter of alliances and nuclear weapons.[5] Interestingly enough, the official inquiry into the failure of the negotiations undertaken by the British government immediately came to a similar conclusion. No matter what economic or institutional concessions the United Kingdom might have made in the negotiations, it argued, the General would have still forbidden British entry on strategic and foreign policy grounds.

There can be no doubt that Prime Minister Harold Macmillan did seek entry into the EEC for foreign policy purposes, to preserve what he could of the United Kingdom's world interests. Most of the conversations between de Gaulle and Macmillan, the sources which have been most used in recent publications, are about foreign policy and the long-term position of their countries.[6] But to draw the sweeping inference from this that for de Gaulle the EEC existed primarily for foreign policy and defence reasons seems unwise and premature. The complexity of the motives which led France to sign the Treaty of Rome has recently been elaborated. Although the essential reason for accepting the Treaty was indeed to secure France's place in the world, this was also defined as securing France's place in the international economic framework. The Treaty defended France against the arrival of an international economic regime whose only regulatory agencies were GATT (General Agreement on Tariffs and Trade) and the IMF (International Monetary Fund), and incorporated the restructured French empire into the commercial framework and supranationally regulatory regime within Western Europe. The Quai d'Orsay was not on balance in favour of the Treaty.[7]

The arrival in power of de Gaulle could hardly have cancelled the conclusions of the long and anxious debate in Paris which finally led to the decision to sign in spite of the misgivings and reluctance of the Ministry of Foreign Affairs. Indeed the failure of his early attempt to modify the system of agricultural income support in France suggests that de Gaulle, for all his great powers, was bound by the same long-run political and economic circumstances which led the Fourth Republic to the EEC. De Gaulle's opposition to British entry was only clearly communicated to the British government through the British ambassador in Paris on 22 May 1962, and even then the opposition was not absolute and the negotiations in Brussels were allowed to continue despite the general's pessimism about their success. The harsh conclusions of the official British inquiry, that de Gaulle never wanted Britain in the EEC and that his opposition was decisive, can certainly not be accepted until the French archives have been properly examined.

But there may well have been further limitations to the powers of de Gaulle and Macmillan which the narrow concentration of recent publications on their diplomacy fails to take into account. Suppose de Gaulle had not been opposed to British entry and on strategic grounds had preferred British membership. Could France, could even all the other member states, have accepted the large and numerous exemptions from the economic and social clauses of the Treaty of Rome which the United Kingdom was still demanding when the negotiations were broken off? This was not put to the test. Little is known accurately about the paths of decision-making in the first years of the Gaullist regime. We cannot be certain that de Gaulle's veto was uninfluenced by economic and social considerations. We do not know that it was he alone, as much of the comment implies, who took the decision. We can see from the British record that the French economic bureaucracy was divided, and some strongly opposed to British membership. Moreover, within the British government Macmillan had few unequivocal supporters in his pursuit of membership, and equivocation was, it seems, often based on economic, social and cultural grounds, or even on prejudice.

There seems therefore little reason why a preliminary history of the British application, based so far almost entirely on Foreign Office and Cabinet papers, should be allowed to encourage the retreat of political science to mere pragmatism and the growing assumption that the EEC was simply an alliance system – a form of interdependence and not a second stage of supranational integration. Were it so, no theory of integration would be needed, because the assumption would then follow that the Treaty of Rome was a rejection of the ideas implicit in the Treaty of Paris. To come to such a conclusion, which would also be to ignore the conclusions of research from other sources than Foreign Ministry papers, would perhaps best expose the danger of pursuing the history of diplomacy as though it had nothing to do with the history of economy and society. It would be wiser to consider the recent spate of publications on the first British application as interesting preliminary comments, from a strictly British perspective, based on a very narrow selection of evidence and paying only scant attention to the history of the Communities themselves.[8]

In reality, many of the underlying assumptions in earlier comprehensive theories of integration remain untested by historians. This is particularly the case with assumptions made about long-run social and economic developments. The underlying assumption of Karl Deutsch's 'community' theory, for example, that within Western Europe and the North Atlantic area there was a sudden upward leap in the frequency of contacts between élites, has not been studied in any systematic way. Neither have the many assertions of theorists of the international economy that increasing international trade in goods and capital has combined with changes in technology to make controls on national frontiers, and thus the demarcation of the nation-state's boundaries, meaningless, together with the concept of 'national income' which governments in the 1950s used as a basic tool of government. There are only observations about these ideas, no chronologically or technologically specific history which could confirm, refute or modify them or make them operable for detailed historical analysis. These are not the only examples. If historical research into the history of European integration is now to have its own proper agenda, including its own theoretical hypotheses, it should certainly not reject the assumptions of earlier integration theory, except where they have been disproved. The working hypotheses of historians in the present state of ignorance have to be heuristic. They must encourage and facilitate as wide a field of inquiry as possible.

At the moment there seem to exist four different, but overlapping, ideas about the fundamental causes of the process of European integration. One is the idea, which the recent literature on the British application seems to support, that it responded to the traditional objectives of the foreign policy of states, a sort of alliance system adjusted to the realities of the world after 1945. Another is the idea that it originated in the modification, perhaps even the rejection, of the traditional objectives of the foreign policies of states. This idea emphasizes the altruism of integration and reposes on the belief that its profoundest cause is the will to unify Europe, or parts of it. Integration springs from a deeply held desire to change, for ever, the nation-state structure of the continent.[9] A third idea is that the process of integration was deliberately conceived and developed to preserve the nation-state by supporting a range of new social and economic policies whose very purpose was the resurrection of the nation-state after its collapse

between 1929 and 1945.[10] A fourth idea is that the loss of sovereignty of
the European nation-state is inevitable because of the long-run path of
economic and social development.[11] The state, this idea emphasizes, has
lost all control of its own destinies because of the permeability of its
frontiers. Its domestic policies can differ from those of other states only
in such insignificant ways as to make resistance to integration pointless
and costly. Proponents of these four ideas write about different things.
The first attracts historians who write about diplomacy and defence.
The second attracts those who write about ideas and people and search
for hidden motivations behind the public record. The third attracts
those who write about the state, its policies, economic growth, the
interactions between policy and markets, and the links between democracy and social change. The last attracts historians of the international
economic system and its long-run evolution.

The problem in the present stage of research is how to construct a
hypothesis about integration which has the same heuristic usefulness as
each of these separate lines of inquiry, but which brings them together.
At the least, historians working in these different fields should be
brought to confront each other; at the best, such a confrontation might
lead them to adopt each other's techniques and instead of working in
an isolated intellectual tradition reach a new synthesis.

European integration, if we define it as the voluntary surrender of
some elements of state sovereignty, may not be new, in principle. There
are plausible examples from medieval history. But in modern history,
on the scale in which it has occurred since 1945, it is a new phenomenon. It is, however, a phenomenon whose only new institutional
characteristics are the supranational institutions of the successive European Communities and the European Union. With every respect for the
aspirations of those who support these institutions, they have not been
the locus of power and decision-making. Everything else than those
institutions must have a historical continuity; people and their ideas, the
states themselves, which were in most cases much more assertive and
securely founded than in the interwar period, and the gradual long-run
developments in the European economy and the societies of which it
was composed. The backward linkages of historical continuity must
therefore be built into any hypothesis.

Where such backward linkages appear in the present historiography
they are as separated as the ideas on present trends. Those who see
integration primarily as the outcome of the traditional foreign policy
objectives of states see the historical continuities in that recently
fashionable subject 'the rise and fall of nations'.[12] The United Kingdom,
France and Germany all 'fell' and with them Europe, excluding Russia
and the Soviet Union which, like the USA, 'rose'. The European

Communities were then an attempt to protect Europe from the worst effects of its fall – on the whole a predictable foreign policy response to the relentless flow of historical change.[13] From this idea comes the interest in discovering a prehistory of post-1945 integration in the interwar period, in the way in which it may have been foreshadowed by French diplomacy in the post-1918 settlement or in the Briand proposals, for example.[14] Those who see integration as an act of human will, similarly seek its intellectual prehistory in the interwar period, particularly in European federalist thinking and in the small number of marginal political figures, such as Coudenhove-Kalergi, who propagandized the idea of a European 'unity'.[15] The assumption seems to be that there were intellectual links to the founding fathers of the European Community, although if there were they are proving remarkably hard to discover. Those who interpret integration as the refoundation of the nation-state see a historical continuity from the institution of universal suffrage after the First World War, the growth of mass democratic political parties and their growing domination of both parliaments and executive government, and the interwar experiments with welfare and employment policies.[16] The Weimar Republic peeps shyly from their work as an infant prototype of the ambitious post-1945 state.

For those, lastly, who see integration as a culmination of irreversible long-run economic trends, the continuities are more broken. The permeability of European national frontiers to the movement of goods, capital and people was on all measurements greater between 1870 and 1914 than in the interwar period and especially greater than in the 1930s. It is thus the interwar period with its temporary reversal of these inexorable economic trends which is the historical puzzle. European integration becomes the predictable political response to the development of a universal international capitalist economy, a universal path of technological development, and the inevitable fact that the proportion of 'national' income earned outside the frontier will grow as a universal pattern of development requires national economies to choose between being open or being poor. It is the next step after the gold standard, and taken the more readily after 1945 because interwar experiments with steps in the opposite direction proved so calamitous.[17]

One concept which may link these allegedly separate continuities together in a single hypothesis, from which an eventual model of integration might be constructed, is that of allegiance. By allegiance is meant the range of all those elements which induce citizens to give their loyalty to institutions of governance, whether national, international or supranational. It excludes repression. While accepting that repression has never been absent as an element of governance of Western European democracies, and even allowing for the possibility

that it may have increased in the last twenty years, few would doubt the
validity of the generalization that in all the member states of the
successive European Communities government has been in its essentials
rule by consent. The transition to a greater measure of government by
consent seems indeed to have been a fundamental requirement for
Greek, Portuguese and Spanish membership. For Western Europe
outside the Iberian peninsula parliamentary democracy, in which political parties have been the main conduits between public opinion and
government policy, has been the norm. The growing influence of the
media does not weaken this statement, for those who react to that
influence have almost invariably done so in respect of their function
within a political party. Why has this system retained the allegiance of
national populations – 'citizens' might be the appropriate term if
democractic continuities were to be traced back to the French Revolution – while at the same time a measurable secondary allegiance to the
supranational institutions of the European Union has also grown?[18]

Establishing and retaining allegiance was not a task accomplished
with any great success by nineteenth-century European states. About 34
million people voluntarily and permanently left European states
between 1815 and 1914, for a life elsewhere. Perhaps 20 million of these
took citizenship of the United States of America. By contrast, only a very
small proportion of emigrants to Argentina and Brazil had taken
citizenship of those countries before 1914. Even if, as seems to be the
case, the preference for a more democratic and participatory form of
governance was the main factor in the choice of departure for only a
very small proportion of the emigrants, allegiance to European nation-
states was not high. This was not true only of states like Romania or
Russia, where much of the population had little to hope for in their
lifetime, politically or economically. It applied notably to Norway, which
by 1914 could have laid reasonable claim to being the most democratic
of the European states, at least in terms of its suffrage, and to the United
Kingdom, which was indubitably the richest and most powerful of them.
Norway had the highest proportion of its population leaving the country
permanently of all European countries. The United Kingdom provided
the largest absolute number of emigrants from Europe, and not only
because of emigration from Ireland. The failure of many emigrants to
take up the formal citizenship of a non-European country suggests that
allegiance was not especially valued, but regarded by large numbers as
something to avoid in all but the most formal sense. This impression is
greatly strengthened when it is remembered that the number of
emigrants moving within Europe was much greater over the same
period than 34 million.

A large body of historical work has concerned itself with the question of how nineteenth-century European states used a mixture of policy, political symbolism and institutions such as primary education and a conscript army to instil the concept of allegiance to a central national state into their 'subjects'. Although the general pertinence of this sort of work to post-1945 European societies is evident, its specific methodological value as an explanatory historical tool in the postwar period is very limited, because of the marked change in the nature of democratic party politics, and its relationship – of a type, scope and scale utterly different from earlier periods – to newspapers, radio and television. Its relevance is, however, diminished above all by the much greater complexity of the mutual demands made on each other by governments and voters in post-1945 democracies. Some elements of this analysis of nineteenth-century practice are still valuable, of course. Until the last ten years the publicly owned media and the measure of public control over private media meant that government still carried on the national educational role of the nineteenth-century state. But the choice of models and images of education for the nation grew so rapidly after 1950 that to study the role of single institutions over the long term in shaping national allegiance – as historians of the nineteenth century have done – would be methodologically unrewarding.

It is a reasonable assumption that allegiance still remains partly determined by the ability of national institutions to protect the citizen, whether from internal or external threats. But all post-1945 historical study shows that what the citizen has demanded as 'security' from the state has widened in range and complexity to the point where protection in the sense of physical safety has rarely been that definition of security which had the highest priority at critical moments of political choice. In short, allegiance since 1945 has been given, sold or bought within a complex pattern of relationships between individuals, families and government which would require a wholly different analysis from that used for earlier periods. The fundamental questions for the history of European integration are why allegiance to the Communities grew, and whether the present allegiance to the institutions of the European Union is permanently subsidiary to, and dependent on, or will eventually replace, that tendered to national or regional government.

A pragmatic analysis of that question should probably first concentrate on those issues which have been shown mainly to influence voters' choices in general and European elections in all member states. Except in moments of perceived danger, or when issues relating to one dominant personality have emerged, personal and family income and the perspective of future income through the life-cycle have been the major determinants of voting. This may mean that they are also major determinants of allegiance. Since 1945 it has been increasingly difficult

to separate them from personal security, because it is long-run expectations of security of income and employment through the life-cycle which
have also determined voting patterns.

It would, though, be absurdly mechanistic to suppose that the
disposition of allegiance between the different forms of governance on
offer has been – or will be – determined by accurate materialistic
calculations or even solely by materialistic perspectives. It is obvious that
in some member states the European Communities came to symbolize
both physical security, as a guarantee against future wars, and personal
security, as the guarantee of social and welfare 'rights'. It is obvious, too,
that at most moments both these guarantees had at least as high a
symbolical as a practical content.

Secondly, the economic and social issues determining the disposition
of national allegiance since 1945 must be fully explored. This requires a
programme of research into the public finances and fiscal history of
post-1945 Western European states. It is an odd fact that whereas we are
extremely knowledgeable about levels of public taxation in the formation of eighteenth-century German states, no research at all has been
undertaken on how voters in West European states were persuaded
between 1945 and 1974 to pay continually increasing levels of personal
taxation, which in most countries culminated in tax rates double those
in the 1930s. That was a change in the nature of allegiance of the
greatest possible significance both to national states and to the Community – as the reversal of the trend since 1984 is also. The connection
between personal income, taxation, security in the widest sense of the
word, and the accepted common policies of the Communities needs
therefore to be explored as an issue in both economic and social history.
Why did people pay to central government in the 1950s and 1960s so
much more money, with no diminution, and perhaps an increase, in
allegiance?

What was purchased with this extra taxation was not primarily a more
robust system of national defence, although that was a big item, but
a complex system of social welfare and personal benefits throughout
the family life-cycle. National governments became giant insurance
companies. How far did the growth of 'the welfare state' correspond
with, and how far did it induce, an increase in national allegiance?
President Lyndon B. Johnson, copying much of what had happened ten
years earlier in Western Europe, put it explicitly when he called the
expansion of the welfare programme 'giving people a stake in society'.
Where primary education and conscription had failed to induce mass
allegiance in the nineteenth century, did the welfare state and its
accompanying employment policies and agricultural income support
policies succeed?

Thirdly, the symbolic role of 'Europe' in political rhetoric, and the changing way in which it enters into national political discourse is a crucial area of research. One weakness of earlier theories borrowed from political science was a false assumption about the causes of jpopular support for the idea of a united Europe: that it was welcomed as something better than the nation-state. But there has been no diminution in national allegiance, even though there has been a growth of secondary allegiance to 'Europe'. A more valid historical explanation of the symbolical and rhetorical meaning of 'Europe' in its non-material aspects, for national voters and political parties, has to be found. What is 'European' allegiance? Is it primarily cultural, economic, idealistically political, realistically political, or simply born from fear or prejudice? And how has it changed since 1945?

Such a pragmatic programme could well uncover only a small part of the answer to the question of what induces allegiance. Its pragmatism would be based essentially on what market research and public opinion polls tell political parties about what will win an election, together with the conclusions of historians of the nineteenth century about the way states then tried to create allegiance. As a working hypothesis for future research, however, it has the one great virtue of bringing together into a common hypothesis the four separate currently prevailing ideas about European integration.

Both the materialist and the symbolic motives for allegiance to national and to supranational institutions are relevant to the formulation and execution of an effective foreign policy. Consider the issue of the United Kingdom's first application for membership. It was, certainly, an important change in the country's foreign policy, as all commentators have pointed out. But why did the decision to make that change drag out for so long? Even before the Treaty of Rome was signed it had been firmly decided by the British government that it would be harmful to the United Kingdom's interests not to become a signatory, but that membership of the EEC was nevertheless impossible. It was considered impossible because of the Commonwealth relationship, but also because it would not be acceptable to public opinion. Between 1956 and 1961 the economic argument for retaining special Commonwealth commercial links weakened to the point where a small majority of the population accepted that the commercial framework of the EEC was more to Britain's economic advantage than that of the Commonwealth. But that did not necessarily lead people to accept the idea of Community membership, because the argument about the Commonwealth was not just an economic one. For public opinion the links with the Commonwealth had a symbolic value, partly created by seventy-five years of imperialist indoctrination in the school system and partly created by cultural affinities and the ties of personal relationships. Distant Australia and Canada were still in the 1950s more real culturally to the government's supporters and most of the population, no matter how distorted their vision of them, than those brief and unsatisfactory next-door wartime allies Belgium and France, to say nothing of the wartime enemies. Foreign policy towards the Community, in short, could not be made solely on rational strategic and economic grounds. The symbolic aspect of allegiance to the United Kingdom contained within it the symbolic value that the United Kingdom was the centre of a vast Commonwealth, for most of whose members the symbolic head of government reigned in London.

Consider, also, that the sharpest divide between the current British government and its chief opposition party over policy towards the European Community is over social policy. This divide was in fact already becoming apparent at the time of the first application, but it ran in the opposite direction. Then the popular fear was thought to be that membership of the Community might reduce levels of personal social benefits by diluting the welfare state or burdening it with payments to poorer foreigners. When the Labour Party opposed the application this train of thought was important in its decision to do so. Now, the European Union is seen by the Labour Party as the last defence of what is left of employee protection and trade-union rights in the United Kingdom and a better guarantor of accumulated welfare benefits than the national government. Unless opinion polls are entirely wrong, the Labour Party's foreign policy has been reorientated partly through the development of a European allegiance for those specific social reasons among its supporters.

These points are made here about the United Kingdom, because that has been the country most under discussion in the recent literature. But they are equally valid for the foreign policies towards the Communities of all other member states. A remarkable exception to the narrowness of recent diplomatic history on European integration is the excellent official history of the Coal and Steel Community by Poidevin and Spierenburg, as inquisitive and informative on business and social history as on diplomacy.[19] Working with the hypothesis suggested here might help further scholars to emulate the effort made by Poidevin and Spierenburg and put the history of European business and domestic politics into the foreign policy formulation process.

As for the intellectual history of European integration, the same point is almost too obvious to make. Jean Monnet was surely an interesting and persuasive man in the corridors of government. But he was never required to win an election. If European integration has been an act of political will, how has the idea spread and what forms has it taken at a *popular* level? This is a question from which historians have fled.[20] It has been much easier to write the history of federalist groups; they were very small and unimportant, so their papers and speeches are easily mastered. But what has 'Europe' meant to the electorate when governments have had to win elections, and how have they used it? We are as yet only scratching the surface of that history. We need to dig more deeply to find the roots of European allegiance, and that must mean linking intellectual history to the mechanics of the society in which it evolves.

Is it true – for it is currently a matter of dispute – that the social and economic policies of Western European governments after 1945 success-fully recreated the nation-state on a much solider basis of popular allegiance than before? If so, how *exactly* was this done? We have no thorough history of the welfare state in any country which identifies the precise beneficiaries of particular acts of policy.[21] Who gained and who lost from these complex redistributional structures seems essential knowledge to explaining the extent of national allegiance, and sub-sequently of allegiance to the Communities. This is difficult, technical, statistical work if it is done on a comparative basis, but its absence means that argument about the validity of the hypothesis that integration was one aspect of strengthening the nation-state expires in baffled ignorance of the real historical detail needed to confirm or refute it.

Lastly, what proportion of national populations has responded to the long-run trends of international economic development in such a way that its national allegiance has been weakened? Is it in fact correct, as much of the literature on the evolution of the international economy implies, that the policies by which nation-states may actually have increased national allegiance between 1945 and 1968, ceased to be possible thereafter, so that national allegiance becomes in part a pointless romanticism? What proportion, for example, of those French taxpayers notorious for tax evasion before the mid-1950s, who then faithfully paid swingeing tax increases in return – it could be assumed – for massive increases in state welfare from the mid-1950s onwards, now avoid paying taxation by devices which, if not strictly legitimate, are at least in conformity with modern economic trends and the state's new policies? Has the proportion of 'citizens' with untaxed foreign bank accounts increased? Has the proportion of the income of a significant proportion of private individuals earned abroad increased? Or have these considerations only been of real financial significance for multi-national corporations? Has de-control of capital movements allowed citizens to escape the ties of national allegiance? Has that and the weakening of other controls, including within the Union controls over

Union citizens, returned the situation to that of the nineteenth century when national allegiance was much weaker? Has the trend of national allegiance over the long run been one in which it was maximized during the 1960s by state benefits and has been diminishing ever since? To what extent de-control has been a considered trend in policy and to what extent it has been merely accepting the inevitable, as this fourth idea of European integration would imply, is another unanswered historical question. But the implications for allegiance are unmistakable, and since all social policies or their abandonment have to be put to the test of general elections, the research hypothesis proposed here would embrace them too.

Of course, the idea that everyone can write every kind of history is unrealistic. Yet any review of the present state of research into the history of European integration is bound to come to the conclusion that we are far from being able to explain it convincingly. The historiography of the subject has been effectively destructive, sweeping aside inapplicable and inapposite theory. But where it is constructive it appears to be engaged, like children on a crowded beach, in building separate small sandcastles, all of which look very vulnerable to an incoming tide. The suggestion made here for a common working hypothesis does at least deal with the central political issue of the whole story. It is only intended to persuade or help scholars to consider the kind of history they write about European integration in the light of the sorts others write.

1995

Notes

1. An important stage in this retreat was marked by the publication of R.O. Keohane and S. Hoffmann, 'Conclusions: Community Politics and Institutional Change', in W. Wallace, ed., *The Dynamics of European Integration,* London 1990, and 'Institutional Change in Europe in the 1980s', in R.O. Keohane and S. Hoffman, eds, *The New European Community. Decision Making and Institutional Change,* Boulder 1991. The enthusiastic reception given to A. Moravcsik, 'Preferences and Power in the European Community: A Liberal Intergovernmentalist Approach', *Journal of Common Market Studies,* vol. 31, no. 4, 1993, which dispenses entirely with the theory of supranational institutions in offering a model of present integration, shows how far the retreat has gone.

2. A. J. Boekestijn, 'Economic Integration and the Preservation of Post-War Consensus in the Benelux Countries', *Economic and Social History in the Netherlands,* vol. 5, 1993.

3. For an interesting attempt to measure the difference made by institutional arrangements to rates of national income growth and a discussion of the possible influence of European cooperative and integrationist arrangements on economic growth, see B. Eichengreen, 'Institutions and Economic Growth: Europe after World War II', paper presented to the Centre for Economic Policy Research Conference on the Economic Performance of Europe after the Second World War, 17–19 December 1993, Oxford.

4. S. Burgess and G. Edwards, 'The Six Plus One: British Policy-Making and the Question of European Economic Integration, 1955', *International Affairs,* vol. 64, 1988; A.

Dobson, 'The Special Relationship and European Integration', *Diplomacy and Statecraft*, vol. 2, no. 1, 1991; S. George, *Britain and European Integration Since 1945*, Oxford 1991; G. Warner and A. Deighton, 'British Perceptions of Europe in the Postwar Period', in R. Girault, ed., *Les Europes des Européens*, Paris 1993; J.W. Young, *Britain and European Unity 1945–1992*, London 1993.

5. On the role of nuclear weapons in the first negotiations for the United Kingdom's entry into the EEC, see I. Clark, *Nuclear Diplomacy and the Special Relationship. Britain's Deterrent and America 1957–1962*, Oxford 1994. For an appreciation of the role of the EEC in French security policy, see G.G. Soutou, 'La France, l'Allemagne et les Accords de Paris', *Relations internationales*, no. 52, 1987, and 'Les problèmes de sécurité dans les rapports franco-allemands de 1956 à 1963', *Relations internationales*, no. 58, 1989.

6. It is a mixture of the records of those conversations and private papers left by Macmillan which led his biographer to this conclusion. A. Horne, *Macmillan, Volume 2, 1957–1986*, London 1989. But Horne was not concerned with the rest of the government.

7. F.M.B. Lynch, 'Restoring France: the Road to Integration', in A.S. Milward *et al.*, *The Frontier of National Sovereignty, History and Theory 1945–1992*, London 1993.

8. For the best recent summary of the relationship between the history of the separate states and that of the Community up to the signing of the Treaty of Rome, and one which puts the diplomatic history of integration into a more balanced perspective, see P. Gerbet, *La Naissance du Marché Commun*, Paris 1987.

9. For a recent example of a work in which this is the underlying idea, see C. Hackett, *Cautious Revolution: The European Community Arrives*, Westport, CT 1990. For one in which it is also a prominent, but not the sole, idea, see P. Winand, *Eisenhower, Kennedy and the United States of Europe*, New York 1993.

10. Recent expositions of this idea are A.S. Milward, *The European Rescue of the Nation-State*, London 1992; L. Tsoukalis, *The New European Economy. The Politics and Economics of Integration*, 2nd edn, Oxford 1993.

11. A. Bressand and K. Nicolaidis, 'Regional Integration in a Networked World Economy', and M. Sharp, 'Technology and the Dynamics of Integration', in Wallace, *The Dynamics*; A. Bressand, 'Beyond Interdependence: 1992 as a Global Challenge', *International Affairs*, vol. 66, no. 1, 1990.

12. P. Kennedy, *The Rise and Fall of the Great Powers. Economic Change and Military Conflict from 1500 to 2000*, London 1988.

13. An argument specifically made by B. Supple, 'Economic History and the Decline of Britain', *Economic History Review*, vol. XVII, no. 3, 1994.

14. 'Britain's First "No" to Europe: Britain and the Briand Plan 1929–1930', *European Studies Review*, vol. 10, 1980; P. Stirk, ed., *European Unity in Context: The Interwar Period*, London 1989.

15. A. Bosco, 'Federal Union and the Origins of the "Churchill Proposal"', *The Federalist Debate in the United Kingdom from Munich to the Fall of France 1938–1940*, London 1992. S. Pistone, 'Il ruolo di Altieri Spinelli nella genesi dell'art. 38 della comunità Europea di Defesa e del progetto di Comunità Politica Europea', in G. Trausch, ed., *Die europäische Integration vom Schuman-Plan bis zu den Verträgen von Rom, Beiträge des Kolloquiums in Luxemburg 17.–19. Mai 1989*, Baden-Baden 1993.

16. A.S. Milward and V. Sørensen, 'Interdependence or Integration? A National Choice', in Milward *et al.*, *The Frontier*.

17. M. Aglietta, A. Brender and V. Coudert, *Globalisation financière: l'aventure obligée*, Paris 1990.

18. For the measure of these two allegiances, see M. Hewstone, *Understanding Attitudes to the European Community: A Social-Psychological Study in Four Member States*, Cambridge 1986.

19. R. Poidevin and R. Spierenburg, *The History of the High Authority of the European Coal and Steel Community. Supranationality in Operation*, London 1994.

20. Useful thoughts about how it may be approached can be found in A.D. Smith, 'National Identity and the Idea of European Unity', *International Affairs*, vol. 68, no. 1, 1992. See this volume, pp. 318–41.

21. For valuable categorizations of European welfare states and typologies of their social and class differences, see P. Baldwin, *The Politics of Social Solidarity: Class Bases in the European Welfare State 1875–1975*, Cambridge 1990; G. Esping-Andersen, *The Three Worlds of Welfare Capitalism*, Cambridge 1990.

2

Rescue or Retreat? The Nation State in Western Europe, 1945–93

William Wallace

My first guideline is this: willing and active cooperation between independent sovereign states is the best way to build a successful European Community. To try to suppress nationhood and concentrate power at the centre of a European conglomerate would be highly damaging. ... Europe will be stronger precisely because it has France as France, Spain as Spain, Britain as Britain, each with its own customs, traditions and identity.

Margaret Thatcher, British prime minister, speech to College of Europe in Bruges, 20 September 1988.

The nation state was the twin of the industrial society, and like industrial society it is becoming outworn. ... The evolution of Europe in the next decades will be shaped by the phasing in of the information society to replace the industrial culture and industrial technology which have served us so well for almost two hundred years.

Poul Schluter, Danish prime minister, speech to the America–European Community Association, London, 20 September 1988.

Nations are not everlasting. They have a beginning, they will have an end. Probably a European confederation will replace them.

Ernest Renan, *Qu'est-ce qu'une nation?* Lecture to Sorbonne, Paris, 11 March 1882.

Both the nation state and integration appear as fortunate accidents of the time, fundamentally contradictory tendencies, which nevertheless in promoting economic growth fortuitously complemented each other.

Alan S. Milward, *The European Rescue of the Nation-State*, p. 24.

The European State and West European Integration

The tension between the nation-state and international integration is central to any discussion of the development of the European political

21

system since the Second World War – as to its likely development during the 1990s. Three overlapping questions are at stake. How far were the processes of European integration deliberately designed to undermine national sovereignty and create instead a European federal state? How have the autonomy and integrity of European nation-states been affected by the evolution of economic, social, technological and political integration over the past forty-five years? How far were both the reconstruction of West European nation-states and their development of intense patterns of cooperative management and formal and informal integration dependent upon the provision of security and hegemonic political and economic leadership by the United States within the Cold War 'Western' order, rather than on the efforts of European leaders themselves or the dynamics of intra-European politics?

The main concern of this essay is with the second of these questions rather than with the first or the third – though it notes that the passion with which proponents of federalism and defenders of sovereignty argued their case in the 1950s and 1960s served to obscure the more subtle impact of economic, social and technological trends, and remarks the extent to which the American role and the importance of a stable security framework were underplayed in the analysis of West European integration in the 1960s and 1970s. It argues (with Milward, Hoffmann and others) that there was – at least until the end of the 1960s – a positive-sum relationship between the security and economic frameworks which the institutions of European integration (including those American-sponsored frameworks for European cooperation, NATO and OEEC/OECD) had built, and the maintenance – or re-establishment – of national legitimacy and autonomy.[1] The ability of national governments to satisfy the aspirations of their citizens and to achieve their own economic and political objectives was strengthened, not weakened, by the institutional containment of West Germany within the EEC, the confidence in continuing economic growth which progress in economic integration provided, and the additional resources which that continuing growth gave national governments to spend on welfare, industrial and technological policies, and defence.

Two definitional points must briefly be noted before our discussion proceeds. First, there is a subtle but vital distinction between the concepts of sovereignty and autonomy. Some nineteenth-century theorists, building on seventeenth- and eighteenth-century models, claimed for the state itself as the expression of the nation an authority unchecked by internal or external constraints; others saw sovereignty as both legitimized and checked by 'the consolidation of the community–state relationship' in the democratic nation-state. Both saw the essence of sovereignty in 'the ultimate primacy of the power of the state': its formal independence from any superior authority.[2] Autonomy is a relative, not an absolute, concept: to be assessed in comparative terms with reference to external constraints and domestic vulnerabilities to outside developments. Sovereignty is formal, legal; autonomy informal, shaped by economic, social and security factors. Second, the processes of regional international integration within Western Europe must be placed within the context of the wider – but looser – processes of globalization which flow from the transformation of communications and the emergence of a global economy. Distinctive elements of West European experience since 1945 include: the presence of an accepted external hegemon (the USA) with surplus security and economic resources available to lessen the costs of integration to the participating states; a degree of shared identity and community sufficient to support compliance with common rules and the limited transfer of resources within the region; the establishment of formal institutions for regional international cooperation – OEEC, NATO, and for the core states the EC (and WEU) – marking mutual limitation of sovereignty for mutual benefit; and the marked demographic and geographical concentration of the region, above all of its core area around the Rhine valley and delta.[3]

'There is', Karl Deutsch wrote forty years ago, 'apt to be confusion about the term "integration"' – most of all between the deliberate political process of institution-building which constitutes formal integration and the largely undirected processes of economic and social interaction which constitute informal integration.[4] The early theorists of European integration saw the institution-building framework as setting in train new patterns of cross-border transactions which would in time create new cross-border shared interests, and so raise perceptions of political community, identity and loyalty 'beyond the nation state'.[5] Working together, through the newly established structure of inter-governmental committees and through the economic associations and social and political groups which increasing interactions would encourage, would lead to a process of informal political integration, through which participants would come to recognize their common interests and to transfer their loyalties to this wider European entity. This constituted – as will be argued in the section following – an ideology of integration much more than an analytical theory.[6]

The relationship between formal and informal integration, it is now clear, is much more complex. The framework of rules and regulations which formal institution-building establishes serves to channel and direct – as well as to inhibit and redirect – informal flows. But economic and social development, aided by technical change, may in time raise those flows to an intensity which faces governments with the dilemma of limiting further development or adjusting rules to accommodate their consequences; so setting off a push–pull process between formal and informal integration, moving from partial bargains among governments to adjust the formal balance between autonomy and common policies to further intensification of informal exchanges, and so to renewed pressures for changes in rules and structures.[7]

The impact of economic and political integration on national autonomy since the end of the 1960s is much more open to question. Paradoxically, the years in which *formal* political integration seemed to be making least progress – between 1972 and 1984–85 – appear in retrospect to have witnessed a progressive erosion of national autonomy, arising out of changes in technology (particularly in its impact on communications), in methods of production and management, and in the explosion of cross-border movement throughout Western Europe. These trends have been reinforced by the integration of financial markets and investment flows, which has been such a marked development during the 1980s.[8]

The dramatic clashes between proponents and opponents of European union in the early 1960s obscured the relatively limited incursions on national autonomy then proposed. Conversely, the relative caution with which most national governments in the 1980s approached formal proposals for the transfer of power and authority from states to European agencies and institutions obscured the progressive erosion of national autonomy through informal (economic and social) integration and the increasingly intensive interlocking of governments and administrations which has marked the nation-state response to these trends.[9]

Any assessment of how far these developments have undermined the core functions of the nation-state – or, alternatively, forced nation-states to adapt to increasing interdependence without severely affecting their core functions – depends partly on one's perception of the role and function of the nation-state as such: a perception which differs to some degree from one European state to another, reflecting the distinctive historical experience of different European states. States have probably lost most autonomy in the economic sphere: where 'national champion' strategies have given way, to one degree or another, to acceptance of multinational cooperation and external and internal investment, and where the instruments of national economic management have been blunted by economic integration. They have lost considerable autonomy over national defence – and more over defence procurement; and are beginning to lose autonomy over the central state functions of public order and maintenance of territorial boundaries. Rule-making and decision-making – law and government – are increasingly becoming caught up in multilateral bargaining: not (as postwar idealists hoped) bypassing the nation-state, but collectivizing national decisions through inter-governmental negotiations.

For the nation-state as a focus for popular identity and a basis for legitimacy, by contrast, little has changed; despite the remarkable increase in social interchange and media integration over the past twenty years. A certain diffusion of loyalties, a certain expansion of horizons from the national to the European (and the global), are evident both among élites and – more faintly – among mass publics. But challenges to the legitimacy of national institutions and élites have come largely from within existing states: leading to fragmentation, not integration. Throughout Western Europe the national community remains the broadest focus for political life and group identity. This growing discrepancy between the political sphere and the economic and social (and even military and public order) spheres was already unsettling national politics in some Community member states in the late 1980s, and became a focus for argument over national autonomy, and even national identity, during the ratification process for the Treaty on European Union in 1992–93.

Assessment of the impact of political and economic integration on the nation-state depends partly upon the observer's perception of the stability or developmental character of the European state. Margaret Thatcher (and Charles de Gaulle), seeing the nation-state as a natural and permanent framework for political life, have seen both the creeping flow of informal integration and the deliberate bargaining and rule-making of formal integration as a fundamental threat – and an impossible dream. Poul Schluter, and those who see the modern nation-state as itself the creation of an earlier process of political, economic and social integration over the past 100–200 years, are less fundamentalist; the nation-state for them is a product of modernization, and technological and economic innovation may indeed be rendering the concept of the autonomous nation-state obsolete. Academic analysts can be found in both camps, defending the state as the only political reality or emphasizing the relative novelty of the developed nation-state and the radical implications of the adjustments West European states are gradually making in the face of rapid internal and external changes.[10]

Ideology and Integration

The idealists who defined the rhetoric of European integration were anti-nationalists: shaped by the bitter experiences of the Second World War, the pathological mutation of nationalism into Fascism and National Socialism, the military defeat of Germany's neighbours and the corrosive impact of occupation. Later historians have questioned whether the reality of inter-governmental bargaining – over the Schuman Plan, the European Defence Community proposals, the Messina 'relaunch' – ever approached the rosy picture of Euro-idealism which the early apologists painted. But the enthusiasm which suffused the Commission in its early years represented an explicit challenge to national governments – and to the opposing rhetoric of national sovereignty – which aroused (under President de Gaulle) the French government's vigorous opposition and made the British and Scandinavian governments deeply suspicious of the whole process of institutionalized integration.[11]

The characteristically 'technocratic' approach of the early theorists and practitioners of 'the Community Method' was not only implicitly anti-national, but also anti-political.

> It relied on technology as the fuel, and on the logic of the market as the motor of integration: the drive for economic modernization would lead to political unity. It was the old Saint-Simonian dream of depoliticized progress, accompanied by one idea that, at first sight, seemed quite political: the idea that the gradual dispossession of the nation-state and the transfer of allegiance to the new Community would be hastened by the establishment of a central quasi-federal political system.[12]

But the new system was itself conceived of in largely technocratic terms: its dynamism to be derived from a professional élite within the Commission, to whose disinterested proposals national governments had to respond. The immediate model was the post-Second World War French planning system, which was successfully rebuilding the state and modernizing the economy even while the political class was squabbling over the disintegrating institutions of the Fourth Republic. 'The development of French planning in the 1950s can be viewed as an act of collusion between senior civil servants and the senior managers of business. The politicians and the representatives of organized labour were both largely passed by.'[13]

The drama of institutionalized (or formal) European integration as a challenge to the nation-state was thus played out in the early years of the European Community, most directly in the clash of perspectives and wills between the first Commission president, Walter Hallstein (a German *Beamte* rather than a French *fonctionnaire*), and President de Gaulle. The Commission package of proposals of 1964–65 on EEC revenues and expenditure, linked to the completion of the Common Agricultural Policy, majority voting in the Council of Ministers, and increased powers for the European Parliament/Assembly represented a dash towards supranationalism; and as such aroused an intransigent response from de Gaulle and the French government. The Luxembourg Compromise, on this interpretation, represented a clear victory for inter-governmental cooperation under the careful control of state administrations over supranational integration. That was, after all, how it was interpreted in the Commission, which issued defiant statements on its continuing commitment to the 'European ideal', as well as within most national governments. British politicians and officials, for example, were much reassured; a Community in which national governments retained firm vetoes over undesired developments was a Community which it might be safe to enter without jeopardizing parliamentary sovereignty.

This was, however, a Brussels-centred drama: enthralling for those who looked to the Community and its institutions as *the* focus for European politics, but of only secondary importance to the large majority of national politicians and officials on whose responsibilities and concerns the three Communities (ECSC, Euratom and the EEC) had not yet impinged. Once we step outside the committed perspective of those who battled over the Brussels institutions, it becomes clear that national political systems throughout most of Western Europe were more strongly entrenched, and more effective in delivering material and symbolic benefits to their citizens, in the 1960s than they had ever been before.

A major element in this was due to sustained economic growth: international cooperation plus Keynesian demand management, with national economies still for most purposes firmly under national control while benefiting from increasing *trade* across national frontiers. Governments large and small across Western Europe sponsored nationally owned companies and followed different interpretations of corporatism both in their handling of relations among government, workers and managers and in the relations between government, public and private financial institutions and industry. The percentage of each national economy accounted for by taxation and by the distributive and redistributive impacts of public expenditure was far higher in most democratic 'mixed economies' than in their predecessor regimes of the interwar period. This in turn enabled state administrations to provide substantial welfare benefits to all their citizens: the nation-state strengthening its legitimacy and its hold on its citizens' loyalty by becoming 'the welfare state'.[14]

The contrast with the interwar period is evident. Then, national governments and state administrations which found themselves unable to guarantee employment to a large minority of their citizens, and cut welfare benefits as recession set in and public revenues fell, suffered revolutionary challenges from right and left. Some collapsed into authoritarianism, even into civil war. The stable framework of rules which the OEEC provided, and the confidence that stability would continue, gave governments a far stronger base for national economic development. The acceptance of Keynesian economic policy – or more

broadly of social partnership, economic management and social democracy – legitimized the active state. National industrial development and
rising public revenues also enabled West European governments to
spend more on defence, and on nationally designed and manufactured
military equipment. Alan Milward, deliberately attacking the historical
school of 'Euro-enthusiasts', concludes that 'the power of the European
nation-state reached its highest point at the end of the 1960s ... the
period 1945–1968 may be considered as that of its [final] achievement:
the apogee of a pre-existing process and not the beginning of a new
phenomenon'.[15]

One may expand on this image of the consolidated nation-state
twenty years after the end of the Second World War, reinforced in its
ability to meet the expectations of its population. Modernization had
rebuilt national infrastructures, without yet developing extensive new
communication channels across national boundaries. Europe's motor-
way network was developing on a national pattern radiating out from
capitals to provinces without stretching beyond the national boundary –
following the pattern of Europe's railways of sixty to eighty years before,
which had thinned out towards each border (and each well-manned
border post) as they integrated each national territory. National telephone networks (without exception national monopolies) had expanded,
international links were only beginning to be built. International STD
across Europe was initiated from the early 1960s, to revolutionize
contacts among business and governments over the following decade.[16]

National education shaped perceptions, with only a small minority
involved in cross-border study and exchanges. The massive Franco-
German exchanges started in the mid-1960s; rising numbers in further
education throughout Europe during that decade brought an increase
in foreign student flows. But the largest body of students from abroad
in Britain and France came from their former imperial possessions, not
from other European states; and the first country of destination for
European university students going abroad was the United States.[17]
Migration within Europe was rising, as economic growth and labour
demand in rich northern Europe drew in *Gastarbeiter* from southern
Europe; but it had not yet reached a point where it was seen as
threatening national solidarity. Mass tourism began to shift balance
from an intra-national to an inter-national phenomenon in the course
of the 1960s, but it was not until the late 1960s and early 1970s that
large numbers of young people across Europe began to treat their
continent – rather than their country – as the space within which they
expected to move.

Both the apologists for the idealistic project of European union as
pursued in the 1950s and 1960s and the revisionists underplay the

immense importance of the American presence in shaping the structure
of postwar Western Europe, and in influencing the character of its
politics. American wartime planning for a postwar Europe promoted
the idea of a 'United States of Europe'; John Foster Dulles was the
secretary of 'the American Committee for a United States of Europe' in
1947–48.[18] The conditions attached to Marshall Plan aid forced its
European recipients into close cooperation, through the Organization
for European Economic Cooperation and the European Payments
Union. American pressure on the European allies to integrate the
reconstructed West German economy, without which (it was argued) a
prosperous pattern of European economic growth could not be established, did much to push the French government into the proposal for
a European Coal and Steel Community, as the only way to reconcile
national security with economic recovery.[19] Intense American pressure,
after the North Korean invasion of South Korea, to allow the rearmament of West Germany similarly pushed the governments of France and
the Low Countries into pursuing the directly federal proposal for a
European Defence Community, with the necessary corollary of a European Political Community to follow.

The collapse of the EDC proposals left security issues firmly within
the Atlantic framework, with the commitment of six American (and
four British) divisions to Germany providing a guarantee of German
good behaviour as well as protection against the Soviet threat; while
political integration was pursued less directly through 'functional'
economic channels. But the argument between de Gaulle and Hallstein
(and the governments of the 'other five') was as much about rejection
of American patronage and the American-dominated political and
security framework as it was about the integrative or inter-governmental
character of European union. The Fouchet proposals were intended to
displace NATO as the main framework for foreign policy cooperation; a
third of the Elysée Treaty of 1963 was devoted to defence and foreign
policy cooperation.[20] Looking back, Milward indeed sees the alliance
between American theorists and Commission institution-builders as an
aspect of the Cold War, through which 'neo-functionalism in the 1950s
and 1960s became the intellectual foundation for a hegemonic foreign
policy architecture'.[21]

Western Europe was 'America's Europe'. The reconstruction of the
nation-state in a postwar Western Europe was built on a number of
contradictions and compromises between the reassertion of sovereignty
and the acceptance of integration. Acceptance of a degree of dependence on the USA – direct and substantial for Italy and Federal
Germany, indirect for Britain and France – was the first of these
compromises; from which West European states gained a great deal, not

only in terms of security but also in terms of the transformation of their economies through the transfer of American technology, the introduction of American managerial and production methods, and the stimulus of American investment. Acceptance of a semi-sovereign Germany, with which its neighbours around the Rhine valley and delta agreed to share sovereignty, rather than risk full independence for the successor to Europe's would-be hegemon of the previous half-century, was for them as significant a compromise. A further self-conscious compromise was the recognition, most directly by the Benelux states, that the only way to provide their citizens with full employment and economic growth – and the public services which the revenue generated through economic growth would finance – was through acceptance of intensified international trade regulated through tighter international regimes. Paul-Henri Spaak, speaking as foreign minister in the Belgian government-in-exile to the Belgian Institute in London in the bleak winter of 1941, spelt out the limitations of autonomy necessary to re-establish postwar autonomy: 'What we shall have to combine is a certain reawakening of nationalism and an indispensable internationalism'.[22]

If we nevertheless accept on the above evidence that the 1960s *were* the high point of national consolidation and state management of economy and society, the crucial question to pose is: what trends have strengthened or weakened the centrality of states in the European political system since then? The forces of economic integration, industrial modernization and technological innovation had so far operated to reinforce national political systems; have they continued to do so, or has there been a qualitative shift in their impact over the twenty to twenty-five years following? But before we address that question it may be useful to consider whether we can talk about a single model of *the* European nation-state, or whether we should accept that different relations between state, economy and society, different national traditions and myths, make it necessary to treat the concept of 'the nation-state' and 'national sovereignty' as to some extent contingent on the particular states to which they are applied.

Nation-States – and Nation-States

The 'nation-state' is an artificial construct, an ideal type heavily dependent upon the historical experience of only two of Western Europe's states: Britain and France.[23] Since Britain and France have developed very different traditions on the role of the state and the relationship between state and society, and state and economy, it is not easy to construct a universally agreed model of the nation-state and its core functions against which to test the impact of formal and informal integration over the past twenty – or forty – years. Any such attempt is complicated further by the weight of German (and Austrian) theory on the authority and functions of the state, from Hegel and von Humboldt to Weber via Marx and many others – and still further by the evolution of Catholic doctrine as Germany and Italy were unified as secular states.[24] To some extent, as Dyson argues, Britain has been the 'odd state out' in comparison with the Continent, never developing a full concept of the state as an autonomous entity, nor achieving any stable consensus on the economic role of the state. But it would be enormously rash to suggest that German concepts of statehood and nationhood obtained unmodified in Protestant Norway and Catholic Portugal, in Orthodox Greece or in the consociational Netherlands.

We have to recognize that there is *no* permanently valid corpus of sovereign powers and state authority – though it has been a frequent assertion of national politicians and political theorists that there is. One may see the late-nineteenth-century European nation-state as representing one apogee of centralized authority and territorial integrity, the states of the 'Trente Glorieuses' of postwar growth as representing another: each taking advantage of advances in technology, administration and communication, and each adapting to changes in the external environment.[25] But it must be emphasized that the West European states of the 1960s differed substantially from those of sixty–seventy years before, not only in their size and territorial boundaries but also in their military, foreign policy, economic and social characteristics. Just as industrialization, railways, the telegraph and the development of efficient state administration transformed the capacities of the nineteenth-century state and its relations with its citizens, so mass-production, the telephone, Keynesian techniques for national economic management, technological advance (often also under state sponsorship, and defence-led) and the development of the 'welfare state' transformed those capacities again in the 1950s and 1960s. 'The basis of the rescue of the nation state was an economic one', Milward argues – though the economic necessity of including the German economy within the broader framework required to sustain growth imposed underlying political, as well as economic, constraints on that rescue. 'The combination of welfare state and employment policy' which northern European states were enabled through sustained growth to pursue 'represents the apogee of the concept of the nation[-state] as the improver of man's lot'.[26]

Even within the same period and under the same domestic and international constraints, the diversity of state/society, state/economy and state/interdependence or autonomy relations is striking. 'Economic viability and political legitimacy can be secured in many ways ... and these ways are shaped by history and politics'.[27] Large states have more resources with which to maintain national autonomy, defend national integrity and promote national prosperity than small states; but such small states as Sweden, Austria and Finland have managed to maintain (and even expand) a high degree of autonomy over the past forty years through the pursuit of carefully judged mercantilist and welfare policies within the limits imposed by the rules of the postwar Western order.

The irreducible minimum of the concept of a state is a body which exercises an accepted monopoly of violence within its boundaries, and a willingness to use violence against outsiders to defend those boundaries. Internal order, external defence (and the diplomacy needed to maintain and reinforce that defence): Hobbes, Machiavelli, John Austin and Albert Dicey all recognize that necessity. The concept of sovereignty asserted that no other authority had the right to summon or convict those under the protection of the sovereign, and that the sovereign conversely had the sole right to conduct political – or military – relations with other territorially organized states. 'This realm of England is an Empire' (the Act of Supremacy of 1534: arguably a more important document in the evolution of the English state than the much more frequently quoted Magna Carta) excluded the claim of the Roman Church to exercise jurisdiction – and to mete out punishment – in England alongside the temporal power.

Legitimacy is as much a part of the core concept of the state: *accepted authority*, laying down and applying rules which have the status of law.[28] Early European states rested their claim to legitimacy – to acceptance by their subjects as representing and identifying them as a 'community', a 'commonwealth', a 'nation' – on sacred or mythical claims: 'the divine right of kings', the inheritance of ancient kingship symbolized by investiture and ritual. Modern states have increasingly rested their claim to internal legitimacy on two different grounds, one ideological, the other rational: first, their identification with (or personification of) 'the nation'; and second, their ability to deliver security, prosperity and welfare to their citizens.

The immensely powerful idea of the nation-state as providing a focus for social and political identity in mass urban societies was a development of the nineteenth century in Western Europe – and of the early twentieth century in Eastern Europe. The integrating power of national identity, propagated through 'national education' and national history by an active state, was perhaps most sharply demonstrated in July and August 1914, when the populations of European states mobilized in response to their governments' commands to defend their nation-states against each other. The harrowing experience of the Second World War brought a wave of revulsion against this mutual identification of nation and state; but the intellectuals who led this revolt aroused little response from populations who continued to live almost entirely within the boundaries of their particular nation-state, to work for companies owned within that state, and to buy products manufactured within that state.

The promotion of national wealth was a central part of most states' aims and activities in the seventeenth and eighteenth centuries – the mercantilist era, in which European governments fought for control of trade routes and sugar and spice islands, and saw tariffs as a means of raising revenue from one another and of protecting national agriculture and manufactures from foreign attack.[29] Mercantilist aims were central to Alexander Hamilton's vision – in *The Federalist Papers* – of a strong United States, and to Friedrich List's vision of a powerful united Germany. The rapid industrialization of Germany in the final decades of the nineteenth century was, after all, a case-study in public and private interests mobilized in pursuit of common national objectives – as was the similarly rapid industrialization of Japan. Bismarck saw it as sound policy to give all German subjects a strong sense of common benefits from common citizenship by developing the foundations of national welfare policies; an example soon copied by others. Well before the postwar period, therefore, the pursuit of prosperity and the provision of welfare were seen by European states as essential tasks for the nation-state.[30] Keynesianism, however, added to their confidence in promoting state-guided capitalism in 'mixed economies'.

The *core* functions of the nation-state may thus be seen as: the preservation of internal order, the maintenance of national boundaries and the defence of national territory against foreign attack; the provision of 'legitimate' government, through an established and well-ordered state apparatus, equipped with the symbols and institutions needed to 'represent' the nation and to give its citizens a sense of participation in the national community; the provision of services, and of welfare, to reinforce this sense of national community; and the promotion of national prosperity – which in the Keynesian era became the pursuit of balanced and sustained economic growth. All these were successfully provided to their citizens by West European states in the 1960s. How successfully were they still being provided in the 1980s? How likely is it that West European states will still be successfully providing these over the next decade?

After the Apogee: The Long Retreat?

Just as the apparent early successes of formal European integration and the reconsolidation of the nation-state had gone together, so at the end of the 1960s and through the early 1970s both faltered. Part of the explanation for both is to be found in a more disturbed global environment, with international economic recession and changes in US policies – still, as in the 1950s, a crucial factor in West European political and economic developments. The student revolts which flashed across Western Europe in 1968–69 – shaking the state itself in France, challenging authority and hierarchy elsewhere – were at once imitative of the American student revolt which the Vietnam war had inspired, and fuelled by domestic discontents and the impatience of the first entirely postwar generation. The legacy they left behind into the 1970s, of student radicalism souring into terrorism, presented a longer-term challenge to state authority.

A more pervasive loss of self-confidence was reflected in the widespread concern over 'ungovernability' which burst out in the 1970s. Sustained economic growth had fuelled popular and interest-group expectations of increasing state provision; social democracy had granted representatives of organized interests an entrenched position in the policy-making process. With slower growth such expectations could be satisfied only through rising levels of taxation, instead of the hoped-for dividends from expanding revenue. Industrial restructuring, needed as heavy industries lost their place as the 'commanding heights of the economy', was inhibited by the mechanism of corporatist consultation. Economic adjustment, necessary to cope with the successive shocks of the US suspension of dollar convertibility and the rise in the oil price, was inhibited by the ethos of social democracy as well as by the entrenchment of economic interests in national policy-making. Technical advance and managerial innovation were enabling transnational companies to move towards multinational production for regional and global markets, while bargaining with competing national governments over the location of production and new investment. 'Ungovernability' was followed by 'Euro-sclerosis' as a Europe-wide fear. European nation-states appeared to be losing power and authority not to any new supranational authority to which decision-making capacities and loyalties were being transferred (as the neo-functionalists had hoped) but into a void.

Yet from the perspective of the early 1980s 'the most striking reality' was 'not the frequent and well-noted impotence of the nation-state'. It was its 'survival, despite the turmoil'.[31] The passing of deference left governments more dependent on the provision of services and visible economic benefits than their predecessors – but did not destroy their legitimacy. The challenge which terrorism presented to several of the larger European states was successfully withstood. Both political and administrative élites, shaken by the turmoil of 1968–74, adjusted through generational change and the turnover of government office, without weakening the state apparatus as such – in sharp contrast to the debilitating stagnation of élites throughout Eastern Europe.

The 1980s, however, were marked by increasing awareness within West European states of the contradictions in which they were caught up: with governments negotiating new bargains over the decision-making rules and regulations of formal integration, while attempting to satisfy electorates who wished to gain the benefits of continuing prosperity and welfare – and of easy access across West European frontiers – without accepting the costs in reductions in national autonomy. The Single European Act was a classic compromise, in which governments committed to the maintenance of as much autonomy as possible nevertheless agreed a new package of rules under what seemed to them powerful economic and political imperatives.[32] The impetus which carried them on to agree on a further inter-governmental conference, and then to negotiate and sign the Maastricht Treaty on European Union, followed from the same pattern of adjustment to the flow of intensifying economic and social interaction – complicated in the course of 1990–91 by the transformation of the security context within which the whole framework of 'civilian' political integration in Western Europe had developed, with the unification of Germany and the beginnings of American (and Soviet) military withdrawal.

Economic logic made for moves towards a single currency, and for the transfer of competition rules and market regulation to the European level. The transformed *security logic* supported closer cooperation among police and intelligence agencies as well as among armed forces. The Maastricht Treaty, it should be noted, touches on almost all the core functions of the European nation-state: control of the national territory and borders, police, citizenship and immigration, currency, taxation, financial transfers, management of the economy, promotion of industry, representation and accountability, foreign policy and defence. Only welfare remained securely in the hands of national governments: though even there the argument over the 'Social Chapter' showed the determination of some participants to transfer rule-making and standard-setting to the Community level. But *political logic* imposed a contradictory impulse, with governments attempting to reassure their publics that this was only a further limited package, and that the focus for political identity and accountability would remain firmly at the national level: a message which their publics, now able through the integration of communications and élites to understand very well what other governments were telling *their* domestic publics and what was being claimed in Brussels, were reluctant to accept.[33]

Perhaps the most striking shift has been in *the pursuit of national prosperity*: the recognition – throughout Western Europe – of the futility of national industrial strategies, and of the increasing limitations on national economic policies. 'National champions' – Philips, Rolls-Royce, Dassault – had been the focus for much industrial (and technological) policy in the 1960s. Government commitment began to falter during the 1970s, most strikingly in Britain (and least so in France and in several of Europe's smaller states); and to give way in the 1980s to deregulation and (or) collaboration, through strategic alliances, even mergers. Industrial 'sponsorship' shifted from the national to the European plane, with governmental and company support for the plethora of initiatives which began with the 'Esprit' programme and developed with 'Eureka', FAST, JESSI and a lectionary of other acronyms. Indeed, many observers see this shift of industrial and technological imperatives as a key factor in the 'revival' of formal European integration in the 1980s.[34]

National governments continued to fight, and to win or lose, national elections on their 'record' of national economic management – or their promises of superior achievement. But the contrasting experiences of the governments of Britain and France which came into power in 1979 and 1981 provide powerful evidence of the erosion of national control. Britain's domestic monetary squeeze of 1979–81 led to a 30 per cent rise in the external value of sterling, sparking off a much sharper recession than anticipated: the beginning of a long learning process in the limits of national autonomy in pursuing deregulation and free market policies which led, through the (remarkably successful) efforts of the mid-1980s to extend deregulation from the national to the European plane with a programme to 'complete' the internal market and through pressure for stricter Community policies on competition and state aids, to acceptance of membership of the Exchange-Rate Mechanism of the European Monetary System in 1990. The French experience of a 'dash for growth' in 1981–83, complete with programmes for the 'reconquest of the domestic market', provided a more direct shock – and thus a more rapid learning process, demonstrating vividly to every West European government that it was no longer possible even for major European economies to pursue national priorities without careful coordination with their partners. If monetary sovereignty is indeed 'the core of the core' of national sovereignty, as Mrs Thatcher once remarked, then both Western Europe's most sovereignty-conscious states are losing control of that core: the British in 1992–93 deeply confused over national or European monetary strategy, the French more determined than ever to gain a degree of compensating control over dominant German monetary policy through closer integration – even monetary union.

Nation-states no longer control national economies in Western

Europe. Advances in technology, communications, management of multinational companies and techniques of multinational production, as well as the integration of financial markets through electronic communications and the displacement of inter-national trade by flows of foreign direct investment linked to intra-company trade, have irreversibly undermined their autonomy.[35] Smaller states, which had survived the downturn of the 1970s through national policies of industrial adjustment and social/corporatist partnership, shifted during the late 1980s towards an acceptance that regional integration was now the only viable national economic strategy. The neutral states of EFTA excluded the question of full membership in the EC before 1989, seeing the EC as too closely linked to the US-led Atlantic alliance; but their need for as close an involvement as possible in setting the rules of the regional economy within which they lived led them to pursue all forms of association short of membership.[36] After the revolution in European security of 1989–90 such political inhibitions no longer held them back. First Austria, then Sweden and Finland, applied for full membership, even before the EC/EFTA European Economic Area (EEA) agreement had been implemented. The Swiss government's announced intention to follow suit, under the same pressures of economic logic, was undermined by the political logic which holds the Swiss Federation together; all but two of its German-speaking cantons produced a majority against ratifying even the EEA in a referendum in December 1992.[37] The gap between government recognition of the advantages of trading a degree of autonomy for the benefits of full access to EC markets, free movement and shared decision-making, and popular resistance to the loss of autonomy (and the feared implications for national identity) was as evident within states approaching EC membership in the 1990s as within existing member states.

Yet it would be rash to conclude that national economic policies have been *entirely* displaced by the pressure of financial markets, multinational investment and production flows, instant communication and market integration. The successful partnership between several German Länder governments – most notably Baden-Württemberg – and high-technology industries, involving cooperation with financial institutions, support for research institutes and relevant university education, shows that adaptive strategies are still practicable. The support given by several European governments to state-owned industries to become European 'multinationals' – Nokia, Matra, Thomson, most recently Renault – provides further evidence. The arguments advanced by Michael Porter[38] on the importance of 'the home base' to multinational company success will be music to the ears of those governments pursuing such 'multinational–national' policies. National economic *autonomy*, we may

conclude, has now substantially been lost. But national abilities to shape
the balance of advantage within European and global markets, through
education and training expenditure, research and development, part-
nerships with banks and (private or public sector) companies, remain;
and are likely to remain for some years to come. French European
strategy is the clearest example of government moving on to a European
plane in pursuit of national objectives no longer achievable on a
national basis; but there are elements in German, Dutch, Italian and
Spanish industrial and economic strategies which illustrate the same
pursuit of harnessing European cooperation to national ends. The
development of a common agricultural policy thirty years earlier, and
the development of common policies on coal and steel even earlier, had
after all attempted the same trade-off between national interests and
European cooperation.[39]

A 'crisis of the welfare state' has been identified – and examined –
since the early 1970s. Facing a shift in the age balance of their
populations as well as rising expectations from their younger generation,
all West European governments have to differing degrees cut back on
the provision of welfare. Further ageing of Western Europe's population
will force them to economize more during the coming decade. Recent
reforms in Sweden mark a major retreat from the principle of universal
welfare provision through financial transfers and benefits. But what is
remarkable here is how much of the structure of national welfare
provision – in unemployment benefits, old-age pensions, health insurance and housing subsidies – has survived, despite the gloomy predictions of the 1970s. What we have seen has been retrenchment and
adjustment, rather than retreat or abandonment. 'Compared to most
aspects of the postwar political economy . . . the welfare state has proved
to be remarkably durable . . . in large part because of a broad and deep
base of political support' which serves also to maintain the instrumental
legitimacy of the nation-state as welfare provider.

> This strength at the national level helps to explain why social initiatives have
> lagged behind other actions in Brussels. But at the same time, the popularity
> of social protection means that if national welfare states should falter under
> the mounting pressures of regional and global integration, the European
> Community will be under intense popular pressure to extend its activities[40]

or, more disruptively, to demand a return to the protection of national
economies and of national social standards seen to be threatened by
international integration. The arguments over the 'Social Chapter' of
the Maastricht Treaty rehearsed these possible developments, with
German trade-union leaders pressing their government to insist on

common employment standards to discourage the movement of production from *Standort* Germany to less-regulated states.

Loss of control over national economies, and the declining importance of national defence, have left the provision of welfare and related public goods as the most significant function of West European nation-states: legitimizing national government and national taxation, redistributing resources among the national community. The combination of slow growth, high unemployment and huge deficits in social budgets which emerged in the early 1980s therefore represented not only a crisis of the European welfare state, but also a potential crisis for the nation-state as such. So far that crisis has been managed, despite persisting high unemployment and consequent heavy demands for redistribution of income through taxation throughout Western Europe. Adverse demographic trends suggest that the strains on national budgets and on popular acceptance of high levels of redistribution will grow further over the next decade.[41] The close link between national solidarity and social welfare in the evolution of the modern nation-state suggests that any substantive moves to dismantle the structures of national redistribution would undermine this legitimizing link between community and state.

The development of modern nation-states was accompanied by the development of *national communications and national media*, formally controlled by domestic censorship laws and informally constrained by domestic political and social pressures. National values and perspectives were fostered through state support for national theatres and literature, and through close relations between the national press and the government. The barriers of language maintained a high degree of autonomy among European media despite the increasing social interactions of the 1970s and 1980s. International newspapers were slow to emerge; the *Financial Times* sold fewer than 17,000 copies in Germany in 1993, after fourteen years of printing in Frankfurt. National licensing arrangements for radio and television also helped to maintain separate national styles (and ownership).

Yet improvements in television transmission, and the spread of cable networks offering a range of channels from several countries, have gone some way to erode national autonomy in this sphere in the geographically concentrated European region. Most of the population of the German Democratic Republic received, and watched, West German television in preference to their own by the mid-1980s: a development which deprived their government of influence over the news its citizens heard or the symbols and images they acquired.[42] Development of satellite television is accentuating this loss of national control, and increasing the incentives to produce 'international' programmes rather

than transmissions which relate to specifically national myths and values.
The French government's resistance to American demands for deregulation of the audio-visual sector reflected its acute awareness of the
threat to national particularity posed by this combination of technological and entrepreneurial challenges. But it was less clear whether any
West European state had the financial capacity – or the support of its
viewing public – to resist these globalizing pressures.

In *defence and public order*, in contrast, little has happened on the
surface of European politics in the 1970s and 1980s to alter the
perception of clear national responsibility, subject to straightforward
national accountability and control. I want to suggest, however, that
these were the areas in which sovereignty – this *is* the most appropriate
term for areas so fundamental to any concept of the state – was
undermined during that period, though formally registered only in the
1985 Schengen Agreement and in Titles V and VI of the Maastricht
Treaty.

The explosion of cross-border movement which was such a remarkable European phenomenon in these years forced governments progressively to ease, and now in some cases to abandon, protection of their
national territories through control of their boundaries. Jet aircraft and
cross-border motorways, complemented by improvements in cross-
border railway links, allowed for a massive increase in trans-European
travel: for business, for tourism, for study, even commuting across
borders to work. The 5 million journeys across the Channel made by
British subjects and residents in the mid-1960s allowed for careful
controls both of their passports and their luggage at either end –
complete with chalkmarks on each suitcase and a thorough examination
of each passport. For the 40–45 million journeys made annually in the
early 1990s, the small increase in immigration officers (and reduced
numbers of customs officers) attempted in most cases a brief glance and
a cursory nod as the waves of tourists, students and business people
swept through: mute acceptance, perhaps, that the European continent
is no longer regarded as 'foreign' or hostile territory, and symbolized by
the single queue for 'European Community Nationals' at British ports
and airports.[43]

First five, then nine countries on the European continent went
further, in the Schengen Agreement of 1985; which provides for the
abolition of internal frontier controls both on goods and on people,
together with consequent measures for cooperation among police,
immigration, customs and intelligence services, for common procedures
on rights of entry and residence. This involves the abandonment of one
of the most basic tenets of the nation-state; and as such was vigorously
resisted by many within national administrations and politics, delaying

implementation of the provisions of the agreement again and again. Yet national police forces, and intelligence services, had come to cooperate extensively with their counterparts in other European countries during the 1970s and 1980s (through the inter-governmental Trevi and Pompidou groups, and other little-reported bodies) against terrorism, drugs traffic, international money-laundering and financial fraud, and against the growth of cross-border organized crime. There is a powerful security logic in this development: that the internationalization of crime necessitates the internationalization of police work, and that the freer movement of goods, people, information and money across frontiers necessarily means that national police forces must move also. Chancellor Kohl in a speech in 1988 even floated a proposal for a European Federal Bureau of Investigation, as a necessary response to the internationalization of crime. The 'third pillar' of the Maastricht Treaty set out to formalize the extensive existing patterns of 'cooperation in the fields of Justice and Home Affairs', while retaining control of that formalized structure within an inter-governmental framework beyond the reach of the European Parliament and with only a consultative role for the Commission.[44] Before either full implementation of the Schengen Agreement or ratification of the Treaty on European Union, the Schengen Bureau, the newly established European office of Interpol and the complex network of committees which link governments and executive services in dealing with terrorism, drug-smugglers, asylum-seekers and immigrants have taken Western Europe a long way from the traditional concept of the territorially sovereign state.[45]

European defence integration was an early aspiration, forced on to the agenda by American insistence on the rearmament of West Germany. The traumatic failure of the European Defence Community proposals, in 1954, took the issue off the agenda – its taboo status strengthened by French Gaullist polarization of the choices between *European* and *Atlantic* defence cooperation in the 1960s. The Western European Union was revived, in the mid-1980s, into a sickly life as a vehicle for inter-governmental cooperation – and as a framework for European defence cooperation, under American leadership, in the Red Sea and the Gulf. Demolition of the Berlin Wall, and the prospect of German unification, led the French and German governments in April 1990 to add defence and foreign policy explicitly to the agenda of the planned inter-governmental conferences (supporting and expanding on the earlier Belgian proposal for a 'political' IGC to meet and negotiate in parallel with the economic IGC already agreed). Redefinition of NATO strategy in the course of 1991 interacted with competing Franco-German and Italian-British proposals for bringing defence and security more closely together with the civilian framework of the European

Union. The 'Provisions on a Common Foreign and Security Policy' in the Maastricht Treaty are tortuously worded and deliberately ambiguous: faithfully representing the immense sensitivity of this area for sovereign nation-states, and the consequent contradictions of almost every government's position. Yet, with the dissolution of the Soviet Union almost as the European Council met in Maastricht, and with the rundown of US forces in Europe well under way, the strengthening of the WEU and its relocation in Brussels, agreed in a protocol to the treaty, moved ahead during 1992 without waiting for national ratification.[46]

The pressures which have been pushing European governments together on defence issues have come much more, however, from technological and budgetary factors than from inter-governmental agreement. The increasing inefficiency of national procurement, producing limited numbers of sophisticated and highly expensive weapons, has forced the major European countries – France, Britain, Germany, to a lesser extent Italy and even Spain – into collaboration. Joint procurement requires some agreement on tasks and threats to be met by the weapons systems to be produced, and so consultations on strategy and tactics: half-way towards coordination of policy as such. Shrinking numbers, and hopes of reducing defence expenditure, pushed governments during the 1970s and 1980s further together: into joint training, into mutual dependence for logistical support, and increasingly into specialization of roles. The Anglo-Dutch marine force and the Franco-German brigade represented the most visible indicators of a trend about which *all* West European governments were schizophrenic, with many defence professionals acknowledging the irrationality of attempting to maintain the myth of independent national capabilities while also acknowledging the immense symbolic and practical (command) obstacles to moving much further.[47] Until the security revolution of 1989–91 American leadership, and the ability of European contingents to fit into American-led forces with all-round capabilities, enabled European defence ministries to avoid difficult choices. The unification of Germany, the disappearance of the Soviet threat, the shift in American security priorities away from Europe, domestic expectations of cuts in national defence budgets, the challenges posed by the growing conflict in Yugoslavia and by outbreaks of disorder in Africa and in the former Soviet Union: all these posed central questions to West European states about the role and purpose of national military forces and about appropriate responses to threats which, while diffuse and distant, nevertheless affected long-term national security. Even before 1989, Western Europe had already passed well beyond the traditional model of the independent nation-state, or even the model which France and Britain proudly presented in the 1950s and 1960s of independent

military power. After 1991 West European states were moving, no longer
under firm leadership from the USA, into previously uncharted waters.

States themselves, the very apparatus of government, have in many
ways been most transformed by the developments of the past twenty
years. No British prime minister before Edward Heath thought it a
necessary part of his duties to travel round the capitals of Europe on a
regular basis, or to devote a considerable amount of his time to the
intricacies of European affairs. Scarcely any members of the British
cabinet beyond the foreign secretary and the president of the Board of
Trade found it useful to devote much time to Continental travel – nor,
below them, did more than a few of their officials. NATO from 1949 to
1950 provided a framework for consultations on security and defence –
involving a small and discrete group of officials from foreign and
defence ministries – and for biannual ministerial councils and
occasional heads of government summits. For their six member governments, the ECSC and the EEC from the early 1950s had demanded
multilateral diplomacy – though the numbers of officials and ministers
involved remained limited to the areas of national policy over which
competence had been transferred to these institutions. France and
Germany had deliberately created an intensive bilateral network of
consultations alongside this multilateral network, under the 1963 Elysée
Treaty. By the end of the 1960s all EEC member governments were
concerned to maintain national control over these spreading transgovernmental links – the French government, with its strong sense of
state sovereignty and national interest, more than its partners.[48]

But the interpenetration of governments across Western Europe has
advanced astonishingly since the early 1970s, as governments have
responded to international economic disturbances, political crises and
new cross-border issues – if initially largely by calling conferences and
setting up working groups. Direct and secure telex and telephone lines
linked foreign offices and central banks; officials from every department
of state developed regular contacts with their counterparts in other
European capitals, bilaterally and multilaterally, assisted by improvements in telephone links, telex and fax; embassies, previously the main
channel of communication between European states, found themselves
arranging hotels and appointments for a constant flow of ministers and
officials; local authorities skirted round national governments in their
contacts with each other and with the European Community; national
officials took training courses together, and even began to work on
exchange within other national administrations.[49] This gradual transformation crept up on European governments so imperceptibly that the
cumulative impact has been easy to overlook – except where such
prominent innovations as the creation of the European Council or the

institution of the rotating Community presidency reveal the reorientation of national business and ministerial and official time. But, again, it
has taken us far from the nation-state model as, for example, Anthony
Eden or Harold Macmillan knew it, and a good deal further than
President de Gaulle, a pioneer of summitry and inter-governmental
consultations, would ever have wished to go.[50]

The sharpest and most formal incursion into national sovereignty,
however, has been the acceptance of European Community law as
superior to domestic law in all areas of Community competence under
the Treaties. The high level of compliance with Community law throughout the EC – and beyond, in its effective incorporation into domestic
law by EFTA associates and aspiring ex-socialist 'Europe Agreement'
states, and in the gradual spread of extra-territorial jurisdiction – is one
of the most remarkable and distinctive aspects of West European
regional integration over the past twenty-five years.[51] The federal quality
of Community law was remarked by the British foreign secretary,
Douglas Hurd, who told Conservative students in February 1992 that it
is 'now right to think of the Treaties as part of the [British] Constitution'.[52] This clear emergence of an operating legal order above the
nation-state negates the absolutist concept of unitary sovereignty pro-
pounded by nineteenth-century theorists; it has to be understood in
terms of relations among multiple levels of government, not between
sovereign powers.[53]

Multi-level government implies multiple loyalties and identities, dis-
tributing a degree of legitimacy to each: citizens who define themselves
as Bavarian in some contexts, German in others, and European in
perhaps the broadest political context (or Catalan, Spanish and European – or Scots, British and European . . .). European élites move easily
between such levels, benefiting from the cosmopolitan patterns of their
work while holding on to national and regional roots – where they wish
to do so – in their private lives. European publics are much less
convinced of the benefits which integration has brought and conscious
of its psychological costs: national identities shaken, the link between
citizens and accountable governments weakened by the displacement of
policy-making into the transgovernmental maze of the Community
process. There is an underlying crisis of national identity in most West
European states, expressed in different forms of popular disillusion with
established institutions and élites – but without any indication of the
transfer of loyalties to any new, European, institutions for which the
early idealists of European integration had hoped. Intermarriage,
migration, cross-border movement, even the purchase of large numbers
of second homes by West European nationals in other countries and the
emergence of a significant north–south 'drift' of the well-to-do elderly

from Germany, Britain and Sweden to Spain, Italy and Portugal have diffused identities, and shaken established assumptions about national political communities.[54] A degree of disorientation is evident within the domestic politics of most West European states: demands for the reassertion – or redefinition – of national identity in the light of the development of 'multicultural' societies or transformed relations with other European countries, or for its restatement in resistance to these 'cosmopolitanizing' trends.[55] The single focus for loyalty and identity which the nation-state model promoted has loosened; but it has not been replaced by any clear pattern of multiple loyalties and identities, like that which predominated in West European Christendom before the seventeenth century and which idealists hoped would come again to characterize the modern European Community.[56]

Is There an Underlying Crisis?

The great achievement of the late-nineteenth-century West European nation-state – the very model of the nation-state which aspirant nation-alists in Eastern Europe and their imitators beyond attempted to emulate – was to link accountability, loyalty and legitimacy to authority and power: to tie political community to state power, as Hinsley put it. The experience of Western Europe over the past twenty-five years is that this link is now loosening. The nation as a political and social community is disconnecting from the state as provider of security and welfare. Both nation and state have lost coherence, as borders have become more permeable, national myths harder to maintain, ethnic diversity more evident, personal prosperity more dependent on local or transnational factors than on national protection.

State administrations have struggled to adapt to the implications of technical change and economic and social integration. They have adapted relatively successfully to the demands of shared policy-making, but at the cost of losing the confidence of a rising proportion of their national publics. The territorial and administrative congruence of state, society and economy which Germany, France, Britain, Belgium repre-sented a hundred years ago has given way to an almost Marxian contra-diction: between forces of production (and of services) operating across wider spaces, social communities seeking to revive regional loyalties or splintering into divided ethnic and social groups, and states attempting to maintain the old territorial and authoritative patterns. The rescue of the West European nation-state after 1945 was guided and assisted by the benevolent hegemony of the United States, and contained by common recognition of a clear and present danger from the Soviet Union. Half a century later there is no definable threat to focus civic loyalty on the state, or to provide nation-states with a common purpose and a shared sense of direction; and there is no benevolent hegemon to redefine objectives or to distribute resources to gain wider consent.

'The strength of the European Community . . . lies in the weakness of the nation state'.[57] The weakness of the European Community lies in the strength of national and sub-national identities. Economic integration, driven by technological change and global competition, is counterbalanced by political disintegration. The crisis of the Belgian nation-state – that model of nineteenth-century modernization – may well be terminal. The crisis in the Italian state, never entirely integrated, may yet prove less severe. The maintenance of the United Kingdom of Great Britain and Northern Ireland has been questioned by its own government, signalling a willingness to reconsider the 'Union' with Northern Ireland for which its Conservative predecessors of eighty years ago were prepared to fight. Disintegrative tendencies in Spain and elsewhere appear, at the end of 1993, much less severe. Integrative capacity, however, in a region faced with complex and difficult demands for political adaptation – to integrate the former socialist countries of Central and Eastern Europe, with all the redistributive and security consequences that implies – is low.

The European nation-state is in retreat. It might again be rescued, through striking a further bargain between sovereignty and integration and adjusting the idea of national sovereignty to a more explicitly confederal regional framework. But that would require a redefinition of the European nation-state, and a political leadership to persuade disillusioned publics to accept that redefinition, of which in 1993 there was little sign.

1994

Notes

I am grateful for comments and advice on an earlier draft from participants in the *Political Studies* conference on 'the crisis of the nation state' in Cambridge, September 1993; and also to Anne Deighton, Ralf Dahrendorf, Anthony Forster, Jack Hayward, Alan S. Milward, Julie Smith, Helen Wallace and Vincent Wright.

1. Stanley Hoffmann, 'Obstinate or Obsolete? The Fate of the Nation-State and the Case of Western Europe', *Daedalus*, summer 1966, pp. 862–915. Alan S. Milward, *The European Rescue of the Nation-State*, London 1992; Alan S. Milward *et al.*, *The Frontier of National Sovereignty*, London 1993.

2. F. H. Hinsley, *Sovereignty*, London 1966, p. 230.

3. The distinctiveness of West European integration is explored further in W. Wallace, *Regional Integration: The West European Experience*, Washington 1994.

4. Karl Deutsch *et al.*, *Political Community and the North Atlantic Area*, Princeton 1957, p. 2. Mica Panic, in *National Management of the International Economy*, London 1988, p. 142, uses the term 'spontaneous integration' to describe informal economic integration.

5. Ernst Haas, *Beyond the Nation State*, Stanford, CA 1964. For a survey of the extensive theoretical literature on West European integration see Carole Webb, 'Theoretical

Perspectives and Problems', in Helen Wallace *et al.*, eds, *Policy-making in the European Communities*, New York 1983.

6. Theorists, largely American, and Commission officials shared these perceptions of the dynamics of the process; see, for example, Walter Hallstein, *Europe in the Making*, London 1972. Its original German title was *Der unvollendete Bundesstaat.*

7. William Wallace, 'Introduction: The Dynamics of European Integration', and Robert O. Keohane and Stanley Hoffmann, 'Conclusions: Community Politics and Institutional Change', in William Wallace, ed., *The Dynamics of European Integration*, London 1990.

8. Richard O'Brien, *Global Financial Integration: The End of Geography*, London 1992; Albert Bressand, 'Regional Integration in a Networked World Economy', Margaret Sharp, 'Technology and the Dynamics of Integration', in Wallace, *Dynamics of European Integration.*

9. For the distinction between formal and informal integration, see William Wallace, *The Transformation of Western Europe*, London 1990, chapter 4.

10. Thus Milward starts 'from the realist position that the modern nation state is still the arbiter of its own destiny' (*The Frontier of National Sovereignty*, p. 20) and – in spite of including Belgium within his compass – equates nation with state throughout. Compare W. Wallace, *The Transformation of Western Europe*, chapters 3 and 4.

11. Alan S. Milward, *The Reconstruction of Western Europe, 1945–51*, London 1984, provides the most vigorous – and convincing – presentation of the 'revisionist' interpretation against those who portrayed the history of European integration in terms of the intellectual leadership and influence of the 'Europeans'. Contributors to Raymond Poidevin, ed., *Histoire des débuts de la construction européenne*, Brussels 1986, support the same view that the influence of intellectual idealists was limited, the role of national governments central.

12. Stanley Hoffman, 'Reflections on the Nation-State in Western Europe Today', *Journal of Common Market Studies*, 21, 1982, p. 29.

13. Ralph Miliband, *The State in Capitalist Society*, London 1969, p. 53.

14. On the role of the major West European states in economic planning and management, see Peter Hall, *Governing the Economy: the Politics of State Intervention in Britain and France*, New York 1986; and the classic work by Andrew Shonfield, *Modern Capitalism*, London 1964.

15. Alan S. Milward, 'Etats-nations et communauté: le paradoxe de l'Europe?', *Revue de Synthèse*, July/September 1990, p. 255. (My translation.)

16. Interviewing British civil servants in 1972 about the impact on British government of Community membership, I was struck by the official who answered that the revolution in relations with the Continent had already happened, over the previous ten years, with the shift from formal dispatches through embassies to telephone conversations with opposite numbers in other capitals.

17. Federico Romero, 'Cross-border Population Movements', in Wallace, *The Dynamics of European Integration*, surveys these and other flows.

18. On American wartime plans, see David Ellwood, 'The American Challenge and the Politics of Growth', in M.L. Smith and P.M.R. Stirk, eds, *Making the New Europe: European Unity and the Second World War*, London 1990. See also Max Beloff, *The United States and the Unity of Europe*, Washington 1963. Jean Monnet's wartime position in Washington gave him and his associates – Robert Marjolin and others – privileged access to postwar US administrations, as close as those which British officials enjoyed.

19. On the central importance of the US–German relationship in this period, see Thomas A. Schwartz, *America's Germany: John J. McCloy and the Federal Republic of Germany*, Cambridge, MA 1991.

20. H. van B. Cleveland, *The Atlantic Idea and its European Rivals*, New York 1966. Atlanticists in the Bundestag added a rider to the Elysée Treaty on ratification, to de Gaulle's fury, which delayed the activation of this chapter until the early 1980s; William Wallace, 'European Defence Cooperation: The Reopening Debate', *Survival*, vol. 26, 1984, pp. 251–61.

21. Milward, *The Frontier of National Sovereignty*, p. 5.

22. Quoted in Milward, *European Rescue*, p. 320.

23. 'It is . . . a case of Western myopia: we have equated the "nation" and the "state",

because that is the form they took in the two historically influential societies – Britain and France – at the very moment when nationalism burst forth.' A.D. Smith, 'State-making and Nation-building', in J.A. Hall, ed., *States in History*, Oxford 1986, p. 230. See also Charles Tilly, 'Reflections on the History of European State-making', in Charles Tilly, ed., *The Formation of National States in Western Europe*, Princeton 1975.

24. Kenneth Dyson, *The State Tradition in Western Europe*, Oxford 1980.

25. Hinsley's classic *Sovereignty* provides a developmental interpretation of the rise of the nineteenth-century sovereign state on the back of improvements in administration and education, industry and communication; but then draws back in the final chapter from accepting the parallel logic that 'these [contemporary] changes in international conditions [which] have proceeded from precisely those technical, social and economic forces which have been producing the highly integrated community and the modern nation state' would progressively weaken the community–state link which an earlier stage of development had supported a century before (p. 221).

26. Milward, *European Rescue*, pp. 43, 45.

27. Peter Katzenstein, *Corporatism and Change: Austria, Switzerland and the Politics of Industry*, Ithaca, NY 1984, p. 246.

28. I am drawing on the extensive discussion in Dyson, *The State Tradition in Western Europe*, here.

29. Istvan Hont, 'Free Trade and the Economic Limits to National Politics', in John Dunn, ed., *The Economic Limits to Modern Politics*, Cambridge 1990, pp. 121–41.

30. Mercantilist policies and state-building thus went together. Deliberate promotion of national competitiveness, and the protection of the national economy against over-dependence on foreign investors or suppliers, were part of the doctrine of state sovereignty – against which free-traders argued a deliberately internationalist, anti-strong-state, line. The Thatcher government's attempt to defend state sovereignty while at the same time pursuing free market policies thus led to a number of fundamental contradictions in British policy. See W. Wallace and H. Wallace, 'Strong State or Weak State in Foreign Policy? The Contradictions of Conservative Liberalism, 1979–87', *Public Administration*, vol. 68, 1990, pp. 83–102.

31. Hoffmann, 'Reflections on the Nation–State Today', p. 22.

32. Andrew Moravesik, 'Negotiating the Single European Act', in R.O. Keohane and S. Hoffmann, eds, *The New European Community: Decision-making and Institutional Change*, Boulder, CO, 1991.

33. The best description of the Maastricht negotiating process so far available is Philippe de Schoutheete, 'The Treaty of Maastricht and its Significance for Third Countries,' *Österreichische Zeitschrift für Politikwissenschaft*, winter 1992–3, pp. 247–60. On Danish reactions see Morten Kelstrup, ed., *European Integration and Denmark's Participation*, Copenhagen 1992.

34. Wayne Sandholtz and John Zysman, '1992: Recasting the European Bargain', *World Politics*, vol. 42, 1989, pp. 95–128; Margaret Sharp, 'Technology and the Dynamics of Integration', in Wallace, *Dynamics of European Integration*.

35. Albert Bressand, 'Regional Integration in a Networked World Economy', in Wallace, *Dynamics of European Integration*; R. O'Brien, *Global Financial Integration: The End of Geography*; Deanne Julius, *Global Companies and Public Policy: The Growing Challenge of Foreign Direct Investment*, London 1990.

36. Helen S. Wallace, ed., *The Wider Western Europe: Reshaping the EC/EFTA Relationship*, London 1991.

37. Anna Michalski and Helen Wallace, *The European Community: the Challenge of Enlargement*, London 1992. Katzenstein, *Corporatism and Change*, provides an excellent study of the struggles of small European states to balance economic autonomy and interdependence as the European economy was transformed by industrial, financial and technological innovation. I am drawing here also on draft chapters of the Oxford D. Phil. in progress by Olli Rehn, 'The Nation State Revisited: Small European States in the New Dynamics of World Economy and Integration'.

38. Michael Porter, *The Comparative Advantage of Nations*, London 1990.

39. Milward, *European Rescue*, chaps 3 and 5, provides an excellent description of the trade-offs involved in the development of the ECSC and CAP.

40. Stephan Liebfried and Paul Pierson, 'Prospects for Social Europe', *Politics and Society*, vol. 20, 1992, pp. 356–7.

41. Jean-Pierre Jallade, 'Is the Crisis behind Us? Issues Facing Social Security Systems in Western Europe', in Z. Ferge and J. E. Kolberg, eds, *Social Policy in a Changing Europe*, Frankfurt 1992, pp. 37–56.

42. Richard Davy, 'The Central European Dimension', in Wallace, *Dynamics of European Integration*, chap. 8.

43. I am drawing on material from a seminar organized by the Royal Institute of International Affairs in collaboration with the Association of Chief Police Officers and the Home Office in the spring of 1989.

44. Title VI, *Treaty on European Union*, Official Publications of the EC, Brussels 1992.

45. So far very little has been published on this whole field. But see Malcolm Anderson and Monica den Boer, eds, *European Police Cooperation: Proceedings of a Seminar*, Edinburgh University, Department of Politics, 1992, and working papers 5 and 8 of their series on 'A System of European Police Cooperation in 1992'; and Malcolm Anderson and Monica den Boer, eds, *Policing across National Boundaries*, London 1994.

46. A. Menon, A. Forster and W. Wallace, 'A Common European Defence?' *Survival*, vol. 34, 1992, pp. 98–118.

47. Pierre Lellouche and Karl Jaiser, eds, *Le Couple franco-allemand et la défense d'Europe*, Paris 1986; Karl Kaiser and John Roper, eds, *British-German Defence Cooperation: Partners within the Alliance*, London 1988; Yves Boyer, P. Lellouche and J. Roper, eds, *Franco-British Defence Cooperation: A New Entente Cordiale?*, London 1989.

48. H.S. Wallace, *National Governments and the European Communities*, London 1973.

49. The largest number of exchanges so far among major European governments has been between France and Germany; some smaller countries, in particular the Scandinavians, have exchanged officials for many years. There have to my knowledge also been exchanges between the British and German foreign ministries; a German official was working in the (British) FCO Planning Staff in 1993–94.

50. Wolfgang Wessels, 'Administrative Interaction', in Wallace, *Dynamics*, provides detailed figures for multilateral meetings within the EC and other European organizations. William Wallace, *Britain's Bilateral Links within Western Europe*, London 1984, detailed the growth of bilateral consultations in parallel with these multilateral meetings.

51. The leading case on extra-territoriality is Ahlström Osakyhtio v Commission, ECR 5193 1988: the 'Woodpulp' case, in which Finnish, Swedish, Canadian and American suppliers of wood pulp were fined for infractions of EC competition rules for concertation of pricing on sales into the EC.

52. Speech to Cambridge University Conservative Association, 7 February 1992 (FCO Verbatim Service).

53. Joseph Weiler, 'Journey to an Unknown Destination: A Retrospective and Prospective of the European Court of Justice in the Arena of European Integration', *Journal of Common Market Studies*, vol. 31, 1993, pp. 417–46; Ann-Marie Burley and Walter Mattli, 'Europe before the Court: A Political Theory of Legal Integration', *International Organization*, vol. 47, 1993, pp. 41–76.

54. Occasional papers 34, 35 and 36 of the Department of Geography, King's College London (1992), illustrate an interesting dimension of this move towards living across borders: the growth of British second-home ownership in France. BNP and Barclays Bank estimated in 1990 that in 1989, 15,000 British subjects bought property in France, bringing the total of British owners of French property to over 200,000; *Independent*, 31 March 1990. Between 75,000 and 100,000 more owned property in Spain, Italy, Portugal and Greece; for some these were retirement homes, from which (under recent British legislation) they retained the right to vote in British elections. Large numbers of Germans and Dutch also owned property outside their own national boundaries.

55. William Wallace, 'Foreign Policy and National Identity in the United Kingdom', *International Affairs*, vol. 67, 1991, pp. 65–80; Emmanuel Le Roy Ladurie *et al.*, *Entrer dans le XXIème siècle: essai sur l'avenir de l'identité française*, Paris 1990; Peter Merkl, 'A New

German Identity?', in Gordon Smith *et al., Developments in German Politics*, London 1992, chap. 17; William Wallace, 'British Foreign Policy after the Cold War', *International Affairs*, vol. 68, 1992, pp. 423–42.

56. A.D. Smith, 'National Identity and the Idea of European Unity', *International Affairs*, vol. 68, 1992, pp. 55–76 (see this volume, pp. 318–42); Smith, *National Identity*, London 1991, chapter 7.

57. Milward, *European Rescue of the Nation-State*, p. 446.

Under the Sign of the Interim

Perry Anderson

Mathematically, the European Union today represents the largest single unit in the world economy. It has a nominal GNP of about $6 trillion, compared with $5 trillion for the US and $3 trillion for Japan. Its total population, now over 360 million, approaches that of the United States and Japan combined. Yet in political terms such magnitudes continue to be virtual reality. Beside Washington or Tokyo, Brussels remains a cipher. The Union is no equivalent to either the United States or Japan, since it is not a sovereign state. But what kind of formation is it? Most Europeans themselves are at loss for an answer. The Union remains a more or less unfathomable mystery to all but a handful of those who, to their bemusement, have recently become its citizens. It is well-nigh entirely arcane to ordinary voters; a film of mist covers it even in the mirror of scholars.

The nature of the European Union must have some relation to the origins of the Community which it now subsumes – although, in a typically alembicated juridical twist, does not supersede. Some political clarity about the genesis of its structure seems desirable as a starting-point for considering its future. This is a topic on which there is still no uncontroversial ground. The historical literature has from the outset – a clear sign that few familiar assumptions can be taken for granted – tended to be unusually theoretical in bent. The dominant early scholarship held to the view that the underlying forces behind the postwar integration of Western Europe should be sought in the growth of objective – not only economic, but also social and cultural – interdependencies between the states that made up the initial Coal and Steel Community and its sequels. The tenor of this first wave of interpretation was neo-functionalist, stressing the additive logic of institutional development: that is, the way modest functional changes tended to lead to complementary alterations along an extending path of often involuntary integration. Cross-national convergence of economic transactions, social exchanges and cultural practices had laid the basis for gradual advance towards a new political ideal – a supranational union of states. Ernst Haas, who thought the beginnings of this process relatively contingent, but its subsequent development path-determined, produced what is still perhaps the best theorization of this position in his *Uniting of Europe*, in the late 1950s.

The second wave of interpretations, by contrast, has stressed the structural resilience of the nation-state, and seen the postwar integration of Western Europe not as a glide-path towards any supranational sovereignty, but on the contrary as the means of reinvigorating effective national power. This neo-realist theme comes in a number of different versions, not all of them concordant. Far the most powerful and distinctive is the work of Alan Milward. There is some irony in the fact that the country which has contributed least to European integration should have produced the historian who has illuminated it most. No other scholar within the Union approaches the combination of archival mastery and intellectual passion that Milward has brought to the question of its origins.

His starting-point was at a productive tangent to it. Why, he asked, did economic recovery in Europe after the Second World War not repeat the pattern after the First – an initial spurt due to physical restocking, followed by erratic fits and starts of recession? In *The Reconstruction of Western Europe 1945–51* (London 1984), he set aside conventional explanations – the arrival of Keynesianism; repair of war damage; larger public sector; high defence spending; technological innovation – and suggested that the basis of the completely unprecedented boom, which started as early as 1945 and lasted till at least 1967, lay rather in the steady rise of popular earnings of this period, against a background of long-pent-up unsatisfied demand. This model of growth, in turn, was sustained by new arrangements between states, whose 'pursuit of narrow self-interest'[1] led both to trade liberalization and to the first limited measures of integration in the Schuman Plan.

It is on the way these developed into the European Economic Community that Milward's subsequent work has focused, with a mass of empirical findings and increasingly sharp theoretical thrust. Both his great study of *The European Rescue of the Nation-State* and its coda, *The Frontier of National Sovereignty*, are sustained polemics against neo-functionalist overestimation of the importance of federalist conceptions of any kind – dismissed as a pack of pieties in a caustic chapter on 'The

Lives and Teachings of the European Saints' – in this process.[2] Milward's central argument is that the origins of the Community have little or nothing to do with either the technical imperatives of interdependence – which may even have been less at mid-century than fifty years earlier – or the ethereal visions of a handful of federalist worthies. It was rather a product of the common disaster of the Second World War, when every nation-state between the Pyrenees and the North Sea was shattered by defeat and occupation.

From the depths of impotence and discredit into which prewar institutions had fallen, a quite new kind of structure had to be built up after peace returned. The postwar states of Western Europe were laid, Milward contends, upon a much wider social basis than their narrow and brittle predecessors, for the first time integrating farmers, workers and petty bourgeoisie fully into the political nation with a set of measures for growth, employment and welfare. It was the unexpected success of these policies within each country that prompted a second kind of broadening, of cooperation between countries. Morally rehabilitated within their own borders, six nation-states on the continent found they could strengthen themselves yet further by sharing certain elements of sovereignty to common advantage. At the core of this process was the magnetic pull from an early date of the German market on the export sectors of the other five economies – complemented by the attractions for German industry of easier access to French and Italian markets, and eventual gains for particular interests like Belgian coal and Dutch agriculture. The European Economic Community, in Milward's vision, was born essentially from the autonomous calculations of national states that the prosperity on which their domestic legitimacy rested would be enhanced by a customs union.

The strategic need to contain Germany as a power also played a role. But Milward argues that it was an essentially secondary one, which could have been met by other means. If the driving force behind integration was indeed pursuit of security, the kind of security that really mattered to the peoples of Western Europe in the 1950s was social and economic: the assurance that there would be no return to the hunger and unemployment and dislocations of the 1930s. In the age of Robert Schuman, Konrad Adenauer and Alcide de Gasperi, the desire for political security – that is, reinsurance against German militarism or Soviet expansionism, and even the wish for 'spiritual' security afforded by Catholic solidarity, were so to speak extensions of the same basic quest. The foundation of the EEC lay in the 'similarity and reconcilability'[3] of the socio-economic interests of the six renascent states, set by the political consensus of the postwar democratic order in each country. In Milward's view, this original matrix has held fast down to the present, unaltered by the enlargement of the Community or the elaboration of its machinery.

The one significant further advance in European integration, the Single Market Act of the mid-1980s, reveals the same pattern. By then, under the pressure of global economic crisis and mounting competition from the US and Japan, the political consensus had shifted, as electorates became resigned to the return of unemployment and converted to the imperatives of sound money and social deregulation. Milward does not conceal his dislike for the 'managerial clap-trap and narrow authoritarian deductions from abstract economic principles'[4] which orchestrated this change of outlook. But it was the general turn to neo-liberalism, sealed by Mitterrand's abandonment of his initial Keynesian programme in 1983, that made possible the convergence of all member states, including the UK in Thatcher's heyday, on the completion of the internal market – each calculating, as in the 1950s, the particular commercial benefits it would reap from further liberalization within the Community. Once again the nation-state remained master of the process, yielding certain of its juridical prerogatives only to enhance the sum of its material capacities to satisfy the domestic expectations of its citizenry.

The cumulative power of Milward's account of European integration, hammered home in one case-study after another, each delivered with tremendous attack – institutional detail and theoretical drive racing imperiously across the keyboard, individual portraits pedalled sardonically below – has no equal. But its very force raises a number of questions. Milward's construction as a whole rests on four assumptions, which can perhaps be formulated without too much simplification as follows.

The first, and most explicit, is that the traditional objectives of international diplomacy – the rivalrous struggle for power in an inter-state system: 'world politics' as Max Weber understood it – were always of secondary weight in the options that led to postwar European integration. Milward argues this truth remains as valid today as it ever did. Whether the states of the Community proceed with further integration, he writes in his conclusion, 'depends *absolutely* on the nature of domestic policy choices' (my italics).[5] Foreign policy, as once conceived, is not dismissed: but it is taken to be ancillary to the socio-economic priorities of the nation-state. Inverting the classical Prussian axiom, Milward postulates a virtually unconditional *Primat der Innenpolitik*.

The second assumption – logically distinct from the first – is that where external political or military calculations entered the balance of policy-making, they did so as extensions of the internal pursuit of popular prosperity: security in a complementary register. Diplomatic objectives are germane, but only in continuity, rather than conflict, with the concerns of a domestic consensus. The latter in turn – here we reach a third assumption – reflects the popular will as expressed at the ballot box. 'The preponderant influence on the formulation of national policy and the national interest was always a response to demands from electors', and 'it is by their votes that citizens will continue to exercise the preponderant influence in defining the national interest'.[6] It was because the democratic consensus, in which the voices of workers, clerks and farmers could at last be properly heard, was so similar across Western Europe that nation-states inspired by the new aims of social security could take the first momentous steps of integration. Here – least prominently, yet still discernibly – is a final suggestion: that where it really mattered, there was an ultimate symmetry in the participation of the states that formed the original customs union, and completed the internal market.

Primacy of domestic objectives, and continuity of foreign goals with them; democracy of policy formation, and symmetry of national public opinions. An element of caricature is inseparable from all compression, and Milward's work is subtle and complex enough to contain a number of counter-indications, some of them quite striking. But roughly speaking, these four claims convey the main emphasis of his work. How robust are they? One way of approaching the question is to notice how Milward treats his starting-point. The absolute origin of movement towards European integration is located in the Second World War. Few would dissent. But the experience of the war itself is viewed in a quite particular light, as a cataclysm in which the general brittleness of prewar political structures – lacking any broad democratic base – was suddenly revealed, as one nation-state after another crumpled in the furnace of conflict.

This is one legitimate and productive way of looking at the Second World War, which does set the stage for the story of postwar reconstruction leading to integration that Milward tells. Yet, of course, the war was not just a common ordeal in which all continental states were tested and found wanting. It was also a life-or-death battle between Great Powers, with an asymmetric outcome. Germany, which set off the struggle, never actually collapsed as a nation-state – and least of all because of any narrowness of popular support. Its soldiers and civilians resisted the Allies unflinchingly, to the end.

It was the memory of this incommensurable experience during the war – of the scale of German military supremacy, and its consequences – that shaped European integration quite as much as the commensurate tasks of rebuilding nation-states on a more prosperous and democratic basis after the war, on which Milward concentrates. The country centrally concerned was inevitably France. It is no accident that the

French contribution to the construction of common European institutions has been out of all proportion to the weight of France within the
overall economy of Western Europe. The political and military containment of Germany was a strategic priority for France from the outset,
well before there was any consensus in Paris on the commercial benefits
of integration among the Six. Once Anglo-American opposition ruled
out any re-run of Clemenceau's attempt to hold Germany down by main
force, the only coherent alternative was to bind it into the closest of
alliances, with a construction more enduring than the temporary
shelters of traditional diplomacy.

At the centre of the process of European integration has therefore
always lain a specifically bi-national compact between the two leading
states of the continent, France and Germany. The rationale for the
successive arrangements between them, principally economic in form,
was consistently strategic in background. Decisive for the evolution of
common European institutions were four major bargains between Paris
and Bonn. The first of these was, of course, the Schuman Plan of 1950,
which created the original Coal and Steel Community. If the local
problems of French siderurgy, dependent on Rhenish coal for its supply
of coke, were one element in the inception of the Plan, its intention was
far broader. Germany possessed much the larger heavy industrial base
of the two countries. France feared its potential for rearmament. On
the other hand, Germany feared continued international military control of the Ruhr. Pooling of sovereignty over their joint resources gave
France safeguards against the risk of renascent German militarism, and
freed Germany from Allied economic tutelage.

A second milestone was the understanding between Adenauer and
Guy Mollet that made possible the Treaty of Rome in 1957. Overriding
reservations from the Finance Ministry in Bonn and the Foreign Ministry
in Paris, the two governments reached an accord that secured German
and French goods industries free entry into each other's markets, on
which each was already highly dependent for its prosperity, while
holding out the prospect of increased imports by the Federal Republic
of French farm produce. Adenauer's *placet* for this deal, in the face of
fierce liberal opposition from Ludwig Erhard – who feared higher
French social costs might spread to Germany – was unambiguously
political in inspiration. He wanted West European unity as a bulwark
against communism and guarantee that eventual German reunification
would be respected by France.

In Paris, on the other hand, economic counsels remained divided
over the project of a Common Market until rival proposals from London
for a free trade area looked as if they might be more attractive to Bonn,
threatening the primacy of Franco-German commercial ties. But it was

not the technical opinion of *hauts fonctionnaires* that decided the issue,[7] nor the personal preference of Mollet himself – who had always favoured European integration but been quite unable to carry his party two years earlier, when the EDC was killed off by SFIO votes. What swung the balance was the political shock of the Suez crisis.

Mollet headed a government far more preoccupied with prosecution of the Algerian war, and preparations for a strike against Egypt, than with trade negotiations of any sort. Anglophile by background, he was committed to an understanding with Britain for joint operations in the Eastern Mediterranean. On 1 November 1956 the Suez expedition was launched. Five days later, as French paras were pawing the ground outside Ismailia, Adenauer arrived in Paris for confidential talks on the Common Market. In the middle of Adenauer's discussions with Mollet and Pineau, Anthony Eden suddenly rang from London to announce that Britain had unilaterally called off the expedition, under pressure from the US Treasury. In the stunned silence, Adenauer tactfully implied the moral to his hosts.[8] The French cabinet drew the lesson. America, far from supporting the war in Algeria, as it had the campaign in Indochina, was sabotaging it. Britain was a broken reed. For the last governments of the Fourth Republic, still committed to the French empire in Africa and planning for a French bomb, European unity alone could furnish the necessary counterweight to Washington. Six months later, the Treaty of Rome was signed by Pineau; and in the National Assembly it was the strategic argument – the need for a Europe independent of both America and the USSR – that secured ratification.

The third critical episode came with the advent of de Gaulle. The first really strong regime in France since the war inevitably altered the terms of the bargain. After clinching a Common Agricultural Policy to the advantage of French farmers in early 1962, but failing to create an inter-governmental directorate among the Six, de Gaulle initiated talks for a formal diplomatic axis with Bonn in the autumn. France was by now a nuclear power. In January 1963 he vetoed British entry into the Community. Two weeks later Adenauer signed the Franco-German Treaty. Once this diplomatic alliance was in place, de Gaulle – notoriously hostile to the Commission headed by Walter Hallstein in Brussels – could check further integration of the EC so long as he was in power. The institutional expression of the new balance became the Luxembourg Compromise of 1966, blocking majority voting in the Council of Ministers, which set the legislative parameters for the Community for the next two decades.

Finally, in a period of relative institutional standstill, in 1978 Valéry Giscard d'Estaing and Helmut Schmidt together created the European

Monetary System to counteract the destabilizing effects of the collapse of the Bretton Woods order, when fixed exchanges rates disintegrated amid the first deep postwar recession. Created outside the framework of the Community, the EMS was imposed by France and Germany against resistance even within the Commission, as the first attempt to control the volatility of financial markets, and prepare the ground for a single currency within the space of the Six.

For the first three decades after the war, then, the pattern was quite consistent. The two strongest continental powers, adjacent former enemies, always led European institutional development, in pursuit of distinct but convergent interests. France, which retained military and diplomatic superiority throughout, was determined to attach Germany to a common economic order, capable of ensuring its own prosperity and security, and allowing Western Europe to escape from subservience to the United States. Germany, which enjoyed economic superiority already by the mid-1950s, needed not only Community-wide markets for its industries but French support for its full reintegration into the Atlantic bloc and eventual reunification with the zone – still officially Mitteldeutschland – under the control of the Soviet Union. The dominant partner in this period was always France, whose functionaries conceived the original Coal and Steel Community and designed most of the institutional machinery of the Common Market. It was not until the Deutschmark became the anchor of the European monetary zone for the first time that the balance between Paris and Bonn started to change.

The high politics of the Franco-German axis tell a story older than that of voters in pursuit of consumer durables and welfare payments. But if it suggests neither a new primacy of domestic concerns nor, inevitably, symmetry of national publics – the other member states scarcely match the significance of these two – it does appear to confirm the overwhelming importance Milward gives to purely inter-governmental relations in the history of European integration. Yet if we look at the institutions of the Community that emerged from it, there is a shortfall. A customs union, even equipped with an agrarian fund, did not require a supranational Commission armed with powers of executive direction, a high court capable of striking down national legislation, a parliament with nominal rights of amendment or revocation. The limited domestic goals Milward sees as the driving force behind integration could have been realized inside a much plainer framework – the kind that would have been more agreeable to de Gaulle, had he come to power a year earlier, and can be found in the Americas, North and South, today. The actual machinery of the Community is inexplicable without another force.

That, of course, was the federalist vision of a supranational Europe developed by, above all, Monnet and his circle, the small group of technocrats who conceived the original ECSC, and drafted much of the detail of the EEC. Few modern political figures have remained more elusive than Monnet, as Milward observes in the couple of wary pages he accords him. Since he wrote, however, there has appeared François Duchêne's excellent biography, which brings him into much clearer focus.[9] In an acute and graceful work, that does not minimize the anomalies of Monnet's career, Duchêne draws an arresting portrait of the 'Father of Europe'.

The provincial reserve and propriety that surrounded his person were misleading. Monnet is a figure more out of the world of André Malraux than of Roger Martin du Gard. The small, dapper Charentais was an international adventurer on a grand scale, juggling finance and politics in a series of spectacular gambles that started with operations in war procurements and bank mergers, and ended with schemes for continental unity and dreams of a global directorate. This was a career that moved from cornering Canadian brandy markets to organizing Allied wheat supplies; floating bond issues in Warsaw and Bucharest to fighting proxy battles with Giannini in San Francisco; liquidating Kreuger's empire in Sweden to arranging railroad loans for T.V. Soong in Shanghai; working with Dulles to set up American Motors in Detroit and dealing with Flick to sell off chemical concerns in Nazi Germany. Such were the staging-posts to the postwar Commissariat au Plan and the presidency of the High Authority, to the Companion of Honour and the first Citizen of Europe.

Monnet's marriage gives perhaps the best glimpse of his life, still visible only in part, between the wars. In 1929 he was floating a municipal bond in Milan, at the behest of John McCloy, when he fell in love with the newly-wed wife of one of his Italian employees. There was no divorce under Mussolini, and a child was born two years later. Attempts to get the marriage annulled were resisted by the husband and father, and refused by the Vatican. By 1934 Monnet's headquarters were in Shanghai. There one day he headed for the Trans-Siberian to meet his lover in Moscow, where she arrived from Switzerland, acquired Soviet citizenship overnight, dissolved her marriage, and wed him under the banns of the USSR. His bride, a devout Catholic, preferred these unusual arrangements – he explained – to the demeaning offices of Reno. Why Stalin's government allowed them, Monnet avowed, he could never understand. It was a tense time for a wedding: Kirov was assassinated a fortnight later. Subsequently, when her repudiated Italian spouse attempted to recover his four-year-old daughter in Shanghai, Madame Monnet found refuge from the kidnapper in the Soviet consulate – an establishment of some fame in the history of the Comintern. At the end of 1935, still holding a Soviet passport, she obtained residence in the US, when Monnet re-located to New York, on a Turkish quota. We are in the corridors of *Stamboul Train* or *Shanghai Express.*

Cosmopolitan as only an international financier could be, Monnet remained a French patriot, and from the eve to the end of the Second World War worked with untiring distinction for the victory of his country and the Allies, in Paris, London, Washington, Algiers. In 1945, when he was appointed by de Gaulle to head France's new planning commission, Monnet was a logical choice. The organizer of the Plan for Modernization and Equipment is with reason described by Milward as 'a most effective begetter of the French nation-state's post-war resurgence'.[10] Here, however, he was in a substantial company. What made Monnet different was the speed and boldness with which he slipped this leash when the occasion arose. His opportunity came when in late 1949 Acheson demanded of Schuman a coherent French policy towards Germany, for which the Quai d'Orsay had no answer. It was Monnet's solution – the offer of a supranational pooling of steel and coal resources – that set the ball of European integration rolling. The larger part of the institutional model of the EEC eight years later descended directly from the ECSC Monnet's circle designed in 1950.

There is no doubt that, as Milward suggests, Monnet's initiatives in these years owed much to American encouragement. His decisive advantage, as a political operator across national boundaries in Europe, was the closeness of his association with the US political élite – not only the Dulles brothers, but Acheson, Harriman, McCloy, Ball, Bruce and others – formed during his years in New York and Washington, abundantly documented by Duchêne. Monnet's intimacy with the highest levels of power in the hegemonic state of the hour was unique. He was to become widely distrusted in his own country because of it. How much of his European zeal, both compatriots at the time and historians since have asked, was prompted by his American patrons, within the strategic framework of the Marshall Aid Programme?

The structural interconnection was indeed very close. It is possible that Monnet was first set thinking about postwar integration by discussions in the US, and certain that his subsequent achievements depended critically on US support. But his political inspiration was nevertheless quite different. American policy was driven by the relentless pursuit of Cold War objectives. A strong Western Europe was needed as a bulwark against Soviet aggression, on the central front of a worldwide battle against communist subversion, whose outlying zones were to be found in Asia, from Korea in the north to Indochina and Malaya in the south, where the line was being held by France and Britain.

Monnet was strangely unmoved by all this. In France itself he got on well with CGT leaders after the liberation. He considered the colonial war in Indochina, financed by Washington, 'absurd and dangerous'; feared the Korean war would escalate American pressure for German rearmament to a point where French public opinion would reject the sharing of sovereignty envisaged in the Schuman Plan; thought Western fixation with the Soviet menace a distraction. As late as June 1950 he told the editor of the *Economist* that the underlying purpose of the ECSC was 'the setting up of a neutralized group in Europe – if France need not fear Germany, she need have no other fears, i.e. Russia'.[11] The important task was to build a modern and united Europe, capable in the long run of an independent partnership with the United States. 'We would transform our archaic social conditions', he wrote in 1952, 'and come to laugh at our present fear of Russia'.[12] American power set the limits of all political action in Europe, and Monnet knew better than anyone how to work within them. But he had an original agenda of his own, which was diagonal to US intentions.

Where did it come from? Monnet had lived through two devastating European conflicts, and his overriding goal was to bar the road to another one. But this was a common preoccupation of his generation, without inspiring any general vision of federalism. Part of the reason was that the passions of the Cold War so quickly succeeded the lessons of the World War, displacing or surcharging them in another set of priorities for the political élites of Western Europe. Monnet was detached from these. His career as a deracinated financial projector, adrift from any stable social forces or national frontiers, left him at a psychological angle to the conventional outlook of his class. As Duchêne points out, people thought Monnet 'lacked political values', because he did not care very much about the 'struggles over economic equality springing from the French and Russian Revolutions'.[13] It was this relative indifference – not exactly the same as insensibility – that freed him to act so inventively beyond the assumptions of the inter-state system in which these struggles were fought out.

Although he was proud of his country, Monnet was not committed to the framework of the nation-state. He opposed the French nuclear deterrent and tried to dissuade Adenauer from signing the Franco-German Treaty. From the conception of the ECSC onwards, he worked consistently for supranational goals in Europe. He was initially cool towards the idea of the EEC, which he did not originate, thinking the Common Market to be a 'rather vague' scheme – he was anyway not particularly impressed with doctrines of free trade. Milward makes much of his paradoxical underestimation of the potential of a customs union for integration, but the question Monnet put as early as 1955 – 'Is it possible to have a Common Market without federal social, monetary and macro-economic policies?'[14] – is still the central issue before the European Union forty years later. The order of the phrasing is significant. A banker by profession, Monnet was not economically conservative. He always sought trade-union support for his schemes, and late in life even expressed sympathy with the student movement of 1968, whose warning of social injustice stood for 'the cause of humanity'.[15]

On the other hand, Monnet was a stranger to the democratic process, as conventionally understood. He never faced a crowd or ran for office. Shunning any direct contact with electorates, he worked among élites only. From Milward's standpoint, in which European integration flowed from the popular consensus inside each nation-state, as expressed at the polls, this was in itself enough to condemn him to the irrelevance that affected federalism more largely. It is more plausible, however, to draw the opposite lesson. Monnet's career was emblematic, in a particularly pure way, of the predominant character of the process that has led to the Union we have today. At no point until – ostensibly – the British referendum of 1976 was there any real popular participation in the movement towards European unity.

Parliamentary majorities, of course, had to be stitched up, and corporate interests squared: there was room for alert lobbies or cross-grained deputies to put in their word. But the electorates themselves were never consulted. Europe was scarcely mentioned at the polls that in January 1956 brought the Republican Front to office in France – they were fought over the Algerian conflict and the appeal of Poujade. But the Archimedean point on which the fate of the EEC finally turned was the switch of a few dozen SFIO votes in the National Assembly that had blocked the EDC, in response to the climate after Suez. The weakest performer in Milward's theoretical quartet is here. The democratic foundations he ascribes to the whole process of integration were quite notional. There was an absence of popular opposition to plans designed and debated on high, which received mere negative assent below. In his most recent writing, Milward himself comes close to conceding as much. The reality is the one Duchêne describes: 'The situation was not revolutionary, and voters were neither a motor nor a brake'.[16]

But if this is so, what enabled Monnet and his associates to play the role they did in the bargaining between chancelleries? If we ask why the outcome of European integration was *not* as lop-sidedly inter-governmental as a neo-realist logic would appear to imply (was not, in other words, something closer to the kind of framework that – let us say – Mendès-France or de Gaulle, or later Thatcher or Major, would have approved), the answer is twofold. Firstly, among the Six the smaller nations were predisposed to federalist solutions. The Benelux countries, whose own customs union was adumbrated in exile as early as 1943, were states whose only prospect of significant influence in Europe lay in some kind of supranational framework. It was two foreign ministers from the Low Countries – Beyen in the Netherlands and Spaak in Belgium – who originated the key moves that led to the eventual brokerage of the Treaty of Rome. Beyen, who first actually proposed the Common Market, was not an elected politician but a former executive for Philips and director of Unilever parachuted straight from the IMF straight into the Dutch cabinet. Milward, forgetting his strictures on Monnet, rightly salutes him.

There was, however, a second and much heavier weight that descended on the federalist side of the scales. That was, of course, the United States. Monnet's strength as an architect of integration lay not in any particular leverage with European cabinets – even if he eventually came to enjoy the confidence of Adenauer – but in his direct line to Washington. American pressure, in the epoch of Acheson and Dulles, was crucial in putting real – not merely ideal – force behind the conception of 'ever greater union' that came to be enshrined in the Treaty of Rome. In so far as it tends to underplay this role, Milward's account can be taxed with not excess but insufficiency of realism.

At the same time US policy throws into sharp relief the last of Milward's postulates. For consistent American patronage – at critical moments, pressure – for far-reaching European integration did not correspond to the interests or demands of any important domestic constituency. In the decisions reached, US voters counted for nothing. More significantly, when the potential for economic competition from a more unified Western Europe, equipped with a common external tariff, was registered by the Treasury, the Department of Agriculture and the Federal Reserve, they were firmly overridden by the White House and the State Department. American politico-military imperatives, in the global conflict with communism, trumped commercial calculation without the slightest difficulty. Eisenhower informed Pineau that the realization of the Treaty of the Rome would be 'one of the finest days in the history of the free world, perhaps even more so than winning the war'.[17] Pregnant words from the Allied Supreme Commander.

Milward is entirely clear about US priorities, which he describes with his customary trenchancy. But he does not pursue the theoretical issue they pose for his interpretative scheme. In America, at least, continuity between domestic agendas and foreign objectives did not obtain. There was a clear-cut conflict between them. Was this just an American exception, without echo in Europe? Milward himself provides the evidence that it was not. For there was, after all, one major country of Western Europe which did not take the path of integration.

Why did the United Kingdom, under both Labour and Conservative rule, reject the logic of the Six? Surely the domestic consensus behind rising popular standards, based on the maintenance of full employment and the welfare state, was even more complete in Britain than in France or Italy, with their still intransigent mass Communist Parties, or Germany with its doughty champions of economic liberalism? On the chequerboard of major political forces, there were no English counterparts of Marty or Erhard; and in the vocabulary of Continental Europe no equivalents to Butskellism. If the predominant impetus to integration was a popular quest for socio-economic security codified in a strong national consensus, should Britain in the age of Attlee or Macmillan not have been foremost in it?

Although he points out the elements of an economic configuration that set the UK somewhat apart from the Six – the structure of agricultural subventions, the role of sterling, the salience of Commonwealth markets – Milward does not argue that it therefore made sense for Britain to stay out of Europe. On the contrary, he judges that 'failure to sign the Treaties of Rome was a serious mistake'.[18] His explanation for the error is that the British political establishment, arrogant and provincial, clung to the belief that the UK was 'still in some sense a great power whose foreign policy should reflect that position'. Its ignorance of the nearby world was richly distilled by Harold Macmillan's remark to his intimates that it was 'the Jews, the Planners and the old cosmopolitan element' who were to blame for the supranational tendencies of the European Commission.[19]

What the detail of Milward's account suggests is that for fifteen years after the war British policy towards European integration was essentially settled by rulers who put calculations – or miscalculations – of political power and prestige before estimates of economic performance. The misfit between this pattern and the overall framework of *The European Rescue of the Nation-State* is too plain to escape his notice. On a more tentative note than usual, he offers the ingenious suggestion that because in the interwar and wartime years the crisis of the British state was less acute than on the Continent, 'so the search for a new consensus after 1945 was more limited', and – despite appearances – the result 'perhaps weaker'. He goes on to remark: 'The prosperity it brought was also more limited and the United Kingdom was eventually to lead the attack on the post-war consensus of which it had only been one of the lesser beneficiaries'.[20]

The possibility of a provocative revision of Paul Addison's *Road to*

1945 can be glimpsed here. The assumption remains, however, that it was the degree of social consensus that governed the pace of economic growth and the fate of European policy. But 'consensus' is an evasive term, notoriously close to euphemism, which parades rather than defines a democratic will. Its usage is best confined to the élites that like to talk of it. In this sense, there was indeed a consensus in Britain, and – *pace* Milward – a singularly strong one: but it had little or nothing to do with elections.

The overstatement in Milward's argument comes from an attractive political impulse. A radical and humane attachment to the achievements of the postwar welfare state – the material improvements in the lives of ordinary people it brought – is the underlying motif of his work. If these were the product of democratic choices within the nation-state, can the same pressures not be given credit for the new forms of cooperation between states? The temptation of this move leads to a quizzical heuristic hybrid – what might be called, stressing the oxymoron, a diplomatic populism. But if Milward yields to this out of one side of his radical temper, the other side – a robust impatience with sanctimonies of any kind – repeatedly checks him.

So his recent writing strikes a more ambivalent note. 'Votes and voters', he now concedes, 'are less important than our original hypothesis suggested'.[21] Instead of relying on the claims of consensus, Milward now proposes the notion of allegiance – 'all those elements which induce citizens to give loyalty to institutions of governance' – as the key to understanding European integration.[22] The substitution is salutary. Compared with consensus, a democratic emulsion, allegiance is an older and stiffer physic. The feudal cast of the term Milward now recommends as capable of integrating the different strands involved in the emergence of the Community is more appropriate. It bespeaks not civic participation but customary adhesion – obedience in exchange for benefits: Hobbes rather than Rousseau. This is certainly closer to Western realities.

'The only defence for national government since 1945 we have offered', Milward writes, 'is that it has better represented popular will than in the past, even if still only partially and imperfectly. That is, for us, the historical reason why it has survived' – a survival, however, that he judges to have been 'finely balanced'.[23] Has reinforcement by European integration put it beyond danger? By no means. The rescue may prove only a temporary reprieve. After the promise of its title, Milward's major book closes with what seems like a retraction: 'the strength of the European Community' lies after all 'in the weakness of the nation-state'.[24]

If these contrary notes do not reach harmony, the historical richness of Milward's work exceeding its theoretical scheme, this is also partly because his later work – unlike his earlier – proceeds by topical selection rather than systematic narration. Without simultaneous tracking of the different forces which he in principle admits were at work, the relative contribution of each to the process of integration cannot be adjudicated on equal terms. Such a narrative waits on a fuller opening of the archives. In its absence, what provisional conclusions are reasonable?

There were at least four principal forces behind the process of integration. Although these overlapped, their core concerns were quite distinct. The central aim of the federalist circle round Monnet was to create a European order that would be immune to the catastrophic nationalist wars that had twice devastated the continent, in 1914–18 and 1939–45. The basic objective of the United States was to create a strong West European bulwark against the Soviet Union, as a means to victory in the Cold War. The key French goal was to tie Germany down in a strategic compact leaving Paris *primus inter pares* west of the Elbe. The major German concern was to return to the rank of an established power and keep open the prospect of reunification. What held these different programmes together was – here Milward is, of course, entirely right – the common interest of all parties in securing the economic stability and prosperity of Western Europe, as a condition of achieving each of these goals.

This constellation held good till the end of the 1960s. In the course of the next decade, two significant shifts occurred. The first was an exchange of Anglo-Saxon roles. The belated entry of the UK brought into the Community another state of nominally comparable weight to France and West Germany; while, on the other hand, the US withdrew to a more watchful stance as Nixon and Kissinger started to perceive the potential for a rival great power in Western Europe. The second change was more fundamental. The economic and social policies that had united the original Six during the postwar boom disintegrated with the onset of global recession. The result was a sea change in official attitudes to public finance and levels of employment, social security and rules for competition, that set the barometer for the 1980s.

Thus the last effective step of integration to date, the Single European Act of 1985, exhibits a somewhat different pattern from its predecessors, although not a discontinuous one. The initiative behind the completion of the internal market came from Delors, a convinced federalist recently appointed as French head of the Commission. At governmental level the critical change was, as Milward rightly stresses, the conversion of the Mitterrand regime at Delors's prompting to orthodox liberal discipline the year before – which coincided with the turn to the right that brought Kohl to office in Germany. This time, however, a third power played a role of some significance – Mrs Thatcher collaborating in the interest of deregulating financial markets, in which British banks and insurance companies saw prospects of large gains; while Cockfield in Brussels gave the project its administrative thrust.

The higher profile of the Commission in this episode was testimony to a certain change in the balance of institutional forces within the Community, which the Act itself modified by the introduction (more properly: reinstatement) of qualified majority voting inside the Council of Ministers. On the other hand, the French stamp on the proto-federal machinery in Brussels was never more pronounced than during the Delors presidency, while Paris and Bonn retained their traditional dominance within the web of inter-governmental relations. The resultant of thirty years of such integration is the strange institutional congeries of today's Union, composed of four disjointed parts.

Most visible to the public eye, the European Commission in Brussels acts as – so to speak – the 'executive' of the Community: a body composed of twenty-three functionaries designated by member governments, headed by a president enjoying a salary considerably higher than that of the occupant of the White House, but commanding a bureaucracy smaller than that of many a municipality, with a budget of little more than 1 per cent of area GDP – revenues, moreover, collected not by the Commission, which has no direct powers of taxation itself, but by the member governments. In a provision of which conservatives can still only dream in the US, the Treaty of Rome forbids the Commission to run any deficit. Its expenditures remain heavily concentrated on the Common Agricultural Policy, about which there is much cant both inside and outside Europe – US and Canadian farm support being not much lower than European, and Japanese much higher. A certain amount is also spent on 'structural funds' to aid poor or rust-belt regions. The Commission administers this budget; issues regulatory directives; and proposes new enactments – possessing the sole right of initiating European legislation. Its proceedings are confidential.

Secondly, there is the Council of Ministers – the utterly misleading name for what are in fact a parallel series of inter-governmental meetings between departmental ministers of each member state, covering different policy areas (about thirty in all), whose decisions are tantamount to the legislative function of the Community: a hydra-headed entity in virtually constant session at Brussels, whose deliberations are secret, most of whose decisions are sewn up at a bureaucratic level below the assembled ministers themselves, and whose outcomes are binding on national parliaments. Capping this structure, since 1974, has been the so-called European Council composed of the heads of government of each member state, which meets three times a year and sets broad policy for the Council of Ministers.

Thirdly, there is the European Court of Justice in Luxembourg, composed of twelve judges, appointed by the member states, who pronounce on the legality or otherwise of the directives of the Commission, and on conflict between Union and national law, and have over time come to treat the Treaty of Rome as if it were something like a European constitution. Unlike the Supreme Court in the US, no votes are recorded in the European Court, and no dissent is ever set out in a judgment. The views of individual judges remain unfathomable.

Finally there is the European Parliament, formally the 'popular element' in this institutional complex, as its only elective body. However, in defiance of the Treaty of Rome, it possesses no common electoral system; no permanent home – wandering like a vagabond between Strasbourg, Luxembourg and Brussels; no power of taxation; no control over the purse – being confined to simple yes/no votes on the Community budget as a whole; no say over executive appointments, other than an unusable threat to reject the whole Commission; no rights to initiate legislation, merely the ability to amend or veto it. In all these respects, it functions less like a legislature than a ceremonial apparatus of government, providing a symbolic façade not altogether unlike, say, the monarchy in the Britain.

The institutional upshot of European integration is thus a customs union with a quasi-executive of supranational cast, without any machinery to enforce its decisions; a quasi-legislature of inter-governmental ministerial sessions, shielded from any national oversight, operating as a kind of upper chamber; a quasi-supreme court that acts as if it were the guardian of a constitution which does not exist; and a pseudo-legislative lower chamber, in the form of a largely impotent parliament that is nevertheless the only elective body, theoretically accountable to the peoples of Europe. All of this superimposed on a dozen nation-states, determining their own fiscal, social, military and foreign policies. Up to the end of the 1980s the sum of these arrangements, born under the sign of the interim and the makeshift, had nevertheless acquired a respectable aura of inertia.

In the 1990s, however, three momentous changes loom over the political landscape in which this complex is set. The disappearance of the Soviet bloc, the reunification of Germany and the Treaty of Maastricht have set in motion processes whose scale can be compared only to the end of the war. Together, they mean that the European Union is likely to be the theatre of an extraordinary conjunction of divergent processes in the coming years: the passage to a European monetary union; the return of Germany to continental hegemony; and the competition among ex-communist countries for entry. Can any predictions be made about the kinds of outcome that might emerge from a metabolism of this magnitude?

At this historical cross-roads it is worth thinking back to the work of Monnet and his circle. Historically, state-construction has proceeded along three main lines. One is a gradual, unplanned, organic growth of governmental authority and territory, such as occurred in – let us say – late mediaeval France or early modern Austria, whose architects had little or no idea of long-term objectives at all. A second path is conscious imitation of pre-existing models, of a kind that first really emerges in Europe in the eighteenth century, with the emulation of French Absolutism by its Prussian or Piedmontese counterparts. A third and historically still later path was deliberate revolutionary innovation – the creation of completely new state forms in a very compressed time, under the pressure either of popular upheavals like the American and Russian revolutions, or of élite drives like the Meiji Restoration in Japan.

The process of statecraft set in train by the projectors – the term of Burkean alarm can be taken as homage – of a federal Europe departed from all these paths. It was without historical precedent. For its origins were very deliberately designed, but they were neither imitative of anything else nor total in scope; while the goals at which it aimed were not proximate but very distant. This was an entirely novel combination: a style of political construction that was highly voluntarist, yet pragmatically piecemeal – and yet vaultingly long-range. Relying on what he called a 'dynamic disequilibrium', Monnet's strategy was an incremental totalization, *en route* to a hitherto unexampled objective – a democratic supranational federation. The implications of his undertaking did not escape him. He wrote: 'We are starting a process of continuous reform which can shape tomorrow's world more lastingly than the principles of revolution so widespread outside the West'.[25] It is one of the great merits of Duchêne's biography that it seeks so intelligently to take the measure of this innovation, which he calls – by contrast with conquest, adjustment or upheaval – 'that rarest of all phenomena in history, a studied change of regime'.[26] This is a striking formula. Yet there is at once a certain overstatement and understatement in it. The changes were more improvised than studied; but at stake was more than a regime.

Looking back, who can deny the genius of this conception of political advance – as if the ambitions of Napoleon could be married to the methods of Taaffe? On the other hand, it exacted a characteristic price. If all historical undertakings are subject to the fatality of unintended consequences, the more deliberate they are the more pronounced the gap may become. The 'construction of Europe' set in train by Monnet and his circle was an enterprise of unrivalled scope and complexity, which yet nearly always relied on drab institutional steps and narrow social supports. Historically, it was bound to lead to what it did – that is, a persistent pattern of consequences that disconcerted and foiled the intentions of its architects.

The series of these bafflements has been continuous down to the present. In the 1950s Monnet wanted Euratom and was landed with the Common Market; working for a supranational union, what he eventually got was an inter-governmental consortium dominated by the statesman most opposed to everything he stood for, de Gaulle. The general in turn thought his procedural fixture in the 1960s would stymie the bureaucratic pretensions of the Commission – which in fact rebounded more strongly than in the long run. In the 1980s, Mrs Thatcher believed the Single European Act would repeat and extend the deregulated internal market she championed in the UK – only to discover it leading towards the single currency she most detested. The hopes of Jacques Delors are still with us. Is it likely their fate will differ in the 1990s?

1996

Notes

1. Alan S. Milward, *The Reconstruction of Western Europe 1945–51*, London 1984, p. 492.

2. See Alan S. Milward, *The European Rescue of the Nation-State*, London 1992, pp. 318–344.

3. Alan S. Milward and Vibeke Sørensen, 'Interdependence or Integration? A National Choice', in Alan S. Milward *et al.*, *The Frontier of National Sovereignty. History and Theory 1945–1992*, London 1993, p. 20.

4. Milward, *The European Rescue of the Nation-State*, p. xi.

5. Ibid., p. 447.

6. Alan S. Milward, 'Conclusions: The Value of History', in Milward *et al.*, *The Frontier of National Sovereignty. History and Theory 1945–1992*, pp. 194, 201.

7. For the extent of hostility to integration in the administrative élite, see Gérard Bossuat, 'Les Hauts Fonctionnaires français et le processus d'unité en Europe occidentale d'Alger à Rome (1943–1958)', *Journal of European Integration History*, vol. 1, no. 1, 1995, pp. 87–109.

8. Christian Pineau, *Le Grand Pari. L'Aventure du Traité de Rome*, Paris 1991, pp. 221–3.

9. François Duchêne, *Jean Monnet. The First Statesman of Interdependence*, New York 1994.

10. Milward, *The European Rescue of the Nation-State*, p. 334.

11. Duchêne, pp. 226–8.

12. Ibid., p. 228.

13. Ibid., p. 364.

14. Ibid., p. 270.

15. Jean Monnet, *Mémoires*, Paris 1976, p. 577.

16. Duchêne, p. 357.

17. Milward, *The European Rescue of the Nation-State*, p. 375.

18. Ibid., p. 433.

19. Ibid., pp. 395, 432.

20. Ibid., p. 433.

21. Milward, *The Frontier of National Sovereignty*, p. 195.

22. Alan S. Milward, 'Allegiance – The Past and the Future', *Journal of European Integration History*, vol. 1, no. 1, 1995, p. 14. See this volume, pp. 5–20.

23. Milward, *The European Rescue of the Nation-State*, p. 186.
24. Ibid., pp. 446–7.
25. Cited in Duchêne, p. 390.
26. Ibid., p. 20.

PRESENT

Politics

4

Pursuing a Chimera

Conor Cruise O'Brien

Nationalism and federalism in Europe are not necessarily antithetical, at least on the surface. British nationalism, indeed, resists the federal project, but it was a particular conception of French national interest and capacities which gave rise to the project in the first place. In French thinking – which is nationalist at the core and federalist on the surface – the tighter the federal arrangements are, the more Germany will be under French control. According to Janet Flanner, an American journalist living in Paris and reflecting prevailing assumptions there, 'France is the planning brain of Europe.' Or as Christopher Tugendhat put it, in his useful book *Making Sense of Europe* (1986): 'For the French, Europe is, in a certain sense, an extension of their own personality.'[1] French officials were much attached to an equestrian metaphor: of the skilful French rider, controlling and directing the powerful German horse.

For a long time, and until very recently, the Germans appeared as meekly accepting the modest equine role assigned to them. They needed to be accepted by the Western Allies and to be integrated with them. They were afraid of the Soviet Union and also – especially in the first two postwar decades – they were afraid of their own selves. If France wanted to tie the Germans, the Germans also wanted to be tied, in case they should again hurt themselves, among others. The Preamble to the German Basic Law of 1949 includes a policy leading to a United States of Europe as one of the constitutional foreign-policy goals of Germany. So when, in the following year, Robert Schuman, then French foreign minister, inspired by Jean Monnet, proposed the formation of a European Coal and Steel Community, he knew that he was knocking at an open door where West Germany was concerned. This began the process which led to the Treaty of Rome (January 1958) and then in the 1970s and 1980s to the expansion of the original 'Europe of the Six' to the present 'Europe of the Twelve'.

Strictly speaking, the European Community is no more than a confederation of twelve states, each of which remains politically sovereign. But it is a confederation whose official documents are federalist in character.

The official general guide is a booklet called (in its English-language version) *European Unification: The Origins and Growth of the European Community*, published in Luxembourg for Official Publications of the European Communities. I am using the third edition of this booklet, which appears to be a translation from the German; the title-page declares that it is 'by Klaus-Dieter Borchardt. July 1989'. The text reflects the Franco-German federalist consensus which, as it happened, had reached its high-water mark in the year in which the booklet was composed. It has no room for British reservations about federalism. A section headed 'Political integration' (p. 25) opens with the words: 'Although the principles and measures laid down by the Treaties relate only to the establishment and operation of the common market, economic integration is not meant to be an end in itself but merely an intermediate stage on the road to political integration.' There follows a section on 'Methods' which begins thus: 'European integration had been shaped by two fundamentally different approaches – the "confederalist" and the "federalist".'

The 'confederalist approach' is then dismissed in five cold lines, ending with the words, 'This is the principle underlying the work of the Council of Europe and the OECD.' One can detect there a federalist sniff of distaste at the mention of such inadequately European institutions. Then the writer, warming to his work, gives us two paragraphs dedicated to the right approach, the federalist one:

> The federalist approach, on the other hand, aims to dissolve the traditional distinctions between nation States. The outdated notion of inviolable and indivisible national sovereignty gives way to the view that the imperfections of social and international co-existence, the specific shortcomings of the nation State system, and the dangers of the predominance of one State over others (so frequent a phenomenon in European history) can only be overcome by individual States pooling their sovereignty under a supra-national community. The result is a European federation in which the common destiny of its peoples – still retaining their individual identities – is guided, and their future assured, by common (federal) authorities.
>
> The European Community is a product of this federalist approach, though in a somewhat modified form owing to the Member States' reluctance simply to abandon altogether their sovereignty [*sic*] and the old nation State

structure which they had only just regained and consolidated after the Second World War in favour of a European federation. Once again a compromise had to be found which, without necessarily establishing a federal structure, would provide more than mere cooperation along confederal lines. The solution, both brilliant and simple, was to seek to bridge the gap between national autonomy and European federation in a gradual process. Rather than relinquish all sovereignty overnight, the Member States were asked merely to abandon the dogma of indivisibility.[2]

The key word is 'overnight'. The states are not being asked 'to relinquish all sovereignty overnight', but they are expected to move in the direction of relinquishing all sovereignty, beginning by abandoning 'the dogma of indivisibility.

Most citizens of the twelve states which make up the European Community would probably be disagreeably surprised if they knew that the sovereignty of their own state is already scheduled for liquidation in official publications of the Community to which it belongs. Fortunately for the Eurocrats, very few citizens read their documents, although they are available free of charge in every European language in all the European capitals, not more than one of which can remain a capital if the authors of these documents get their way.

But do they even *want* to get their way? I suppose some of them do; bureaucrats, for example, and Belgians. But I don't think the principal politicians who have been making the running, rhetorically, in the direction of the federalist goal, really mean that they want to get there. To travel hopefully is just fine, but to *arrive*? Ugh! I can't believe that President François Mitterrand (for example) really yearns to see the day when he can announce to the French people that French national sovereignty has become a thing of the past. Nor do I believe that Chancellor Helmut Kohl cherishes any corresponding ambition. When both men, in certain contexts, seek to give the impression that they are more 'European' than they are French, or German, I don't believe them.

Paradoxically, in both France and Germany, the language of federalism, on the lips of political traders, has become a coded way of appealing to rival bodies of nationalists in the two countries. French nationalists, listening to their president recommending federalism, are expected to think: '*We* will outsmart *them*, because we are so much cleverer, and we will run Europe, as well as our own country.' German nationalists, listening to virtually identical language on the lips of their chancellor, are expected to think: 'We must necessarily dominate a Federal Europe, because of our size, our numbers, our strength of character, and our national habits of thrift and hard work, reflected in the strength of our national currency, the DM.'

The two sets of nationalist interpretations are mutually incompatible. And by the end of 1991, it had become clear that it is the German expectation, alone, that is soundly based. The French interpretation has already acquired the pathos of a fading national fantasy. The degree of plausibility that interpretation once commanded derived from its apparent acceptance by the Germans. Throughout the period in which West Germany was a distinct polity, the Germans seemed willing, even eager, to play second fiddle to the French. By doing so, they projected an image of a new Germany: modest, unassuming, even deferential, threatening nobody, not even by so much as a vocal intonation. As long as a Soviet threat was there, it was a German interest and top priority in Bonn to reassure the West, thereby guaranteeing the continuance of the security arrangements that were vital to Germany's defence. It was important to the West that Germany should appear eager to bind herself, under French tutelage, into federal institutions. But after the Soviet threat disappeared, the need to reassure the West, while still felt to some degree, had lost the status of an absolute imperative.

I mentioned earlier that 1989 – the year in which Klaus-Dieter Borchardt composed his federalist thesis for publication by the Community – was the high-water mark of Franco-German federalist enthusiasm. In that year, the Germans were trying to allay French fears of German unity, by displays of eagerness to press forward with European federation, of which a united Germany would be an integral part. These displays did not have their intended effect. The French clearly did not find the idea of being 'tied' with a united Germany particularly reassuring. They now tried to rein in that putative horse of theirs, but the powerful beast bolted off down the road to Berlin. Its rider, François Mitterrand, having been thrown, made his way to Moscow in a bid to avert, or at least to delay, the coming of German unity. He failed even to delay it.

The attainment of German unity, in 1990, in the teeth of French opposition, marked not so much the end of a honeymoon, as the first stage in the breakdown of a marriage of convenience that had lasted for forty years. Appearances are still kept up, on public occasions, but the circumstances that dictated the union in the 1950s have changed radically, and the husband no longer feels quite the old need to keep up appearances.

The first major symbolic act of the new European era, which began with the unification of Germany at the beginning of the present decade, was the re-interment of the bones of Frederick the Great in Berlin. This was both an appeal to German national pride, and an assertion of German national independence. Germany was saying, in effect, to the West, including its putative partners in new federal arrangements: 'We know you don't like this sort of thing, coming from us. We had to defer to your wishes when we were divided and threatened from the East, but we don't feel a need to defer any more, now that we are united and no longer threatened. You people out there had better get used to a new German style. You may not enjoy that, but the Germans will, and that's what matters most to us now.'

The Frederick affair was merely a symbolic expression of the new style, whose first definitive manifestation in practical politics came over Croatia and Slovenia. Germany was in favour of the recognition of the two republics. The rest of the Community was against, and the United States strongly so. Faced with such an apparently powerful 'Western consensus', on any such matter, the old pre-1990 Bundesrepublik would have respectfully backed away. The new united Germany simply ignored the United States, and turned the Community round. Germany recognized the independence of Croatia and Slovenia, and the rest of the Community followed suit within a few days. The reversal of the Community position was particularly humbling for the French. It represented a further degeneration of the cherished equestrian metaphor. Over German unity, the horse had thrown the rider, but over Croatia and Slovenia it had dragged the rider in its wake. The two new republics are now part of a vast German sphere of influence to the east, which includes the former European subjects of the Soviet Empire. The whole area marked out as a French sphere of influence after 1918 is now a German one.

German economic hegemony in Europe is now a fact of life, to which the rest of us Europeans must adjust as best we can. And it is clear that this brings with it a degree of political influence not far short of political hegemony. That was proved in the case of the recognition of Croatia and Slovenia. To press ahead with federal union, under these conditions, would not 'rein in' the mighty power of united Germany. It would subject the rest of us to German hegemony in its plenitude. The sovereignty of national parliaments is only an imperfect barrier against the intrusions of German hegemonic power, but it is the principal barrier we have, and we should take care to hold on to it.

William Cash, MP, in his powerful polemic, *Against a Federal Europe: The Battle of Britain,* has a chilling quotation from Bismarck, who is talking about Prussian hegemony over the other states of the German Empire:

I will use my strength to guarantee you and, in return, you must follow my lead with regard to other powers, and give me support and assistance when I call upon it ... Hegemony is typically an unequal relationship established between a great power and one or more smaller powers which is nevertheless based on the juridical or formal equality of all the states concerned. It is not an empire. It is not based on 'ruler' and 'ruled' but on 'leadership' and 'followers'. It is held together not by command and obedience but by influence and what may be called allegiance. Great powers seek to guarantee their position by establishing a 'buffer' or 'barrier' of smaller powers friendly or aligned to themselves . . . but hegemony is not a one-way relationship.[3]

As Cash suggested, this statement seems to prefigure the condition of the European states within a European federal union dominated by a united Germany. I think, however, that federal union is not about to happen. The partnership that drove on towards it is now holed below the waterline. France let down Germany, over unity, in 1989–90. Germany humiliated France, over Croatia and Slovenia, in 1991. The partnership still exists, in habitual rhetoric, and along with it the federal idea, but both now have a hollow ring to them. The movement towards European political union faltered at Maastricht; John Major did not have as much difficulty as expected in eliminating the word 'federal' from the draft. And the vague formula of Maastricht will probably remain the high-water mark of European federalism.

The French still pay lip-service to the idea of a federal Europe, but the reality, as they now know, is something to be avoided. A federal Europe would be dominated by the new, confident, united Germany, and not by themselves. The federal reality would in fact be precisely that which the French had hoped to avert, through their own self-indulgent version of how federalism would work. So the French are still 'in favour' of federalism, but they don't actually want it any more.

Nor, I think, are the Germans much keener than the French on federal union, under present conditions. To reassure, by showing willingness to be 'tied in', was always a prime ingredient in their federalist zeal. In the post-unification period, however, their interest in the question of whether other people find them reassuring or not has been sensibly diminished. As for hegemony, I think they probably already have as much of that, or almost as much, as they need. European Monetary Union, around the Deutschmark, will consolidate their economic dominance. In the matter of political hegemony, if they have Community support for their policies in relation to Eastern Europe, that is probably as much as they require. The decisions on Croatia and Slovenia suggest that support will be forthcoming, even in the absence of federal structures. Once that support is assured, the idea of responsibility within such structures is probably unattractive. Its exercise would be a distraction from the huge opportunity and problems opening before Germany in its economic *Drang nach Osten*.

Polls show that German support for a federal Europe has greatly diminished since the advent of German unification. In 1988, 51 per cent of West Germans favoured increasing the pace of European unification, while just 6 per cent wanted to slow the pace down. An Altenbach poll in January 1992 showed that support for acceleration is down to 10 per cent, while 29 per cent want to slow the pace down. This means that European political union is not on. Even European Monetary Union is now unpopular with Germans. Only 29 per cent of Germans are prepared to see the Deutschmark exchanged for a common European currency, while 49 per cent refuse the change. These figures should be moderately reassuring to those in the West who fear German hegemony in an increasingly integrated Community. Hegemonically minded Germans are looking east, rather than west, at least for the present.

As for the future, Germany has an opportunity, in this decade, to refute Churchill's dictum that it will 'always be either at your feet or at your throat'. It has not been at anyone's feet since 1990, and it has yet to show any signs of wishing to be at anyone's throat. Yet German nationalism is on the rise, and it seems likely that Germans, in the near future, will interpret their own past in an increasingly nationalist manner, placing strain on relations within the Community. The present 'Europe of States' should be sufficiently flexible to take such strains. A tightly integrated federal Europe might explode under them.

In the book which I quoted earlier, Christopher Tugendhat refers to German reactions to Allied celebrations of the fortieth anniversary of the final period of the Second World War. In 1984–85, he says, the wartime Allies engaged in 'an apparently ceaseless round of celebrations commemorating the Normandy landings, VE Day and various connected events which were bound to arouse difficult psychological and emotional problems for the Germans'.[4]

The fiftieth commemorative cycle of the same events starts in a little more than two years' time. The wartime Allies are likely to hear more outspoken German response to these 'problems' in 1994–95 than they did ten years before.

Although both the Allied celebrations of 1984–85, and the German 'problems' about these, were nationalist in character, the collective wisdom of the period (up to the end of the decade) among the federalists was that nationalism was a thing of the past. A representative federalist politician, the Belgian foreign minister, Leo Tindemans, declared in 1984: 'The old Adam of nationalism is banished forever.' It was easy for Tindemans to say that, since there is no such thing as Belgian nationalism. Yet the antipathy between Fleming and Walloon in Belgium is only a minute aspect of the same old Adam who takes more formidable shape in the major European nationalisms.

That old Adam is now on the rampage in Eastern, and especially South-eastern Europe, and throughout the former Soviet Union. The nationalisms of Western Europe are also still there. The establishment of common transnational economic institutions, transcending national rivalries, was a brilliant and successful innovation. But if the federalists were able to press on towards their United States of Europe through a serious attempt at dismantling the national sovereignties, they would find that they had done the opposite of what they intended. They would have awakened the sleeping giant of nationalism.

Fortunately, they are not likely to get that far. Yet they got far enough to produce some small symptoms of what would have been the results had their enterprise succeeded. There was more than a touch of xenophobia in some of the British reactions to the mere talk of federalism. And in France, such talk, more copious there than anywhere else, contributed to the rise of Jean-Marie Le Pen. Sophisticated French people understood that what was intended was a federal Europe controlled by the French. Unsophisticated French people, however, see their country as about to be taken over by foreigners, and vote for Le Pen. A serious attempt to impose a United States of Europe would have been a bonanza to the Le Pens of every nation – including the most dangerous ones: those of Germany.

The idea of the United States of Europe is a dangerous mirage, deriving from the two meanings of the word 'state'. In Europe, the states concerned are not remotely like states in the American sense. The European states with the exception of Belgium are also nations. The results of attempting to federate nations are visible in Yugoslavia.

1992

Notes

1. Christopher Tugendhat, *Making Sense of Europe*, London 1986, p. 85.
2. Klaus-Dieter Borchardt, *European Unification: The Origins and Growth of the European Community*, Luxembourg, Official Publications of the European Community, January 1990.
3. William Cash, *Against a Federal Europe: The Battle of Britain*, London 1991, p. 94.
4. Tugendhat, *Making Sense of Europe*, p. 95.

5

From Albert Speer to Jacques Delors
John Keegan

What has the fortieth anniversary of the foundation of the European Coal and Steel Community (ECSC) – which fell this week – got to do with the great debate about Europe? How could the establishment of a body so banal help us to find answers to the two great 'whys': why do the British – and the Danes – dislike Europe so much and why do the other members of the Community not dislike it more than they do?

Help none the less it does, for two reasons. The first is that the ECSC was the direct precursor of the European Community and that the debate over its powers and institutions – High Authority, Council of Ministers, Court of Justice, parliamentary assembly – exactly anticipated those current in the EEC member states, which have abruptly woken up and realized how much more sovereignty they are called upon to surrender by the Maastricht Treaty. The second is that the motives underlying the foundation of the ECSC, represented at the time and still today as the first manifestation of the 'European' ideal, are open to an entirely different interpretation.

The ECSC was the child of Jean Monnet and Robert Schuman, the two Frenchmen who share the title of 'father of Europe'. No one – certainly not I – would disclaim their reputation as both genuine patriots and European idealists. Both made their way from France to England to serve de Gaulle when Vichy had declared him a traitor. Both returned to France determined to restore their country's economy and to put its relations with Germany on a footing of permanent friendship. Prosperity and harmony are the central European ideas. Little fault, it might seem, is to be found therefore with the ECSC; none at all, indeed – unless one sees the ECSC as a reconstitution of a German instrument of wartime economic rationalization, organized in a form designed to distribute rather than concentrate German power.

There are two histories of 'Europe'. The first runs something like this. Enlightened Europeans, after 1918 and before 1939, were moving towards an ideal of internationalism. They had been horrified by the hatreds released in 1914. They had come to share the view of José Ortega y Gasset that 'the State has become a puny thing' (though capable of bringing European civilization close to collapse), and that 'only the determination to construct a great nation from the group of peoples of the Continent would give a new life to the pulses of Europe'. After 1939, this noble ideal was taken up by the Resistance in the countries subordinated to German conquest, between whose writings on the European future a narrow congruence can be demonstrated. United by a hatred of Nazism and fascism, the internal Resistance in all countries liberated in 1945 joined hands – among themselves and with the returning external Resistance, personified by Monnet and Schuman – to work together towards Ortega y Gasset's prewar vision.

The common agency of cooperation was Christian Democracy – MRP in France, CDU in Germany and so on – and its chosen instruments such bodies as the Council of Europe (1949), the Western European Union (1954), the European Defence Community, the Organization for Economic Cooperation and Development (1959), as well as the ECSC. Some of these bodies were more successful than others – the Defence Community failed altogether – but all tended towards the same end. In retrospect, the ECSC may be seen as the most significant, because it was the first to which the individual states made actual transfers of sovereignty. Its High Authority's powers over the member states' coal and steel industries so exactly anticipated those of the European Commission over general trade and industry that the two bodies were simply merged in 1967. Between Ortega y Gasset's brilliant vision and its realization in the Treaty of Rome, therefore, the Coal and Steel Community had provided the crucial bridge.

The other history of 'Europe' runs quite differently. It begins with the uncomfortable reminder that the coal and steel resources of France, Belgium and western Germany had twice before been run as a single unit, once during the First World War, once during the Second, as a result of German conquest. In both wars, north-eastern France was placed under the authority of the military governor of Belgium and its industrial resources administered as an entity. There were not, as is often thought, two governmental zones in France between 1940 and November 1942 but three: Vichy, the occupied zone and the north-east.

This arrangement suited German purposes; but it was not wholly inimical to French interests either. Indeed, German occupation policy throughout western Europe was tailored to circumstances. Its aim was to yield Germany the largest possible returns for the least possible outlay on security measures; its method was the greatest measure of indirect rule consistent with that aim. Hence Vichy and hence, too, the policy of leaving constitutional government intact in Denmark, where free parliamentary elections were held as late as 1943. (Those who leap to the conclusion that Denmark's 'No' vote in the Maastricht referendum reflects pride in the continuity of the country's parliamentary institutions may be on to something.)

The more brutish sort of Nazi occupation official despised the indirect principle. Otto Sauckel, commissioner for forced labour, paid no heed to it in his campaign to strip western as well as eastern Europe of skilled manpower. The technocrats, Albert Speer foremost among them, came eventually to a more subtle view. Speer was enormously impressed by the skills shown by Jean Bichelonne, Vichy's industry minister, in manipulating the Franco-German Armistice Commission towards policies that met the needs of German industry while keeping French industrial capacity intact. He eventually succeeded in having Bichelonne received at Berlin as a guest of the state, where together they discussed plans for creating, in effect, a European common market. Speer had decided that exploitation was inefficient and that the future lay in cooperation. 'It would have been the supposition,' he explained to his interrogators after the war, 'that the tariff was lifted from this large economic area and through this a mutual production was really achieved. For any deeply thinking individual it is clear that the tariffs which we have in western Europe are unbearable. So the possibility for producing on a large scale only exists through this scheme.'

Speer's conception – greatly influenced by the ideas of Carl Schmitt, which included not only that of the *Grossraumwirkschaft* (large economic area) but also of a European 'Monroe doctrine' designed to exclude 'alien powers' – made some headway; during 1943–44, genuine measures of cooperation between French and German industrialists were agreed. It could not prevail, however, in circumstances where the finance of international trade was entirely dominated by the system of 'occupation costs' levied at a rate of exchange fixed by the *Deutsche Verrechnungskasse* (German Clearing Bank). All occupied countries were forced to pay the cost of their occupation by German troops out of export earnings from accounts held in the Clearing Bank. The bank so overvalued the mark, however, that exports could never bridge the deficit, which had to be made good by increasing direct taxation at home; as a result in France, for example, payments to the Clearing Bank totalled 49 per cent of public expenditure between 1940 and 1944.

Speer's common market proved, therefore, to be Europe through the looking-glass, but experienced as a nightmare rather than a dream. It taught the whole of western Europe – including Italy, one of the worst sufferers after Mussolini's fall – how punitive German economic primacy could be, and how essential it would be, after liberation came, to set permanent limits to German power. Disarmament would be a necessary but not sufficient limitation. The intrinsic capacity of German industry and banks to set the terms of trade, once war damage had been repaired, demanded institutional measures. Jean Monnet, on his return to France, saw so at once. He recalls in his memoirs how the German coal and steel cartels had robbed their French equivalents of markets during the 1930s and how horrified he was to discover that the French coal and steel masters' one thought, after 1945, was to win measures of tariff protection that would shield their inefficiencies from renewed competition.

He had different intentions. One was to replicate in France the machinery of centralized economic organization which Speer had so brilliantly directed. The outcome was the Ministry of Planning and Equipment, whose young executives – among them Jacques Delors – were eventually to achieve a genuine modernization of French industry. The second was to avert the effects of German cartelization by restoring the wartime integration of the German, French and Belgian coal and steel enterprises, but under conditions that would not only outlaw tariffs, price-fixing and subsidies but levy enforceable sanctions against transgressors. The Coal and Steel Community, which was the result, forced the non-German members into uncomfortable competition but denied the Germans the opportunity to use extra-industrial means – in particular, tax concessions levied on a larger fiscal base – to heighten their competitive advantage.

From the Coal and Steel Community to the Treaty of Rome was but a short step, for the Treaty introduced nothing new. It merely extended over the whole of the economic life of the Six the authority of the institutions the ECSC had set up. Thirty-five years on, the Delors plan – to which the Treaty of Maastricht was to give force – did go much further. Delors was motivated by the fear that, unless the greatly enlarged European Community took wider powers, those it already possessed would be eroded. He therefore hurried the Twelve into the Single European Act and the Exchange-Rate Mechanism, and urged them towards federalism, a single currency and a common foreign and defence policy.

It was at this point that the Danes jibbed and the British Euro-sceptics in parliament threatened to block ratification. The Euro-sceptics have many objections to Maastricht. One way of encapsulating them, however, is to say that they do not understand why all that seems so important to them – above all, the accountability of the executive to elected representatives, hard won over centuries of history – is something that Continental politicians should be so ready to surrender for as yet undelivered economic advantages.

It is a genuine incomprehension, because the British, whether declared Euro-sceptics or not, have not undergone in their lifetime the awful experiences through which the Delors generation lived. They might buy the idealized Ortega y Gasset 'history' of Europe. They simply do not grasp the reality of the other 'history', because, while it was unrolling, their own wartime generation was fighting frantically against it. Their version of the Second World War is a simple one of how a brutal German conquest of the continent was rolled back by the military efforts of the United Kingdom, the United States and the Soviet Union, which eventually brought liberation to its enslaved peoples. They do not perceive the complexities of the German wartime empire, which was simultaneously fiscal and industrial as well as military. An understandable Continental silence on the extensiveness of 'collaboration' – no more than a necessity for proprietors with a business to run – hinders any attempt they might make to see how Delors's 'federal Europe' and Speer's 'large economic area' overlap in the Continental consciousness.

The two may indeed be seen as equivalent to each other in 'good' and 'bad' forms. The European Commission is a version of the Franco-German Armistice Commission in a good form, since in it the French are the equals of the Germans. The Exchange-Rate Mechanism, with the Deutschmark as its key currency, is certainly a better version of the German Clearing Bank with its 'occupation costs' mark, even if parities are effectively set by the Bundesbank for German domestic purposes. Paying for German reunification is a great deal less onerous than paying for the war in the east. The European Parliament, however feeble, is a great deal better than nothing, since wartime Europe, except Denmark, had no parliamentary life at all. The European Court is very much better, since the rule of international law disappeared altogether in Europe between 1940 and 1944. There are even personal analogies: Jacques Delors, the product of a Vichy lycée, may be seen as a 'good' version of Jean Bichelonne, to whom, in his overpowering intelligence and relentless energy, he bears a striking resemblance. Bichelonne, moreover, was in his own way a patriot, who sought to curb German power from a position of weakness. Delors, from a position of strength, is pursuing the same object as patriotically as Monnet and Schuman at the outset.

It is there that those who underwent occupation and those who did not come to the parting of the ways. The Euro-sceptics, whatever our short-term difficulties, are probably wrong in thinking that Britain has any economic future outside Europe. They are right, however, in their political anxieties, which the prime minister has best expressed in his warnings about the growth of a 'European superstate'. To the Continental politicians, whose polities were subsumed in a monstrous German superstate in 1940, the surrenders of sovereignty their quite infant parliamentary systems are now called upon to make must look of trifling significance when contrasted with the outright robbery of sovereignty they experienced in that terrible year. Delors's 'federal Europe' is a comfortable place by comparison even with Speer's 'large economic area'.

Yet Delors, as the Danish vote has perhaps brought home to him, has gone too far. The permanent constraint of German economic power need not entail the surrender of sovereignties to Brussels by the Community's member states that his plan demands. To re-read the objections made in 1950–52 by French, Dutch, Belgian and even German constitutionalists to the intended nature of the Coal and Steel Community – that it required 'jumblings of legislative, judicial and executive functions', that its High Authority would be 'autocratic', its parliamentary assembly 'powerless' and its court an instrument of 'economic review', and that 'a permanently outvoted member would not be able to threaten to withdraw', in which case 'how would unity be preserved if one member wanted to leave?' and 'how would the infidel be punished?' – is to be carried not into the past but face to face with the present. The objections were not answered then. They have resurfaced to torment us now. If they are not met, and if constitutional measures are not framed to accommodate them while Britain – the one member state unafflicted by memories of occupation – holds the Community's presidency, the EEC is unlikely to survive as an entity.

1992

6

British Euro-solipsism

Peter Gowan

The spasms of furious argument about the European Union which have been convulsing British political parties over the last thirty years possess one quality to a far greater extent than is common in political debate. They are not just conflicts about whether the EU is a good or a bad thing: they are at least as much about what kind of thing the EU is: about analysis and explanation as much as about attitudes and values. Indeed, much of the venom, as well as the chaotic and seemingly uncontrollable character of the debates, probably derives from cognitive shocks as British preconceptions have failed to adjust to the evolution of this historically peculiar ensemble of institutions.

One source of these intellectual difficulties lies in the fact that the EU cannot easily be framed within any one of the conventional frameworks for understanding political and economic phenomena. It is evidently a treaty-based international organization, yet unlike other such bodies it possesses a wide jurisdiction within its member states. It evidently carries some weight in international politics, yet it lacks the instruments of force and of diplomacy usually considered to be prerequisites for the wielding of international influence. It has institutional attributes which look similar to the internal institutions of a state, yet on closer inspection its Parliament, Commission and Council turn out to be *sui generis.* Only its Court of Justice and its projected central bank look like analogies with equivalent institutions at the level of a nation-state. And it lacks that most elementary attribute of a state – an enforcement apparatus of its own.

Some have viewed the EU as the institutional materialization of a political movement for a clear and precise programmatic goal: a federal Europe. They have thus viewed it as, at any historical moment, a snapshot of a dynamic process of ever deeper political integration. Yet attempts to identify the deeper mechanisms of the realization of this telos seem to encounter as many contingencies as determinations.

In Britain for decades, the dominant paradigm for understanding the EC was signified by its popular name: the Common Market. The EC was to be understood as an economic arrangement without fundamental political significance. Yet over the last ten years, this minimalist conception has seemed entirely insufficient and misleading, perhaps especially to British observers. The dominant topic of British intellectual enquiry has rather become the significance of the EU for the sovereignty of its member states.

International relations theorists have never taken the EC very seriously as an autonomous actor in international politics. During the Cold War, books on European international politics would characteristically scarcely mention the Community, concentrating instead upon the confrontation between the two blocs and treating what autonomous politics there was in Western Europe as the product of the British, French and German executives. At most, the EC's informal network of European political cooperation would gain a paragraph for its work in the Helsinki process or a footnote for a declaration on the Middle East.

This 'realist' way of thinking has continued to downgrade the EU in the 1990s. But both in the United States and in Britain some of the more extreme proponents of this way of looking at politics, such as John Mearsheimer, have raised concerns which have had a major impact on perceptions of what the significance of the EU may be. The concerns, in a nutshell, are that the United States' dominance in European politics may be coming to an end, and could be replaced either by renewed rivalry and conflict between the West European powers or by a new German regional hegemony.

In the France of François Mitterrand, such realist concerns seemed to lead towards demands for a rapid consolidation of an EU bloc through the building of a common foreign and security policy (under French leadership). In the Britain of Margaret Thatcher and John Major, the concern of the Right was that the banner of 'Europe' would corral a continent bereft of American leadership into a new German *Grossraum*. Within this perspective, the EU had no autonomous existence in its own right. It was, instead, in the striking phrase of Nicholas Ridley, 'a German racket'. Europe had come full circle between 1942 and 1992. Lord Ismay's remark about NATO's purpose being to keep the Americans in, the Russians out and the Germans down was being turned on its head: the Americans were to be out, the Russians down and the Germans up. On this reading the EU is to be a cover for German power.

There is a small grain of truth in this view: Germany is by far the largest economy within the EU and the entire integration process from the 1950s did take forms deliberately tailored to assist German revival as a pivotal ally against the USSR and the international Left. Key features of the European Community were thus constructed to offer the FRG a major economic stake in the Western alliance, compensating for its loss of its eastern provinces to the USSR and Poland and the subtraction of its central region by the GDR. Bonn's diplomacy was also strengthened by its ability to project its influence through such multilateral bodies as the EC and NATO. In the post-Cold War context the EU and the 'European idea' were vital mechanisms for protecting German interests and avoiding German isolation, while the projected form of monetary union is tailored, at least on paper, to fit with German economic ascendancy.

But the realist argument is not principally about economics. On any traditional realist reckoning, the notion of American retreat and German political ascendancy in European politics is simply wrong. The United States remains overwhelmingly the dominant European military power, while the West European states remain subaltern and fragmented in the military-strategic field. They lack the logistic and intelligence-gathering sinews essential to strategic action; they lack internal political unity and the commitment to build the institutions which could cement such unity. The France of Jacques Chirac is shifting its location: within the Atlantic alliance the old pattern of France posing as an alternative for the Germans to a US-led NATO has been replaced by a German interest in deepening Europe's defence identity, faced by a French state re-integrating into NATO and posing as the United States' most potentially vigorous ally; while British policy remains committed both to maintaining a dominant US presence in Europe and to seeking a fragmented political order in Europe held together by traditional mechanisms of power balances.

The source of the anti-German rhetoric on the British realist Right has less to do with German political dominance than with British political marginalization at the end of the Cold War. The increasingly illusory 'British racket' of claiming Number Two status after the USA within the Western alliance has been cruelly exposed under the Bush and Clinton administrations, as Washington has become ever more open in giving priority to contacts with Bonn and Paris over its link with London on so many major European issues. This marginalization is all the more painful against the background of Thatcher's brief moment of prominence at the height of the second Cold War and during the first two years of the Gorbachev period, itself the freak result of Germany's political marginalization as a result of Pershing deployments.

There is abundant evidence that there are residues of anti-German sentiment in the core countries of the European Union which are at least as strong as in the UK. If realist power politics were driving Germany to establish itself as a regional hegemon, these cultural resources of anti-German sentiment would surely have become activated in wider European circles than the right-wing British press. Two conclusions thus seem inescapable. First, the German state's added strength from unification and the collapse of its Soviet-bloc enemy has not led to attempts to rebalance power in Western Europe on the part of Germany's neighbours by ganging up against Bonn. Second, it is at least likely that one of the reasons for the lack of efforts to form such a bloc is the European Union itself: the other member states do not view the post-Maastricht EU as a 'German racket' but rather consider that their own states have too big a stake in the preservation of the EU to sacrifice its functioning on the altar of the balance of power.

If this is the case, then the entire realist argument to the effect that power politics in the traditional senses of the term drives state behaviour is shaken. For realists the member states of the EU should be concerned above all with relative power gains rather than absolute power gains. A government facing a choice between securing its state a gain of 3 per cent while giving Germany a gain of 4 per cent, or alternatively accepting a loss for itself of 1 per cent while ensuring a German loss of 2 per cent, would always choose the latter (relative gain) over the former (larger absolute gain). Yet the post-Maastricht behaviour of the Continental member states of the EU suggests that this realist logic is simply not working. The driving forces of support for the EU today do not derive directly from the calculus of power politics.

However, a radically different perspective on the European Union has also gained currency on the British Right during the first half of the 1990s. This views the EU as in essence an institutional materialization of a political movement and, taking its evidence from the information services of the European Commission, insists that the Union is above all an impulse towards a united federation replacing the balkanized Europe of nation-states.

One could argue that the paradigm shift in Mrs Thatcher's own perspective on the European Union towards this view has been a defining moment in the contemporary history of the British Right. During the early years of her administration, particularly after she had settled the budget issue at Fontainebleau in 1984, the British prime minister could have claimed to have been at the very heart of 'Europe'. She had, after all, through the work of her chancellor, Sir Geoffrey Howe, blazed the trail for what in many ways is the core of the single-market programme through the first major act of her government on coming to office in 1979: the ending of all currency controls, which launched the drive for the free movement of capital across the EC. Her trusted lieutenant Lord Cockfield then led the drive for the single market, while she signed the Single European Act, assured by the Foreign Office that the remarks in it of a political nature were the usual Commission Euro-waffle. Yet by the time of the Rome European Council she was under siege from Continental Christian Democrats who insisted on taking pledges of political unity, not least through monetary union, seriously.

There is no doubt about the real elements of support to be found for this view of the EU in the ideals of Christian Democratic and Socialist parties of the Continent. Both these movements committed themselves to the building of a federal state in Western Europe after the war, and that goal has become virtually enshrined in what might be called the national ideologies of those states in which Socialist and Christian Democratic parties have had predominance – Germany, Italy, the Benelux countries and, more recently, Spain. Indeed the postwar rebuilding of state authority in many of these countries was powerfully assisted precisely by their broad commitment to the inspiring goal of European unity.

Awareness of this dimension of the Community was long delayed in Britain, where neither of the main political parties has had a federalist commitment and where the national strategy was first to revive the old imperial idea and then to embrace what might be called a goal of Little England punching, in Douglas Hurd's phrase, 'above its weight'. British entry into the Community was legitimated almost entirely in economic terms: the Community was simply a 'Common Market'. All the more shocking, therefore, to British political ears was the revival of federal rhetoric by continental parties and by Delors during the late 1980s. During the 1990s, the tendency in Britain has thus been to view the federal impulses within the Union as potentially the shaping influence on its future development.

Yet this federalist perspective also, surely, is exaggerated. In the first place, what might be called the 'constitution' of the Union is constructed more for political immobilism than for political development.[1] The powers of resistance of minorities among governments are entrenched and the possibilities of circumventing such resistance through the use of popular mandates are non-existent: the power of initiative for any constitutional development lies exclusively with national governments operating under the unanimity principle. And the institutional development of the EU has been more in the direction of inter-governmentalism than towards a democratic federation. The creation of the European Council of heads of state and government in the early 1970s has been followed by a steady increase in the Council's salience, culminating in the pivotal position allocated to it in the Maastricht Treaty.

Moreover, the influence of the party ideals of both the Christian Democrats and the Socialists, when the occasions for federal transformation have arisen, have tended to be overridden by other forces. This was most marked at the Maastricht inter-governmental conferences at the end of 1991 when federalism seemed to be on the agenda and when Christian Democrats or Socialists governed in Germany, France, Italy, Spain and most of the rest of the Community. They might have opted for a stride towards a democratic federal policy while offering the British escape routes, yet they failed to do so. Today, of course, the party political landscape in Europe has changed; with Chirac's neo-Gaullist presidency, Italy in the throes of a regime crisis, and more uncertain political leadership in Spain.

The failure of the seemingly powerful 'federalist' coalition at Maastricht was all the more striking since the principal policy task there was deemed to be the achievement of monetary union. The detailed institutional design for this laid down the arrangements for an entirely independent central bank which would take charge of monetary policy. It was widely accepted that such a framework would make fiscal coordination and therefore what Delors called an 'economic government' more or less a functional necessity – and if there was to be such an economic government, the argument for it to be democratically responsible would surely carry the day. In theory, the task of designing such a democratically accountable 'economic government' would be straightforward: the Commission could become a democratically authoritative executive by being formed out of the party or parties with a majority of seats in the European Parliament.

Yet the public quasi-federalist rhetoric of President Mitterrand and the French Socialists turned out to be a bluff: no breakthrough was achieved, Delors's hopes for the Treaty were disappointed and instead the European Parliament was given 'greater powers' – in other words, powers to block legislative progress, whereas the parliament's actual concerns are not to contribute further to EU decision-making gridlock but to streamline institutional development.

Federalist defenders of Maastricht still argue that their goal will be achieved through the pressure of functional necessities. They assert that economic and monetary union will unblock a cascade of functional and political spillovers: a single monetary policy will call forth a coordinated fiscal policy followed by 'economic government', followed by overwhelming pressure for effective democratic control of the economic policy executive: and European parliamentary control will itself necessitate a fully fledged federal constitution. Those on the Tory Right who argue that monetary union will lead to a federal superstate essentially share this prognosis of the 'federalist functionalists'.

This view would carry more weight if its proponents could demonstrate at least one of two propositions: first, that the logic of events
themselves will impel governments down this route; or, second, that
popular pressures in reaction to monetary union will impose a democratically accountable government upon the Union. Yet neither of these
arguments carries conviction. As to the first, the 1996 IGC demonstrated
no will on the part of any significant government in the Union to press
for construction of a democratically accountable European executive
leadership. Such impulses today seem weaker even than five years ago
at Maastricht. As to popular pressures, they will no doubt arise, perhaps
quite strongly, if the monetary union is wide in geographical scope. But
such movements, whether in defence of jobs or welfare rights or wages,
can only have a national focus in the absence of a prior construction of
a European Union governmental authority. The reason for this lies not
in resurgent nationalist ideology but in elementary institutional realities.
A movement for jobs or welfare rights – indeed, any popular political
movement – must seek out an authoritative negotiating partner with a
credible claim to be able to deliver on any deal struck round a
bargaining table. No such executive bargaining partner exists at Union
level, unless it were to be the Council of heads of state and government.
Jacques Santer could have no mandate to deliver on anything of
substance. The only such credible interlocutors are organized at the
nation-state level.

Of course, Britain's Euro-sceptics are on strong ground in so far as
they argue that the European Union's policy-making powers lack liberal-
democratic legitimacy. Most varieties of liberalism would require that
policy-making should be open to public scrutiny and debate, while
representative democracy demands that the policy-making process
should be dominated by officials who are electorally accountable. But
the integration process has never been driven by democratic will-
formation. Its core decision-making institution – the Council of Ministers – is closed to public scrutiny, while the European Parliament
remains more decorative than effective. The élite federalists in the
tradition of Monnet surely have much to answer for here.

Yet the current democratic clamour from British Euro-sceptics is rich
in humbug as well as irony. For the British Right, while denouncing the
lack of democracy within the Union, has also to reinforce the democratic deficit by confining all power in the Council of Ministers.
Meanwhile, the new concentrations of unaccountable decision-making
lie precisely in those areas where the capitalist nation-state itself has
always resisted democratic encroachment most trenchantly: monetary
policy, internal security, foreign policy and judicial management.

If in such areas the European nation-states had functioned as free,

democratic associations of citizens engaged in a sovereign and largely
transparent process of policy-making, the transfer of such jurisdictions
to an unaccountable EU would surely have raised a storm of criticism.
Yet this liberal vision of the European nation-state has always been an
ideal one with only the most distant relationship to reality.

Thus, in matters connected to welfare-state issues, the details of tax
policy or matters concerned with public ethics, crime and punishment,
the policy-making process in European states has tended to be relatively
fragmented and open to democratic contestation. It is precisely in these
areas that the European Union still plays a very small part. But in
monetary policy, foreign and internal security, the nation-state has been
very largely closed, with policy-making being confined within executives
in dialogue with the private élites of the country concerned.

In the policy-making systems of what might be called normal capitalist states, the notion of democratic control over monetary policy has
always been largely alien. In Britain, where Treasury control of the
Bank of England has been officially presented as absolute, at least
during the brief period since the Bank of England was nationalized
after the war, the degree of involvement in monetary policy on the
part of elected politicians has typically been minimal. In the 1970s,
Callaghan did manage to gain a seat at the committee making monetary
policy, known at the time as the 'Tuesday Seminar'. But even Mrs
Thatcher was evidently unaware for a long time that the Treasury's
sterling policy involved shadowing the Deutschmark. The Bank of
England has, in truth, acted more as a conduit of private City influence
upon great swathes of public policy-making than as an instrument of
the will of elected politicians over monetary or private financial
institutions.

The story has been very similar in the fields now tackled within the
justice and home-affairs pillar of the Union. Matters concerned with
internal security, policing, migration and asylum have been notoriously
impermeable to parliamentary scrutiny, while management of the
judicial system, hived off in the mysteries of the Lord Chancellor's
office, has been answerable mainly to the House of Lords rather than
the Commons. Foreign and security policy in the UK is famous for the
lack of influence on it even of select groups of aficionados in bodies like
Chatham House. Furthermore, it was the British government which led
the successful campaign at Maastricht to maintain these fields separate
from the legislative procedures of the European Community itself. Their
incorporation within the EC pillar by the current IGC would actually
mark an advance in transparency over the status quo ante at the level of
the British state.

The EU has, of course, as a result of the single-market programme, acquired very extensive legislative powers over the regulation of industry. This field has traditionally been governed by the parliamentary process at a nation-state level. Yet here also the ceremonial must be distinguished from the effective in the exercise of legislative power. In the UK the real process of legislative interchange in this area has tended to become increasingly confined to bilateral discussions between the executive and business interests, before bills are even published for scrutiny by MPs. The most important business interests have rarely had to devote their lobbying resources to the cultivation of backbench opinion for the passage of bills through the House of Commons. The paradigm illustration of this is the famous occasion when a British cabinet decided to break with its normal practice of closed policy-making and to introduce a major piece of industrial regulation without consulting the representatives of big business: the Heath government's introduction of its 1971 Industry Act. The government was for once attempting to legislate in activist ways which it knew would not be to the liking of the Confederation of British Industry. The CBI was then confronted for the first time with the need actually to lobby MPs, and its leaders discovered to their consternation that they had no files with any list of Conservative MPs who had significant influence on the cabinet! In effect, ever-wider areas of legislative activity have passed, through 'delegated legislation', into the hands of the executive. It would be difficult to find many members of the administrative élites of European states who would view the throwing open of these areas of policy-making to the scrutiny of the general citizenry as a strengthening of state capacity.

It is precisely in these largely closed areas that EU encroachment upon the liberal vision of state sovereignty has been so extensive – incursion managed to a great extent by the very same officials who kept the doors of the nation-state closed against public scrutiny in the past: the senior functionaries of Coreper and the Council of Ministers and the latter's satellite committees. Thus, the shift of policy-making in these closed areas to a European collegial plane is not, in most cases, a significant loss of democratic accountability at the member-state level, since little or no such democratic control has ever existed.

We are therefore confronted with a genuine puzzle in our efforts to understand the sources of the bitter hostility to the European Union since Maastricht on the part of a powerful section of the Conservative Party. Could it really be the result of multiple misunderstandings: exaggerated fears of German dominance, phantasmagorias of a federal superstate or confused anxieties about democratic accountability? The puzzle is deepened when we appreciate the remarkable degree of congruence between the public objectives of the British governments since 1979 and those of the single-market programme.

For dominant developments within the EU since 1985 have, paradoxically, dovetailed with the goals of the Conservative Party during the
Thatcher period – at least in so far as these goals were articulated by the
party's deputy leader, if not by Thatcher herself during the eleven years
of her rule. If we were to think of the battle for the future of the
European Union as one between the politics of Jacques Delors and the
goals of Sir Geoffrey Howe, it would surely be Howe who could claim
his vision had proved victorious. It was his drive for the ending of
controls on the free movement of capital which Delors was to take up
and which formed the basis for the entire single-market programme.
That programme in turn has 'quasi-globalized' the institutions of the
West European economies in the ways in which Sir Geoffrey, along with
his American counterparts, would have wished – a process that involves
a dense network of legal regulation invigilated by the European Court
of Justice without which the Single European Act could not have been
implemented.

The result has been the characteristic economic pattern with which
we have all become familiar, both in the UK and on the Continent
during the 1980s and 1990s: slower growth or semi-stagnation at a
macroeconomic level, combined with a revival of the profitability of
oligopolistic businesses – i.e., the breaking of the traditional link
between high growth and high profits; large structural pools of unemployment (partially concealed in the UK by statistical massaging and the
counting of part-time jobs as if they were full-time) and a constriction of
effective demand, coupled with neo-mercantilist efforts to open up
peripheral markets so that large European multinationals can restore
their profits through scale economies and the extraction of monopolistic
rents in 'emerging markets' (notably in east Central Europe); pressures
for lower taxation upon the wealthy and business, combined with fiscal
strains and even crisis at the nation-state level. All this has been achieved
with minimal success for Delors's efforts to build a countervailing
structure of 'social cohesion' – the various modest investment packages
to stimulate job creation offered by the Commission have easily been
emasculated by German and British votes, most recently at the Florence
Council of June 1966. When Howe provoked the final downfall of
Thatcher's premiership, it is no accident that he used the device of
reading out a letter allegedly written by an anonymous businessman
warning of the dire economic consequences of anti-European British
nationalism. No Thatcher loyalist thought to challenge him by demanding to know the signatory of the letter or by suggesting that he might
have written it himself. All were only too aware how plausible was his
invocation of widespread corporate opinion, and of the reasons for it.

Strangely enough, one might even say that five years after Maastricht, the vision of Europe outlined in Mrs Thatcher's Bruges speech is closer to realization than seemed conceivable at Maastricht. This development has been masked by the continuities of political forms in the current IGC: the UK in a minority of one (on the common foreign and security policy) or a minority of two (on the third pillar, of justice and home affairs) and a prime minister posing once again as a truculent defender of 'Britain' against 'Europe'. Yet the striking feature of the IGC agenda is how very limited its ambitions are. Indeed, it is largely a pragmatic schedule for ensuring that decision-making in the Council of Ministers will remain viable on single-market issues in the context of any future eastward enlargement. In the present phase of European construction, ambitions have been curtailed to little more than ensuring a robust framework for preserving the internal market while preparations both for the single currency and for eastward enlargement proceed. The federalist and democratic impulses which seemed strong at the start of the decade have largely dissipated, at least for the moment.

We are thus driven to a paradoxical conclusion: that Tory Euro-scepticism is incomprehensible as a cognitive response to changes within the European Community/European Union during the last decade. Its sources must be found within the pathology of the British state and within the Conservative Party itself. There is first the particular politics of the Thatcherite drive for neo-liberal restructuring during the 1980s. While on the Continent these restructuring efforts have proceeded piecemeal and cautiously, often under Socialist governments legitimat-ing their efforts by reference to the single-market programme and the need to respect the parameters of the EMS and convergence criteria, in Britain they were mounted under the banner of a nationalist-populist assault on domestic labour, and assorted external foes – including the 'socialism' of the European Community. The failure of neo-liberalism as an inclusive programme of modernization has merely radicalized Tory nationalism in a Poujadist direction reminiscent at times of the rhetoric of Jean-Marie Le Pen. Each disaster in domestic management, from the ERM debacle of 1992 to the BSE crisis of 1996, is simply expelled abroad into a confrontation with 'Europe'.

'Neo-liberalism' Conservative-style has also, through its very social successes in enriching the Home Countries core of the party's following, undermined the cultural basis of the old conservative coalition. Thatch-erite nationalist populism has been combined with free-market ideo-logies which have corroded respect for the traditional institutions of the British state and unleashed centrifugal forces within the UK. Attempts to reconsolidate the Tory coalition through anti-EU rhetoric have deeply split its own business constituencies. While most of the largest manu-facturing companies in the UK (whether British owned or Japanese,

German or American) feel themselves to have a massive stake in
Britain's continued full integration within the EU, such groups have
never had a monopoly of influence within the Conservative Party.
Under Mrs Thatcher a rentier class was born again through the
rebuilding of very large portfolio investments in North America and in
other parts of the non-European world, and much of it dreams of
turning the country into a European off-shore Hong Kong or Singapore,
unfettered by the welfare state concessions made to the Left during the
Cold War, or indeed by the whole tradition of social and political
liberalism in Britain.

These dreams have gained added lustre from an unpleasant truth
about the British political economy which no Conservative politician
can publicly acknowledge but which is a source of deep concern for the
future: the German-style regulatory regime under EMU would expose
the British economy's continuing lack of competitive strength and could
subject large regions to deepening economic decline. For a quarter of a
century the weaknesses of the domestic economy relative to its continental partners have been both cushioned and concealed by a strategy of
creeping currency devaluation. Monetary Union would remove that
cushion and expose the relative poverty of the bulk of the British
population. Yet to stay out of EMU will risk making the UK a far less
attractive centre for inward investment within the EU for foreign capital.

Once again, the source of problems stems not from a German
challenge but from Britain's economic weakness in comparison with the
majority of its partners in the EU. A decade and a half of a kind of Tory
vulgar Marxism – attempting to revive competitiveness by undermining
the incomes, security and bargaining power of employees – has left the
key problems of contemporary competitive strength unresolved: levels
of investment remain low, infrastructure is decaying, trade performance
continues to be weak. The legacy, apart from the enrichment of a small
minority, is a state weaker in effective political influence abroad and in
domestic authority. A xenophobic and solipsistic nationalism against the
EU is the result.

The banks and firms that gained a large stake in the EU in these
years have thus been driven by the need to preserve their market
positions, to turn for security in new directions. The letter from the
industrialist which Sir Geoffrey Howe pulled out of his jacket in the
House of Commons back in 1990 now rests quite comfortably in the
pocket of Tony Blair. The Labour Party, which might be thought to
have better grounds than a business-oriented Conservative Party for
being sceptical about the direction of the EU in the 1990s, has become,
for the moment at least, somewhat more accommodating. But as the
campaign Union Jack blazoned behind the new leader reminds us, it

would be unwise to assume the solipsist syndrome is an exclusive property of the outgoing regime. The example of Gaitskell, New Labour *ante diem*, should be warning enough: the passion of Brighton exceeded that of Bruges. Times have changed, but the cult of macho politics has not.

1996

Notes

1. See Michael Newman, *Democracy, Sovereignty and the European Union*, London 1996, for an excellent discussion of the policy-making mechanism of the Union.

7

Strengthening the Hard Core
Karl Lamers

I. The Situation

The process of European unification has reached a critical juncture in its development. If, in the next two to four years, no solution to the causes of this critical development is found, the Union, contrary to the goal of ever closer union invoked in the Maastricht Treaty, will in essence become a loosely knit grouping of states restricted to certain economic aspects and composed of various sub-groupings. It would then be no more than a 'sophisticated' free-trade area incapable of overcoming either the existential internal problems of the European societies, or the external challenges they face.

The main causes of this situation are:

- Overextension of the EU's institutions which, originally set up for six member countries, must now cater for a membership of twelve – soon (it is to be expected) to rise to sixteen.
- A growing differentiation of interests, fuelled by differences in the level of socio-economic development, which threatens to obscure the basic commonality of interests.
- Different perceptions of internal and, above all, external priorities (e.g., Maghreb/Eastern Europe) in a European Union stretching from the North Cape to Gibraltar.
- A process of profound structural economic change. With its mass unemployment, which it will be impossible to overcome in the short term, this crisis poses a threat to already overstretched social systems

and to social stability. The economic crisis is one aspect of the general crisis of modern society in the West.

- An increase in 'regressive nationalism' in (almost) all member countries, which is the product of deep-seated fears and anxieties caused by the internal crisis of modern society and by external threats, such as migration. Fear and anxiety tempt people to seek, if not a solution, then at least refuge in a return to the nation-state and all things national.
- The highly debilitating effect of the enormous demands placed on national governments and parliaments by the above problems.
- The open question, at least as regards the 'when' and 'how', of the involvement of the countries of (Eastern) Central Europe in the European Union. For the present members of the European Union, eastward expansion constitutes both a challenge and a test, not only in terms of the material contribution they are able and willing to make but also in terms of their moral and spiritual self-conception. The Union's response will show whether it is able and willing to become the main pillar of a continental order, alongside a democratized and once again stable Russia and in alliance with the USA.

II. Germany's Interests

Owing to its geographical location, its size and its history, Germany has a special interest in preventing Europe from drifting apart. If Europe were to drift apart, Germany would once again find itself caught in the middle between East and West, a position which throughout its history has made it difficult for Germany to give a clear orientation to its internal order and to establish a stable and lasting balance in its external relations. Germany's attempts to overcome its position at the centre of Europe's conflicts through hegemony failed. The military, political and moral catastrophe of 1945 – the consequence of the last such attempt – not only made Germany realize that it lacked the necessary resources; in particular, it led to the conviction that security could be achieved only by radically transforming the system of states in Europe into one in which hegemony appeared neither possible nor desirable. This conviction became the cornerstone of German policy. In this way, the problem of security 'against' Germany was solved in the West by creating a system of security 'with' Germany. This new system combined control over Germany by its partners with control over these partners by Germany. A condition for its establishment was that the western part of Germany became indispensable for the security of the West *vis-à-vis* the Soviet Union and that in the military field NATO, under American leadership, assumed this dual task of integrating Germany. In the economic sphere, and also increasingly in the political sphere, the solution was to integrate Germany into the EC/EU. This was in line with the need to establish joint institutions to handle the increasingly dense network of relations among the countries of (Western) Europe. Within this system, Germany's relative economic superiority did not have a dominating effect but proved beneficial for all. In this way, Germany – or at least its larger part – for the first time in its history clearly became a part of the West with regard both to its internal order and to the orientation of its foreign policy. For Germany, there was no alternative to this extraordinarily stable and successful postwar system since, as a result of the East-West confrontation and Germany's total defeat in 1945, the option of pursuing an independent policy towards the East, or indeed of seeking alignment with the East, simply did not exist.

Now that the East–West conflict has come to an end, a stable order must be found for the eastern half of the continent too. This is in the interest of Germany in particular since, owing to its position, it would suffer the effects of instability in the East more quickly and directly than others. The only solution which will prevent a return to the unstable prewar system, with Germany once again caught in the middle between East and West, is to integrate Germany's Central and Eastern European neighbours into the (West) European postwar system and to establish a wide-ranging partnership between this system and Russia. Never again must there be a destabilizing vacuum of power in Central Europe. If (West) European integration were not to progress, Germany might be called upon, or be tempted by its own security constraints, to try to effect the stabilization of Eastern Europe on its own and in the traditional way. However, this would far exceed its capacities and, at the same time, erode the cohesion of the European Union, especially since everywhere memories are still very much alive that historically German policy towards the East concentrated on closer cooperation with Russia at the expense of the countries in between. Hence, Germany has a fundamental interest both in widening the Union to the East and strengthening it through further deepening. Indeed, deepening is a precondition for widening. Without such further internal strengthening, the Union would be unable to meet the enormous challenge of eastward expansion. It might fall apart and once again become no more than a loose grouping of states unable to guarantee stability. Only if the new system set up after 1945 to regulate conflicts, to effect a balancing of interests, to promote mutual development and to ensure Europe's self-assertion in its external relations can be further developed and expanded to take in Germany's neighbours in Central and Eastern Europe, will Germany have a chance of becoming a centre of stability in the heart of Europe. This German interest in stability is essentially identical with that of Europe.

Owing to its position, its size and its close relations with France, Germany bears a special responsibility and has a major opportunity to play a leading part in promoting a course of development which will benefit both it and Europe. Following its assumption of the presidency of the European Union on 1 July 1994, for Germany the tremendous long-term efforts needed to achieve this goal have begun.

III. What Must Be Done? Proposals

The above goal can be achieved only through a combination of measures in the institutional sphere and in a number of policy fields. The following five proposals are mutually dependent and reinforcing, and form an integrated whole:

- further develop the EU's institutions and put subsidiarity into effect, including the retransfer of powers;
- further strengthen the EU's hard core;
- raise the quality of Franco-German relations to a new level;
- improve the Union's capacity for effective action in the field of foreign and security policy;
- expand the Union towards the East.

It goes without saying that, especially with a view to enhancing public acceptance of European integration, these measures must be accompanied by efforts to combat organized crime, establish a common policy on migration, fight unemployment, establish a common social policy, ensure Europe's continued competitiveness and protect the environment.

1. Further Developing the EU's Institutions

The further development of the EU's institutions, which is on the agenda of the inter-governmental conference in 1996, should be based on the following principles.

- The goal must be to strengthen the EU's capacity to act and to make its structures and procedures more democratic and federal.
- To this end, the question of who does what must be answered. This should be done in a quasi-constitutional document which, in clear

language, describes the division of powers between the EU, the nation-states and the regions, and defines the fundamental values on which the Union is based.

- This document must be oriented to the model of a 'federal state' and to the principle of subsidiarity. This applies not only to the division of powers but also to the question of whether public authorities, including those of the Union, should perform certain functions or should leave them to groups in society. Germany, at whose request the principle of subsidiarity was incorporated in the Maastricht Treaty, and which has experience in applying it, is called upon to put forward recommendations not only on how the principle of subsidiarity can be applied to future measures of the EU but also on how existing regulations can be adapted to it.

- All existing institutions – the Council, the Commission, the presidency and the European Parliament – must be reformed. Numerous reform proposals have been put forward, by among others the CDU/CSU parliamentary group. The reforms must be geared to concepts for a new institutional balance, according to which the European Parliament will increasingly become a genuine law-making body with the same rights as the Council; the Council, in addition to performing tasks in the inter-governmental field in particular, will assume the functions of a second chamber, i.e., a chamber of the member states; and the Commission will take on features of a European government.

- In addition to greater efficiency, democratization must be acknowledged as the guiding principle of all reforms. Naturally, this applies first and foremost to the European Parliament which is to be closely involved from the outset in the preparations for the inter-governmental conference in 1996. This should be accompanied – not preceded – by efforts to enhance participation by national parliaments in the decision-making process within the EU. With regard to the Council, democratization means striking a better balance between the basic equality of all member states, on the one hand, and the ratio of population size to number of votes in the Council, on the other.

- The further development of the EU's institutions must combine coherence and consistency with elasticity and flexibility. On the one hand, they must be flexible enough to absorb and compensate for the tensions inherent in a Community stretching from the North Cape to Gibraltar and differentiated enough to cope with differences in member countries' ability (and willingness) to pursue further integration. On the other, they must be strong enough to ensure that, even in the face of tremendous challenges, the Union retains its ability to act.

- To achieve this, the 'variable geometry' or 'multi-speed' approach should as far as possible be sanctioned and institutionalized in the Union Treaty or the new quasi-constitutional document, despite the considerable legal and practical difficulties involved. Otherwise, this approach will continue to be limited to inter-governmental cooperation, which might well encourage a trend towards a 'Europe *à la carte*'. It must therefore be decided whether, in the case of amendments to the Maastricht Treaty, the principle of unanimity laid down in Article N should be replaced by a quorum yet to be more clearly specified. It is essential that no country should be allowed to use its right of veto to block the efforts of other countries more able and willing to intensify their cooperation and deepen integration.

Developing flexible approaches to integration, as envisaged for monetary union in the Maastricht Treaty and as already practised outside the Treaty within the framework of the Schengen Agreement, appears all the more imperative in view of the immense difficulties the above institutional changes will cause even with membership at its present level. As the negotiations on the accession of the EFTA countries showed, these difficulties are unlikely to diminish in the future. Just preventing a standstill in the process of integration, which would in fact constitute a step backwards, would be a major achievement.

2. Further Strengthening the EU's Hard Core

In addition to ensuring that the decision-making process within the European Union becomes more efficient and democratic, the existing hard core of countries oriented to greater integration and closer cooperation must be further strengthened. At present, the core comprises five or six countries. This core must not be closed to other member states; rather, it must be open to every member state willing and able to meet its requirements.

The task of the hard core is, by giving the Union a strong centre, to counteract the centrifugal forces generated by constant enlargement and, thereby, to prevent a South-West grouping, more inclined to protectionism and headed in a certain sense by France, drifting apart from a North-East grouping, more in favour of free world trade and headed in a certain sense by Germany.

To this end, the countries of the hard core must not only participate as a matter of course in all policy fields, but should also be recognizably more Community-spirited in their joint action than others, and launch common initiatives aimed at promoting the development of the Union. Belgium, Luxembourg and the Netherlands must therefore be more closely involved in Franco-German cooperation – especially since the Netherlands, too, has revised its earlier sceptical attitude towards the essential function of these two countries as the driving force behind European integration. Cooperation among the core countries must focus in particular on the new policy fields added to the Treaty of Rome by the Maastricht Treaty.

In the monetary field, too, there are strong signs that a hard core of five countries is emerging. They (together with Denmark and Ireland) are the ones which come closest to meeting the convergence criteria stipulated in the Maastricht Treaty. This is especially important since monetary union is the cornerstone of political union (and not, as is often believed in Germany, an additional element of integration alongside political union).

If monetary union is to be completed within the set timetable, it will encompass probably no more than a small number of countries – in line with the procedure outlined in the Maastricht Treaty. Even so, it will be completed only if the hard core of five work towards this objective systematically and with great determination. To this end, in the fields of monetary policy, fiscal and budgetary policy and economic and social policy, they should strive for ever closer coordination and aim to establish common policies, thereby – irrespective of the formal decisions taken in 1997 or 1999 – laying the foundations for monetary union among themselves by that time.

The core countries must convince all the other members of the EU – in particular founder member Italy, but also Spain and, of course, Great Britain – of their unreserved willingness to involve them more closely as soon as they have overcome their current problems and in so far as they themselves are willing to work towards the common objectives. The formation of a core group of countries is not an end in itself but a means of reconciling the two ostensibly conflicting goals of widening and deepening the European Union.

3. Raising the Quality of Franco-German Relations to a New Level

The quality of Franco-German relations must be raised to a new level if the historic process of European unification is not to peter out before it reaches its political goal. Therefore, no significant action in the foreign or EU policy fields should be taken without prior consultation between France and Germany. Following the end of the East–West conflict, the importance of Franco-German cooperation has not diminished; on the contrary, it has increased yet further.

Germany and France form the core of the hard core. From the outset, they were the driving force behind European unification. Their special relationship faces a stiff test because it too is beginning to show signs of the above-mentioned differentiation of interests and perceptions, which might cause them to drift apart as well. In France there are fears that the process of enlargement, taking in first the Scandinavian countries (as well as, in particular, Austria) and later the countries of Central and Eastern Europe, could transform the Union into a loose grouping of states in which Germany might acquire far greater power and thus assume a dominant position. For France, therefore, the issue of deepening the Union prior to enlargement is of vital importance. Now that Germany is reunited and – more importantly in this context – now that it can once again pursue an active foreign policy in the East and enjoys the same freedom of action as its partners in the West, the old question of how to integrate a powerful Germany into European structures, which arose when the process of European unification – limited initially to Western Europe – began, assumes a new, if not in fact its real, meaning.

It is important for Franco-German relations in particular that this question be addressed frankly in order to avoid misunderstandings and mistrust. An initial answer can be given by pointing to the fact – important for Germany too – that a desire not to become too dependent on Germany is, to a not inconsiderable degree, the reason why its eastern neighbours (like the EFTA countries before them) are keen to join the EU. However, this can only be achieved in a community which is more than just a free-trade area. It is vital, of course, that precisely at this point in time Germany should, through its policies, demonstrate its unwavering commitment to the goal of a strong and integrated Europe capable of effective action. (Germany believes it has long since provided proof of its commitment but, as the criticism of the way it proceeded with regard to the accession of the Scandinavian countries and Austria shows, this view is not shared everywhere.) Germany must furnish the required proof in proposals on ways to deepen the Union in institutional and political terms before further enlargement. These proposals must nevertheless also be made with a view to the future enlargement of the Union.

If Germany puts forward clear and unequivocal proposals, then France must make equally clear and unequivocal decisions. It must rectify the impression that, although it allows no doubt as to its basic will to pursue European integration, it often hesitates in taking concrete steps towards this objective – the notion of the unsurrenderable sovereignty of the 'État-nation' still carries weight, although this sovereignty has long since become an empty shell.

In view of the importance of monetary union for Franco-German relations in particular, attempts must be made – in addition to preparations within the hard core of countries – to overcome differences of opinion between France and Germany on fundamental issues of economic policy. These include the substance of 'industrial policy' and competition law. In this connection, it would be a positive step if agreement could be reached on a European cartel office. There must also be a debate on the long-term objectives of the Common Agricultural Policy and on the basic features of the Union's future financial system.

The same goes for the frequent divergence of views in France and Germany on the central issue of a common European defence and its relationship to NATO (as evident, for instance, in the current discussions on ways to implement the decision on the so-called combined joint task forces (CJTF) taken at the NATO summit in January 1994).

On both issues, the corresponding Franco-German councils (Economic and Social Council, Defence Council) should be used as a forum for a thorough, unbiased and undoctrinaire debate. More than ever before, Germany's relations with France are the yardstick by which to measure its sense of belonging to the West's community of shared political and cultural values, as opposed to the tendency, gaining ground once again, especially among intellectuals, to seek a 'German special path'. This is especially important since, now that the East–West conflict has come to an end, the USA can no longer play its traditional role in the same way. Conducting a serious and open dialogue on the attitudes which underpin such tendencies, and on the mutual sentiments and resentments in the Franco-German relationship, is just as important as enhancing the quality of political cooperation between the two countries.

4. Improving the Union's Capacity for Effective Action in the Field of Foreign and Security Policy

Giving the Union the capacity to take even more effective action in the field of foreign and security policy is of vital importance for the future. The nation-states of Europe are no longer capable of guaranteeing their external security individually, especially in view of the fact that other security problems to have been overcome in Europe have re-emerged and that, following the end of the East–West confrontation, the USA's assistance in resolving every kind of conflict is no longer certain.

A state's ability to guarantee its external security – its ability to defend itself – is, however, the precondition for, and the quintessence of, sovereignty. This applies in turn to the EU as a community of states inasmuch as only within the community can nation-states preserve their sovereignty. Moreover, because a nation's awareness of its sovereignty determines not only its self-perception but also its relations with other nations, the common defence capability of this European community of states constitutes an indispensable factor in endowing the EU with an identity of its own, an identity which, however, at the same time leaves room for the sense of identity of each individual state.

In the few years since the end of the East–West conflict, a common foreign and security policy has become more important and more urgent than envisaged in the Maastricht Treaty. Not even the larger member states are capable of addressing the new external challenges alone. All opinion polls show that a large majority of citizens would like to see a common foreign and security policy. The inadequacy of the Union's response to the dramatic developments in the eastern part of Europe has led to a clear drop in public support for the process of European unification. The question of the security status of future members is of decisive importance for the political make-up of Europe, and for its entire political order.

Action by the European Union in the field of foreign and security policy must be based on a strategic concept which clearly defines common interests and objectives and stipulates the conditions and procedures as well as the political, economic and financial means. The common foreign and security policy must give priority to the following fields:

- a common policy geared to stabilizing Central and Eastern Europe;
- development of relations with Russia with the aim of establishing a wide-ranging partnership;
- a common policy in the Mediterranean, where stability is of fundamental concern not only to the littoral states but to Germany as well;
- development of a strategic partnership with Turkey;
- reorientation of transatlantic relations: transatlantic relations are especially important because they encompass all the issues arising in the context of the common foreign and security policy. For this reason, the European Union and the USA must formulate a joint policy in these fields. They must also coordinate their efforts to address the global challenges.

The creation of a common European defence is a matter of much greater urgency than envisaged in the Maastricht Treaty. It should be done now, rather than 'in time' as stated in the Treaty. The urgency of this demand has been underlined by the European countries' difficulties among themselves and with the USA over the war in the former Yugoslavia. The efforts to establish a common defence must therefore be intensified. The Europeans must assume a far greater share of the responsibility for their own security. This goes, on the one hand, for measures to preserve and to enforce peace. On the other, it applies even more to the question of the security status of future members of the Union. In a community of states which sees itself as a genuine union, all members must enjoy the same status with regard to their security. That is a precondition of membership. But if the USA is to be expected to show a willingness not only to maintain its commitment in the present territory of the Alliance but to extend it (at least) to those countries which become members of the Union, then in the non-nuclear field Europe must itself make the main contribution to its own defence.

Looking ahead, this means transforming NATO into an alliance within which Europe and the USA and Canada carry equal weight and form a unit capable of effective action. In this sense, the inter-governmental conference in 1996 must reorganize the relations between the EU and the WEU in accordance with Article J.4, paragraph 6.

With regard to the current issue of restructuring the relations between the WEU and NATO as to tasks not covered by Article 5 of the North Atlantic Treaty (CJTF), a solution must be found which, on the basis of a decision by the NATO Council in each individual case (and thus, of course, with the involvement of the USA), allows the Europeans to take independent action using NATO resources and parts of the NATO staffs. As President Clinton made clear in a speech in Paris in June this year [1994], the USA not only welcomes but indeed calls for the creation of a European defence identity.

An active and effective common foreign and security policy requires a more flexible and efficient system of management and coordination. To this end, a high-level planning cell with access to national policy-makers, and concerned exclusively with forward-looking planning work, must be set up.

Excursus

To propose the formation of a hard core in Europe and the further intensification of Franco-German cooperation does not, however, imply the abandoning of hopes that Great Britain will assume its role 'in the heart of Europe' and thus in its core. Rather, these proposals are born of the conviction that determined efforts to spur on the further development of Europe are the best means of exerting a posi-tive influence on the clarification of Great Britain's relationship to Europe and on its willingness to participate in further steps towards integration.

Enlarging the EU towards the East

Poland, the Czech and Slovak Republics, Hungary (and Slovenia) should become members of the European Union around the year 2000. Their accession should depend on the implementation of the measures outlined above and also be their objective.

The certain prospect of EU membership, and membership itself even more so, is more likely to promote the political and economic development of these countries than any form of external assistance. Apart from the clear political and psychological advantages, accession at that time would, however, impose such a serious economic strain on members old and new that it will be possible only through a combination of measures. They include not only the approximation of laws in the acceding countries, already provided for in the Europe agreements, but also changes in various fields of EU policy, above all with regard to agriculture. In addition, to allow for economic adjustment there must be very long transitional periods (probably varying in length from country to country), which will be a case for the application of the concept of 'variable geometry'. The result must be that the costs for both sides are no higher than would be the case if accession were to take place at a later date. It must be borne in mind that the later accession takes place, the higher the costs are likely to be.

The accession of these countries must take place in stages and be accompanied by a further deepening of cooperation. Hence the following proposals:

- implement fully the opening of markets envisaged in the Europe agreements;
- coordinate trade policy;
- promote free trade and cooperation among the reforming countries;
- extend the participation of Central and Eastern European countries as regards certain areas of the EU's common foreign and security policy, i.e., multilateralize cooperation;
- implement cooperation in the security field in line with the Kirchberg Declaration on 'associate partnership' with the WEU;
- with regard to justice and home affairs, involve these countries in cooperation in the fields of aliens, migration, asylum and visa policy as well as with EUROPOL.

The integration of the Central and Eastern European countries into the European Union must be accompanied by the establishment of a wide-ranging partnership between the EU and Russia. As far as it is possible from outside, this policy must give Russia the certainty that, alongside the EU, it is acknowledged as the other centre of the political order in Europe. The agreement on partnership and cooperation with Russia is a first major step in this direction. It must be followed by security agreements in connection with the accession of the Central and Eastern European countries to the EU/WEU and NATO.

Implementation of the programme proposed above offers the best chance of overcoming the current uncertainties among our citizens with regard to the process of European unification. Unlike some intellectuals – and occasionally politicians too – who express views and opinions which are not only ill-considered and ill-informed but also far removed from reality, that is, purely theoretical and legalistic and politically dangerous, the large majority of citizens clearly recognize the need for European unity. However, they quite rightly expect more democracy, openness and transparency, and, above all, successful policies by the EU in the above fields. Basically, our citizens know full well that Germany's interests can only be realized in, with and through Europe, and that, far from posing a threat to the nation, this in fact safeguards its essence because it safeguards its future.

1994

8

Catching the Wrong Bus?

Timothy Garton Ash

Five years ago, in the euphoria at the end of the Cold War, it looked as if we could discern the shape of the twentieth century in Europe. That shape seemed to be a V. The line descended from the first and second Balkan wars before 1914, through what Churchill called Europe's second Thirty Years War, to the depths of Auschwitz and the Gulag, but then gradually rose again from mid-century, through the reconstruction of Western Europe to the liberation of Eastern Europe in 1989. For Poland, VE Day came only in the summer of 1989 – just forty-four years late. And for Germany, that autumn. 'Only today is the war really over', said an improvised poster in East Berlin as the Wall came down. So in 1989 the shape of the century looked like a V for victory. But since then the upward line has faltered, perhaps even turned downward, as we once again witness a Balkan war.

Fifty years on, we remember Britain's unique contribution to the victory in Europe with wholly justified pride. But we had to fight that war partly because of an earlier British policy based on the mistaken belief that Britain could, by a diplomacy of detachment, insulate itself from those European quarrels in far-away countries of which Chamberlain knew nothing. Wrong then, even more wrong now.

So, fifty years after the end of what we still call *the* war in Europe, and five years after the end of the Cold War, what has Europe come to, and where, if anywhere, is it going? And is there, could there be, a British way of thinking Europe?

Most contemporary British discussion of 'Europe' is not about Europe at all. At best, it is about EU-rope: that is, some aspects of the collective political and economic life of the west, north and south European states now organized in something rather misleadingly called the European

117

Union. But mainly, it is about Britain. Our so-called 'European debate' is part of a tortured national self-examination, an English, Scottish, Welsh and Irish agonizing about self. In this debate, 'Europe' appears as a threat to the very existence of Britain for (mainly English) 'Euro-sceptics' of the Right; as a chance to transform the very nature of Britain for (often Scottish or Welsh) 'Euro-enthusiasts' of the Left; as both opportunity and problem for the large centre; but for all sides as something basically external. There is 'Europe' there and 'Britain' here, and the argument is about the relationship between them and us.

Penser l'Europe is a French book-title[1] which is almost inconceivable as a British one. Thinking Europe is an un-British activity. Those who do it (even as consenting adults in private) risk being stigmatized as 'Euro-intellectuals' – a neologism which neatly combines two things the British deeply mistrust.

In the circumstances, it is not surprising that most of our Continental partners regard the very notion of 'a British idea of Europe' as a contradiction in terms. This is a pity. It is a pity for Britain: we lose influence because we are seen on the Continent to be opposed or at best marginal to the mainstream of European development. But it may also be a pity for Europe, since Europe, and specifically EU-rope, could perhaps use a little more British thinking at the moment – with 'British' here meant in the deeper sense of our particular intellectual tradition: sceptical, empirical and pragmatic.

For 'Continental' ways of thinking about Europe also have their problems. To use a simple dichotomy of 'British v. Continental' would, of course, be to make precisely the British mistake: there is a huge variety of different ways of thinking about Europe across the Continent. Yet certainly there are some common characteristics of at least the main French and German approaches which have had a formative influence on the development of EU-rope over the past half-century.

Whereas British politicians make an artificial separation of the national and the European, ignoring the degree to which the two are already intertwined, French and German politicians utterly conflate the national and the European, so it is almost impossible to distinguish when they are talking about Europe and when about their own nations. Now the instrumentalization of 'Europe' for the pursuit of national ends is an old European habit. Bismarck famously observed that he had always found the word 'Europe' in the mouths of those politicians who wanted from other powers something they did not dare demand in their own name. His conclusion was: 'Qui parle Europe a tort. Notion géographique.' British Euro-sceptics applaud Bismarck.

Yet in truth things are now a little more complicated. For in the half-century since 1945 there has also been a great deal of genuinely idealistic commitment to Europe among French and German politicians and opinion-formers – a commitment born from personal experience of revolution, war, genocide, defeat and occupation. The trouble is that the conflation of national and European -- part instrumental, part idealistic – has become so habitual that they themselves sometimes don't quite know when they are talking about Europe and when about France or Germany.

Idealism in a different though related sense – the tendency to represent things in an ideal form rather than as they are, idealism as opposed to empiricism – is the other salient common characteristic of this French and German Euro-thinking. The 'Europe' of which they have spoken for the past half-century is an idea and an ideal, a dream, a vision or a grand design; this is *faire l'Europe, Europa bauen,* Europe as project, process, progress towards some *finalité européenne*; Europe as telos. At its most vertiginous, this comes as dialectical idealism. *Europa der Gegensätze auf dem Wege zu sich selbst,* proclaims a German publication: 'The Europe of contradictions on the way to itself'. Which, in English, makes about as much sense as 'the London of traffic jams on the way to itself'. 'No, I'm afraid Europe will not come to pass,' says a French friend, and I want to reply, 'But Pierre, you're in it!' The very name 'European Union' is a product of this approach. A Union is what it is meant to be, not what it is.

The difference between the teleological–idealistic and the empirical–sceptical approaches leads to profound misunderstandings. For the former, the great end justifies the often unsatisfactory means. Eurocratic nonsense from Brussels is a price worth paying for the larger political sense. But the teleologists are in trouble. In the Continental élites' building plans for EU-rope, from Messina to Maastricht, the telos was a substitute for the absent demos – with the hope of eventually contributing to the creation of a new European demos, from above, by education and example. But it has not happened. There is still no European people, or demos. And after the signature of the Maastricht Treaty, the peoples of the very heartlands of EU-rope turned to question what was being dished up in their name. 'For we are the peoples of Europe, that never have spoken yet', as Chesterton might have written.

In this sense, EU-rope is perhaps now ready for a more (intellectually) 'British' approach. But is any constructive 'British' approach on offer? An approach, that is, which cares about Europe as Europe and not just as a threat or opportunity for a greater or lesser Britain. What follows is an attempt to 'think Europe' in English: to see Europe plain and to see it whole.

In the index to Arnold Toynbee's *Study of History*, we read 'Europe: as a battlefield', then: 'as not an intelligible field of historical study'.

And he makes a strong case. This most ill-defined of continents has, after all, been open for long stretches of its history not just on one but on three sides: to the south across the Mediterranean, throughout most of what we call 'ancient history' and in some ways again today; to the east where Europe does not end but merely fades away into Asia; and to the west, across the Atlantic, especially in our post-1945 'West'. The 'globalization' caused by the technological developments of the past half-century further calls into question the coherence or validity of the unit 'Europe' as compared with smaller (state, region, firm) or larger (Euratlantic, OECD, world) ones.

And what of its internal make-up? What are Europe's essential constituent parts? Its hundreds of millions of individual people who more or less – mainly less – identify themselves as 'Europeans'? Its regions? Classes? Societies? Nations and states? But to say 'nation-states', as most British politicians do, misses the huge diversity of European combinations of nation and state, from the national state, with citizen-ship rights conditional on membership of one dominant ethnic *Volk*, or the classic east European variant of ethnic nations distributed between several states, through the French civic *état-nation*, to Britain itself: a nation-state containing several nations.

None the less, in most of western, southern and now also northern Europe, these individuals, regions, societies, nations but above all *states* are now organized in something new – EU-rope – which differs qualitatively both from any previous arrangement of European states and from any current arrangement of states on any other continent. The nature of this arrangement is, however, very hard to define. The German Constitutional Court has described it as a '*Staatenverbund*'. In English, we might call it a thing. This thing is less than a federal superstate but more than an alliance: an unprecedented, unique and horribly complex combination of the supranational and the inter-governmental, of economic integration and political cooperation.

This thing evolved in the Cold War, like NATO and with NATO, as the western half of a European order which we called in shorthand 'Yalta'. Its development was directly and indirectly influenced, to a degree many devoted advocates of European unification find hard to acknowledge, by that of the Cold War – and of *détente*, the Siamese twin of Cold War. But five years ago, this 'Yalta' order ended in a way quite different from that in which previous European orders, whether of 'Versailles', 'Vienna' or 'Westphalia', had ended. Essentially, its eastern half just fell away, with the largely peaceful death of communism in Eastern Europe and the rather less peaceful dissolution of the Soviet Union. The western half remained intact; or at least, apparently so.

So today this now slightly expanded western part, this EU-rope, with its fifteen states and some 370 million people, faces the other Europe from which it was so long insulated by the Iron Curtain. (For we lived, as the Hungarian writer György Konrád put it, with our backs to the Berlin Wall.) This other Europe may itself be very crudely sub-divided into a second and a third Europe. The second Europe has in all some twenty states, of which fifteen have only recently been liberated from communism, and some 140 million people. The states of this second Europe, among which I do not include Turkey, are mainly small: except for Poland and Romania, none has more inhabitants than Greater London and most have far fewer. Most of them, or at least most of their political élites, more or less clearly want to join the Europe of EU and NATO – to 'return to Europe', in the slogan of 1989. More important, their theoretical claim to belong, sooner or later, is more or less accepted by the political leaders of the EU – although with the emphasis in practice often on the less and later.

Clearly this is to paint with a very broad brush. Having spent much of the past fifteen years trying to explain to Western readers that Prague, Budapest and Warsaw belong to Central not to Eastern Europe, I am the last person to need reminding of the immense differences between Poland and Albania. But to suggest that there is some absolutely clear historical dividing line between the Central European democracies in the so-called Višegrad group and, say, the Baltic states or Slovenia would be to service a new myth.

The third Europe comprises two much larger states, Russia and Ukraine, together with Belarus and perhaps also Serbia. They, however, have a very large combined population of more than 210 million (or 220 million if one includes Serbia). These states are themselves, especially in the case of Russia, somewhat more ambivalent about their own historical belonging to Europe and current desire to join the first Europe of EU and NATO. But more important, the political leaders of the EU and NATO do not agree even on the long-term principle of these states' claim to membership.

Again, the division between the second and third Europe is crude, probably unfair to Ukraine and may understate the longer-term possibility of a democratic Serbia reoriented towards Europe. But wherever the exact lines fall at any given moment, for the foreseeable future the other Europe will certainly be sub-divided between states which are recognizably set on a course towards EU-rope and those which are not; with, no doubt, a number straggling in between.

The central political question about the composition of Europe today is therefore whether and how EU-rope can gradually include an ever larger part of the second Europe, while itself still continuing to 'work' in the unique, complex, unsatisfactory but none the less real way it does;

and how this process will both affect and be affected by relations with the third Europe, above all with Russia.

At issue right across the other Europe is not just the choice between democracy and dictatorship but also that between war and peace. Banishing the spectre of war between European states and peoples was, of course, the first great purpose of EU-rope's founding fathers. Economic integration was the indirect means chosen to achieve that end, especially after a more direct approach – the European Defence Community – was voted down in the French National Assembly. Now it is a fair question how far it really was the (then still) EEC/EC which kept the peace in Europe (inasmuch as it was kept) up to 1990, and how far NATO and the East–West nuclear stand-off in the Cold War. But certainly the habits and institutions of peaceful conflict-resolution and permanent cooperation in the EC made a large contribution.

Yet while our leaders still mouthed the platitude that 'war has become unthinkable' in Europe, war had not only again become thinkable across much of post-communist Europe but was actually being waged, even as they spoke, bloodily and brutally and – with almost too crude an irony – in a place called Sarajevo.

One lesson of the short twentieth century is that political ends are not separable from the means used to attain them. Today, EU-rope's means are threatening its ends. The process of 'making Europe' proceeds *pars pro toto*. The élites negotiate for the people and ask them only afterwards – if at all – whether they agree. In this sense, as process, what is happening now is already 'Maastricht 2'. EU-rope also decides for Europe, and future members have to accept the given shape. The Poles send up their old cry, 'Nic o nas bez nas' ['Nothing about us without us!'] but as usual the West hardly listens.

Within the EU, a number of states, and crucially France and Germany, are contemplating 'going ahead': *pars pro toto* again. Following German unification, France's political leaders feel it to be more urgent than ever to bind Germany into Europe and – curious but true! – Germany's current political leaders want their own country to be bound in, so they are not left alone to face the temptations of the past in the centre of Europe. True to the functionalist tradition of proceeding through economic means to political ends, the chosen path is monetary union. This, with its inevitable and desired political consequences, is to make the process of integration 'irreversible'. The Franco-German avant-garde will form a 'magnetic core' of a uniting Europe, with monetary union as the hard core of the hard core. But where they lead, other states, including Britain, are to follow, as they have done through-out the previous history of the EEC-EC-EU. EU-rope after Maastricht (1 and 2) will be 'multi-speed' but still moving in one direction.

Here, stripped to essentials, is the bold – even breathtaking – Franco-German project for EU-rope in the closing years of the century, and the immediate European challenge for Britain. The trouble is that this project is very likely to fail. Monetary union itself might fail, obviously, at the first or second fence, because even the core economies are not close enough to stand the strains, or because either French or German political opinion turns against it. Both countries have parliamentary elections in 1998, which according to the Maastricht timetable should be a decisive year. In fact, German public opinion is already loath to give up the Deutschmark, and even Chancellor Kohl is now saying that the convergence criteria are more important than the timetable. Monetary union might also fail after the event; nothing except death is irreversible, and European history offers several examples of failed monetary unions.

Yet it may also fail by succeeding. That is: succeed in the narrow, technical sense but fail in the broader purpose. The countries in the single market but not in the core monetary union would face both pressures and temptations to pursue a different economic policy from the core. How, for example, would the core-group countries react to a flooding of their markets by devaluation? (That would be short-sighted of us, to be sure, but most governments are.) A single market is perhaps difficult to sustain without a single currency, but it may be even more difficult to sustain with a clear, formalized division between monetary core and periphery. And how would this work in the councils of EU-rope? Would representatives of the core states have separate meetings on those fundamental issues of fiscal and macroeconomic policy on which they would now have to reach a common stance? (The idea of EMU as gold standard, with each state bound to keep its own budgetary house in order or go broke, is theoretically attractive but not practical European politics.) Or would the core group be a permanent caucus, coming to each Council with an agreed position? One of the great strengths of the EU is its flexibility: you have changing national alliances on different issues. Set one alliance in concrete, and you risk breaking the whole structure.

The great gamble of this continental project is that the Franco-German core will indeed be magnetic, that where Bonn and Paris lead, others will sooner or later follow; and the reason people in Bonn and Paris (and quite a few older 'pro-Europeans' in London) think this will happen is that that is roughly what did happen for about thirty-five years, from 1955 to 1990. But a process that worked, almost with the regularity of a physics experiment, in the air-cooled laboratory of 'Western Europe' in the Cold War will by no means necessarily work in the same way in the much larger, messier post-Wall Europe of today.

Anyone who has played with flat magnets as a child knows that they can have two effects: one way round they attract, the other they repel. There is now a serious danger of the would-be magnetic core exerting magnetic repulsion. The best can be the enemy of the good. The rationalist, functionalist, perfectionist attempt to 'make Europe' or 'complete' Europe through a hard core built around a rapid monetary union could well end up achieving the opposite of the desired effect. A procedure aimed at finally overcoming the bad old European ways of competing nation-states and alliances risks hastening a return to precisely those bad old ways. Press the fast-forward button, and you go backwards.

Yet even if it succeeds, both economically and politically, even if Britain and others in the EU once again follow where France and Germany have led, this in itself offers nothing to the rest of Europe knocking at our door. Indeed, the whole 'IGC' process threatens to be 'Maastricht 2' in another sense: with the leaders of EU-rope so totally preoccupied with the EU's own (in this case, bold) internal reforms that they simply don't have enough time, energy and attention left for the parts of Europe where our actions might actually make the difference between democracy and dictatorship, war and peace. They'll still be fiddling in Brussels while Sarajevo burns.

Yet it is not enough just to point out – empirically, sceptically and pragmatically – the flaws and dangers in a Franco-German project which is, characteristically, at once teleological, idealistic and instrumental. For the French and Germans will quite rightly retort: do you have a better one? For anyone who cares about Europe, the task is therefore to come up with a better one. Or, at the very least, to ensure that there is something else under way so that the whole 'European enterprise' at the end of the twentieth century is not seen to stand or fall with this hair-raising adventure, this *Europe as Will and Idea*, of unification through money.

That 'something' should, I believe, be a detailed project both for the enlargement of the present EU to include, over the next twenty years, the recently liberated second Europe, and simultaneously, for a more closely coordinated, and in some respects 'common' foreign, security and defence policy, to meet the challenges and dangers both within Europe itself and from the dangerous world around. This project would therefore approach the political goal directly, by political means, not by the functionalist diversion through economics. Unlike EMU, it would be not one simple big thing but a whole jigsaw of complex, piecemeal things, since it would necessarily involve many other, overlapping European institutions, and, above all, EU-rope's second true pillar: NATO. But however precisely it were done, it would require more sharing of power and sovereignty; both in the form of Qualified Majority Voting, without which an EU of twenty and more member states would simply not work, and in the rather different procedures for what one might call Qualified Minority Acting (by varying groups of states, but usually involving France, Germany and Britain) which are what is needed in foreign, security and defence policy.

But if you don't care about Europe as Europe, just about Britain as Britain, why bother and why pay the price? For two reasons: because if we don't we'll be left out, and because if we don't we'll be dragged in. Left out, in the short term, from the next stage of Franco-German EU-ro-building, with (at the very least) high risks for Britain, but then dragged in by the probable failure of that design and by the disorder of the rest of Europe which that design does so little to address.

There is a surreal, even a grotesque, discrepancy between the contorted, rapid-sleep-inducing, acronym-ridden, polit-bureaucratic detail of the current 'IGC' debate about reforming EU-rope, and the huge, fateful, almost melodramatic challenges facing us across the rest of Europe after the end of the Cold War. And yet our answer to the latter must start from the former; for where else should we start except where we are?

And going where? All divisions of time are artificial, and perhaps the last five years of the twentieth century and the second millennium AD should be considered no differently from any other five years. But the millennial deadline does concentrate the mind. In these next five years, we probably have a larger chance but also a larger danger than at any time in the past fifty. The chance is that in the year 2000 more of Europe will be more peaceful, prosperous, democratic and free than ever before in its history. The danger can also be simply described. If we get things wrong now, then some time in the early part of the next century we will stop talking about 8 May 1945 as the end of *the war* in Europe – because there'll be another.

1995

Notes

1. Edgar Morin, *Penser l'Europe*, Paris 1987.

The Europe to Come

Perry Anderson

On New Year's Day 1994, Europe – the metonym – changed names. The dozen nations of the Community took on the title of Union, though, as in a Spanish wedding, the new appellation did not replace the old but encompassed it. Has anything of substance altered? So far, very little. The number of member states has risen to fifteen, with the entry of three former neutrals. Otherwise things are much as they were before. What is new, however, is that everyone knows this is not going to last. For the first time since the war, Europe is living in anticipation of large but still imponderable changes to the part that has stood for the whole. Three dominate the horizon.

The first is, of course, the Treaty of Maastricht. We can set aside its various rhetorical provisions, for vague consultation on foreign policy and defence, or ineffectual protection of social rights, and even ignore its mild emendations of the institutional relations within the Community. The core of the Treaty is the commitment by the member states, save England and Denmark, to introduce a single currency, under the authority of a single central bank, by 1999. This step means an irreversible move of the EU towards real federation. With it, national governments will lose the right either to issue money or alter exchange rates, and will be able to vary rates of interest and public borrowing only within very narrow limits, on pain of heavy fines from the Commission if they break central bank directives. They may still tax at their discretion, but capital mobility in the single market can be expected to ensure more or less common fiscal denominators. European monetary union spells the end of the most important attributes of national economic sovereignty.

Secondly, Germany is now reunited. The original Common Market

126

was built on a balance between the two largest countries of the Six, France and Germany – the latter with greater economic weight and slightly larger population, the former with superior military and diplomatic weight. Later, Italy and Britain provided flanking states of roughly equivalent demographic and economic size. This balance started to break down in the 1980s, when the EMS proved to be a zone pivoting on the Deutschmark, as the only currency never to be devalued within it. A decade later, Germany's position has been qualitatively transformed. With a population of over 80 million, it is now much the largest state in the Union, enjoying not only monetary but increasingly institutional and diplomatic ascendancy. The process of European integration is now, for the first time in its history, potentially confronted with the emergence of a hegemonic power, with a widely asymmetrical capacity to affect all other member states.

The third great change has followed from the end of communism in the countries of the former Warsaw Pact. The restoration of capitalism east of the Elbe has further transformed the position of Germany, both by reinstating it as the continental *Land der Mitte* which its conservative theorists always – with reason – insisted it would once again become, and – a less noticed development – by reducing the significance of the nuclear weapons that France or Britain possess and it lacks. Yet more significant, however, is the currently expressed desire of virtually all the East European countries, and some of the former Soviet lands, to join the EU. As things stand, the total population of these candidates is about 130 million. Their inclusion would make a community of half a billion people, nearly twice the size of the United States. More pointedly still, it would approximately double the membership of the European Union, from fifteen to some thirty states. A completely new configuration would be at stake.

Historically, these three great changes have been interconnected. In reverse order, it was the collapse of communism that allowed the reunification of Germany that precipitated the Treaty of Maastricht. The shock-wave moved from the east to the centre to the west of Europe. But causes and consequences remain distinct. The outcomes of these processes obey no single logic. More than this: to a greater extent than in any previous phase of European integration, the impact of each is quite uncertain. We confront a set of *ex ante* indeterminacies that, adopting a Kantian turn of phrase, might be called the three amphibologies of post-Maastricht politics. They pose much more dramatic dilemmas than is generally imagined.

I

The Treaty itself offers the first. Its origins lie in the dynamism of Delors's leadership of the Commission. After securing passage of the Single Market Act in 1986, Delors persuaded the European Council two years later to set up a committee largely composed of central bankers, but chaired by himself, to report on a single currency. Its recommendations were formally accepted by the Council in the spring of 1989. But it was the sudden tottering of East Germany that spurred Mitterrand to conclude an agreement with Kohl at the Strasbourg summit in the autumn, which put the decisive weight of the Franco-German axis behind the project. Thatcher, of course, was implacably opposed.

But she was comprehensively outmanoeuvred, not least by the continental regime she most disliked, which sat in Rome. The otherwise impregnable self-confidence of *The Downing Street Years* falters disarmingly whenever its heroine comes to Europe. The titles of the chapters speak for themselves. The ordinary triumphal run – 'Falklands: The Victory', 'Disarming the Left', 'Hat Trick', 'Not So much a Programme, More a Way of Life', 'The World Turned Right Side Up' – is interrupted by a faintly woeful note. We enter the world of 'Jeux Sans Frontières' and 'Babel Express', with its 'un-British combination of high-flown rhetoric and pork-barrel politics', where 'heads of government would be left discussing matters that would boggle the mind of the City's top accountants', and 'the intricacies of European Community policy really test one's intellectual ability and capacity for clear thinking'.[1]

The uncharacteristic hint of humility is well-founded. Thatcher appears to have been somewhat out of her depth, as a persistent tone of rueful bewilderment suggests. The leitmotif is: 'Looking back, it is now possible to see', but 'I can only say it did not seem like that at the time'.[2] Many are the occasions that inspire this mortified hindsight. Exemplary in its comedy is the Milan summit of the European Council in 1984, which ensured the inclusion of qualified majority voting in the Single European Act. 'Signor Craxi could not have been more sweetly reasonable ... I came away thinking how easy it had been to get my points across' (*sic*). But lo and behold on the following day: 'To my astonishment and anger, Signor Craxi suddenly called a vote and by a majority the council resolved to establish an IGC.'[3] Six years later, the precedent set at Milan proved fatal at Rome. This time it was Andreotti who laid the ambush into which Thatcher fell head over heels, at the European summit of October 1990. 'As always with the Italians, it was difficult throughout to distinguish confusion from guile', she haplessly writes. 'But even I was unprepared for the way things went.'[4] Once more, a vote to convene an IGC was sprung on her at the last minute, this time on the even more provocative topic of Political Union. Her explosion at Andreotti's silken trap finished her. In London, Geoffrey Howe took a dim view of her reaction, and within a month she was ejected from office. No wonder she hated her Italian colleagues so cordially, to the point of saying: 'To put it bluntly, if I were an Italian I might prefer rule from Brussels too'.[5]

Thatcher respected Delors ('manifest intelligence, ability and integrity'), liked Mitterrand ('I always have a soft spot for French charm') and could put up with Kohl ('style of diplomacy even more direct than mine'). But Andreotti she feared and detested from the start. At her very first G7 summit, within a few months of coming to power, she found that 'he seemed to have positive aversion to principle, even a conviction that a man of principle was doomed to be a figure of fun. He saw politics as an eighteenth-century general saw war: a vast and elaborate set of parade-ground manoeuvres by armies that would never actually engage in conflict but instead declare victory, surrender or compromise as their apparent strength dictated in order to collaborate on the real business of sharing the spoils. A talent for striking political deals rather than a conviction of political truths might be required by Italy's political system and it was certainly regarded as *de rigueur* in the Community, but I could not help but find something distasteful about those who practised it'.[6] Andreotti's judgement of Thatcher was crisper. Emerging from one of the interminable European Council sessions devoted to the British rebate, he remarked that she reminded him of a landlady berating a tenant for her rent.

The increasing role of Italy as a critical third in the affairs of the Community was a significant feature of these years. The 1989 *Report on Economic and Monetary Union* that laid the basis for Maastricht was drafted by an Italian, Tommaso Padoa-Schioppa, the most trenchant advocate of a single currency, and it was also an Italian initiative – Andreotti again – that at the last minute wrote an automatic deadline of 1999 into the Treaty, to the consternation of the British and of the Bundesbank. Nevertheless, the final shape of the bargain reached at Maastricht was of essentially French and German design. The central aim for Paris was a financial edifice capable of replacing the unilateral power of the Bundesbank as the *de facto* regulator of the fortunes of its neighbours, with a *de jure* central authority over the European monetary space in which German interests would no longer be privileged. In exchange Bonn received the security system of 'convergence criteria' – in effect: draconian conditions for abandonment of the Deutschmark, which Italian theorists of a single currency had always rejected – and the fixtures and fittings of 'political union'.

The diplomatic origins of the Treaty are one thing. Its economic effects, if implemented, are another. What is the social logic of the monetary union scheduled to come into force by the end of the 1990s? In a system of the kind envisaged at Maastricht, national macroeconomic policy becomes a thing of the past: all that remains to member states are distributive options on – necessarily reduced – expenditures within balanced budgets, at competitive levels of taxation. The historic commitments of both Social and Christian Democracy to full employment or social services of the traditional welfare state, already scaled down or cut back, would cease to have any further institutional purchase. This is a revolutionary prospect. The single obligation of the projected European Central Bank, more restrictive even than the charter of the US Federal Reserve, is the maintenance of price stability. The protective and regulative functions of existing national states will be dismantled, leaving sound money as the sole regulator, as in the classical liberal model of the epoch before Keynes.

The new element – namely, the supranational character of the future monetary authority – would serve to reinforce such a historical reversion: elevated higher above national electorates than its predecessors, it will be more immune – not only by statute – from popular pressures. Put simply, a federal Europe in this sense would mean not a super-state – as Conservatives in Britain fear – but *less* state. Hayek was the lucid prophet of this vision. In his 1939 essay on 'Economic Conditions of Interstate Federalism', he set out the current logic of European monetary union with inspired force and clarity. After arguing that states within such a union could not pursue an independent monetary policy, he noted that macroeconomic interventions always require some common agreement over values and objectives, and went on: 'It is clear that such agreement will be limited in inverse proportion to the homogeneity and the similarity of outlook possessed by the inhabitants of an area. Although, in the national state, submission to the will of a majority will be facilitated by the myth of nationality, it must be clear that people will be reluctant to submit to any interference in their daily affairs when the majority which directs the government is composed of people of different nationalities and different traditions. It is, after all, only common sense that the central government in a federation composed of many different people will have to be restricted in scope if it is to avoid meeting an increasing resistance on the part of the various groups it includes. But what could interfere more thoroughly with the intimate life of the people than the central direction of economic life, with its inevitable discrimination between groups? There seems to be little possible doubt that the scope for regulation of economic life will be much narrower for the central government than for national states; and since, as we have seen, the power of the states which comprise the federation will be yet more limited, much of the interference with economic life to which we have become accustomed will be altogether impracticable under a federal organization.'[7]

On this reading, Maastricht leads to an obliteration of what is left of the Keynesian legacy that Hayek deplored, and most of the distinctive gains of the West European labour movement associated with it. Precisely the extremity of this prospect, however, poses the question of whether in practice it might not unleash the contrary logic. Confronted with the drastic consequences of dismantling previous social controls over economic transactions at the national level, would there not soon – or even beforehand – be overwhelming pressure to reinstitute them at supranational level, to avoid an otherwise seemingly inevitable polarization of regions and classes within the Union? That is, to create a European political authority capable of re-regulating what the single currency and single-minded bank have deregulated? Could this have been the hidden gamble of Jacques Delors, author of the plan for monetary union, yet a politician whose whole previous career suggests commitment to a Catholic version of social-democratic values and to suspicion of economic liberalism?

On this reading, Hayek's scenario could well reverse out into its opposite – let us say, the prospect drawn by Wynne Godley. As the Treaty neared ratification, he observed: 'The incredible lacuna in the Maastricht programme is that while it contains a blueprint for the establishment and modus operandi of an independent central bank, there is no blueprint whatever of the analogue, in Community terms, of a central government. Yet there would simply *have* to be a system of institutions which fulfils all those functions at a Community level which are at present exercised by the central governments of the individual member countries'.[8]

Perhaps because he feared just such arguments, Hayek himself had changed his mind by the 1970s. Influenced by German fears of inflation if the Deutschmark was absorbed in a monetary union (by then he was based in Freiburg), he decided that a single European currency was not only a utopian but a dangerous prescription.[9] Certainly, it was more than ever necessary to take the control of money out of the hands of national governments subject to electoral pressures. But the remedy, he now saw, was not to move it upwards to a supranational public authority; it was to displace it downwards to competing private banks, issuing rival currencies in the market-place.

Even on the principled Right there have been few takers for this solution – which Padoa-Schioppa, perhaps with a grain of malice, commends as the only coherent alternative to his own.[10] But misgivings about what the kind of single currency envisaged by the Treaty of

Maastricht might mean for socio-economic stability are widely shared, even among central bankers. With nearly 20 million people currently out of work in the Union, what is to prevent huge permanent pools of unemployment in depressed regions? It is the governor of the Bank of England who now warns that, once devaluations are ruled out, the only mechanisms of adjustment are sharp wage reductions or mass out-migration; while the head of the European Monetary Institute itself, the Belgian-Hungarian banker (and distinguished economist) Alexandre Lamfalussy, in charge of the technical preparations for the single currency, pointedly noted – in an appendix to the report of the Delors Committee, of which he was a member – that if 'the only global macroeconomic tool available within the EMU would be the common monetary policy implemented by the European central banking system', the outcome 'would be an unappealing prospect'.[11] If monetary union was to work, he explained, a common fiscal policy was essential.

But since budgets remain the central battle-ground of domestic politics, how could there be fiscal coordination without electoral deter-mination? The 'system of institutions' on whose necessity Godley insists is only conceivable on one foundation: it would perforce have to be based on a genuine supranational democracy at Union level, embodying for the first time a real popular sovereignty in a truly effective and accountable European Parliament. It is enough to spell out this con-dition to see how unprepared either official discourse or public opinion in the member states is for the scale of the choices before them.

II

What, secondly, will be the position of Germany in the Europe envisaged at Maastricht? The accelerator towards monetary union was pressed not merely by the hopes or fears of bankers and economists. Ultimately more important was the political desire of the French government to fold the newly enlarged German state into a tighter European structure in which interest rates would no longer be regulated solely by the Bundesbank. In Paris the creation of a single currency under supra-national control was conceived as a critical safeguard against the re-emergence of German national hegemony in Europe. At the same time, even sections of the German political class and public opinion, some-what in the spirit of Odysseus tying himself to the mast to protect himself from temptation, were inclined – at any rate declaratively – to share this view. On both sides, the assumption behind it was that a European monetary authority would mean a reduction in the power of the nation-state that was economically strongest, namely the Federal Republic.

No sooner was the Treaty signed, however, than exactly the opposite prognosis started to take shape, as German interest rates at levels not seen since the 1920s inflicted a deep recession on neighbouring countries, and German diplomatic initiatives in the Balkans – once again, as in the early years of this century, shadowing Austrian manoeuvres – stirred uneasy memories. Conor Cruise O'Brien has expressed the alternative view most trenchantly. Commenting on the Yugoslav crisis, in which Bonn claimed to be moved only by the principle of national self-determination – less applicable, of course, to lesser breeds: Chechens, Kurds or Macedonians – he wrote: 'Germany was in favour of the recognition of [Croatia and Slovenia]. The rest of the Community was against, and the United States strongly so. Faced with such an apparently powerful "Western consensus", on any such matter, the old pre-1990 Bundesrepublik would have respectfully backed away. The united Germany simply ignored the United States and turned the Community round. Germany recognized the independence of Croatia and Slovenia, and the rest of the Community followed suit within a few days. The reversal of the Community position was particularly humbling for the French. ... The two new republics are now part of a vast German sphere of influence to the east ... German economic hegemony in Europe is now a fact of life, to which the rest of us Europeans must adjust as best we can. ... To press ahead with federal union, under these conditions, would not "rein in" the mighty power of united Germany. It would subject the rest of us to German hegemony in its plenitude.'[12]

Just this fear, of course, was the mobilizing theme of the campaign against ratification of Maastricht in the French referendum a few months later. The French electorate split down the middle on the issue of whether a single currency would reduce or enhance the power of the strongest nation-state in the continent. The majority of the political élite, led by Mitterrand and Giscard, in effect argued that the only way to neutralize German predominance was monetary union. Their opponents, led by Séguin and De Villiers, retorted that this was the surest way to bring it about. The dispute was fought out against the background of the first monetary tempest set off by the raising of the German discount rate in June, which ejected the lira and the pound from the ERM in the final week of the campaign. A year later it was the turn of the franc to capsize in waves of speculation whipped to storm-height by the line of the Bundesbank.

We now have a vivid inside account of these events in Bernard Connolly's book *The Rotten Heart of Europe*.[13] The coarseness of its title and cover are misleading: signs more of the self-conscious *encanaillement* of smart publishing than of authorial quality. The book suffers from an occasional lapse of taste, and liking for melodrama. But for the most part it is a highly literate and professional study. Indeed, piquantly so. A crypto-Thatcherite at the highest levels of the Community's financial apparatus in Brussels, Connolly is at the antipodes of Thatcher's bemusement in the field of European politics. His book displays an unrivalled mastery of the nexus between banking and balloting in virtually every member state of the EC: not just France, Germany, Italy and the UK but also Belgium, Denmark, Portugal and Ireland are covered with dash and detail. (The only significant exception is the Netherlands, whose ambivalence between liberal economics and federal politics is consigned to an exasperated footnote.) Chauvinist convictions have produced a cosmopolitan *tour de force*.

Connolly's standpoint is based on a principled hostility not merely to a single currency but to fixed exchange rates between different currencies – in his eyes, a dangerous and futile attempt to bridle the operation of financial markets, which can only stifle the economic freedom on which the vitality of a disorderly economic system depends. 'Western capitalism contained is Western capitalism destroyed', as he pithily puts it.[14] Describing the dogfights of 1992–93 inside the ERM, his sympathies are with the most adamant German opponents of concessions to their neighbours' concerns over interest rates, above all the crusty figure of Helmut Schlesinger, then chairman of the Bundesbank. But the sympathy is strictly tactical – Schlesinger is applauded for an intransigence whose effect was to undermine any prospect of stability in the ERM, so exposing in advance the unviability of EMU. It involves no idealization of the Bundesbank, the myth of whose 'independence' of political influence Connolly punctures effectively – its policies corresponding with remarkable regularity to the needs of the CDU/CSU in the electoral arena.

Today the German political class, in which nationalist reflexes are no longer so dormant, is having second thoughts about monetary union, as the prospect of a single currency has come to look ambiguous on the other side of the Rhine too. Could it be that Germany received shadow rather than substance in the bargain at Maastricht? In chorus, Waigel for the ruling coalition and Tietmeyer for the central bank have been upping the ante for monetary union, with stentorian demands for 'strict compliance' with the convergence criteria appended to the Treaty (public debt no higher than 60 per cent and public deficit no higher than 3 per cent of GDP, inflation within 1.5 per cent and interest rates within 2 per cent of the three best performers in the Union), and a 'stability pact' beyond them. This orchestrated clamour has no legal basis, since in the text signed at Maastricht the convergence criteria are not unconditional targets to be met, but 'reference values' to be moved towards; and whether or not sufficient movement has been achieved is in the first instance for the Commission – not the German or any other government – to decide. These provisions were the work of Philippe Maystadt, foreign minister of Belgium, a country with good reason to insist on flexibility, and certain memories. In its disregard for legal niceties, or small neighbours, the tone of current German diplomacy has become increasingly Wilhelmine.

Nevertheless it is a striking fact that so far this 'Teutonic tirading', as Adorno once called it, has met no rebuff. Paris, far from reacting vigorously, has been eager to accommodate. For Connolly, this is only to be expected. Since Mitterrand's capitulation in 1983, the attitude of the French élite has been a Vichy-like subservience to German economic power. In its pursuit of a *franc fort* requiring punitive interest rates to maintain alignment with the Deutschmark at the cost of massive unemployment, this establishment has committed treachery against the French people. Noting the widespread alienation from the political class evident in every recent poll, and recalling with relish the country's long traditions of popular unrest, Connolly – who describes himself as a Tory radical – looks forward with grim satisfaction to the explosion of another revolution in France, when the population becomes aware of the price it is paying for monetary union, and rises up to destroy the oligarchy that sought to impose it.[15]

Premonitions of this kind are no longer regarded as entirely far-fetched in France itself. For the moment the prospect is less dramatic, but still fraught enough. The Maastricht referendum revealed the depth of the division in French opinion over the likely consequences of a single currency – would it lead, in the stock question, to a Europeanized Germany or to a German Europe? The victory of Jacques Chirac in the subsequent presidential election guarantees that the tension between antithetical calculations will continue to haunt the Elysée. For no French politician has so constantly oscillated from one position to the other, or opportunely reflected the divided mind of the electorate itself. Clambering to power on a platform challenging the bi-partisan consensus of the Rocard–Balladur years – *la pensée unique* – that gave higher priority to a strong franc than to job creation, Chirac in office – after a few mis-starts – has reverted frantically to financial orthodoxy again. The Juppé government is now administering even tougher doses of retrenchment to force the deficit down to Maastricht levels.

Yet even the tightest budgetary rectitude is no guarantee of a *franc fort*. The 'convergence criteria', as Connolly rightly insists, are completely unrealistic in their exclusion of growth and employment from the indices of a sound economy. Designed to reassure financial markets, they satisfy only central bankers. The markets themselves are not mocked, and will sooner or later mark down the currency of any country where there is widespread unemployment and social tension, no matter how stable are prices or balanced are public accounts – as the French Treasury discovered in the summer of 1993. The current domestic course of the Chirac regime can only tighten already explosive pressures in the big cities at the cost of its electoral credibility, on which that of its exchange rate also depends. The massive street protests of November 1995 could be a harbinger of worse trouble to come. The regime's slump in the opinion polls is without precedent in the Fifth Republic. An image of zealous compliance with directives from the Bundesbank involves high political risks.

Chirac's resumption of nuclear tests can be seen as a clumsy attempt to compensate for economic weakness by military display – demonstratively flexing the one strategic asset the French still possess and the Germans do not. The result has been merely to focus opprobrium on France. Partial or hypocritical though much of this reaction has been (how many pasquinades have been written against the Israeli bomb?), Chirac's experiments remain pointless. Forcible–feeble in the style of the man, they can scarcely affect the political balance of Europe, where nuclear weapons are no longer of the same importance. At a moment when French diplomacy ought to have been engaged in winning allies to resist German attempts to harden the Treaty of Maastricht, for which France's immediate neighbours, Italy, Belgium and Spain, were more than ready, it was gratuitously incurring a hostile isolation. On present performance, Chirac could prove the most erratic and futile French politician since Boulanger.

Nevertheless, contrary to received opinion, in the end it will be France rather than Germany that decides the fate of monetary union. The self-confidence of the German political class, although swelling, is still quite brittle. A cooler and tougher French regime, capable of public historical reminders, could prick its bluster without difficulty. Germany cannot back out of Maastricht, only try to bend it. France can. There will be no EMU if Paris does not exert itself to cut its deficit. The commitment to monetary union comes from the political calculations of the élite, and the world of classical statecraft – a foreign policy determined to check German and uphold French national power. The socio-economic costs of the *franc fort* have been borne by the population at large. Here, absolutely clear-cut, there is a conflict between external objectives and domestic aspirations of the kind Alan Milward would banish from the record of earlier integration. How much does it matter to ordinary French voters whether or not Germany is diplomatically master of the continent again? Are not the creation of jobs and growth of incomes issues closer to home? In France the next years are likely to offer an interesting test of the relative weights of consumption and strategy in the process of European integration.

Meanwhile the pressures from below, already welling up in strikes and demonstrations, can only increase the quandaries above. On the surface, the French élite is now less divided over Maastricht than at the time of the referendum. But it is no surer that the single currency will deliver what it was intended to. Germany bound – or unbound? In the space of the new Europe, the equivocation of monetary union as an economic project is matched by the ambiguity of its political logic for the latent national rivalries within it.

III

Finally, what of the prospects for extending the European Union to the east? On the principle itself – it is a striking fact – there has been no dissent among the member states. It might be added that there has also been no forethought. For the first time in the history of European integration, a crucial direction has been set, not by politicians or technocrats, but by public opinion. Voters were not involved; but editorialists and column-writers across the political spectrum, before the consequences were given much consideration, with rare unanimity pronounced any other course unthinkable. Enlargement to the east was approved in something of the same spirit as the independence of the former republics of Yugoslavia. This was not the hard-headed reckoning of costs and benefits on which historians of the early decades of European integration dwell: ideological goodwill – essentially, the need to recompense those who suffered under communism – was all. Governments have essentially been towed in the wake of a media consensus. The principle was set by the press; politicians have been left to figure out its applications.

Here the three leading states of Western Europe have divided. From the outset Germany has given priority to the rapid inclusion of Poland, Hungary, the former Czechoslovakia and, more recently, Slovenia. Within this group, Poland remains the most important in German eyes. Bonn's conception is straightforward. These countries, already the privileged catchment area for German investment, would form a security glacis of Catholic lands around Germany and Austria, with social and political regimes that could – with judicious backing for sympathetic parties – sit comfortably beside the CDU. France, more cautious about the tempo of widening and mindful of former ties to the countries of the Little Entente – Romania, say, or Serbia – has been less inclined to pick regional favourites in this way. Its initial preference, articulated by

Mitterrand in Prague, was for a generic association between Western and Eastern Europe as a whole, outside the framework of the Union.

Britain, on the other hand, has pressed not only for rapid integration of the Višegrad countries into the EU, but for the most extensive embrace beyond it. Alone of Western leaders, Major has envisaged the ultimate inclusion of Russia. The rationale for the British position is unconcealed: the wider the Union becomes, in this view, the shallower it must be – for the more national states it contains, the less viable becomes any real supranational authority over them. Once stretched to the Bug and beyond, European union will evolve in practice into the vast free-trade area it should – in the eyes of London – always have been. Widening here means both institutional dilution and social deregulation: the prospect of including vast reserve armies of cheap labour in the East, exerting downward pressure on wage costs in the West, is a further bonus in this British scenario.

Which outcome is most likely? At the moment the German design has the most wind in its sails. In so far as the EU has sketched a policy at all, it goes in the CDU's direction. One of the reasons, of course, is the current convergence between German calculations and Polish, Czech and Hungarian aspirations. There is some historical irony here. Since the late 1980s publicists and politicians in Hungary, the Czech lands, Poland and more recently Slovenia and even Croatia have set out to persuade the world that these countries belong to a Central Europe with a natural affinity to Western Europe, that is quite distinct from Eastern Europe. The geographical stretching involved in these definitions can be extreme. Vilnius is described by Czesław Miłosz, for example, as a Central European city.[16] But if Poland – let alone Lithuania – is really in the centre of Europe, what is the east? Logically, one would imagine, the answer must be Russia. But since many of the same writers – Milan Kundera is another example – deny that Russia has ever belonged to European civilization at all,[17] we are left with the conundrum of a space proclaiming itself centre and border at the same time.

Perhaps sensing such difficulties, an American sympathizer, the *Spectator*'s foreign editor, Anne Applebaum, has tacitly upgraded Poland to full occidental status, entitling her – predictably disobliging – inspection of Lithuania, Belarus and Ukraine *Between East and West*.[18] Another way out of them is offered by Miklos Haraszti, who argues that while current usage of the idea of Central Europe may make little geographical sense, it does convey the political unity of those – Poles, Czechs, Magyars – who fought against communism, as distinct from their neighbours who did not.[19] More Romanians, of course, died in 1989 than in the resistance of all three countries combined for many years. Today, however, the point of the construct is not so much retrospective as stipulative: originally fashioned to repudiate any connection with Russian experience during the Cold War, it now serves to demarcate superior from inferior – i.e., Romanian, Bulgarian, Albanian, etc. – candidates for entry into the EU.

But geopolitical concepts rarely escape their origins altogether. The idea of Mitteleuropa was a German invention, famously theorized by Max Weber's friend Friedrich Naumann during the First World War. Naumann's conception remains arrestingly topical. The Central Europe he envisaged was to be organized around a Germanic nucleus, combining Prussian industrial efficiency and Austrian cultural glamour, capable of attracting satellite nations to it in a vast customs community – *Zollgemeinschaft* – and military compact, extending from 'the Vistula to the Vosges'.[20] Such a unified Mitteleuropa would be what he called an *Oberstaat*, a 'superstate' able to rival the Anglo-American and Russian empires. A Lutheran pastor himself, he noted regretfully that it would be predominantly Catholic – a necessary price to pay – but a tolerant order, making room for Jews and minority nationalities. The Union it created would not be federal – Naumann was an early prophet of today's doctrine of subsidiarity too. All forms of sovereignty other than economic and military would be retained by member states preserving their separate political identities, and there would be no one all-purpose capital, but rather different cities – Hamburg, Prague, Vienna – would be the seat of particular executive functions, rather like Strasbourg, Brussels and Frankfurt today.[21] Against the background of a blueprint like this, it is not difficult to see how the ideological demand for a vision of Central Europe in the Višegrad countries could find political supply in the Federal Republic.

But given that widening of some kind to the east is now enshrined as official – if still nebulous – policy in the Union, is it probable that the process *could* be limited to a select handful of former communist states? Applications for admission are multiplying, and there is no obvious boundary at which they can be halted. Europe, as J.G.A. Pocock has forcibly observed, is not a continent but an unenclosed subcontinent on a continuous land-mass stretching to the Bering Strait.[22] Its only natural frontier with Asia is the strip of water once swum by Leander and Lord Byron, the Hellespont. To the north, plain and steppe unroll without break into Turkestan. Cultural borders are no more clearly marked than geographical: Muslim Albania and Bosnia lie a thousand miles west of Christian Georgia and Armenia, where the ancients set the dividing-line between Europe and Asia. No wonder Herodotus himself, the first historian to discuss the question, remarked in Book IV of the *Histories* that 'the boundaries of Europe are quite unknown, and no man can say where they end ... but it is certain that Europa [he is referring to the beauty borne away by Zeus] was an Asiatic, and never even set foot on the land the Greeks now call Europe, only sailing [on her bull] from Phoenicia to Crete'. The irony of Herodotus perhaps still retains a lesson for us. If Slovakia is a candidate for entry into today's Union, why not Romania? If Romania, why not Moldova? If Moldova, why not Ukraine? If Ukraine, why not Turkey? In a couple of years, Istanbul will overtake Paris to become the largest city in what – however you define it – no one will contest is Europe. As for Moscow, it is over two centuries since Catherine the Great declared in a famous *ukaz* that 'Russia is a European nation', and the history of European culture and politics – from the time of Pushkin and Suvorov onwards – has enforced her claim ever since. De Gaulle's vision of a Europe 'from the Atlantic to the Urals' will not lightly go away. All the stopping-places of current discussion of widening the EU are mere conveniences of the ring of states closest to it, or of the limits of bureaucratic imagination in Brussels. They will not resist the logic of expansion.

In 1991, Pocock remarked that ' "Europe" is once again an empire in the sense of a civilized and stabilized zone which must decide whether to extend or refuse its political power over violent cultures along its borders but not yet within its system: Serbs and Croats if one chances to be Austrian, Kurds and Iraqis if Turkey is admitted to be part of "Europe". These are decisions to be taken not by the market but by the state.'[23] But as Europe is not an empire in the more familiar sense of the term – a centralized imperial authority – but merely (as he put it) 'a composite of states', with no common view of their borderlands, it is not surprising that the *limites* have yet to be drawn by the various chancelleries. Since he wrote, however, there has been no shortage of expert opinion to fill the gap.

For example Timothy Garton Ash, one of the first and keenest advocates of a PCH fast track, has recently adjusted his sights. 'Having spent much of the past fifteen years trying to explain to Western readers that Prague, Budapest and Warsaw belong to Central not Eastern Europe, I am the last person to need reminding of the immense differences between Poland and Albania', he wrote in the *Times Literary Supplement*. 'But to suggest that there is some absolutely clear historical dividing line between the so-called Višegrad group and, say, the Baltic states or Slovenia, would be to service a new myth'.[24] Instead, the dividing line must be drawn between a Second Europe numbering some twenty states whom he describes as 'set on a course' towards the EU; and a Third Europe that does share this prospect, comprising Russia, Belarus, Ukraine and – a cartographical nicety – Serbia.

A dichotomy so visibly instrumental is unlikely to be more durable

than the mythical distinction it has replaced. At the end of his
Orchestrating Europe, a capacious and strangely zestful guide through the
institutional maze and informal complications of the Union, Keith
Middlemas looks out on a somewhat broader scene.[25] Europe, he
suggests, is surrounded by an arc of potential threat curving from
Murmansk to Casablanca. To hold it at a distance, the Union needs a
belt of insulation, comprising a 'second circle' of lands capable of
integration into the Community, shielding it from the dangers of the
'third circle' beyond – that is, Russia, the Middle East and Black Africa.
In this conception the respective buffer zones logically become Eastern
Europe; Cyprus and Turkey in the Eastern Mediterranean; and the
Maghreb. Middlemas, however, explains that, while the first two are
ultimately acceptable into the Union, the third remains inconceivable.
For 'the countries of the Maghreb are irrelevant as a barrier to sub-
Saharan Africa, which presents no threat except via small numbers of
illegal immigrants'. In fact, on the contrary, 'the *threat* comes from
North Africa itself'.[26] If this is a more ecumenical approach than that of
Garton Ash, who expressly excludes Turkey from Europe, it traces the
same movement, common to all these tropes – a slide to aporia. Every
attempt so far to delimit the future boundaries of the Union has
deconstructed itself.

For the moment, it is enough to register that 'Europe Agreements',
formally designated as antechambers to entry, have been signed by six
countries: Poland, the Czech Republic, Hungary, Slovakia, Romania and
Bulgaria; and that four more are impending (Slovenia and the Baltic
states). It is only a matter of time before Croatia, Serbia, Macedonia,
Albania and what is left of Bosnia join the queue. Does this prospect –
we might call it an inverted domino effect, in which the pieces fall
inwards rather than outwards – mean that the British scenario will come
to pass? Harold Macmillan once spoke, with a homely national touch,
of his hope that the Community, when exposed to the beneficent
pressure of a vast free-trade area, would 'melt like a lump of sugar in a
cup of tea'.[27] Such remains the preferred vision of his successors. Their
calculation is that the more member states there are, the less sovereignty
can practically be pooled, and the greater is the chance that federal
dreams will fold. How realistic is it?

There is no doubt at all that enlargement of the Union to some two
dozen states would fundamentally alter its nature. The most immediate
effect of any extension to the east, even of modest scope, would be a
financial crisis of heroic proportions. The cost of integrating the
Višegrad quartet alone would mean an increase of 60 per cent in the
Union budget today – rising to nearly 75 per cent by the end of the
century. There is no chance of the existing member states accepting

such a burden, at a time when every domestic pressure is towards tax reduction. That leaves either decimating current support to farming communities and poorer regions within them, composed of voters with the power to resist, or abandoning the *acquis communautaire* altogether to create a second-class membership for new entrants, without benefit of the transfers accorded to first-class members.

These are just the fiscal headaches attending rapid expansion. There are also the material consequences for the former communist econom- ies. If the effort of adhering to the convergence criteria for monetary union is already straining prosperous Western societies to breaking- point, how can impoverished Eastern ones be expected to sustain them? No previous candidates, however initially disadvantaged, had to scale such a macroeconomic cliff. Contemplating the requirements of EMU, it is not surprising that enthusiasts for expansion are starting to call for the whole idea of a single currency to be dropped. For Garton Ash, the needs of Warsaw and Prague dovetail with what is anyway the wisdom of London. 'Europe could perhaps use a little British thinking at the moment', he writes of monetary union, 'with "British" meant in the deeper sense of our particular intellectual tradition: sceptical, empirical, pragmatic.'[28]

As might be expected of this trio, the result is a grander castle in the air than any folly of the Commission: in place of economic integration through monetary union in Western Europe, political embrace of the whole of the Eastern Europe under the guidance of NATO, complete with power-sharing from Albania to Ireland, topped up by 'qualified minority acting' for the UK and its peers. This, as Garton Ash puts it in another native image, is jumping off 'the wrong bus' and catching the right one. If the leap is not made in time, he adds, Europe will soon be engulfed in another world war. The euphoric construction needs an apocalyptic conclusion – why otherwise, it might be asked, take it seriously? The conviction that EMU and Eastern enlargement are incompatible, on the other hand, is entirely reasonable. It is shared from the opposite standpoint by the unlikely figure of Jacques Attali, who regards the single currency as a valid but now lost cause, and enlargement as a German project that will lead away from a federal Europe, for which most of the national élites, mesmerized by American culture, anyway have no appetite, 'L'Europe ne s'aime pas,' he glumly observes at the end of the Mitterrand experience.[29]

Maastricht is unlikely to evaporate so easily. But the hazards of enlargement do not lie only in the economic pitfalls it poses for new or old members. Even if derogations of various kinds – from the Common Agricultural Policy, from the structural funds, from the single currency – were to be made for what were once the 'captive nations', a still more fundamental difficulty would remain, of a purely political nature. To double its membership would cripple the existing institutions of the Union. Already the original balance of the Six or the Nine has been thrown out of kilter in the Council of Ministers. Today the five largest states – Germany, France, Italy, Britain and Spain – contain 80 per cent of the population of the Union, but command only just over half the votes in the Council. If the ten current ex-communist applicants were members, the share of these states would fall even further, while the proportion of poor countries in the Union – those now entitled to substantial transfers – would rise from four out of fifteen to a majority of fourteen out of twenty-five.

Adjustment of voting weights could bring the *pays légal* some way back towards the *pays réel*. But it would not resolve the most intractable problem posed by enlargement to the east, which lies in the logic of numbers. Ex-satellite Europe contains almost exactly as many states as continuously capitalist Europe (at the latest count, sixteen in the 'East' to seventeen in the 'West', if we include Switzerland), with a third of the population. Proliferation of partners on this scale, no matter how the inequalities between them were finessed, would threaten institutional gridlock. *Rebus sic stantibus*, the size of the European Parliament would swell towards eight hundred deputies; the number of Commissioners rise to forty; a ten-minute introductory speech by each minister attending a Council yield a meeting of five hours, before business even started. The legendary complexity of the already existing system, with its meticulous rotations of commissarial office, laborious inter-governmental bargains and assorted ministerial and parliamentary vetoes, would be overloaded to the point of paralysis.

In such conditions, would not widening inevitably mean loosening? This is the wager in London, expressed more or less openly according to venue, from the FCO to the *TLS*. In the long term, the official line of thinking goes, expansion must mean defederalization. Yet is this the only logical deduction? Here we encounter the final amphiboly. For might not precisely the prospect of institutional deadlock impose as an absolute functional necessity a much more centralized supranational authority than exists today? Coordination of twelve to fifteen member states can just about operate, however cumbersomely, on a basis of consensus. Multiplication to thirty practically rules this out. The more states enter the Union, the greater the discrepancy between population and representation in the Council of Ministers will tend to be, as large countries are increasingly outnumbered by smaller ones, and the weaker overall decisional capacity will become. The result could paradoxically be the opposite of the British expectation – not a dilution, but a concentration of federal power in a new constitutional settlement, in which national voting weights are redistributed and majority decisions become normal. The problem of scale, in other words, might force just the cutting of the institutional knot the proponents of a loose free-trade area seek to avoid. Widening could check or reverse deepening. It might also precipitate it.

Each of the three critical issues now facing the European Union – the single currency, the role of Germany, and the multiplication of member states – thus presents a radical indeterminacy. In every case, the distinctive form of the amphibology is the same. One set of meanings is so drastic it appears subject to capsizal into its contrary, giving rise to a peculiar uncertainty. These are the political quicksands on which the Europe to come will be built.

1996

Notes

1. Margaret Thatcher, *The Downing Street Years*, London 1993, pp. 727, 729–30.
2. Ibid., p. 536.
3. Ibid., pp. 549–51.
4. Ibid., pp. 765–76.
5. Ibid., p. 742.
6. Ibid., pp. 70, 742, 736.
7. Friedrich Hayek, *Individualism and Economic Order*, Chicago 1948, pp. 264–5.
8. Wynne Godley, 'Maastricht and All That', *London Review of Books*, 8 October 1992. See this volume, pp. 173–7.
9. Friedrich Hayek, *Denationalisation of Money. The Argument Refined*, London 1978, pp. 19–20.
10. Tommaso Padoa-Schioppa, *L'Europa verso l'unione monetaria*, Turin 1992, pp. xii, 189. See this volume, pp. 162–72.
11. Alexandre Lamfalussy, 'Macro-coordination of Fiscal Policies in an Economic and Monetary Union', *Report on Economic and Monetary Union in the European Community*, Luxembourg 1989, p. 101.
12. Conor Cruise O'Brien, 'Pursuing a Chimera', *Times Literary Supplement*, 13 March 1992. See this volume, pp. 77–84.
13. Bernard Connolly, *The Rotten Heart of Europe. The Dirty War for Europe's Money*, London 1995.
14. Ibid., p. 64.
15. Ibid., pp. 391–2.
16. Czesław Miłosz, 'Central European Attitudes', in George Schöpflin and Nancy Wood, eds, *In Search of Central Europe*, London 1989, p. 116.
17. Milan Kundera, 'The Tragedy of Central Europe', *New York Review of Books*, 26 April 1984; see also George Schöpflin, 'Central Europe: Definitions and Old and New', in *In Search of Central Europe*, pp. 7–29.
18. London 1994. Like most writers in this genre, Applebaum is not always consistent: in the mediaeval period, Poland is accounted an 'average central European country' (p. 48).
19. Personal communication.
20. Friedrich Naumann, *Mitteleuropa*, Berlin 1915, pp. 3, 129–31, 222ff., 254ff.
21. Ibid., pp. 30, 67–71, 232–8, 242.
22. J.G.A. Pocock, 'Deconstructing Europe', *London Review of Books*, 19 December 1991. See this volume, pp. 297–317.
23. Ibid.

24. Timothy Garton Ash, 'Catching the Wrong Bus?', *Times Literary Supplement*, 5 May 1995. See this volume, pp. 117–25.

25. Keith Middlemas, *Orchestrating Europe*, London 1995.

26. Ibid., pp. 664–5.

27. François Duchêne, *Jean Monnet: The First Statesman of Interdependence*, New York 1994, p. 320.

28. Garton Ash, 'Catching the Wrong Bus?'

29. Jacques Attali, *Europe(s)*, Paris 1994, pp. 15, 147–50, 181–99. See this volume, pp. 345–56.

Economics

10

The Social Bases
of Monetary Union?

Alan S. Milward

What has happened to the once relatively democratic and humane
national governments of Western Europe that they now contemplate
the harshness in present circumstances of monetary union? Why is
France, a society as socially unjust as Britain and with an ever higher
unemployment rate, contemplating putting yet more people out of
work? Why is sluggish Germany, where those in employment now put
in an average of twelve hours a week less than their British counterparts, ready to endanger their welfare benefits, so hard-earned in
earlier times, and therewith perhaps the democratic stability they have
brought, in return for the euro? Why is the United Kingdom wondering whether sterling, backed by a low-wage, low-welfare, low-safety-
regulation economy, might not after all successfully resist the euro and
preserve London as Europe's greatest financial centre? These questions
are prompted by a book by a former European Community official,
Bernard Connolly.[1]

For the fact that no one has a plausibly consistent theoretical
explanation of this political change the Left has much to answer for.
When the European Community started in 1950–52 there was nothing
in the dried tea-leaves of Marxist analysis that referred to it. The
Protestant, nationalist Left mistakenly thought it was another old enemy.
'Church, capitalism and cartels', cried Kurt Schumacher, propped on
one stump and waving another towards a crowd of what still, at that
date, looked like the authentic pre-Nazi working class. Plump, intact,
Hugh Gaitskell – product of a life in which resistance had had a lesser
meaning – told the Labour Party in 1962 that Britain should never
abandon its thousand years of separate existence. Like other Fabian
efficiency experts, he preferred the British Empire. French socialism

149

generated as many opinions about the Community as it did deputies to
the National Assembly, but no one's opinion is remembered as relevant
or illuminating.[2] Much of the Dutch Labour Party took refuge in a
dreamy federalism which misunderstood everything.[3] Scandinavian
socialists had scarcely heard of the whole idea.

Yet the conservative Right proved equally inept and unaware. In
Britain and France it erroneously set about defending the nation against
that very train of developments which would so strengthen it. In France
it passed quickly into the same political isolation as the anti-republican
Catholics of the Third Republic. In Britain it took power and launched
its project of the 'one-world system', no regional customs unions and
the like, but an open multilateral world trade and payments system, with
Britain and sterling as sub-hegemons to the dollar and the United
States. There is, unfortunately, no such thing as a sub-hegemon.

Leaving Europe to the Liberals

Both Left and Right in Britain thought the idea of European union
would go away. It was politically unrealistic, because inexplicable by
their own political ideas. The Americans, who encouraged it, would
come to their senses. France would be too weak and divided to carry it
through. Academic writing reflected these political attitudes. Theoretical interpretation was left to resurrected nineteenth-century liberalism.
A burst of historically discredited ideas dominated not only the propa-
ganda pamphlets of the federalist movements but supposedly heavyweight academic literature too. Most of the latter came from America
and repeated what liberals believed had made the United States a great
nation. Removing barriers to trade and enterprise meant greater
economies of scale, which meant a faster growth of incomes, which in
turn meant the growth of democracy and, for the federalists, in a further
turn, as Tennyson, following Cobden, had declared, 'the Parliament of
man, the Federation of the world!' Political science elaborated a range
of progressivist, teleological theories, functionalist and neo-functionalist,
to show that a new epoch of world history had begun.[4] Economic and
political interdependence meant that supranational governance had
begun its inevitable replacement of the now inadequate nation-state.
Moribund in European national politics, liberalism was left to explain
all in supranational politics.

Those in the Labour Party who embraced 'Europe' were most
typically the inheritors of Gladstonian anti-imperialist liberalism, like
Roy Jenkins. They could believe more easily in the teleologies of
economics and political science and saw 'Europe' as a more realistic
and distinct objective than socialism; the class basis for a socialist

programme was so evidently receding in 1950s Britain. 'Europe', since it was foreordained, needed no quasi-Marxist basis of conflictual class interest for its successful creation. Something similar happened on the Right, as the old class landscape of conservatism was rapidly eroded by the most rapid and sustained growth of income, comfort and leisure for more than a hundred years. 'Modernization' became the way to win elections. Modernizers in the Conservative Party like Macleod and Heath equated 'Europe' with efficiently managed, peaceful, and middle-class democracy.[5] Empire became retrograde. In so far as such groups in either party needed any political philosophy other than a practical handbook for gathering votes, they found it in the same inconsistent, historically unfounded superficialities that political scientists and federalists called 'integration theory'.

The Left was silent on this subject, still hoping it would go away, and drawing some comfort from the severe dents that General de Gaulle's policies inflicted on such theories in the 1960s. De Gaulle also caused American political science to veer back towards a 'realist' world, where nation-states were still tough, self-seeking organizations armed with guns and bombs. In Britain two kinds of history of European integration were written; on the one hand, federalist fables in which Europe has one culture and the European Parliament is, after some false turns on the way, the logical consequence of Charlemagne in the *longue durée*,[6] and, on the other, the national diplomatic history of Britain's sub-hegemony.[7] From both, political economy – the interests of most people, why they vote as they do, how the system is shaped from below – was entirely lacking.

It has taken Gorbachev, the demolition of the Berlin Wall, the privatization of Eastern Europe, and monetary union proclaimed for the immediate future in a grand treaty to change things. But now at last the Left begins to understand that it needs a political economy of the European Union, as it once had of socialism. Recent articles by Tom Nairn[8] and Perry Anderson[9] reviewing my work were each that rare thing, a creatively intelligent response, and after fifteen years of scanning marginal comment by the uninterested it should have given me more pleasure than it did to read discourses so purposefully engaged with the real world of social and economic trends in Western Europe as a whole. Satisfaction was diluted by the thought that both should have been helped by the imperfect efforts of an out-of-date, semi-Keynesian social democrat.

The Rationale of European Union

In my work, I have argued that the underlying cause of European integration is to be found in the national policy choices of the re-established postwar Western European nation-states.[10] In most cases, this re-establishment was based on a similar model of participatory democracy in which the nation-state was reformulated in a stronger mould through policies of redistribution towards labour, the farming sector and the lower middle class. Parliamentary parties, searching for a stronger power base, served as conduits to channel policy demands, many of which had accumulated since 1929, to the parliamentary centre where national governments, striving to regain legitimacy after the disasters of 1939–40, adopted them in a strikingly similar pattern of response. The institutions of the Community grew because they made such policies easier, or in some cases possible. Anderson accurately notes that this offered but three-quarters of an explanation of what happened and he tops up the rest with a set of Cold War diplomatic necessities. Some of those I deliberately under-emphasized for purposes of creative exaggeration but others the Left, to my mind, would do well to regard more sceptically. It would seem, however, that we would be in close agreement that where foreign policy considerations mattered – and in the cause of keeping our bit of Germany under control they certainly did – there could only be such consensus about them because of the similar political economies of the separate nations. It was this that made successive surrenders of national sovereignty possible; they have strengthened popular domestic policies.

But in a further article looking at EMU, Anderson seems as puzzled as everyone else by why it should be happening.[11] It may not, after all, be true, he suggests, that the growth of the European Community is primarily to be attributed to national domestic-policy choices, because only foreign-policy considerations could explain agreement on the next planned surrender of sovereignty, and by far the most important one. Who wants EMU? How can we explain the transition from the 1950s and 1960s, when European integration buttressed the nation-state in the pursuit of income, welfare, family security and employment, to a European Union which threatens the immediate personal security and welfare of so many of its citizens in return for empty platitudes about future growth through competitiveness?

Bernard Connolly has an explanation typical of the populist Right: EMU is the work of élites. It can certainly be accepted that the workings of Western European democracies are no longer what they were before 1968, and that the conduits through which policy flows have tended to reverse the direction of that flow. Policy comes from the top down because parties have become more authoritarian in their struggle for the small number of voters who swing in elections. But Connolly's observations are much more sweeping than this, and they suggest that the populist Right is not likely to make a better job of answering these questions than the Left. It has become as Manichaean about the Union as a distortion of the world as the Left was in the 1950s about the Coal, Iron and Steel Community. The world could, after all, still be pure. Its molecules could be individual contracts. Each contract could be a free market, whose regulatory mechanisms would only be money and the law. All that is needed is a central justice system and a better understanding of how to control the money supply to ensure a stable relationship between the demand for money and nominal GDP. Politics could be reduced to management, providing managers have the power to manage. Power is still needed to sweep away 'rigidities', or institutions as they used to be called, and 'inefficiencies', formerly known as dialogue.

The Dragon of the Rhine

European Monetary Union has been devised, Connolly argues, to fight against this vision of individuals freed from history interacting in unencumbered economic advance. It is there to defend an old monster, 'Rhenish corporatism'. Matured in dark Burgundian forests since the time of Charlemagne, this dragon emerged in the personages of Mitterrand, Delors and Kohl to squat balefully in Brussels. It stands for 'the ossification that would keep the same families and castes in political and economic power from one generation to the next'. When Mitterrand abandoned 'socialism in one country' in 1983, Delors led France to the embrace of 'corporatism in one continent', 'along lines similar, as it happens, to those envisaged by Nazi and Vichy theorists, to confront the Anglo-Saxon world'. This plot would have been thwarted by the great burst of productivity improvement and income gains in mid-1980s Britain, attributable to Margaret Thatcher. The Foreign Office – 'it must have been either treachery or incompetence' – and Nigel Lawson's misguided belief that, all domestic ways of controlling the money supply having failed, it could be managed by linking sterling to the Deutschmark in the European Monetary System, bound emancipated, booming Britain to Euro-sclerosis. Margaret Thatcher fell and EMU waits at the door.[12]

This line of thought, like Thatcherism in general, cuts across the conventional divisions of political economy. Connolly is not a journalist on the *Sun*. He was a well-paid Community insider, in the very Directorate-General, in fact, that was supposed to put Delors's plans into practice. The book's cover, however, could not have been bettered by the *Sun*; Belgium's favourite statue directs a well-aimed stream of piss onto the city of Frankfurt-am-Main. This is not an unfair trick by the publishers. They can piss off, the lot of them, the book implies, for we British could still have our own political economy if the government gets back on the Thatcher track and stays out of EMU.

This seems highly fanciful, but liberation from history can make such flights seem normal, and it is a claim that was frequently made in 1980s Britain. What differences can be established in economic and social trends between Britain in the Thatcherite 'revolution' and the rest of Western Europe? There seems to have been a greater number and proportion of new small enterprises founded in Britain between 1983 and 1989. But their rate of collapse after the 1989 downturn eliminated the difference – Lawson's fault, Connolly argues. It can be argued that the higher rate of growth of overall productivity in the United Kingdom than in much of Western Europe between 1983 and 1989 was a consequence of these new enterprises, although there is no hard evidence for this other than temporal coincidence. It was nevertheless certainly a reversal, albeit brief, of the comparative trends since 1945. The diversity of incomes, formerly known as income inequalities, opened more widely in Britain than in other European countries. This was due more to a widening of the spread of wages than to reductions in social-security benefits; indeed post-redistribution incomes at family rather than individual level widened more rapidly in the Netherlands, and other countries in Western Europe were closer to the British experience. The state, we may perhaps conclude, was more involved in subsidizing low individual real wages in Britain as they were reduced, perhaps by the diminution of labour protection and the weakening of trade unions.

The Bullish Right

Nevertheless, even within the European Union, the United Kingdom is now a low-wage country compared to large competitors like Italy or Spain, to say nothing of Greece and Portugal. Trade unions have been legally discriminated against in a way that has not occurred elsewhere, but membership remains very high compared to, say, France. The sharp rate of decline of the manufacturing sector relative to services, which was at its steepest in 1979–83 before the true 'revolution', is being replicated elsewhere, even in Germany. The deregulated financial-services sector did not gain ground over other financial centres. The shifts in fiscal burdens and types of tax have been paralleled elsewhere. The British economy in the 1980s was much more determined by its history than the new Right wishes to believe and the differences between its behaviour and political economy and that of the rest of Western Europe are hard to discern. 'By May 1987', Connolly writes, after the tax cuts in the budget and the Conservatives' election victory – the most 'Thatcher-specific' of their three victories under her leadership – 'the casual visitor could literally see, hear, taste – and almost literally smell and feel – the bullishness in the country.'[13] For the first time, he claims, since the People's Budget in 1909, Britain was standing on its own feet. Might future historians wonder whether 'bullishness' was a misprint for 'bullshit'?

We are usually told that multinationals want a single currency and that Delors was able to use them as a pressure group by appointing some of their heads as advisers in pushing through the single-market initiative. When most intra-Community manufactured exports are made by multinationals, this is plausible. But note who told *France Dimanche* that central bankers are uniting 'to fight inflation when the principal threat to Europe is deflation'.[14] It was the chairman of Peugeot, Jacques Calvet. He argued that for the Treaty of Maastricht, which gives them the power to attempt such a policy in unison, we can blame Delors, who has put 'Europe on the worst possible path'.

It is said that EMU is supported by central bankers – that it is their final victory over the so-called Keynesian State. It was they, under Delors, who staffed the Committee for the Study of Economic and Monetary Union which produced the Delors Report for the Hannover European Council in 1988. The convergence criteria of the report are indeed deflationary, especially in reducing the ratio of public debt to GNP in Belgium and Italy. Yet there are those who hint that the central bankers wrote down these criteria under the prompting of the Bundesbank, so that EMU could not happen. Connolly, who on such matters may well be a knowledgeable inside source, hints throughout that Helmut Schlesinger, the president of the Bundesbank Council who approved the Delors Report in its final stage, thought the wording of the criteria was stiff enough to save the Deutschmark by frightening politicians away.

The élites to which Connolly attributes EMU are French civil servants, the British Foreign Office, ambitious politicians of smaller economies, like González, and businessmen with multinational and transnational interests. Trimming British politicians like Howe, Lawson, Heath, Wilson, Callaghan and others come in for a roasting as non-populist fellow travellers. For a populist, the people can be wrong only if misled. Yet what evidence is there that citizens of the member states are in fact so opposed to EMU, or would be if they knew the truth about it? It seems a rather finely balanced issue in the opinion polls across Europe as a whole, and that is what the Left has to explain better than Connolly's often justified denunciations of the undemocratic procedures by which EMU has been pushed through.

Of course, as in every earlier surrender of sovereignty to 'Europe', the future of Germany, our future, has to be regulated. The single currency is the price that Germany must pay to France for reunification. French voters, at least, did agree to pay it in a referendum, albeit very narrowly. Surely they were not simply doing what the hereditary élites of the Quai d'Orsay were telling them? They may have thought it remarkable that Germany had been reunited so peacefully and had stayed within the complex net of political and economic control that France designed as the European Community. Helmut Kohl's public insistence that Germany benefits from this is strong and frequent. Connolly has another view of reunification. The GDR could have been a dynamic low-wage, low-cost Thatcherite rival to 'Rhenish corporatism', but Bonn imposed on it West German trade unions, wages, social-security systems and West German firms in order to stifle it. It is occupied territory, taken over not reunited. Surely, however, that is what its population wanted, and voted for, massively. They, alone of the Soviet Union's satellites, have jumped the new immigration wall into the Europe of labour protection, institutionalized wage-bargaining and the weekly giro.

Where the price becomes hard to pay is in France's unwillingness, supported by Britain, to allow any genuine democratic decision-making in the supranational institutions of the Community. But this shows no signs of becoming an election issue in Germany. Neither does the struggle between the Bundesbank and the German government over political control of the proposed European central bank.

The Economic Benefits of Integration

French and German voters, like those in the rest of the Union, offer their allegiance to government, national and supranational, by deciding how its actions will affect their long-term family-income prospects. Whenever the control mechanisms of the Community were extended in the past, whenever European nations surrendered parts of their national decision-making power to 'Europe', they did so because it helped national policy to offer material gain to voters. There has always had to be a coincidence between that promise and the need to extend supranational machinery to make it possible, or easier, for such policies to succeed. Margaret Thatcher and her ministers supported the single-market legislation in the 1980s because they believed that making the Common Market more perfect would return European economies to their earlier high rates of income growth. Would not the Left be wiser to suppose that EMU is one more effort, perhaps to be one of the long list of such efforts which were abandoned because they did not fit this criterion, to use the supranational machinery to buttress a national policy choice which, far from being wanted by practically no one, does have a substantial degree of popular support? It would then, beneficially, have to face up to the question of why it had this support. That would prevent a relapse into the three-monkeys attitude of the 1950s.

The concerns of the public about EMU, at least on the evidence of polls, reflect anxieties about interest rates, savings security, transaction costs and employment. Virtually all discussion of the first starts from the assumption that low interest rates are what is wanted, but this is one of the many examples where political economy is still fixed in past assumptions. The proportion of the population that prefers high interest rates is much larger than in the postwar years of fast growth and it is increasing. The prosperous workers and first-time home buyers of the 1950s and 1960s are the rentiers of the 1990s, and the proportion of income that comes from savings is far higher. Contemporary discussion in the media remains dominated by a peculiarly British preoccupation. Low interest rates are the pressing concern of younger voters in countries like Britain, but unlike Germany or Italy, where house-purchasing capacity is determined by flexible mortgage rates and a high ratio of mortgage borrowing to purchase price. The voter interest in deflationary monetary policies is large, whereas in the 1950s it was almost non-existent.

Even on present rates of national income growth, however, per capita income in Western Europe will have increased by more than 20 per cent by 2015. If inherited wealth and savings from the great postwar boom have so altered the political economy of the 1980s and 1990s, that is a trend which will continue. Furthermore, it is the old who as a group are most homogeneously in favour of high interest rates and stable money and most opposed to inflationary stimuli. The old age dependency ratio, the proportion of those over sixty to the working-age population, is at the moment at about 19 per cent in Western Europe. It will be 28 per cent in 2010, in Germany 34 per cent. Only Ireland will not reflect that pattern. At the height of the Thatcher boom, before employment rates again began to fall, the idea that the boom could be better safeguarded by a European central bank with a record like the Bundesbank's rather than by the Bank of England, a subservient tool of inflationary, election-boom-seeking politicians, was in fact surprisingly popular in Britain. Sustained deflationary pressure on the economy through interest rates, even when, on the evidence of the last decade, inflation is one of the least dangers the economy runs, does have a numerous and influential backing in the electorate, and those backers are not deterred by the idea that it is foreigners who will set the interest rate. People are not intelligent enough to know that that is what happens anyway.

The interest in stability of savings is high everywhere. Suppose the United Kingdom were to exercise its opt-out from monetary union. Under the rules from which it has not opted out, it could not impose exchange controls against other members of the Union. Would the British then save in sterling? If financial institutions competed to offer them the chance of saving in euros, would there be a competition to offer higher and more inflationary interest rates or would the euro be the more stable choice? Assuming that the overall European instability which would ensue did not deter voters, they might well prefer the euro option. Sterling has been a pretty poor choice for long-term savings.

Reduced transaction costs, not giving the money-changers their cut every time you go through the Channel Tunnel, has attracted much favourable comment and has electoral appeal, although in reality the savings that would be made from eliminating these costs, even Delors's henchmen had to agree, are tiny compared to the financial estimate of any other gain or loss from EMU.

The Last Bastion of the Working Class

It is when it comes to employment that EMU has far less voter appeal. Harder times since 1989 are the weightiest reason for the miasma of uncertainty that has grown up around it. In most countries in the 1980s, even to maintain social-security benefits at their real level during the 1970s – they had increased in level in Western Europe for the two decades before that – required public deficits as a percentage of GDP well over the Maastricht convergence criterion of 3 per cent. In the peak unemployment years, the average was just over 5 per cent. Of course, big factors in the increase in these deficit ratios were the problem of uncertain expenditure control in health and welfare services, the continued demand for some social services even at higher income levels, and the demographic trend towards an older population. But much the biggest factor was the impact of unemployment on the social-security income stabilizers built into the economy everywhere before 1974. It should be no surprise that it is Germany – last European home of the secure, unionized, blue-collar, manufacturing working class, comfortable enough to reproduce planned middle-class patterns of consumption and investment, that social group from which the Labour Party once drew its political might – that now suddenly asks whether EMU is worth it. But in Europe the whole history of German postwar manufacturing is atypical. There are far fewer jobs and votes of that kind for other, including British, politicians to defend.

If Germany stuns the idea into slumber, some other proposed surrender of sovereignty will have to emerge as politically feasible, for Germany to all appearances still wishes to pay the price of Community membership. But EMU will only slumber. Unlike the late, unlamented European Defence Community, EMU does have national electoral support. Like the Sleeping Beauty, it will be kissed back to life if prosperity returns.

Europe and the Left

I would not for one moment pretend that these brief remarks constitute a full or usable political economy of EMU. They are a plea to the Left that it should not make the mistake of the populist Right, but that it should construct a continuing political economy of European Union based on the irrefutable fact that the social and economic trends in the United Kingdom are those of any other small Western European country. As in every earlier surrender of sovereignty to Europe, the question has also to be asked: what is the alternative? Has national policy succeeded in defending employment? It is not intended to in most countries. Is the alternative to EMU and a real transfer of political power to Europe so attractive to voters? When those transfers of sovereignty were so limited in the great European boom, one reason was that national government brought such manifest benefits. Things look different now.

In constructing a political economy to explain why EMU might follow the model of earlier surrenders of sovereignty, the costs of what the French call social 'exclusion' – the word is now being introduced in Britain – should be discounted. The fact is that, if the excluded are more excluded by EMU, this will not affect the issue in national elections or at the diplomatic level. It took a war to do that for the excluded of the 1930s. What is probably more pertinent is the argument that state-supported social security must come down to permit competition against the non-Community world. Here, the crucial middle-class group of voters whose swing determines elections has much to defend; it is a great beneficiary of state-supported welfare benefits for health care and for care of the aged. Because of changes in family patterns, the decay of the two-parent, single-earner family and the increase in female participation ratios, families are less willing and less able to assume welfare burdens which governments, having taken the money in tax to pay for them, now wish to hand back. The defence of *some* existing social security benefits and of *existing* employment might be pragmatic reasons for resisting EMU. Whether it happens or not, it remains an error to suppose that this is merely the work of diplomats and other élites.

The Right will not abandon its view that the fixed exchange rates that under any system will precede EMU, no matter how wide the permitted spread, are, firstly, a fetter on enterprise and human liberation, and secondly, that in any case, the history of all such attempts to fix rates shows them to be futile. There is much to be said for the second, historical, conclusion. It should also be remembered how many monetary unions have collapsed. But the first conclusion is an abstract, untestable one and the Left should be more pragmatic. Would an accurate political economy show that Mitterrand, González and Blair, in turn, were right to take up the cause of 'Europe', which at the moment means EMU? Asking that kind of question suggests a more accurate appraisal of the real political trends in present European society and thus a more realistic understanding of what contribution the Left could expect to make. It might well, indeed, indicate that monetary union is not the way forward, but the Left would then know the reasons why and come to a closer understanding of the European Union. The Left would understand that the Union exists because it has been a response by national governments to popular demand; that the surrender of sovereignty has been a political instrument of such governments, and that any further cession of it will be successful only if based on a close politico-economic analysis of gains and losses. That idea at last seems to be dawning. How late it was.

1996

Notes

1. B. Connolly, *The Rotten Heart of Europe. The Dirty War for Europe's Money*, London 1995.

2. W. Loth, *Sozialismus und Internationalismus. Die französischen Sozialisten und die Nachkriegsordnung Europas 1940–1950*, Stuttgart 1977.

3. W. Asbeek Brusse, 'The Dutch Socialist Party', in R.T. Griffiths, ed., *Socialist Parties and the Question of Europe in the 1950s*, London 1993.

4. K.W. Deutsch *et al.*, *Political Community and the North Atlantic Area*, Princeton 1947; E. B. Haas, *Uniting of Europe*, Stanford 1968; L. N. Lindberg, *The Political Dynamics of European Integration*, Stanford 1963.

5. J. Turner, '"A Land Fit for Tories to Live in": The Political Ecology of the British Conservative Party 1944–1994', *Contemporary European History*, vol. 3, pt. 2, July 1995.

6. R. Mayne, *The Community of Europe. Past, Present and Future*, New York 1962; R. Vaughan, *Twentieth Century Europe: Paths to Unity*, London 1979. Both were standard teaching materials for some time.

7. J.W. Young, *Britain and European Unity, 1945–1992*, London 1993, is the most useful, but also typical, example.

8. T. Nairn, *The Guardian*, 21 August 1994.

9. P. Anderson, 'Under the Sign of the Interim', *London Review of Books*, 4 January 1996. See this volume, pp. 51–71.

10. Alan S. Milward, *The Reconstruction of Western Europe 1945–51*, London 1984, and *The European Rescue of the Nation-State*, London 1992; Alan S. Milward *et al.*, *The Frontier of National Sovereignty. History and Theory, 1945–1992*, London 1993.

11. P. Anderson, 'The Europe to Come', *London Review of Books*, 25 January 1996. See this volume, pp. 126–45.

12. Connolly, *The Rotten Heart of Europe*, pp. 76, 32, 47.

13. Ibid., p. 52.

14. Interview with Jacques Calvet, *France Dimanche*, 14 January 1996.

Engineering the Single Currency

Tommaso Padoa-Schioppa

I write as one moved by a number of convictions, which have underlain my part in European debates over the years. I believe that a free decision by the peoples of Europe to place the sovereignty of their national states in a common order, founded on the rule of law, is a goal allotted to us by two world wars. Such an order requires institutions empowered to address and resolve common problems. Among them, a single market supposes monetary union, each set on a firm foundation. These ideas are simple and not particularly novel. Their inspiration goes back to the tradition that extends from Immanuel Kant's *Scheme for a Perpetual Peace* to the economic and political teachings of Luigi Einaudi.

Even, however, those of us who had long believed that European monetary union was both necessary and possible, and had done something to lay the groundwork for it, were not merely delighted but astonished when the Community heads of government reached an agreement at Maastricht on the means and timetable for achieving EMU. A proposal that had lain dormant in distant and increasingly ritual declarations of intent was suddenly unearthed, and translated into not just a political objective but a legally binding commitment. In just three and a half years, from June 1988 to December 1991, all the main issues at stake in monetary union were – under strong political pressure – debated, negotiated and codified: a result achieved only by painstaking attention to technical detail and huge organizational effort.

The inter-governmental conference of 1991 alone entailed the direct involvement – i.e., with some degree of influence on the final outcome – of hundreds of people working in the political and technical institutions of the Community and its member countries; not to speak of the even greater number of people who participated in the debate, and indirectly in the decision-making process, through their work in research institutes, media, business or trade unions, local government or national parliaments. The result of this enormously complex undertaking is now a clear and coherent agenda, whatever the immediate problems of its practical implementation.

The zone of Europe that signed the Treaty of Maastricht lost its monetary unity around the seventh century, when barbarian kings began to mint coins bearing their own images instead of that of the emperor, in whose name they exercised authority. The face of the emperor, symbol of an indivisible power – including that of coinage – vanished, as Western Europe itself fractured. In that epoch, the clash of vastly different peoples, customs and laws was mitigated by the emergent principle of *jus sanguinis*, which sanctioned the co-existence of plural jurisdictions within a single territory. Today, with the creation of a union founded on reciprocal recognition of the laws of member countries and a single currency, Europe appears to be retracing its steps along a path which in distant centuries led from the unity of an empire to a multiplicity of kingdoms, legal codes and currencies.

How, in the space of a few years, could such a momentous initiative have been born? It will be some time before the history of the Treaty of Maastricht can be written. The key documents marking each stage in its preparation – the conclusions of the Council of Europe, the Delors Report, the Guigou Report, the documents of the Commission, the Central Bankers' Committee and the Monetary Committee, and the successive drafts of the Treaty itself – have yet to be comparatively analysed. So too the longer-run causes of the process. Personal and institutional archives remain inaccessible, and accounts of diplomatic negotiations partial and incomplete. It is also clear that future historiography of the Treaty of Maastricht will inevitably be affected by its eventual outcome, which we cannot yet foresee.

So to the question 'How was it possible?' I can only offer the subjective answers of an actor reflecting on events while often in the thick of them. But as a witness to many of the episodes that led to the Treaty, I will try to look back at them in the light of events that are now before us.

During the 1980s a latent logic, familiar alike to economists and historians, started to impress itself upon decision-makers in Europe. The logic can be expressed in a proposition: free trade, unconstrained mobility of capital, fixed exchange rates and independent national monetary policies cannot co-exist for long. They form what I have dubbed an 'inconsistent quartet'. The instability of their combination can be resolved in only two ways: either by replacing the last term with a single currency, or by eroding the other three. If more detailed work remains to be done in specifying the dilemma, there is no doubt of the direction in which the Treaty of Maastricht resolves it. My own view is that the construction set up by the Treaty of Rome was afflicted with a structural weakness which, without the decision taken at Maastricht, would eventually have caused the Community to regress to the precarious life of a mere pact for international cooperation. Naturally, this is not a claim amenable to 'analytic proof' – we are in a region where the choice of acceptable solutions is a matter of judgement.

What such judgement needs, however, is a theory of monetary institutions rather than of exchange-rate systems. For it has become increasingly clear over the years that monetary union is *not* an exchange-rate system. It is worth recalling that in the debates over the EMS, distinguished advocates of flexible exchange rates like Milton Friedman or Alan Walters directed their fire more against fixed exchange systems than against a single currency proper. In fact, the true alternative to a single currency is represented by schemes for running *domestic* monetary systems rather than managing international relations between sovereign currencies: not the flexible exchange rates proposed by monetarists, but the kind of currency denationalization and monetary competition favoured by Friedrich Hayek. This was the line of thinking to which the British Treasury turned in its unsuccessful quest for an alternative to the Delors Report.

A second basic proposition derives from Richard Musgrave. It formulates economic policy as a triad of functions – allocation, stabilization, and distribution – which correspond to three goals, efficiency, stability and equity, and argues that a balance between the three functions must be struck at every level and in every system of government, even in the sphere of international relations. In my view, it was the relevant model for analysing the effects of the Single European Act, when the move towards a single market led to an imbalance between the first and the other two functions of economic policy.

But whereas in the 1970s the logic of these two propositions operated regressively, in the 1980s their effect was profoundly positive – transmitting momentum from economic to political decisions, as the success of the EMS led to the creation of the single market and then to a reconsideration of monetary union. It is fair to say that the correction of the twofold imbalance began in 1988. In terms of 'equity' or redistributive policy, the Community gave a new priority to 'cohesion' by doubling the so-called structural funds for poorer regions; while on the front of 'stability', monetary unification was set in train by the creation of the Delors Committee.

A variety of choices and circumstances – as well, of course, as people – contributed to the virtuous dynamic that permitted the 'unthinkable' to happen. Western Europe was enjoying its longest cycle of economic expansion since the war. Most of its governments were led by politicians moulded by the idea of Europe, possessed of a firm grasp of power, unified by familiarity of contacts, and sustained by a favourable social climate. In France, the legacy of prejudice bequeathed by General de Gaulle had substantially diminished. In Germany, the loyalty of the political class – and of Helmut Kohl and Hans-Dietrich Genscher in particular – to the supranational commitments that had come with peace was now so solid that it could withstand even the collision of European integration with the preservation of the Deutschmark, the symbol of German influence in the continent. The importance of the role of Jacques Delors, at the head of the Commission, needs no emphasis.

Finally, between late 1989 and late 1990, the wind of history blew a strong gale from the East, which was skilfully made into a favourable breeze for Europe. From the fall of the Berlin Wall (November 1989) to the first free elections in eastern Germany (March 1990) and the European Council in Rome (October 1990), the unification of Germany and the development of the Community were closely interwoven; and their meshing gave the scheme for EMU a critical push. Here Kohl's resolve, against stiff opposition in his own country, to pursue the twin goals of reuniting Germany and of embedding it within the Community, proved decisive.

At the same time, a change in the intellectual climate made it easier to move towards European integration without unduly upsetting national governments. The rise of a philosophy of 'minimal government' and economic deregulation unlocked the formula that permitted the single market – minimal harmonization and mutual recognition. Those years also saw a growing conviction that monetary policy possessed only limited margins of discretion, given the overriding need to pursue price stability, for which an independent central bank was essential. It was this consensus that allowed the idea to be floated of introducing monetary union by the creation of an independent European banking authority, prior to full political union.

It was a historical irony of the process that European integration was to be furthered even by those who opposed it outright, or others who regarded it with grave disquiet. The free-market outlook of even such a tenacious adversary of the Community as Margaret Thatcher in fact helped to signal the road of the Single European Act. Likewise, the appeal of minimal government could be used to resist inclusion of budgetary policy in EMU, which otherwise might well have overloaded, and sunk, proposals for monetary union at the outset. The Bundesbank, flushed with pride in its institutional model, not only provided a stable anchor for the EMS in the first half of the 1980s, but also pushed for a type of central bank compatible with Community institutions. It was also helpful that a dress rehearsal for the bond between political union and monetary union could be staged in Germany, clarifying the actual distribution of roles between an elected government and a central bank in an inter-German rather than a Community-wide context.

In hindsight, some tactical choices on the road to Maastricht are worth recording. If in 1986 the Commission had not suddenly taken the far-sighted decision to press ahead with liberalization of capital movements, setting 1992 as the deadline for completion, the single market and monetary union would probably not have become parallel issues of debate and negotiation, reinforcing one another as they did. If the composition of the Delors Committee, created at the Hannover meeting of the heads of state in 1988, had not included the central bankers of the interested countries, they might well have adopted a very different attitude towards the prospect of monetary union. Moreover, without their technical competence and authority, it would have been much more difficult to hammer out a scheme comparable in complexity and importance only to the Spaak Report that paved the way for the Common Market.

Once the Delors Committee was set up, the course it selected was also crucial. It was here that the idea of 'subsidiarity' was introduced as a criterion for determining which new areas of competence were to be attributed to the Community. Its most important innovation, however, was the crystallization of a 'fundamentalist' view of monetary union as the creation of a federal equivalent of a 'national' monetary system, rather than as any kind of international agreement. Perhaps this radical approach was quietly preferred by some elements of the Committee in the belief that just because it was more rigorous it was also less likely to come to pass. However that may be, within the first few months of the working life of the Delors Committee, it was this approach that guided the flight-path to Maastricht, as all measures were framed in relation to the final objective rather than a set of intermediate stages; institutional rather than behavioural parameters were set in view; and monetary policy was treated as indivisible.

Maastricht was no foregone conclusion. Inquiry into how the Treaty was actually achieved dispels any notion that it was the only outcome possible. Those who worked for the result that was in the end secured were moved by a conviction that monetary union was desirable and feasible, but not that it was probable, let alone ineluctable. There were innumerable moments when events could have taken a different turn. Strategic choices, political atmosphere, economic conditions, historical context might easily have intersected in such a way as to stop the process in its tracks. Guicciardini's words come to mind: 'faith breeds obstinacy', and 'since the things of the world are subject to a thousand chances and accidents, unhoped-for assistance may come in many ways over the length of time to those who have persevered in obstinacy'. One might even think of a benign conspiracy by history, or Manzoni's conception of providence: but certainly never speak of inevitability.

In fact, even the concept of monetary union itself was far from fixed in advance, and my own ideas on it evolved over time. Although I was convinced by 1982 that 'the two goals of free movement of capital and fixed exchange rates require the creation of a single monetary space and authority' it was not until 1987 that I pressed this point publicly with a concrete proposal – and when I did so, I still envisaged a wide range of possible forms and paths, in a more open-minded way than it was possible to develop during the internal debates within the Delors Committee or in other forums of negotiation. For example, it seemed to me at the time that neither fixed exchange rates nor a formal treaty were indispensable for monetary union, whose sufficient condition – I argued – was simply 'a monetary policy, and therefore single monetary authority, vested with powers of decision and means of operation'.

Similarly, so long as the idea of monetary union seemed unlikely to get serious consideration from official bodies, it was natural for anyone in favour of it to look instead to market dynamics to bring it about – in particular, to the dynamism of the Ecu market. Persuaded that monetary union was a necessary complement to the Treaty of Rome, I then believed that it might be possible to reach, if not EMU itself, at least an antechamber to it, 'from below'. After all, I was aware that, as Karl Menger once put it, 'currencies were not legislated into existence; in origin they are social, not state, arrangements'. This was the path that struck me as most feasible then; not that I ever thought it preferable to institutional innovation 'from above'.

This dilemma was resolved by the Delors Committee, where the fundamentalist line rapidly swung towards the solution 'from above' that in 1987 had struck me as technically attractive but politically tricky. No one can now disprove – or, for that matter, prove – the hypothesis that in the absence of initiatives at governmental level, the Community would in any case have moved towards monetary union from below. Nor is anyone in a position to determine the degree to which the prospect – or, viewed in an opposite light, danger – of market-led pressures for a single currency induced politicians and central bankers to take the road that led to Hannover and Maastricht. But it is worth reflecting on the fact that chief executives of banks and corporations of the magnitude of Philips, Deutsche Bank, Fiat and Total were already publicly calling for a single European currency.

The successful end-result of the work of the Delors Committee, historically striking as it has been, warrants no euphoria. The town of Maastricht, known to the Romans as 'Ad Mosam Traiectum', has been a focus of political contention and strategic crossing-point for the European powers down the centuries. What was signed there in December 1991 was just one in a long series of treaties that has punctuated the history of the European continent. Monetary union has yet to be realized. Today there exists a set of instruments for realizing it which even a short time ago seemed almost beyond reach: a clear-cut plan, a precise timetable and a binding commitment. In short, to the long-run pressures towards monetary union has now been added the force of law. But the road from Treaty to Union is not guaranteed.

For it cannot be taken for granted that the goal set at Maastricht will in practice be attained. I have tried to give some inkling of how imponderable was the combination of factors – no matter how strongly economic reason called for it – that led to the Treaty. Historical precedents caution against any assumption that signature is equivalent to implementation. Key provisions of the Treaty of Rome lay blocked for some fifteen years before the Single European Act – in effect, a fresh treaty – restored momentum to them again. Implementation of the Treaty of Maastricht must advance through conditions very different from those of the 1980s. It would be unwise to count on the balm of economic expansion to spread social optimism and dampen distributive conflicts. Signs of political fatigue and distrust are evident in many member states. For a new generation of rulers the memory of European warfare, hitherto such a strong source of constructive determination, will no longer provide steady counsel.

In the process that led to Maastricht, as in the founding period of the Community itself, it can be said the contribution – both technical and political – of my own country exceeded its relative weight within Europe. The tactical sense and professional competence that Italy brought to the preparatory negotiations were certainly a factor in their success. Still more important, however, is the fact that, perhaps to a greater extent than in any other country, there was a broad consensus of viewpoints on European integration stretching across all the different components of the governmental system: from the office of the prime minister to the Foreign Ministry, the Treasury to the Bank of Italy, parliament to party machines. This unusual unity of purpose, reflecting a widespread European sentiment in the country, acted as an efficiency multiplier on Italy's part in the drive to monetary union. A country often afflicted by internal divisions and administrative failings in this period acted with more coherence than stronger countries which in principle were better equipped for decisive intervention, but in practice were hampered by conflicts of institutional competence or political direction.

Last but not least, Italian initiatives gained enhanced effect by promoting genuinely *communautaire* options and solutions, for in any negotiation whoever seeks and defends a common interest always benefits from doing so. It was less a matter of forgetting Italy's interests than of serving them better. At Hannover, Rome and Maastricht, interventions by Italian premiers and foreign ministers – Ciriaco di Mita, Giulio Andreotti, Gianni de Michelis – were decisive. They remained loyal to a tradition that has been upheld, irrespective of party allegiance, for almost fifty years by the most eminent figures in Italian public life: the conviction that European integration constitutes a fundamental interest for Italy, a country with relatively recent democratic and civil norms that have not yet fully taken root in the country's social and industrial structures. This sense that the Italian interest coincides with the Community interest, consistently reflected in successive Italian governments, made Italy an influential player in these years.

That, of course, does not mean everything went its way. On at least two major issues, Italian positions were rejected. From the Delors Report to the Council at Rome, my country argued that the European Central Bank should come into existence at the start of Stage Two. Between Rome and Maastricht, however, this key clause was jettisoned, in the only major step back from the decisions reached at Rome. Here the German version of the fundamentalist stance, while making it possible to cast the whole issue of monetary union in terms of the creation of a single central bank, also had the effect of making any discussion of the transition very difficult indeed. A refusal to contemplate any – even partial – surrender of sovereignty prior to the 'zero hour' of the final stage was improperly invoked by (above all) the German delegation to postpone the setting-up of the European Central Bank, in flat contradiction of the undertakings given in Rome by Chancellor Kohl. The result is that the transitional stage was entrusted to a temporary body, the European Monetary Institute (EMI). This is a new departure in the history of the Community. The coming period will reveal just which intermediate position the EMI occupies along the continuum that separates the former Governors' Committee from the future European Central Bank.

A second issue over which Italian representations were set aside has since become a much more prominent focus of controversy, not only in Italy but throughout the Community. The insistence by some countries during the course of negotiations on 'convergence conditions' for a single currency reflected intellectual assumptions I could not share. As an economist, I believed the claim that a high degree of nominal convergence (rate of inflation, budgetary policy, public debt, etc.) was a necessary precondition for the implementation of monetary union to be ill-founded. It seemed to me that its advocates were motivated less by solid economic arguments than by – no doubt legitimate – political considerations, in particular a desire to postpone loss of sovereignty for as long as possible, in the hope of making monetary union more acceptable to domestic public opinion. In the event, the Treaty signed at Maastricht includes in an Annexe a detailed set of criteria for macroeconomic convergence, as a condition of participation by member states in monetary union.

It is fair to say that this faces Europe with a real 'Italian question'. For Italy is the only country that is both central to the history of the Community and an economic power of G7 rank – hence capable of affecting the stability of the whole area, yet structurally divergent from the other leading states of the Community in its levels of long-run inflation and public debt. If, before Maastricht, it was in Italy's interests to be pro-European, today to be a good European means getting the Italian economy back on to a sound footing. Here a number of mistaken ideas are to be avoided.

One of these is the illusion that 'they will let us in anyway'. It is self-deception to believe that the element of discretion in the convergence criteria, rightly inserted in the Treaty in part on Italian insistence, will significantly weaken the standards so firmly demanded by the majority of member states. The legal obligation is unequivocal. Moreover, given the argument that monetary union between countries with strongly differing macroeconomic positions would pose inflationary dangers for the whole Community, it would be unwise to underestimate the room for manoeuvre that persistent Italian divergence might concede to the unbowed opponents of a single currency, above all in Germany. Before the Treaty of Maastricht was signed, convergence was still a precondition for implementation of the final stage of monetary union. Now, however, the deadline for transition to the third stage – with its corollary of automatic exclusion of non-convergent countries – has turned it into a precondition of participation at all.

It is also an error to claim that convergence within the timetable laid down is 'a huge task' for Italy, a road strewn with 'blood and tears'. To present the situation in this way is to furnish ourselves with false alibis in advance. The reality is otherwise. In the space of three years, Italy must reduce inflation by roughly 3 per cent and bring its deficit (currently running at over 150,000 billion lire) down by the equivalent of 7 per cent of GDP. As these targets are met, interest rates will come down and the ratio between public debt and GDP will start to fall. This is not the place to consider the hard decisions and specific measures needed to tackle the twin problems of inflation and budgetary deficit. Results will certainly have to be swift, and solutions structural.

But it is misleading to portray the task as gigantic. In the 1980s, several European countries managed within three-year periods to achieve reductions in their deficit equal to or greater than that now required of Italy. Denmark cut its budgetary deficit by almost 11 per cent of GDP, Ireland by just under 8 per cent and Luxembourg by 7 per cent. In just three years, each of these countries broke a climbing ratio of national debt to GDP, setting it on a firmly downward trend. Any macroeconomic policy designed to repress inflation and restore balance to public finances is liable to have an initial deflationary effect. In the medium term, however, no permanent setback is involved; what occurs is rather an investment in growth and stability. For Italy, this is a small price to pay – one that certainly does not jeopardize Italian membership of that small band of countries where living standards are now higher than humankind has ever known. The term 'sacrifice' cannot justifiably be applied to policies of this nature.

Nor should the question of convergence be reduced to a mere matter of numerical ratios. In a more profound sense, the Treaty of Maastricht offers a key to unlock essential changes in Italy. The Italian welfare state was created later than the German, French or British. But the imbalances and excesses which have appeared in these societies, and which are now being painfully corrected, have emerged in Italy as well. Here, however, they are compounded by the dysfunctions of a relatively recent democratic system, which is still beleaguered by an ancient and widespread alienation from the state, that corrupt civic morality and encourages public waste. The social changes needed to 'converge' with Europe are thus in a broader sense the same as those anyway required for Italy's historical maturity as a nation.

But if Italy is a special case in the Community, every country confronts an adjustment of its own. Since the formal and legal ratification of the Treaty of Maastricht, intellectual and psychological ratification is still in train. This must be a salutary process. To move forward to monetary union as if by stealth, while relying on people and institutions to look the other way, would endanger the whole process. The prospect of monetary union remains to be internalized by the various component parts of society: political élites, business and trade unions, and citizens at large. The single currency will be a dramatic change for all. Banknotes are the only industrial products that everybody handles. Although endowed with a purchasing power far beyond their cost of production, they are nevertheless accepted by everyone 'on sight' from complete strangers, with no more than a cursory glance. They symbolize the power of the state and the sense of security that it is the duty of the state to provide. To a far greater degree than economists or central bankers, politicians and ordinary citizens sense that there would be little point in a single currency unless it is a move towards political union.

From 1949 onwards, Europe has evolved in composite fashion, often zig-zagging between different horizons: between an exclusively economic project and a political ideal; between confederation and federation; between a free-trade area and a single market; between technocracy and democracy; between the functionalism of Jean Monnet and the constitutionalism of Altiero Spinelli. These oscillations and ambiguities have made it possible to attract a wide spectrum of support, to work with the grain of the various chancelleries and experts, and to erect a major technical and institutional edifice. But they have also cumulatively stored up a democratic deficit incompatible with Western constitutional traditions, and put major decisions within the Community beyond the reach of public opinion and political participation.

I recall an occasion during the proceedings of the Delors Committee when Jacques Delors, disconcerted by arguments from some of his colleagues from the central banks, wondered aloud whether history could still 'avancer le visage masqué' (continue to advance under a mask). His conclusion was that the risks involved in calling things by their own names, in designing and proposing EMU in a way comparable to the currency of a nation-state, would simply have to be accepted. Today the room for circumlocution and evasion has shrunk, not only for monetary but for political union. Postponed for years, perceived by every critical conscience as vital to cement the unity of Europe, anticipated as the ineluctable encounter between the principles of democracy and the quest for a supranational order, the moment of clarification has at last perhaps arrived.

What is now necessary above all is not just choice but invention; not so much to buttress the union as to define the kind of union we want to create. It was only with the Single European Act that the Community clearly abandoned the premises of the centralized state that was the legacy of the great European monarchies. Still more recently, it has become clear that even the American federation may not after all provide an appropriate pattern, born as it was from a compact between linguistically and culturally homogeneous units, without prior history or much subsequent aversion to centralization. But if it is to be achieved, the unification of Europe will bring into existence a new kind of state, which may have to forge its shape by amending some of the construction already accomplished.

1992
Translated by Chris Woodall

12

The Hole in the Treaty

Wynne Godley

A lot of people throughout Europe have suddenly realized that they know hardly anything about the Maastricht Treaty, while rightly sensing that it could make a huge difference to their lives. Their legitimate anxiety has provoked Jacques Delors to make a statement to the effect that the views of ordinary people should in future be more sensitively consulted. He might have thought of that before.

Although I support the move towards political integration in Europe, I think that the Maastricht proposals as they stand are seriously defective, and also that public discussion of them has been curiously impoverished. With a Danish rejection, a near-miss in France, and the very existence of the ERM in question after the depredations by currency markets, it is a good moment to take stock.

The central idea of the Maastricht Treaty is that the EC countries should move towards an economic and monetary union, with a single currency managed by an independent central bank. But how is the rest of economic policy to be run? As the Treaty proposes no new institutions other than a European bank, its sponsors must suppose that nothing more is needed. But this could only be correct if modern economies were self-adjusting systems that didn't need any management at all.

I am driven to the conclusion that such a view – that economies are self-righting organisms which never under any circumstances need management at all – did indeed determine the way in which the Maastricht Treaty was formed. It is a crude and extreme version of the view, which for some time now has constituted Europe's conventional wisdom (though not that of the US or Japan), that governments are unable, and therefore should not try, to achieve any of the traditional goals of economic policy, such as growth and full employment. All that

173

can legitimately be done, according to this view, is to control the money supply and balance the budget. It took a group largely composed of bankers (the Delors Committee) to reach the conclusion that an independent central bank was the only supranational institution necessary to run an integrated, supranational Europe.

But there is much more to it all. It needs to be emphasized at the start that the establishment of a single currency in the EC would indeed bring to an end the sovereignty of its component nations and their power to take independent action on major issues. As Tim Congdon has argued very cogently, the power to issue its own money, to make drafts on its own central bank, is the main thing which defines a nation's independence. If a country gives up or loses this power, it acquires the status of a local authority or colony. Local authorities and regions obviously cannot devalue. But they also lose the power to finance deficits through money creation while other methods of raising finance are subject to central regulation. Nor can they change interest rates. As local authorities possess none of the instruments of macroeconomic policy, their political choice is confined to relatively minor matters of emphasis – a bit more education here, a bit less infrastructure there. I think that when Jacques Delors lays new emphasis on the principle of 'subsidiarity', he is really only telling us we will be allowed to make decisions about a larger number of relatively unimportant matters than we might previously have supposed. Perhaps he will let us have curly cucumbers after all. Big deal!

Let me express a different view. I think that the central government of any sovereign state ought to be striving all the time to determine the optimum overall level of public provision, the correct overall burden of taxation, the correct allocation of total expenditures between competing requirements and the just distribution of the tax burden. It must also determine the extent to which any gap between expenditure and taxation is financed by making a draft on the central bank and how much it is financed by borrowing and on what terms. The way in which governments decide all these (and some other) issues, and the quality of leadership which they can deploy, will, in interaction with the decisions of individuals, corporations and foreigners, determine such things as interest rates, the exchange rate, the inflation rate, the growth rate and the unemployment rate. It will also profoundly influence the distribution of income and wealth not only between individuals but between whole regions, assisting, one hopes, those adversely affected by structural change.

Almost nothing simple can be said about the use of these instruments, with all their interdependencies, to promote the well-being of a nation and protect it as well as may be from the shocks of various kinds to which it will inevitably be subjected. It has only limited meaning, for instance, to say that budgets should always be balanced, when a balanced budget with expenditure and taxation both running at 40 per cent of GDP would have an entirely different (and much more expansionary) impact than a balanced budget at 10 per cent. To imagine the complexity and importance of a government's macroeconomic decisions, one has only to ask what would be the appropriate response, in terms of fiscal, monetary and exchange-rate policy, for a country about to produce large quantities of oil, to a fourfold increase in the price of oil. Would it be right to do nothing at all? And it should never be forgotten that, in periods of very great crisis, it may even be appropriate for a central government to sin against the Holy Ghost of all central banks and invoke the 'inflation tax' – deliberately appropriating resources by reducing through inflation the real value of nation's paper wealth. It was, after all, by means of the inflation tax that Keynes proposed that we should pay for the war.

I recite all this to suggest, not that sovereignty should not be given up in the noble cause of European integration, but that if all these functions are renounced by individual governments they simply have to be taken on by some other authority. The incredible lacuna in the Maastricht programme is that, while it contains a blueprint for the establishment and *modus operandi* of an independent central bank, there is no blueprint whatever of the analogue, in Community terms, of a central government. Yet there would simply have to be a system of institutions which fulfils all those functions at a Community level which are at present exercised by the central governments of individual member countries.

The counterpart of giving up sovereignty should be that the component nations are constituted into a federation to which their sovereignty is entrusted. And the federal system, or government, as it had better be called, would have to exercise all those functions in relation to its members and to the outside world which I have briefly outlined above.

Consider two important examples of what a federal government, in charge of a federal budget, should be doing.

European countries are at present locked into a severe recession. As things stand, particularly as the economies of the USA and Japan are also faltering, it is very unclear when any significant recovery will take place. The political implications of this are becoming frightening. Yet the interdependence of the European economies is already so great that no individual country, with the theoretical exception of Germany, feels able to pursue expansionary policies on its own, because any country that did try to expand on its own would soon encounter a balance-of-payments constraint. The present situation is screaming aloud for coordinated reflation, but there exist neither the institutions nor an agreed framework of thought which will bring about this obviously desirable result. It should be frankly recognized that if the depression really were to take a serious turn for the worse – for instance, if the unemployment rate went back permanently to the 20–25 per cent characteristic of the 1930s – individual countries would sooner or later exercise their sovereign right to declare the entire movement towards integration a disaster and resort to exchange controls and protection: a siege economy if you will. This would amount to a re-run of the interwar period.

If there were an economic and monetary union, in which the power to act independently had actually been abolished, 'coordinated' reflation of the kind which is so urgently needed now could be undertaken only by a federal European government. Without such an institution, EMU would prevent effective action by individual countries and put nothing in its place.

Another important role which any central government must perform is to put a safety net under the livelihood of component regions which are in distress for structural reasons – because of the decline of some industry, say, or because of some economically adverse demographic change. At present this happens in the natural course of events, without anyone really noticing, because common standards of public provision (for instance, health, education, pensions and rates of unemployment benefit) and a common (it is to be hoped, progressive) burden of taxation are both generally instituted throughout individual realms. As a consequence, if one region suffers an unusual degree of structural decline, the fiscal system automatically generates net transfers in favour of it. *In extremis*, a region which could produce nothing at all would not starve because it would be in receipt of pensions, unemployment benefit and the incomes of public servants.

What happens if a whole country – a potential 'region' in a fully integrated community – suffers a structural setback? So long as it is a sovereign state, it can devalue its currency. It can then trade successfully at full employment, provided its people accept the necessary cut in their real incomes. With an economic and monetary union, this recourse is obviously barred, and its prospect is grave indeed unless federal budgeting arrangements are made which fulfil a redistributive role. As was clearly recognized in the MacDougall Report which was published in 1977, there has to be a quid pro quo for giving up the devaluation option, in the form of fiscal redistribution. Some writers (such as Samuel Brittan and Sir Douglas Hague) have seriously suggested that EMU, by abolishing the balance-of-payments problem in its present form, would indeed abolish the problem, where it exists, of persistent failure to compete successfully in world markets. But as Professor Martin Feldstein pointed out in a major article in the *Economist*, this argument is very dangerously mistaken.[1] If a country or region has no power to devalue, and if it is not the beneficiary of a system of fiscal equalization, then there is nothing to stop it suffering a process of cumulative and terminal decline leading, in the end, to emigration as the only alternative to poverty or starvation. I sympathize with the position of those (like Margaret Thatcher) who, faced with the loss of sovereignty, wish to get off the EMU train altogether. I also sympathize with those who seek integration under the jurisdiction of some kind of federal constitution with a federal budget very much larger than that of the Community. What I find totally baffling is the position of those who are aiming for economic and monetary union without the creation of new political institutions (apart from a new central bank), and who raise their hands in horror at the words 'federal' or 'federalism'. This is the position currently adopted by the British government and by most of those who take part in the public discussion.

1992

Notes

1. Martin Feldstein, 'Europe's Monetary Union: The Case against EMU', the *Economist*, 13 June 1992, pp. 23–6.

13

Building on Maastricht

Sam Aaronovitch and John Grahl

The starting-point in any assessment of the current state of European integration is to recognize how closely the project of European construction has become engaged with a very narrow and dogmatic project for monetary stabilization. This linkage is both damaging and inextricable.

On the one hand it is clear that both the 'convergence process' which is preparing the way for EMU and the immediate consequences of the latter – particularly the division between insiders and outsiders it is bound to bring about – will do nothing to resolve, and may well aggravate, the European social crisis which arises from persistent unemployment and insecurity and expresses itself in a dangerous alienation of populations from political leaderships.

On the other hand, however, it is not possible to undo the Maastricht Treaty or to renegotiate the delicate political compromise on which it rests. No doubt this is to be regretted – one can imagine alternative starting-points which would have been more favourable, both in terms of the objectives set for the Union and in terms of the strategies and institutional structures through which they would be pursued. But these alternatives are no longer real. In practice, political perspectives can only be developed if the real circumstances of the Union are recognized: these include an immense commitment of political capital to the achievement of EMU according to the formulae of Maastricht and an increasing momentum towards that goal.

What is called for, therefore, is a precise strategic orientation within a very narrow space. This space is not wide enough to permit the rejection of Maastricht and EMU. The failure of monetary integration is certainly possible, although it is less and less likely. But failure would leave the Union in a political and economic vacuum, in which it would be impossible to formulate a constructive strategy. The loss of authority and prestige of EU institutions, the break-up of existing coordination procedures, the promotion of anti-European political forces which would follow such failure, would all be severe blows to the wider project of European construction as such. In such a context the EU would be reduced to a mere free-trade zone, which might be widened to include new member states but in which there would be no possibility of deepening the process of integration. Nor would the disabling of central political structures permit a larger choice of strategies at national level. On the contrary, constraints on national economic policy would be tightened by uncontrolled competition to attract investment and economic activity from one territory to another. The pressures on state budgets arising from the Maastricht convergence process would be perpetuated by efforts to advance national competitiveness in a dutch auction of welfare cuts, deregulation and tax give-backs.

However, although rejection of Maastricht leads to a strategic dead end, there is no scope for any strategy which merely accepts the Maastricht agenda. The dysfunctionality of the Maastricht project has become more obvious since the ratification of the Treaty. The political resources and energy of the EU are being absorbed by an absurd war on inflation at a time when inflation has ceased to be a serious economic problem in many EU countries. Even in its own terms, as a counter-inflationary exercise, the Maastricht agenda – both convergence criteria and the European Central Bank (ECB) – may prove self-defeating, by inducing financial disequilibria and social tensions which increase rather than reduce inflationary risks. Beyond this exaggerated concern with price stability, it is clear that Maastricht is obstructing the elaboration of effective EU economic policies and narrowing the range of objectives which can be addressed. The most important example is the attenuation of the employment strategy developed by the Commission in 1994: the failure to carry through even these modest measures carries major political dangers for the Union. European electorates, in France for instance, can see quite clearly the impact of the Maastricht programme on employment, welfare and social stability; if it becomes impossible to point to other EU programmes which promote security for Union citizens, the already alarming gap between the project of European construction and the populations which the project is meant, in principle, to serve will become a threatening gulf.

This is the narrow space in which strategic intervention must be considered: between a rejection which would strike, effectively or otherwise, at integration as such; and the endorsement of a programme so narrow and dogmatically conceived that it has already begun to disorganize the political and economic life of the Union. The only feasible approach is to attempt initiatives inserted into the Maastricht agenda itself – into its incoherences, its lacunae, its limitations – with the aim of *strengthening* the advance to EMU, securing the political and economic basis of a common currency, rationalizing the process by which it is pursued and enhancing the further objectives of the unified currency area.

The organization of political forces behind such intervention also raises very difficult questions. There can be no doubt that discontent with present developments is both intense and widespread: dissatisfaction is experienced not only by the citizenry of several member states but also by significant elements of the political class, including much of the European Commission itself. But it is not clear that these forces can be easily united around a common project for an alternative. One possible line of fracture is along national boundaries; another is between the forces deeply committed to a different vision of European construction and those fundamentally hostile to integration as such. In these conditions the specification of ambitious immediate objectives may have the effect of fragmenting rather than mobilizing the forces for change.

It cannot be denied that programmatic thinking along these lines must be closely confined, both by established political arrangements and by economic imbalances which can only be slowly corrected. But it is nevertheless the most fruitful approach, since it avoids a negative, and probably futile, refusal of the realities of the post-Maastricht period, while still attempting to widen and enrich the Maastricht agenda. In spite of the constraints, there are a number of significant strategic opportunities to promote a more positive interaction between developments at national and EU level. The key policy areas include: an alteration of the macroeconomic stance of member states in order to facilitate the transition to EMU; a stronger and more explicit political commitment to limit exclusions from the monetary union and to shorten the period during which major member states will be outside; a relaunch of the employment initiatives which are, indeed, a necessary political and economic complement to the EMU programme; and efforts to valorize the achievement of EMU both internally and externally, through balancing centralized monetary policy with new fiscal powers and initiatives for global monetary and financial reform. Such ambitions may themselves appear voluntarist, but they have a practical basis in that they are necessary to secure and stabilize the actual strategy for European construction and to control the political and economic risks which Maastricht has begun to generate.

The plan of the present essay is, first, to assess these risks – the literal interpretation of Maastricht, the excessive and uncoordinated drive for fiscal consolidation, the narrowing of EU economic policies, the alienation of Britain from the integration process. On this basis, some of the most promising initiatives can be sketched – these opportunities exist precisely because they would defend and stabilize the EMU process itself by limiting the costs and enhancing the benefits to which it gives rise. Particular attention will be paid to the case of Britain, whose lack of engagement with the current phase of European construction in itself goes a long way to explain the imbalances and inadequacies of the Maastricht agenda.

Locked In

By the summer of 1996 it had become obvious that the drive for monetary union, intended to be the occasion of a new and deeper phase of European integration, had become almost the opposite – a clear sign of the inadequacy of European institutions. The formulae of the Maastricht Treaty, both as regards the convergence process *before* monetary union and as regards the ways in which a common currency is to be managed *after* it is introduced, were more and more clearly damaging to European economic development in the present and more and more threatening for its future. Yet no political process, no forum for discussion, no strong institutions devoted to general European interests, permitted the adaptation or amendment of these formulae. To touch them would be to jeopardize EMU itself and rob the Union of the project which has increasingly monopolized its political energy and its strategic capacities: the inter-governmental conference of 1996 was designed to examine the workings of the Treaty of Union and to bring about such corrections as were necessary. Yet the IGC, it was decided, would not discuss the monetary aspects of the Treaty, since the compromise on which these rested was too fragile to admit of any alteration. In particular, the highly qualified endorsement of Maastricht in the German constitutional court seemed to threaten denunciation of the Treaty by Germany if any of its monetary clauses were to be amended.[1] EMU was kept off the IGC agenda in spite of the fact that the first obvious consequence of the Maastricht formulae would be to exclude the majority of EU member states from early participation in this key project of the Union.

Proposals for a more rational and less costly approach to monetary union were not lacking. They ranged from the daring (De Grauwe's suggestion of an EMU *without Germany*);[2] through the strategic (the European Parliament's argument that the preparatory process should rest on the closest possible collaboration among core countries – above all France and Germany – likely to be the first participants in EMU);[3] to the modest but eminently practical (allow the weakest countries to make

extensive transitional use of capital controls).[4] Yet realistic commentators were gradually forced to recognize that no substantial deviation
from the formulae was politically conceivable because the underlying
political compromise was too delicate.[5] The most that could, perhaps,
be hoped for was to relax, slightly, the criteria for participation in EMU
in exchange for even more solid guarantees of counter-inflationary
rectitude after it begins.[6]

Meanwhile the 'convergence process' put EU citizens, in their
millions, on the rack. Ferocious expenditure cuts were used to reduce
public-sector deficits, even though these budgetary retrenchments,
applied everywhere, rapidly became a major aggravating factor in the
decline of European growth rates and thus of the problems of public
finance they were intended to resolve. The economics involved is
neither complex nor controversial: it is a standard procedure to
distinguish structural (trend) deficits from cyclical deficits, arising from
the decline in tax revenues and increases in welfare expenditure which
take place in a recession. There is no good argument for drastic
measures to reduce cyclical deficits, because they constitute a stabilizing,
counter-cyclical mechanism. But since the Maastricht Treaty does not
pay much attention to the distinction, European governments promoted
ever more stringent economies in an attempt to narrow the deficits
induced, at least in part, by their collective resort to previous measures
of the same kind. The political leadership of the EU was quite incapable
of preventing, or even moderating, this self-destructive process. Increasingly, the Commission has confined itself to calling for ever more
budgetary rigour.[7]

It must be conceded that the drive to restrict public spending does
not arrive simply from the Maastricht agenda. National governments
are to some extent using Maastricht as an alibi for their own projects to
establish more restrictive welfare regimes, to intensify market disciplines
and to favour particular social strata. Only such motives can explain the
tax reductions which, in many cases, accompany expenditure cuts and
make the achievement of Maastricht public finance targets more difficult. But the speed and intensity of the adjustments being attempted,
together with the damaging way in which they are combined with
otherwise inexplicable monetary restriction, indicate that macroeconomic policies are very largely driven by the EMU process in reality
as well as in appearance.

France Paralysed

Ironically, it is in France – the source of European strategy and the
principal inspirer of the EMU project – that the 'convergence process'

has proved most painful and disruptive. The presidential election of 1995 was barely over when Jacques Chirac began to sacrifice his promised programme on the altar of budgetary rigour. The reshuffling of the Juppé government in the autumn had no other purpose than to focus ministerial efforts on the drive for economies. These provoked a huge protest movement by the end of the year, but this lacked the focus of a clear alternative strategy, at least in part because the main opposition grouping, the Parti Socialiste, was committed to the pursuit of identical ends by identical means. As economic activity stagnated, the room for manoeuvre in economic policy virtually vanished: as each new set of data revealed slower growth and, as a result, wider public-sector deficits, the Chirac regime could only put forward more austerity proposals – aggravating the already exceptionally high and persistent unemployment and increasing social tensions which appeared to work only to the benefit of extreme right-wing, anti-EU political forces.

The only possible source of relief would be a decisive relaxation of monetary policy which would both encourage private expenditures and reduce pressure on state finance. But here France and other member states are closely constrained by German policy. Again following the Maastricht formulae, the EU left monetary policy in the transition phase completely at national level: in practice this was to perpetuate the key currency role of the Deutschmark. Once again, however, the Bundesbank was reluctant to assume its inescapable international responsibilities – relaxation came at a grudging pace which did not give sufficient stimulus.

In fact, the post-1992 EMS, with very wide fluctuation margins, may even have taken pressure off the Bundesbank to consider the external effects of its policies, because it is not obliged to intervene in support of the franc while the Banque de France continues to hold it close to the old central rate and thus well above the new floor.[8]

Employment Policy Stagnates

The Commission has always tried to claim that monetary union and the fiscal stabilization which Maastricht necessitates do not exhaust its economic strategy and that it also has plans for tackling Europe's persistently high levels of unemployment.

Since 1994 these plans have centred on the strategy of publicly sponsored investment in Europe-wide transport and communications networks. Ambitious proposals were put forward both by the European Parliament and by the Commission.[9] They had already been very much diluted to win the consent of national governments, but then failed to win agreement on financing at the Florence Council of June 1996. With the Florence Council, the fig-leaf covering the absence of an effective EU employment strategy was stripped away. All that the proposals could have achieved, in any case, was a mobilization and coordination of national efforts to stimulate employment; the network programmes were little more than a symbol of the commitment that might be achieved. The reality so far, however, is that national policy is everywhere committed only to budgetary retrenchment and that Commission activity has been reduced to encouraging the latter in line with the dubious formulae of Maastricht.[10]

Towards a Two-speed Europe

If the *approach* to EMU has become dysfunctional for member-state economies, its *implementation* promises little better. How the ECB will function when it begins operations remains obscure: it is doubtful whether it can do what it is designed to do and replicate the performance and procedures of the Bundesbank, since it will be dealing not with the highly coordinated German economy but with a much more complex and incoherent assembly of economic relations on a continental scale. In this sense, as De Grauwe points out, the initiation rites imposed by Germany for participation in the EMU were always of doubtful effect – there is no way in which the rigours accepted today can guarantee anti-inflationary probity tomorrow.[11] The council of finance ministers at Dublin introduced a post-EMU system of fiscal discipline which may prove effective, but it cannot, in advance, stabilize the environment in which the ECB will work. Certainly the markets remain sceptical: Holtham points out that Deutschmark debts likely to be redeemed in euros carry a substantial interest-rate premium.[12] In any case, the aim, endorsed by Maastricht, of projecting a German institution on to the European plane appears fundamentally misconceived. The ECB will be dealing with such a different, and difficult, situation that only a very wide interpretation of its remit is likely to prevent serious destabilization.

What can be confidently predicted is that EMU in 1999 will immediately split the EU into two zones, according to whether countries are deemed to have met the convergence criteria.[13] This situation itself is dangerous for the EU: frictions between insiders and outsiders may impair both commercial and political relations. Already, France has tried to introduce a disciplinary regime to prevent competitive devaluations by outsiders, only to be told by the Commission that this approach is not acceptable. Nevertheless, the exclusion of a large number, probably a majority, of member states from what will be the EU's most powerful structure could turn EMU into a disintegrating strategy: outsiders will be constrained to accept less favourable positions on international credit markets while insiders such as France will fear the loss of market shares and investments to weak currency countries. Only a real relaxation of the fiscal criteria for entry can resolve this problem, since otherwise Italy, in particular, will be left to wrestle with its disequilibrated public finances for a very long time before it qualifies for the EMU club.[14]

The Two Projects

It has always been a strength of the movement for European integration that it has been able to redefine the content of the process of European construction in order to meet the political and economic priorities of the day. The danger of using other projects as vehicles to carry integration forward is that, although it makes Europe relevant to other programmes of reform, it may tie the fate of European institutions very closely to projects with an uncertain future. Thus, in the 1990s, the two projects of strengthening EU institutions, on the one hand, and, on the other, of pursuing monetary disinflation as this is now understood (that is, with the discretionary but restrictive policies of an independent central bank substituted for yesterday's discredited formula of reliance on some simple quantitative rule for the issue of money) are linked.[15]

Now in most contemporary discussion, it is the second of these projects which is seen as necessary and practical (who does not believe, today, in a rigorous monetary policy?) while the first, European federalism, has come to seem distinctly old-fashioned (surely the last great scheme for a rational reordering of society to survive into the postmodern twilight). Such judgements may be as precarious as they are fashionable.

Disinflation by means of monetary policy alone, to begin with, rests on very shaky intellectual foundations. The fundamental premise of the argument for it, the separability of real and monetary phenomena, is not well established. All the economic reasoning involved relies on models in which one can specify, at any given time, a given set of productive possibilities, formalized as some aggregate production function. But, for short- to medium-term developments, there is no empirical basis for this *a priori*. Few products (except, perhaps, leisure in the sense of Robert Lucas – that is to say, unemployment) can be turned out using purely current inputs to satisfy an immediate want. The vast mass of employment depends on some kind of investment activity, that is, it is part of some future-oriented strategy and thus conditioned by the view taken of future economic developments. The co-existence of these heterogeneous employing activities requires both the respect of monetary constraints by all agents and the perpetual recycling of financial resources from surplus to deficit units among them. The two conditions are intimately related, so that the expectations which govern financial relations bear not only on the small fraction of economic activity which is usually identified as investment but on the monetary constraints faced by almost all enterprises. All the experience of modern economies indicates that these constraints have to be *managed* at an aggregate level to avoid severe disruption arising from financial disequilibria and changing conventional views of the future. This creates a need for centralized refinance which places a constraint on monetary policy. The latter can be safely devoted to price stabilization only in conditions of stability and confidence.[16]

It follows that the project of monetary disinflation depends on the successful control of real economic imbalances and the construction of a healthy and robust climate for investment; it can succeed only as part of a successful economic strategy with much wider objectives.[17]

This raises the question of the other project – European construction – and the contribution it might make to improved real economic performance. The possibilities here have hardly, as yet, been explored, largely because prevailing economic orthodoxies place excessive faith in the power of markets to secure real economic adaptation. Two areas seem of particular importance: the promotion of a favourable environment for long-run investment by the clear specification of developmental priorities – regional, ecological and so on – which can orient market agents; and the stabilization of external conditions through the deployment of the collective influence of EU countries on a global level. Both ambitions certainly inspired the original drive for monetary integration but both have been submerged by the increasingly narrow and restrictive interpretation of the latter as an exercise in disinflation.

However, the balance between the two projects, in spite of Maastricht, is not fixed for all time. EMU itself will create a new situation and bring new priorities into view – above all, the problem of persistently high levels of unemployment for which the Union will no longer be able to escape direct responsibility. It is not only desirable but in fact necessary to begin to enrich the economic objectives of the EU to meet the responsibilities which EMU will place on it. One aspect of this will be the need for policies, beyond mere exhortation, to overcome the exclusion of non-participating states.

Britain without a Project

The argument above has stressed the ambivalence of the projects behind the present phase of European construction. It is now necessary to insist that no project whatsoever, no view of economic reconstruction or of social or political renewal, inspires current British policy or the attitude of rejection fostered by Euro-sceptics. In fact this political force seems only to express the impasse at which British social and economic development has arrived; it constitutes the demand that British institutions escape the otherwise harsh judgement that might be made on them and attempts to exculpate irresponsible national leadership by directing popular discontent against EU institutions, which in truth have little to do with either Britain's lamentable economic performance or its increasingly divided society.[18] It is symptomatic of the vacuity of contemporary British political life that *non*-participation in EMU is virtually the only clear economic strategy that one can detect. On the Right, Euro-scepticism covers the exhaustion of a Thatcherite agenda, of which the few remaining elements are pursued simply as a *fuite-en-avant* from the chaotic consequences of the same strategy; while the Euro-scepticism of the Left has little more to offer than nostalgia for a nationally based economic programme which has been manifestly obsolete for over a decade (certainly since the failure of the experiment carried out in France between 1981 and 1984).

The obfuscation of contemporary British political discourse is so dense that it seems worthwhile to insist on the following clarifications. The logic of each point is direct but none of them is clearly perceived in what has become an unreal debate, concerned with little more than symbols.

Firstly, Britain does not enjoy any significant measure of monetary 'sovereignty'. Its departure from the ERM in September 1992 did indeed permit a rapid and substantial relaxation of policy. This, however, was by no means a simple reassertion of national priorities against external constraints: it was, in fact, made possible only by a unique monetary situation in the global economy. At that time, short-run interest rates in Frankfurt were some 6 per cent higher than in New York. Under these exceptional, and probably unrepeatable, circumstances, it was indeed possible for Britain to cut its own rates in disregard of German policy. This was not an expression of 'independence' but merely a reorientation of policy from a European to an Atlanticist setting. Sterling is a weak and dependent currency; while it survives, it will have to be defended by offering a costly risk premium above the interest rates prevailing in the key currency – dollars, Deutschmarks (or, tomorrow, euros) – which forms the indispensable external reference. The external constraint will always be primary in the formulation of British monetary policy since a 'clean float' and the primacy of internal objectives are possibly only for the very strongest economies – such as Japan – which inspire such confidence in international wealth-holders that a depreciation today does not raise fears of a collapse tomorrow. The exceptional (and, from a European point of view, absurd) policy settings of 1990–92 apart, it is probably to Britain's advantage to link sterling to the Deutschmark rather than to the dollar, because the former is a more reliable point of reference for a country trading largely within Europe, and because interest rates can generally be expected to be lower with a European than with an American orientation.

Secondly, the current heated debate on the question of an EMU referendum is fatuous. Immense industrial, commercial and financial interests are at stake in Britain's adhesion to, or absence from, the single currency. Largely because, until recently, EMU itself has been in doubt, these interests have not yet been expressed in a decisive way, although there are several straws in the wind, such as the increasing anxiety of City banks and financial institutions about lack of access to the euro payments system, TARGET; it seems that access may be limited to participants in EMU in the interests of monetary control.[19] If a clear position in favour of participation in EMU is adopted by the majority of the corporate players, then the consultation of the electorate becomes meaningless and a foregone political conclusion. Britain is too weak in economic and industrial terms to enjoy the luxury of obstructing private-sector strategies on such an issue. It is sometimes observed that the Euro-sceptic drift of the Conservative Party has opened up an unprecedented gap between its political rhetoric and the views held in British boardrooms. It is necessary to draw the corollary that such a gap empties Conservative discourse of force and conviction.

Finally, Britain remains deeply, albeit silently, engaged in the Maastricht process. This is, in fact, the real content of the anguished governmental debate on fiscal relaxation versus consolidation. Chancellor Kenneth Clarke explicitly recognized, some years ago, the claims of the convergence criteria on British public finance (such explicitness seems frequently to get him into trouble). Although this motive for financial prudence is now unlikely to be stated openly, it remains a key determinant of the direction of British budgetary policy and provides a rationale of such cogency as to constrain, or even override, the electoral logic of tax cuts.

Given these realities of British economic and political life, a negotiating position centred on the rhetoric of 'sovereignty' and on 'opt-outs' constitutes a simple failure to articulate authentic national interests. The modalities of EMU are of great importance to Britain; in spite of the country's industrial decline, its political status and its centrality to global financial developments guarantee that it can be influential in European financial and industrial affairs; the simplistic and rigid formulae agreed at Maastricht are not appropriate to British economic circumstances; no player can have the same possibilities as Britain to persuade Germany to amend these formulae or to interpret them with more flexibility. In this sense, the re-engagement of British political discourse with European (and domestic) realities has become one of the key conditions for the constructive implementation of the Maastricht programme.

Failure

One can introduce the programmatic section of this discussion by considering the possibility, real but fading, that EMU will not be achieved, that the experience of the 1990s will in the end replicate that of the 1970s and Delors go the way of Werner.

Although such an outcome would be welcome in Britain, where it would release several political groupings from a most painful dilemma, it seems clear that it is not in Britain's power to block a process from which it has already distanced itself. Britain, it is widely agreed, will not be among the pioneer members of the currency union; but it cannot, on the other hand, obstruct the formation of a union if France, Germany and their smaller neighbours are determined to achieve it. (Ironically, the minimalism of the British government may be reinforcing that determination, since British ministers are systematically blocking all the other paths to further integration at the IGC.)

In fact EMU seems to reproduce the decision-making conditions of the Schuman Plan. When asked how many participants were necessary, Adenauer replied, 'Two.' The same two countries control today the fate of the Maastricht agenda: without France the experiment would collapse, as it would represent a simple extension of German hegemony – a politically unacceptable threat to the European project rather than a contribution to it; without Germany, the euro would be too weak and dependent on external circumstances to constitute a genuine advance of European construction.

It follows that the contingencies which might block or delay (every delay is dangerous as it could lead to blockage) the move to EMU are easy to specify: social revolt in France, if the population, in the street, refuses the final heavy instalment of austerity required to place France at the rendezvous of 1999; bad faith in Germany, if political leaderships, having extracted the highest obtainable price for their participation, nevertheless decide that the sacrifice of the Deutschmark is too great a cost.

Neither contingency can be assigned an objective probability; but neither seems plausible – most of the costs of EMU have already been met; the prize is now less than thirty months away; to retreat at this point would be to devalue vast amounts of political (and financial) capital. Rather than speculate on such an outcome, one can insist on its drastic and unavoidable consequences for the EU. No alternative strategy exists with any lodgement in the European political class; no alternative compromise could be constructed when nations have been brought with such difficulty to hazard some elements of their sovereignty; political recrimination, against leaderships which have demanded such substantial sacrifices in an ultimately futile venture, would be comparable only to those which have overthrown governments in the wake of economic or military catastrophe.

No doubt, the huge industrial and commercial interests linked to European integration would try to contain the most violent of the centrifugal forces that would be released. But that, surely, would be a question of damage limitation. One can easily develop conceptual alternatives to the Maastricht agenda, many of which might, in abstract terms, be preferable to it. But in the aftermath of such a setback they would remain concepts – no political dynamic would exist capable of bringing them into effect.

Easing the Transition

It is appropriate, at this point, to pass from the contemplation of failure to the initiatives which might help to secure and consolidate success. The most concrete and immediate of these is a distinct alteration of macroeconomic stance.

At present, fiscal policy in most EU countries is – largely as a function of Maastricht itself – extremely restrictive. (One can add that immense efforts had already been made in this direction before the recession of 1991–92, induced by the malfunctioning of the EMS, wiped out most of the progress that had been made.) Although one can quarrel with the timing and speed of the fiscal correction being attempted, and the failure to coordinate it across the Union, the necessity for the correction is surely beyond dispute. Even if one maintains the widest Keynesian ambitions for fiscal stimulus, such a stimulus requires, as a first condition, that the governments which undertake it are credit-worthy. Now it is a matter of arithmetic that public finance in the majority of member states is not sustainable. Thus a medium-term correction to limit deficits and stabilize indebtedness is unavoidable.[20]

What can be changed is the monetary context of fiscal policy. The Bundesbank has carried out a significant easing since the climax of its frenzied post-unification squeeze in the summer of 1992.[21] But the steps taken have been too slow and reluctant. They hardly take into account the 30 per cent appreciation of the Deutschmark which has been brought about since 1992, partly as a consequence of the ERM crises which German policy triggered at that time. Bundesbank policies can be criticized on several grounds: they continue to focus on internal developments at a time when it is increasingly clear that the Deutschmark is destined for extinction and monetary policy will be translated to the European plane; they still refer to invariably misleading monetary aggregates, which have long since lost all meaning as intermediate targets, rather than to any objective assessment of inflationary pressures.[22] A consideration of the latter indicates that inflation is subdued in Germany itself, while in France the most sober commentators have begun to measure the risks of a straightforward deflation.[23] Meanwhile, the consequences of the current fiscal retrenchment have not been drawn – it might be rational to use the threat of monetary restriction to concentrate government attention on the stability of public finance; but such pressure is self-defeating if governments are already committed to the most rapid stabilization that can be endured. For countries like France and Germany – each with public debt around 50 per cent of annual GDP – a 1 per cent rise in interest rates adds 0.5 per cent to the PSBR. Likewise, a corresponding reduction moves the deficit substantially downwards. These pay-offs are even higher for heavily indebted states, such as Italy.[24]

There are two dimensions to the necessary relaxation. As regards interest rates, Japan offers a good example of the potency of monetary expansion in an essentially stable economy: discount rates have been reduced to near zero for over a year to promote the refinance of both public and private agents in a situation characterized by financial stress but in which underlying inflationary pressures are small. Even discount policy understates the extent of the relaxation since open market operations have made cash so cheap that banks have little incentive to make use of discount facilities. No doubt such measures strike the Germans as too colourful; but they indicate that there is substantial room for manoeuvre.

The second dimension is exchange rates. The Banque de France portrays any depreciation of the franc as dangerous to confidence and as likely to be counterproductive in provoking a rise in long-run interest rates or a wider risk premium on short rates. This is almost certainly correct if the depreciation results from unilateral French action. The same logic, however, does not apply to a realignment agreed with

Germany which is jointly declared to be the final readjustment prior to EMU. If a realignment is treated in this way, and followed by a qualitative rise in monetary coordination, eliminating sterilization of monetary flows between France and Germany in anticipation of 1999, it could relieve pressure both on French unemployment and on German costs. The dogma of Maastricht is that monetary competence – like God, indivisible – must remain at national level until it is, at one fell swoop, centralized. It would not be necessary to challenge this doctrine explicitly to make room for much closer and more effective monetary coordination.

Some straws in the wind suggest that the logic of this kind of argument is beginning to penetrate even the unimaginative thinking of the German monetary authorities. The Bundesbank Council, addicted to announcement effects, chose on the last occasion to surprise by the scale of their interest-rate cuts rather than by another exercise in immobilism; and Council members have even been quoted as calling for a more proactive approach to the forthcoming currency unification. It is desirable to deepen and accelerate this change of perspective. No doubt, achievements will fall short of what is possible – the optimal decision would be a temporary increase in the 'normative inflation' targets of the German authorities in order to levy an inflation tax on a European scale as the most effective financial preparation for EMU. But already the realities of the European political conjuncture are beginning to shift habitual responses.

Relaunching the Employment Programmes

The political necessity of an extension of EU employment initiatives was put clearly by Klaus Haensch, president of the European Parliament: 'More and more people associate the EU with social breakdown and the destruction of jobs. We must link it again with the creation of jobs and social progress. The success of monetary union depends on this.'[25] To this case we can add that the same kind of development has a solid economic rationale from any but the most one-sided neo-liberal position. As investment, these initiatives can work to lengthen time horizons and stabilize expectations on the condition that they reflect a long-term political commitment. If the priorities are clear, private agents will begin to recognize them: for example, they will recognize that full economic integration does constitute the future for unified Germany to the extent that this has become a solid commitment of the German government. At the European level, such priorities embrace the development of peripheral and decayed industrial regions, respect for the environment, the adaptation of educational structures and so on. One aspect of this is just to guarantee the availability of complementary public inputs to private investors; more generally, uncertainties can be limited only by such positive action.

The second key economic aspect concerns the impact of active measures on employment itself. There is a strong case for EU-wide coordination to limit forms of labour market competition which would tend to nullify active measures or discourage their application at national level: this is clearly the case for moves on hours of work, the conditions of short-term employment and so on.[26] Without EU sanction one can also expect damaging forms of inter-state competition in such fields as job promotion, training schemes and so on – it is at least rational to exclude such expenditure, a recognized Union priority, from the 'convergence' accounting exercise. In a more positive view, tax reform – to reduce impositions on low-paid labour – is a central part of the strategy laid out in the Commission's employment strategy. Such measures, and the corresponding levy of a carbon tax or other environmental sources of revenue, can become the occasion of a new round of fiscal harmonization and coordination. Progress without coordination is at present hardly conceivable because many of the benefits of such action will spill over into other member states, while the costs remain a charge on domestic economic activity.

A first step in this direction would be to return to the Commission's *Pact of Confidence for Employment*,[27] which was refused adequate funding at the Florence Council, and use it as the basis for the promotion of employment issues to the top of the Union's agenda. It can be noted that a change in British policy would be the biggest single contribution to such a development.[28]

Fiscal Centralization

A significant centralization of fiscal policy follows from EMU itself, in spite of the Maastricht formula, according to which monetary unification can take place while the entirety of public finance remains at national level. One can refer, firstly, to the implications of theory: no one has ever seriously argued that the EU constitutes an optimal currency area, but the development of centralized public finance would certainly move it nearer to being so. The issue of fiscal federalism is intensely disputed. Commentators of neo-liberal persuasion argue that decentralization remains critical in order to maximize the territorial congruence between contributions and public services received;[29] on the other hand, comparison with other developed federations indicates that mutual insurance among regions is an almost universal characteristic of actual monetary unions. Beyond this, the political theme of

cohesion in the EU points to more developed redistributional capacities
as a necessary compensation to the losers in the integration process.
(A central authority with monetary, but without fiscal, powers might
seem alarmingly suggestive of nineteenth-century economic policy –
and could be expected to result in nineteenth-century degrees of
instability.)

It seems that, in this field, there are significant opportunities to
encourage a disengagement of the project of European construction –
even though it is centred on monetary stabilization – from the general
thrust towards deregulation, privatization and public service reductions
with which it has become so closely associated over the last ten years.
This is because the success of EMU may well hinge on the emergence
of a centralized economic steering capacity within the currency union
which only fiscal centralization will make possible. Even the restrictive
approach to public finance stemming from the Maastricht criteria
becomes ambivalent in this context: ECOFIN (the Economic and Finance
Ministers' Council) agreed in September 1996 to tighten the centre's
supervisory role over national budgets through the introduction of
sanctions to enforce member states' fiscal discipline. But such power is
likely to attract a measure of responsibility – if weaker nations are
prevented, by central rules, from making a certain range of expenditures then, at least for those public functions regarded as common
priorities, it may become incumbent on the centre to guarantee the
appropriate continuity of policy.

Goodhart has suggested that such a centralization of public finance
is barely hidden behind the EMU project. He points out, in particular,
that monetary union will disturb the existing structures of interest
groups.[30] At present, these are still very largely national; but when
central control over a significant dimension of economic policy has
been established, the congruence between national polities and groups
concerned with taxation and expenditure issues is likely to become
looser, so that fiscal policy at the level of the union will involve not only
the simple bargaining among member states which is seen today but
also the interaction of increasingly transnational groupings.

It is certainly true that little can be done in this direction while fiscal
developments continue to be governed by the outcome of the Edinburgh Council of 1992, which, having established the Cohesion Fund,
placed a ceiling on expenditures for the rest of the decade. Nor should
one underestimate the resistance to any centralization of public finance
mounted by the Major government. The British attitude was well
displayed in its insistence that a windfall underspend on agriculture be
returned to member states rather than used to promote the Trans-
European Networks which are the most prominent budgetary item

arising out of the Commission's employment initiative. But neither of these constraints may be binding for much longer.

In any case, it is clear that a substantial degree of fiscal centralization would follow from any recognition of the arguments put forward in the previous section, for employment-generating actions as a necessary political and economic complement to the Maastricht agenda established so far. This by no means absolves the EU, taken as a whole, from the need for a medium-term stabilization of public debt and state deficits, since otherwise the public agencies which attempt to undertake stimulative action will not be credit-worthy and their initiatives will lose much of their effectiveness. For this reason there is, at present, little chance of significant deficit-financed expenditure at Union level. But fiscal consolidation can be interpreted as a reconstruction and reinforcement of the active state rather than as another step towards the minimal state of the neo-liberals. There are already some signs that this first interpretation finds widespread favour among the European political class – particularly in the readiness of France and Germany, according to recent reports, to introduce an explicit employment commitment into the IGC negotiations.[31] The simple concern to defend the existing, however narrow, project for EMU can, here again, become a stepping-stone to a fuller and more adequate agenda for the EU.

Two-tier Monetary Europe

All the proposals put forward here as possible growth points in a post-Maastricht Europe are mutually reinforcing. For instance, the alteration of macroeconomic stance made necessary by the contractionary effects of 'convergence' would work to accelerate and ease the fiscal correction which, in the medium term, is unavoidable. Again, the relaunch of the EU's employment programme would compensate for these contractionary effects while preparing the way for more active and centralized public finance. The pursuit of fiscal coordination and harmonization is like to present opportunities for some budgetary centralization. The same applies to the most difficult problem which the first achievement of EMU will present to the Union in the next century, that is, the division of member states into insiders and outsiders. This Maastricht-induced division is indeed full of dangers for the EU. In economic terms the outsiders will continue to pay high and variable interest rate premiums as long as the exchange rate at which they will enter EMU is in doubt, even if some EMS-like arrangement pegs their currencies to the euro; at the same time, the single market will be weakened even if the French nightmare of competitive devaluations by the outsiders is not realized. In political terms it is in the about-to-be-excluded countries, particularly Italy, that the will to achieve EMU is strongest. In Italy, the Europeanization of policy areas is seen as a solution to intractable national difficulties, rather than as a source of constraints. If this aspiration is frustrated, the EU will be deprived of the most solid political support that exists at present for European construction.

All these factors imply that the reintegration of the Maastricht-divided Union will have to be given a very high priority in the post-EMU period. Now the conditions which can accelerate and ease the transition of the financially weaker economies are exactly those that have been discussed. An easier monetary stance will further the control of public finance, which is the biggest obstacle for Italy and the Mediterranean countries, while a certain centralization of public expenditure would shield at least some key functions from the dislocation that fiscal stabilization will certainly involve. The defence of a newly emerging EMU – even if one reckons narrowly in terms of price stability – requires the adoption of wider objectives, since otherwise the ECB will face major risks of financial or structural imbalances so acute as to necessitate inflationary refinance; and the exclusion of important member states will not avoid, but may even accentuate, these risks. In this way also, the very commitment of EU leaderships to the Maastricht agenda opens up some possibilities for a wider and more adequate conception of the integration process.

External Implications of EMU

It is impossible to exaggerate the potential implications of EMU for the global financial and monetary environment in which European economies function. The theme is certainly understated, even disguised, in official EU discussions of EMU – partly to avoid alarming other major forces such as the US, partly to accommodate the German preoccupation with internal stability. But there can be no doubt that the reform of global monetary arrangements was a central goal of the EMU project as originally conceived – above all in France.[32] What is at stake is the assertion of elements of social control in a sphere where disorganization and unregulated market forces have given rise to qualitatively greater pressures on individual countries, and to their penetration by financial forces which have rendered whole fields of domestic policy increasingly difficult over the last twenty-five years. EMU cannot transform this situation rapidly; but it does introduce into the global economy a new dynamic which can gradually alter external constraints in small and large ways. It is important to emphasize that nothing of the kind is possible for isolated member states, with the partial exception of Germany. The globalization of economic and financial processes is irreversible; only global intervention and regulation of these processes is conceivable. EMU brings forward a body capable of strategic action at global level.

To avoid suggesting that huge and dramatic change is an early possibility, one may begin with the most modest but most secure example of the kind of developments which can be envisaged. In the territory of the currency union, monetary conditions will be protected from the destabilization which has followed, over more than twenty-five years, every significant variation in the external value of the US dollar. Invariably, internal exchange rates have been put under pressure by dollar depreciation – a pattern that clearly continued into the summer of 1996. These are not trivial disturbances: to this day they place critical pressures on internal monetary policies and, sometimes, on the working of the internal market. EMU will eliminate them overnight in the countries using the euro – an additional motive for the most determined efforts to extend the single currency to as many member states as possible.

A second significant external theme is the taxation of capital income. High degrees of capital mobility have tended to undermine the ability to tax mobile, especially financial resources. Policy reactions are not blocked by US attitudes; on the contrary it is plausibly argued that the US would welcome forceful European measures which could underpin its own fiscal stance, which it is extremely reluctant to dismantle.[33] The key obstacle in this field has been European disunity, and the failure to define a common position: Germany's attempt to introduce a withholding tax on interest payments in 1989, and thus to align its policies with those of France, had to be abandoned because of capital flight to other European countries. EMU will not guarantee an effective, unified position but it will make such a position much easier to achieve.

Macroeconomic policy coordination among the large industrial powers will also be simplified and encouraged by EMU. Certainly conflict is to be anticipated. Germany in particular will resist any external commitments which might threaten the overriding objective of price stability, and the letter of the Maastricht Treaty, to the extent that its Byzantine pronouncements on the matter are capable of any unambiguous interpretation, would seem to be in its favour. But that can hardly be the last word on such a critical theme. Not all external stabilization agreements necessarily have an inflationary bias; the fact that the US and Japan's interlocutor will now not be, as in the past, the Bundesbank and the German government, but agencies constrained to reflect general European interests in itself constitutes an important change. One can hardly imagine anything as inept and damaging, for example, as German reactions to US policy in 1979 and 1980.[34] One should not exaggerate the scale of coordination which is becoming possible, nor the pay-off from it. The most that can probably be aimed at is to avoid flagrantly inconsistent targets for exchange rates or balances of payments among the big three. No player will be ready in the near future to commit its domestic policy stance to any ambitious exercise. But even to avoid the interest-rate wars that took place in the early 1980s and again a decade later would be an important advance.

What can be achieved in terms of control over international credit flows? Both the desirability and the feasibility of steps in this direction are in dispute. The present writers are not qualified to assess such fundamental reforms as the Tobin tax which aim at a decisive assertion of public priorities in this field, but it can be suggested that such experiments, fruitful or otherwise, are hardly conceivable without European monetary unity.[35] In less ambitious terms, EMU itself offers some significant leverage over the capital markets: the avoidance of massive inconsistencies in policy settings would already work towards calming the markets, although they would continue to sanction situations which were obviously unsustainable; the regulatory, like the fiscal, problems arising from the use of off-shore financial centres would be much easier to handle on the basis of EMU, if only because the latter implies a more stringent approach to Europe's own fiscal paradises and deregulated refuges.

More thoroughgoing reform must remain at this time a matter of supposition: the items on a long-run agenda would be global monetary integration or, perhaps less implausibly, the introduction of a supranational reserve currency. The latter, often proposed by the French, would have meaning only if it involved the subordination of commercial creation of international credit. At present there is considerable scepticism about such proposals.[36]

The potential importance of EMU in this general context can be suggested by referring to the work of De Grauwe.[37] He argues that, until the failure of Bretton Woods, national and international monetary systems had developed in analogous ways: from the disorganized issue of different moneys on a competitive basis; to agreement on a common standard (gold); to the promotion of one money-issuer to central prominence – the role of the central bank as it evolved within private banking, the role of the US within Bretton Woods; and finally to the gradual supersession of gold by state-issued money. At this point there is a divergence between the two paths of development: whereas national systems develop through explicit political control and the substitution of fiat money for gold, the international system moves to a plurality of monetary units, scrutinized and perhaps controlled by a sophisticated set of financial markets. It is difficult to justify such different lines of development. If they are inconsistent, which is the correct path? Should political control over monetary processes within nation-states be attenuated, or do we require strong international political institutions to stabilize and direct the global monetary and financial system? If the second perspective is chosen, then European integration would appear to be a precondition of wider reform.

Conclusion

If we take the danger of European war as remote, the EU is, or should be, about world government. To put the point in a less grandiloquent way, it is about social control over the terms and methods which govern the insertion of the European economies into the global economy. Globalization is sometimes perceived in an undifferentiated or exaggerated way.[38] Nevertheless it is an unavoidable and irreversible process, full of dangers for European populations. The EU can influence this process in two ways: internally, by organizing economic life to improve adaptation to external constraints and by redistributing some of the gains and losses that occur. But it can also act externally to modify the constraints themselves, using its immense political, commercial and, tomorrow, monetary powers to obtain advantageous reforms in the global economy itself through compromises with the other principal actors. Monetary union as such is a logical part of this mission: it eliminates an enfeebling fragmentation of European interests and makes possible a wider, more coordinated and deeper influence in a key dimension of the emerging global economy – financial and monetary relations.

However, the forms and modalities of monetary integration agreed at Maastricht turn away from these responsibilities. Under the obsessive, and self-defeating, preoccupation with internal price stability, European institutions were designed in ways that negate the possibilities of enhanced social control that are the only constructive rationale for the EU itself. Influenced by the same worship of spontaneous, market-determined adjustment to all problems that seized the EC during the 1980s, European leaders designed a mechanism that will in fact fail to shield either citizens or member states from the harshest aspects of ever-tightening external constraints.

It is certainly possible for the EU to fail in the only task which gives it meaning – the use of the strength of unity to alter the environment in which its peoples live. In this case European integration will prove, in retrospect, to be a self-liquidating enterprise, a mere moment in the dissolution of its member states into an increasingly uncontrolled global economy. What is not possible is for its present projects – the single market and EMU – to succeed as strategies for internal stabilization and modernization in the absence of wider and more far-reaching objectives.

The fragility and lack of democracy which characterize EU political relations make it impossible to achieve a comprehensive renegotiation of the Maastricht agreement. But to abandon it would not serve European interests because it would only throw European peoples back on national state structures that are increasingly unable to exert decisive leverage over external conditions, and this in circumstances that would make the external environment more dangerous by promoting damaging forms of rivalry among European countries themselves.

It follows that the least bad strategy, for those concerned with the deteriorating social climate and economic performance of European countries, is to accept the Maastricht agenda while proposing gradualist and, initially, piecemeal strategies for its amendment and transformation in the desired directions – priority to employment, rather than price, stability; interventions, internal and external, which genuinely benefit the most disadvantaged groups and regions of the EU. This strategic orientation has to recognize multiple political, financial and economic limits that cannot as yet be overcome. But it can draw strength from the circumstance that the Maastricht agenda, in its present form, is quite unworkable, the reflection of a crippled, utopian, project for a universal market to which all political instances would be subordinated. Thus the gaps, incoherences and inadequacies of the existing pattern of European advance may provide points of entry for a movement aimed at its enrichment and correction.

However, the modesty of the immediate goals which can be formulated in this way should not be confused with a lack of ambition as regards ultimate objectives. The latter include both the comprehensive modernization, in a positive way, of internal systems of social protection and a growing contribution to a more stable and equitable world order. Nothing less, in any case, would be compatible with the values which inspired the project of European integration. Only if a wide vision informs the inevitably constrained attempts at immediate amelioration will these attempts have some prospect of success.

1996

Notes

1. See R. Smits, 'A Single Currency for Europe and the Karlsruhe Court,' *Legal Issues of European Integration*, no. 2, 1994.

2. P. De Grauwe, 'Alternative Strategies towards Monetary Union', *European Economic Review*, vol. 39, nos 3–4, 1995.

3. S. Collignon, with P. Bofinger, C. Johnson and B. de Maigret, *Europe's Monetary Future: A Study Prepared at the Request of the European Parliament*, London 1994.

4. U. Dürkop and R. Naser, 'Back to Basics. Reformen in Europäischen Währungs-system', in C. Thomasberger, ed., *Europäische Geldpolitk zwischen Marktwängen und neuen institutionellen Regelungen*, Marburg 1995.

5. B. Winkler, 'Towards a Strategic View on EMU: A Critical Survey', *Journal of Public Policy*, vol. 16, no. 1, January–April 1996.

6. M. Artis, 'Alternative Transitions to EMU', *Economic Journal*, vol. 106, no. 437, July 1996.

7. European Commission, 'Towards Greater Fiscal Discipline', *European Economy*, reports and studies, no. 3, 1994.

8. C. Thomasberger, 'Europäische Währungsintegration an der Wegscheide. Die Antinomien des Leitwährungssystems und die Notwendigkeit institutioneller Reformen', in C. Thomasberger, ed., *Europäische Geldpolitik zwischen Marktwängen und neuen instituti-onellen Regelungen*.

9. European Commission, *White Paper: Growth, Competitiveness, Employment: The Challenges and Ways Forward into the 21st Century*, Luxembourg 1994.

10. For the debate on investment initiatives, see K. Coates, *Dear Commissioner*, Nottingham 1996.

11. P. De Grauwe, 'Monetary Union and Convergence Economics', *European Economic Review*, vol. 40, nos 3–5, April 1996.

12. G. Holtham, 'The Maastricht Conception of EMU is Obsolete', *Political Quarterly*, vol. 67, no. 3, July–September 1996.

13. For a full assessment, see J. Arrowsmith, 'Economic and Monetary Union in a Multi-tier Europe', *National Institute Economic Review*, vol. 152, no. 2, May 1995.

14. See, for example, European Commission, 'The Economic and Financial Situation in Italy', *European Economy*, reports and studies, no. 1, 1993.

15. For an empirical critique of these views, see A. Posen, 'Why Central Bank Independence Does Not Cause Low Inflation', in R. O'Brien, ed., *Finance and the International Economy. The Amex Bank Review Prize Essays in Memory of Robert Marjolin*, volume 7, Oxford 1993.

16. For the history of central banking in this context, see M. Aglietta, 'Genèse des banques centrales et légitimité de la monnaie', *Annales*, no. 3, May–June 1992.

17. For an analysis of monetary policy which makes this argument, see H. Minsky, *Inflation, Recession and Economic Policy*, Brighton 1982.

18. J. Grahl, 'Euroscepticism and the Major Government', *Annales de l'Université de Savoie*, no. 19, 1995.

19. See Mark M. Iner, 'Call for Full Access to EMU Payments System', the *Guardian*, 6 October 1996.

20. For a comprehensive critique of the Maastricht fiscal programme, see W. Buiter, G. Gorsetti and N. Roubini, 'Excessive Deficits: Sense and Nonsense in the Treaty of Maastricht', *Economic Policy*, no. 16, April 1993.

21. For a discussion of the Bundesbank's policy errors at that time, see W. File, 'Credibility of German Monetary Policy on the Road towards EMU', in A. Steinherr, ed., *30 Years of European Monetary Integration. From the Werner Plan to EMU*, London 1994; and H. Riese, 'Schwäche des Pfundes und Versagen der Deutschen Mark: Anmerkungen zur gegenwätigen Krise des Europäischen Währungssystems', in P. Bofinger, S. Collignon and E.-M. Lipp, eds, *Währungsunion oder Währungschaos*, Wiesbaden 1993.

22. See, for example, OECD, *Economic Survey 1994–95. Germany*, Paris 1995.

23. J.-P. Fitoussi, 'L'Economie européenne prise au piège', *Le Monde*, 29 August 1996.

24. P. De Grauwe, 'Monetary Union'.

25. Klaus Haensch, quoted in Stephen Bates and Alex Duval Smith, 'Europe Divided: Santer Brushes Aside Britain's Euro Doubts', the *Guardian*, 19 September 1996.

26. For the general argument for regulation, see S. Deakin and F. Wilkinson, *Labour Standards – Essential to Economic and Social Progress*, London 1996. For a discussion in the context of the EU, see G. Alogoskoufis et al., *Unemployment: Choices for Europe*, CEPR no. 5, *Monitoring European Integration*, London 1995.

27. European Commission, *Pact of Confidence for Employment*, Brussels 1996.

28. For an argument in favour of a European 'growth initiative' along lines similar to

those proposed by the Commission, see J. Drèze and E. Malinvaud, 'Growth and Employment: The Scope of a European Initiative', *European Economic Review*, vol. 38, nos 3–4, April 1994.

29. For example, A. Alesina, R. Perotti and E. Spolaore, 'Together or Separately: Issues on the Costs and Benefits of Political and Fiscal Unions', *European Economic Review*, vol. 39, nos 3–4, 1995.

30. C. Goodhart, 'European Monetary Integration', *European Economic Review*, vol. 40, nos 3–5, April 1996.

31. See John Palmer, 'Major Tries to Block EU Dublin Summit', the *Guardian*, 13 September 1996.

32. For the French tradition of dissent, see J.-M. Jeanneny, 'De Bretton Woods à la Jamaïque: contestations françaises', *Economie internationale*, vol. 59, no. 3, 1994.

33. A. Giovannini, 'National Tax Systems versus the European Capital Market', *Economic Policy*, no. 9, October 1989.

34. For a first-hand account, see O. Emminger, *D-Mark, Dollar, Währungskrisen*, Stuttgart 1986.

35. See the debate in D. Greenaway, ed., 'Policy Forum: Sand in the Wheels of International Finance', *Economic Journal*, vol. 105, no. 428, January 1995.

36. B. Eichengreen, *International Monetary Arrangements for the 21st Century*, Washington 1994.

37. P. De Grauwe, *International Money: Post-war Trends and Theories*, Oxford 1989.

38. P. Hirst and G. Thompson, *Globalization in Question*, Oxford 1996, can be read as a necessary correction to apocalyptic views of globalization, even if one rejects their argument that constraints on national economies are qualitatively unchanged. For other views, see R. Boyer and D. Drache, eds, *States against Markets: The Limits of Globalisation*, London 1996.

14

The New Insecurities
Guy Standing

For nearly a quarter of a century, Western Europe has experienced mass unemployment, after a quarter of a century of what many described as 'full employment'. The latter was never as impressive as it looked at the time or has seemed to many social scientists and commentators who have referred back to a mystical golden age of welfare capitalism. One reason for reservations about the earlier era was that the postwar variety of full employment was based largely on men only being in regular, secure, full-time wage employment. Welfare provision, in both the Beveridge and Bismarckian variants, essentially provided social 'insurance' protection to cover periods of 'temporary interruption of earning power' and was oriented to the presumed norm of a nuclear family with a male bread-winner. It was a socio-economic arrangement for a predominantly industrial society.

Since the mid-1970s, the character of the Western European labour market has been undergoing fundamental change, in which the prevailing feature has been growing insecurity. It is an economic insecurity that has become pervasive. Those looking back on the history of the second half of the twentieth century will note that the cherished social objectives of the postwar era became perceived by mainstream policy-makers as 'costs' to be avoided in the last two decades of the century. In the initial period, the European economies traded mainly with countries with broadly similar labour rights and a moderately progressive fiscal and welfare policy. In the latter period, trade liberalization and the changing pattern of investment and trade in the context of economic globalization put pressure on governments to roll back the provision of welfare and protective regulations.

Another way of portraying the developments is that as the European

Union has been enlarged and as the international context has evolved, with growing trade and investment competition from industrialized and industrializing economies – and in the 1990s with exposure to a new form of integration with countries of Central Europe – the spread of economic insecurity has been accentuated by governments and employers dismantling elements of the social wage in the interest of reducing labour costs and in the interest of increasing labour market 'flexibility'.

This is the context of debates on employment and unemployment in Western Europe. Yet the public discussion has become somewhat schizophrenic. Governments and commentators claim that reducing unemployment is the top priority, yet macroeconomic policy and the 'convergence criteria' of the 'single-market' strategy for the expanding European Union imply a broadly deflationary posture, as well as a tendency to restrict the scope for independent national monetary and fiscal policies.[1] This is being accentuated by the drive for EMU.

An irony is that Western European governments have been at the forefront of efforts to encourage the growth of international capital markets, which has led to the adoption of higher real interest rates and more deflationary macroeconomic policies that have depressed economic growth, which in turn has raised unemployment. The economic orthodoxy, epitomized by the Maastricht Treaty as well as by the IMF, is that 'budget deficits' must be cut to a small percentage of GDP (3 per cent). This imposed policy imperative has induced a political atmosphere in which all robust politicians intent on obtaining or retaining office have seemed to accept that welfare and other public spending has to be cut and that 'costly' protective labour regulations must be reformed. Whatever the merits or demerits of this perspective, measures being put into effect as a result of it have contributed to the growth of economic insecurity.

The debate on European labour markets is further complicated by the ongoing microeconomic changes associated primarily with electronics and information technology. The crucial point for the labour market is that managements have more options in the way they can organize production and employment. This has been associated with the spread and legitimized use of more flexible types of employment than full-time regular labour and more flexible payment systems – aided in part by changes in regulations, and the 'globalization' of production and investment. The perceived availability of more options has given employers a much stronger bargaining position. Many firms have turned to less binding forms of employment, which have increased insecurity among both the workers in those statuses and others fearful of being pushed into them. They have widened wage differentials and have probably widened differentials in total remuneration by much more, for core employees have been provided with an increasing range of benefits while ordinary workers either have had former benefits monetized or have been excluded from entitlement to them by virtue of their non-regular employment status. There have also been many efforts to seek greater 'functional flexibility' in the organization of work.

All these changes have contributed to what are surely the major developments in Western Europe, the growth of insecurity and the growth of new forms of socio-economic fragmentation that are not easily captured by conventional class analysis.

Flexibility as Insecurity

Since the early 1980s, the conventional view has been that Western European labour markets have been 'rigid' and that the answer to unemployment is to make labour markets more 'flexible'. For a decade and a half, governments have been introducing measures to achieve that, and there can be no doubt whatsoever that on any conventional definition labour markets across Europe are much more flexible than in 1980. Yet unemployment is much higher. In 1996, it was estimated that about 11 per cent of Western Europe's labour force was unemployed, with a further rise forecast for 1997.

The country in which the government has claimed to have proved that a strategy of making the labour market more flexible lowers unemployment is the United Kingdom. But there too, after a decade and a half of measures to increase flexibility, unemployment was nearly 9 per cent, much higher than when the policy started, despite numerous changes to the definition that have substantially lowered the apparent level of unemployment and at the very least made inter-temporal comparisons misleadingly positive. Moreover, the relative erosion of full-time employment has accelerated, particularly among men. Even in 'booms', this has continued. From September 1995 to September 1996, total employment in the UK rose by 198,000, but this included only 14,000 full-time jobs, while male full-time employment fell by 36,000.

Several deductions can be drawn from such figures. First, mass unemployment persists and reflects chronic labour market insecurity. Second, there has been a 'feminization' of employment over the period, in the double sense that women's share of employment has grown considerably and the character of a rising proportion of the jobs being created (part-time, precarious) has been of the type long associated with women's patterns of (intermittent) labour-force participation. Third, the type of employment that has been emerging is quite different from what used to be regarded as the norm and which guided the development of postwar welfare states.

Similar trends have been developing in most parts of Europe. Governments have come to accept levels of unemployment that they would not have dared to allow in the preceding era, and they have tolerated massive long-term unemployment that is also inconsistent with the welfare state envisaged by its founders. One wonders when a minister of labour, such as the Irish minister, Eithne Fitzgerald, says, 'No economy can afford to have a situation in which one in ten, as in Ireland, are in long-term unemployment.' The fact is that countries have been experiencing levels described routinely as unaffordable and intolerable for years, and they have been tolerated, and seem to be tolerable for politicians and enough of the people for enough of the time to allow the policy-makers to pursue other priorities.

With growing labour-market flexibility and the policy stances taken by European governments, one can trace the growth of seven forms of economic insecurity. The first is the labour market insecurity epitomized by the persistently high unemployment. Second, a growing proportion of Europeans have been experiencing employment insecurity, finding themselves in temporary or casual work statuses, on fixed-term employment contracts, being homeworkers, out-sourced, agency workers, and so on. There are more people in casual and temporary jobs than at any time since 1945, and the upward trend is continuing.

Third, there has been growing job insecurity, with people having to change jobs or bundles of work competences more often. In principle, job-changing could be a desirable feature of life, yet there should surely be concern that many people, perhaps a majority, are expected to learn basic skills in conditions of uncertainty about whether those skills will shortly become obsolescent, inadequate or low-paying.[2] Older workers, in particular, will fear for their adaptability to the changing technological requirements. Job insecurity corrodes morale and, at worst, induces anomic despair in those not blessed with good education, good parents, good intelligence, good age, good looks, good health and good luck. There has been a lot that is rotten about Taylorist and related rigid job structures, and nobody should seek to defend them against the charge that they have had deleterious effects during most of the twentieth century. However, in the current era job flexibility has meant that there has been less scope to protect groups of workers with personal characteristics making them intrinsically economically vulnerable and relatively unadaptable to change (or at least presumed to be less adaptable).

Fourth, and related to the employment and job insecurity, there has been a growth of skill reproduction insecurity. People require more technical qualifications for the higher-income, secure forms of employment, yet the conventional forms of training and skill formation either have been shrinking or have become less valuable. For many years,

Germany was cited as the country in the EU with the most advanced system of training. Yet in 1996, over 40 per cent of the unemployed in Germany had been successfully through the country's famed apprenticeship system.

Fifth, with labour cost-saving and the drift to market deregulation, there may have been a growth in work insecurity, arising from more labour-force participants being exposed to unprotected working conditions and not having coverage for occupational health and safety. This form of insecurity is surely greater among those finding themselves outside regular employment in well-established, registered private and public enterprises.

Sixth, there has been a growth in representation insecurity. Except in Northern Europe perhaps, there has been a substantial decline in unionization and in the effectiveness of union representation. Even though an increasing proportion of labour force participants find they cannot identify with traditional craft and industrial trade unions, or with 'labourism' in general, the erosion of the collective voice in the regulation of employment and the labour market intensifies the general sense of economic insecurity.

Seventh, this has become the era of income insecurity. For those in employment of some kind, this is reflected in numerous ways, ranging from the dwindling coverage of minimum-wage legislation and implementation of minimum-wage laws to the spread of more flexible payment systems that effectively place the costs of economic risk on the worker. The employed's income insecurity has been intensified by efforts by employers and governments to shift some of the costs of social protection from enterprises and government authorities onto the worker. Meanwhile, for those out of employment, income insecurity has been intensified by cuts in unemployment benefits (notably through cutting income-replacement rates), tighter conditionality for entitlement to benefits, shorter duration of entitlements, and so on.

One could count hundreds of little measures introduced by European governments in the past decade that have tended to boost labour-market flexibility and the various forms of economic insecurity. Again and again, critics have protested that the measures would not be tolerated. Yet, often after token mass rallies, they have been tolerated. Perhaps the main reason can be stated bluntly: fear changed sides in the 1980s. When the 'working class' was perceived as a large and growing voting bloc, cutting back on social protection was rarely envisaged. Once the working class was perceived as shrinking and fragmented, nothing was sacrosanct. This realization allowed a supply-side economic strategy to be pursued, first by the UK and the USA and then by governments of other EU countries. In more draconian forms, similar policies have been pursued in Eastern Europe under the rubric of 'shock therapy' and in developing countries under the name of 'structural adjustment'.

Whatever the variant, among those drawn to identify with the economically underprivileged, intellectual hesitancy has seemed to match the pervasive sense of insecurity, almost inducing a loss of will to change. By the 1990s, the best that mainstream critics could seem to muster was better management of the insecurity.

From Keynesian Welfare to Active Labour Policy

> You can go to any school in Ireland and mark out certain four-year-olds with long-term unemployment written all over them.
> Eithne Fitzgerald, Irish minister of labour affairs[3]

The debates on employment in Europe have evolved from the consensus of the 1960s that full employment could be preserved by means of macroeconomic demand management to the point where such a view is routinely described as 'discredited'. Having done much to discredit it, the supply-side school of economics initially placed zealous faith in market forces, and then tended to place increasing faith in what has become known as 'active labour-market policy'.

A great deal has been expected of so-called active labour-market policy. Above all, it is expected to lower the fabled NAIRU (the non-accelerating inflation rate of unemployment) by helping to reduce 'structural unemployment'.[4] Albeit for somewhat different reasons, faith in active policy has been one of the points on which political Right, Left and Centre are in harmonious agreement, differences of opinion stemming merely from perceptions of design faults, adequacy of resources, and efficiency of management. The conventional wisdom as to the desirability and strategic virtues of active labour-market policies could almost be described as hegemonic.

Those on the political Left – social democrats and labourists – have tended to favour them in part because they associate active labour-market policy with Sweden, for long regarded as the standard to be emulated. Yet the term originated as part of the postwar Swedish model where it signified counter-cyclical policy – as recessions began the government was meant to pump funds into the economy in order to employ or train more of those who would have been unemployed or who were unemployed. With economic expansions, expenditure on such measures was meant to shrink.

Only in the 1970s did the term acquire its current meaning, and in a sense, as the debate has evolved, the predominant character of active labour-market policy has been transformed. Now the political Right tends to support it because the primary objectives have been to alter the supply side of the labour market. Indeed, those on the Right have favoured active labour-market policy mainly because it has been seen as a way to reduce unemployment and to integrate those on the margins of the labour force into employment while putting downward pressure on the wages and working conditions of those already in (low-paying) employment.

The basic appeal of active policy to those on both the Right and the Left is that it seems to offer a means of regulating the lower end of the labour market. As with all public discourses, it is sensible to be alert to the political content of the key words. The debate here is couched in terms of 'active' versus 'passive' policy, where 'active' covers the provision of training, employment subsidies, public works and other measures intended to take people out of unemployment, and where 'passive' is the provision of income in the form of unemployment benefits and other state transfers. The terms 'active' and 'passive' are scarcely neutral. 'Active' suggests virile, dynamic, constructive and helpful; 'passive' conveys a sense of being unresourceful, unimaginative and even deplorable.

Yet active policy risks turning those on the margins of the labour market into 'passive' clients, to be directed in certain directions, if not coerced and stigmatized. Gradually research is accumulating to show that active policies rarely do what their advocates claim. Often they do not help participants in the schemes, and thus they give support to the rationality of the anomic reaction of many of the unemployed to exposure to active labour-market policy. For example, an extraordinary amount of hope and hype has been devoted to labour-market training schemes. Yet it appears that participation in such schemes may actually lower a person's probability of subsequent employment, and income, relative to someone with otherwise similar characteristics.

Similarly, for this and most other forms of 'active' policy, there are effects that make the attainment of the ostensible objective of reducing unemployment rather unlikely. For instance, providing subsidized training or employment subsidies for certain 'disadvantaged' groups tends to induce very high substitution effects, whereby those targeted for special treatment merely displace others who were doing the jobs. Impressive-sounding placement rates for participants in such schemes may often be misleading in that respect, especially as there is a general tendency for officials to 'cream' from among the unemployed provided with the special assistance, so as to give the appearance of success. For instance, giving subsidies to encourage the employment of teenagers in Sweden was followed by a rise in the absolute and relative unemployment rate of workers aged twenty to twenty-four.

Similarly, the popular policy of giving subsidies to employers who hire those who have been unemployed for more than twelve months (or, in Britain's case, twenty-four months) almost definitionally worsens the job prospects of those who have been unemployed for between six and twelve months. There is also a risk of a stigmatizing effect of involvement in an active labour-market scheme, if employers and others come to believe that such schemes cater for labour-market failures, and so seek to avoid those who have been in them.

There is also an issue that should give more people more intellectual unease than appears to be the case. What is the justification for the state in effect to encourage discrimination against anybody because he or she belongs to a particular group to which he or she did not choose to belong? This is precisely what is involved if active labour-market policy is designed to assist particular target groups. One may like a particular priority being given, yet the equity principle should be debated much more than it has been. For instance, there is little doubt that because active labour-market policy has been largely concentrated on youth, older workers have experienced more serious labour-force marginalization than would otherwise have been the case. So easily, yesterday's 'advantaged' can become today's 'disadvantaged', and vice-versa.

Despite the mounting evidence of its limited capacity to reduce unemployment, much faith is still placed in active labour-market policy across Europe. One view, not advertised with as much fanfare as the aim of improving the employment of one group or another, is that such policies can lower wages at the lower end of the labour market, by increasing labour supply, and putting pressure on other workers for fear of substitution in their relatively secure jobs.

Many of the schemes that have emerged under the umbrella of active labour-market policy across Europe in the current era do have positive features, in that they can impart technical skills, provide some respite from unemployment for numerous people, and so on. Yet the debate ought to be far more critical, in the broadest sense of that word. Active policy risks turning people into passive citizens, and can be used to regulate the poor, whether knowingly or otherwise. Unless the governance of such policies is structured in such a way as to limit those tendencies, those dedicated professionals who, usually with the best of intentions, are required to implement such policies are likely to be used for dubious purposes.

From Active Policy to Workfare?

The debates on flexibility and active labour-market policy have contributed to a powerful trend to workfare in the mid-1990s. Some politicians and commentators have been hesitant about using the term, but have favoured the policy thrust of what it represents. Others have used political code, such as that 'people cannot have rights without responsibilities and obligations'.

Since the 1970s, there has been an erosion in the principle and practice of universalism in the provision of social protection. The key words of the 1990s in this part of the public debate are 'selectivity', 'targeting' and 'social safety net'. This last term has been widely deployed, and has been used to suggest that the state is providing a basic set of social transfers to prevent citizens from falling into the pit of poverty. All are euphemisms, representing the respectable way of presenting measures for cutting back or limiting the growth of social transfers.[5]

There has been a desire to cut expenditure on 'passive' (*sic*) policies, and a drive to attack two of the results of the trend towards greater reliance on means-tested benefits. The latter are usually described as the 'poverty trap' and the 'unemployment trap': that is, the possibility that those with low earnings could lose more in transfers than they would gain from somewhat higher earnings, and that the unemployed would lose almost as much in forgone benefits and social assistance from taking a low-paying job as they would gain from it. One often reads, for example, that to improve the incentives for the jobless to find employment the level of unemployment benefits has been reduced.

Unfortunately for those on the margins of the labour market, the social safety nets across Western Europe (and even more so in Central and Eastern Europe) seem increasingly tattered, so that resource-thin people fall through the holes. One should warn anyone inclined to use the alternative image of a 'floor' of social protection that this can be equally ambiguous. For it has become clear that neither active labour-market policy in its traditional guises nor more selective, means-tested systems of social protection are remedying the problems of mass unemployment and socio-economic detachment at the bottom of the labour market. The poor tend to be visible on the streets; they can be seen begging and disturbing socially responsible people going to and from their work and homes; and they persist on relying on social 'hand-outs'. They display *lumpen* characteristics, and are not socially responsible active citizens, despite the best endeavours of labour-market policies to make them so.

The result has been twofold. Policy has tended to oblige the unemployed, and other marginalized people deemed to be suffering from 'dependency' on state assistance, to take a job or a training place in return for a small income. Or it has denied benefits to those who either refuse to take a designated job or training option or have failed to find a job within a certain period, which itself has been shortened. The 'pure' case of workfare has lost favour since experiments and analyses have suggested that it might be rather expensive. This has encouraged those who believe that there cannot be individual rights without individual obligations to favour the more simple expedients of shorter time-limits on social transfers and the requirement that the poor unemployed must take very low-paid jobs if they wish to receive social assistance.

Of course, the social solidarity principle of social insurance has long been a misnomer for the patchwork of social transfers in most European countries. Yet because of the increasingly flexible and insecure labour market, a larger proportion of the population is finding that they do not build up sufficient contributions to have entitlements to employment-related benefits. Now, whether the drift to workfare or to stricter conditionality continues, one senses that the old debate about the 'deserving' and 'undeserving' poor will figure prominently in the last few years of the twentieth century.

The Influence of 'New Democracy' on the Employment Debate

One feature of the debate on social and labour-market policy in Europe that deserves more attention than it has received is that the debate itself has exhibited its own brand of dependency. Traditionally, policy was conceived, designed and introduced because those developing it believed that it was appropriate, and typically a principal motive would have been somewhat close to the Rawlsian 'difference principle': measures were justified if they could be expected to improve the economic situation of the worst-off groups in society. This no longer seems to be the rule. Increasingly, policy initiatives seem to have become dependent on their perceived appeal to 'the median voter'. Put bluntly, unless a change is perceived as likely to find favour with a key voting bloc it is unlikely to be introduced.

This 'voterism' in part reflects the erosion of traditional notions of class as the basis of production and distribution, and the growth of social fragmentation. When the 'working class' was perceived as the largest bloc of voters and as having an essentially homogeneous set of interests, and when those who saw themselves as its political representatives saw the forward march of labour as the gradual (or rapid) redistribution of income and control, full employment and the welfare state were progressive rallying cries. But the contradictions inherent in such notions have always been there.

Of Convergence and Reports

Another feature of the public debate on employment in the 1990s has been the number of international 'high-level' conferences and 'high-level' reports devoted to the subject. There was the Detroit Jobs Conference in 1995 convened by President Bill Clinton of the USA; there was the Lille Jobs Conference in 1996, convened by President Jacques Chirac of France; there was the United Nations' Social Summit in Copenhagen in early 1995; and governments of several EU members have used their six-month stints of presidency to convene conferences on employment and unemployment. The OECD has issued a massive *Jobs Study*, dedicated to the proposition that Europe suffers from rigid labour markets, the ILO has issued a new annual *World Employment Report*, broadly defensive of Keynesianism with some modest changes in labour regulations, and in 1995 the World Bank devoted its *World Development Report* solely to labour market issues.

In 1994, Jacques Delors issued a European Union White Paper, entitled *Growth, Competitiveness and Employment*, committing the EU to creating 15 million new jobs by the year 2000. The resultant Essen Declaration of December 1994, summarizing the conventional wisdom, set out the European Union's heads of state agreement on five priorities or guidelines to enhance employment dynamism. In brief, these were:

(i) Improving employment by vocational training;
(ii) Increasing the employment intensity of growth by (a) more flexible work organization, (b) wage moderation below productivity improvement, (c) regional job creation taking account of environmental and social service needs;
(iii) Reducing non-wage labour costs;
(iv) Improving labour markets, by moving from 'passive' to 'active' labour-market policies;
(v) Improving the position of disadvantaged groups, i.e., youth, long-term unemployed, women and older workers.

In the two years after the Essen Declaration, employment in the EU continued to decline. In December 1995, the EU summit in Madrid set the seal on the timetable for monetary union. It is the rapidly shrinking calendar for the creation of a single European market that is now spreading political consternation, since many observers fear that it will be associated with more unemployment, economic insecurity and public-spending cuts.

In January 1996, Jacques Santer, president of the European Union, unveiled a proposal for a 'Confidence Pact' between employers, unions and governments. Many commentators and officials have had an interest in denying a link between Maastricht-induced monetary and fiscal austerity and unemployment, because they were committed to both. As a result, in Santer's proposal, once again 'special' measures were advocated to boost jobs, including an appeal to reduce non-wage labour costs and re-allocation of savings from the EU Common Agricultural Policy to 'trans-European networks' and research. There was also talk of an 'employment pillar' for a second Maastricht Treaty, advocated by the Swedish authorities, committing governments to measures to promote employment. But, predictably, the EU Florence Council of June 1996 failed to agree on the financing of trans-European transport and communication networks, setting back the idea of 'active' pan-European employment plans.

There has been something unreal about the employment debate during the early and mid-1990s. Commitments to reduce unemployment have coincided with rising unemployment. Measures to cut non-wage labour costs have been introduced, labour markets have been made visibly more 'flexible', and reforms have been made to social security systems. Yet still unemployment has risen, and in 1996 it was forecast to rise further in 1997. Perhaps more benefits should be cut, perhaps more insecurity generated, perhaps conditionality for state transfers should be tightened further. Is this the Europe that we want?

Debates over the plethora of high-level reports and conferences have taken place alongside the great EMU debate. European Monetary Union will, it is presumed and intended, establish a single currency, the euro, and fuse the monetary policy of European central banks. It will thereby remove monetary policy as one tool of national economic policy, probably contributing to higher interest rates in countries with above-average unemployment than they would otherwise have.

In the economics profession, the optimal area for a single currency is one that coincides with the existence of a single 'flexible' labour market. Moves towards EMU are likely to intensify pressure to have a single labour market (no doubt, designated by an acronym such as SLM). There is no prospect of a European SLM in the near future. However, the trend will mean that there will be greater pressure on Sweden, for instance, to cut social spending from 34 per cent of GDP towards some European norm. What will that norm be? Will it be a path-breaking country, such as the UK, with its social spending of about 23 per cent of GDP, or will it be some continental European average? Or will certain countries effectively browbeat others to adopt their model of social and labour policy? One does not have to be a Euro-sceptic to find this issue somewhat alarming. Will there be overwhelming pressure from some country that pursues what is in effect a beggar-my-neighbour policy of cutting social spending to make it more 'competitive' for investment and trade? Or will the institutional and legislative machinery of the EU succeed in preventing this particular variant of what is sometimes called 'social dumping'?

The answers to these questions are linked to the debate on employ-ment. It is an irony that the pursuit of economic convergence has coincided with widely divergent unemployment rates, with relatively low levels (until yesterday) in western Germany and persistently over 20 per cent in Spain. A less deflationary policy would surely be justified in the high-unemployment country. Yet this is ruled out. An orthodox retort to this dilemma would be to state that the government of the high-unemployment country should make its labour market more flexible. But this is what Spain has done, to a greater extent than in low-unemployment parts of Europe.

The governor of the Bank of England, Eddie George, has not been alone in pointing out that, if the Maastricht criteria are to be main-tained, countries with above-average unemployment will either have to lower nominal and real wages or have to lower their exchange rate. Given the difficulty of doing the former, at least in the short term, such countries would either have to opt out of the convergence process or have to accept the higher level of unemployment. This might be overstating the dilemma slightly, since some measures could be pursued to influence unemployment. However, it was interesting that the governor of the Bank of England in 1995 suggested that if exchange rate changes were not allowed the only two mechanisms for dealing with high-unemployment countries would be labour migration and large-scale transfers from the countries with lower unemployment.

So, if national governments do have diminishing control over mon-etary and fiscal policy, they will be left with only labour-market and social policy to influence employment. Will that induce a policy conserv-atism, or inertia, in that it will become harder for any single country to launch a radical, redistributive policy? One other likely outcome is that the high-unemployment countries will demand and need massive trans-fers from other EU countries to compensate for the high unemployment.

There is also a moral hazard characteristic of the EMU agenda. Governments will be increasingly tempted to attribute their welfare-cutting measures to the dictates of EMU, conveniently trying to shift public opprobrium from themselves to the supranational 'treaty obliga-tions'.[6] That will be close to the reality as well.

Concluding Hopes: Flexibility as Security

The debate on employment in Western Europe is at an impasse. The dominant route being taken is towards a convergence based on acceptance of high unemployment and considerable economic insecurity in a context of repeated vociferous commitments to full employment. It may take time before it becomes acceptable to question the desirability as well as the feasibility of full employment. In an industrial society, with a fairly clear class structure and a strong and growing 'working class', the 'rights of labour' surely included the 'right to employment'. Yet once rights are perceived as entailing obligations in order to be legitimate, the door is open to making that right far from desirable or the route to economic security.

One way of proceeding is to contemplate whether the opposite of the conventional wisdoms would be better or worse. The current trend is to make entitlement to benefits more conditional on passing certain behavioural or means tests, and to penalize those among the poor or detached who do not conform to designated norms of social behaviour. The costs and inequities of that process are considerable. Yet can critics of the alternatives be sure that the alleged costs would be greater?

First, would it not be more conducive to genuine freedom, autonomy and redistribution to move steadfastly away from selectivity, 'means-testing' and 'work-testing' towards giving everybody a minimum income as a right of citizenship? This would not be a panacea, and could not be introduced immediately. Yet gradually de-linking basic income security from wage labour would be a progressive route. Hesitatingly, this has been happening, particularly in the United States, with tax credits. The objections that have been put forward to this ever since Tom Paine are well known, and can be answered. Yet the most important point now is to have the legitimacy of this objective accepted. Only then will ways be sought to obtain it and to avoid the alleged drawbacks of doing so. There is certainly no 'end of work' in prospect, rather the contrary. Yet providing a minimal income security could be essential for liberating the scope for flexible working patterns, and enabling people to pursue diverse combinations of forms of economic and learning activity spread over adult life. Only a 'passive' policy – of non-conditionality – would facilitate 'active' participation in the sense of greater personal autonomy and basic economic security.

Those on the Left seem to find this as hard to accept as those on the Right. Yet a paternalistic, directive state imposing behavioural obligations on the poor is scarcely compatible with a progressive redistributive strategy.

An issue related to proposals for moving towards a citizenship income guarantee that could be mildly subversive of the current economic orthodoxy is the treatment of what is usually described as the 'informal economy'. It is widely argued that this is extensive and growing. What is covered by the term is such that it is unwise to use it as a reliable concept. It ranges from unrevealed full-time working, perhaps characterized as part-time employment to avoid or evade taxes or social security contributions, to undeclared self-employment undertaken by those with wage jobs, and to illegal quasi-criminal activities.

Even with regard to the non-criminal activity, one view has been that it should be controlled. The result has been costly and ineffectual policy, often inequitable in its outcomes, in that those caught have often been the poorer groups. Another view is that most of such activity should be legalized and recognized as economic, so as to increase tax revenue, lower the appearance of unemployment and raise measured GDP, which in turn would lower the public deficit as a percentage share of GDP. For instance, it has been suggested that informal economic activities account for about 10 per cent of Germany's GDP. Incorporating that into the country's national income would lower the government's debt-to-GDP ratio to below 60 per cent, the maximum level allowed by the Maastricht Treaty to permit entry to EMU. Other countries would be able to achieve even more impressive improvements in trying to meet the Maastricht criteria by counting their informal economy as part of their national income.

What has this to do with moving towards a citizenship income guarantee? Quite a lot, since moving in that direction would reduce the unemployment and poverty traps that discourage small-scale involvement in income-earning activities or that encourage those on the margin of the labour market to conceal their work from the authorities because they would lose benefits or other entitlements by revealing them. This could also help to reduce the economic insecurity faced by those in the lower income strata of the increasingly fragmented labour force.

Second, most forms of economic insecurity derive from, or reflect, the weakness of representation security, due in the 1980s and the 1990s to the erosion of trade unions. Unless alternative collective institutions can be fostered that give sustainable potential for effective 'voice regulation' in labour relations, fragmentation and vulnerability will persist. Statutory protective regulations are blunt instruments, at worst abused, evaded and avoided, at best applied through legal and administrative means that impose heavy transaction costs. Some statutory regulations will always be needed. However, bargaining and representative agencies can be more flexible and effective in securing greater equity and efficiency. Organizations capable of representing all vulnerable groups in local labour markets must emerge. Perhaps fiscal and other policies will be required to foster these in the next few years.

Third, the employment debate over the past two decades has been increasingly divorced from the historical concern for distributive justice. Income inequality may be greater in the UK than elsewhere in Western Europe, but it has been increasing faster in some other countries, including Sweden. Research may show that the growth of inequality in terms of economic insecurity has been greater than is captured in income data *per se.*

Once the economic drawbacks of progressive direct taxation were accepted (rightly or wrongly) in the 1980s, and once the welfare state's capacities were exposed as limited, there was a void in redistributive policy. Where in Europe is there an articulated strategy for redistribution to reduce economic inequality and insecurity? Many across the political spectrum argue openly or quietly that we must learn to live with greater inequality. Many have argued that inequality is desirable, with arguments that would have worried their lookalikes two decades ago. Yet if one cannot have full employment, or independent fiscal policy, what redistributive policy is on offer? Perhaps the only feasible way forward is to consider how forms of social sharing of economic surplus, or profits, could be introduced, forms that would spread income more equally while not impeding efficiency and investment.

The specifics of those ideas are for other occasions. Suffice it to reiterate one point by way of conclusion. One of the features of the debate on employment (and on much else) is the unwillingness of most prominent participants in the debate to think, speak or act radically. Besides the dismal spectacle of the numerous spins on themes reiterated in international conferences and reports, there is an intellectual insecurity, which has narrowed the range of imagination and created what almost amounts to a paralysis of disengagement. So much is ruled out as impractical even before it is considered.

The intellectual insecurity has mirrored the growth of economic insecurity, although it stems from different roots. There is an unhealthy concern for the mythical 'median voter', with the fear that the most-polled MV would oppose redistributive reform, and if so that would be that, even if the analyst believed it would be socially just to pursue such reform. This characteristic could also be called 'intellectual flexibility'. One day we might be prepared to use more pithy terms for the pusillanimous way the debate on employment has been conducted in the 1980s and 1990s. The sooner the better.

1996

Notes

The author is a member of the International Labour Organisation. The views expressed here are personal, and should not be attributed to the ILO.

1. Keynes commented that economists could be divided into 'little inflationists' and 'little deflationists'. There can be little doubt which variant has been in the ascendancy during the past two decades. One way of characterizing the major change in economic thinking is that in the 'Keynesian era' (c.1944–74) macroeconomic policy was expected to ensure full employment, while microeconomic policy was expected to check inflationary pressures. In the neo-liberal era (c.1975–96?), macroeconomic policy was intended to control inflation while microeconomic policy was expected to influence employment but not ensure full employment.

2. Employment security must be distinguished from job security. Some analysts have claimed that there has been little reduction in employment security because the average tenure of employment has not changed much over the past decade. This tells us nothing about job-changing within employment. Moreover, the data on employment tenure usually refer to those only in regular full-time employment, whereas it is those in part-time and non-regular forms of employment who tend to have the shorter employment tenures, and it is these who have accounted for growing shares of total employment. The fairly stable tenure figures also probably reflect a compositional change, in that a proportion of the short-tenure employment would have been converted into non-regular work statuses.

3. Opening speech to 'Beyond Essen: Active Employment Measures for Disadvantaged Groups', a European Round Table organized by the European Foundation for the Improvement of Living and Working Conditions, Brussels, 17 October 1996.

4. The latter is a hazy concept that is often used, rarely defined, even more rarely measured other than in an inductive manner. For a critique, see G. Standing, 'The Notion of Structural Unemployment', *International Labour Review*, vol. 122, no. 2, March–April 1983, pp. 137–53.

5. Bear in mind that some commentators have tended to dismiss concern about the European 'welfare state' by pointing to the fact that social welfare spending has remained above 20 per cent of GDP. The difficulty is that this has been an era in which, because of much higher unemployment and economic insecurity, the needs have grown.

6. For a trenchant critique of this tendency, see Sam Aaronovitch and John Grahl, 'Building on Maastricht', this volume, pp. 178–202.

15

Central Bankism
Edward Luttwak

Communism is dead, socialism has been repudiated by the socialists themselves, fewer and fewer Europeans are believing Christians but it seems that a fanatical new religion – also practised in America – has replaced all of them: Central Bankism. Like all religions, it has both a supreme God – hard money – and a devil, inflation. Common sense suffices to oppose high inflation, and to fear hyper-inflation as the deadly disease of the currencies. But it takes the absolute faith of religion to refuse even very moderate inflation at the cost of immoderate unemployment and stagnation, as the Europeans have been doing, or to accept slow economic growth for years on end, as in the United States.

To be sure, the American version of central bankism is much more willing than its orthodox European counterpart to accommodate popular desires – the same is true of the other religions practised on both continents. Just as the Catholic Church is forced to allow more latitude in pragmatic America, where even devoted Jews drive on the Sabbath, the local version of central bankism has restraint imposed on it. The US Congress would legislate the Federal Reserve right out of existence rather than tolerate the horrendous levels of unemployment long prevalent in Europe. But the essential doctrine is identical. In the US, too, central bankism devalues labour rather than money, but instead of unemployment there are falling real wages – more than half of all jobs throughout the US economy pay less now than they did twenty years ago, in constant dollars. No wonder millions of new jobs keep being created, as Clinton keeps boasting: American labour is so cheap.

Like most religions, central bankism has its sanctuaries, which inspire as much awe as any great cathedral: from the majestic Bank of England to the Greek temples of the US Federal Reserve, the massive modernity of the Bundesbank compound and the inevitable Umbertino of the Bank of Italy. The Nihon Ginko of Japan is housed in a solid but otherwise unremarkable office building on a side street, which is appropriate given that until recently it was a servant of the powerful Okurasho, the 'Treasury Ministry', just as the Banque de France was a slave of the Ministry of Finance. As such, both were subject to the corrupting influence – dare one say it – of political decisions, though in truth both ministries are ultra-conservative élite strongholds, scarcely exposed to the vagaries of democracy.

Like many religions, central bankism has its high priests, constantly striving to assert their independence from secular parliaments, politicians and public opinion. Although, like any other public officials, they receive their salaries from the taxpayer, central bankers claim the right to ignore the public will by invoking their duty to a higher authority – the sacrosanctity of hard money. Central bankers in office – invariably for terms of papal length, often prematurely renewed in fear of the fears of financial markets – are surrounded by an aura of sovereign power very properly denied to government ministers or even prime ministers and presidents, mere mortals voted in and out of office by the ignorant masses, or reshuffled at even shorter intervals. And when these high priests do at length retire, they are not uncommonly elevated to financial sainthood, their every fleeting opinion reverentially treasured, their candidacy for any position of special trust eagerly accepted, their very names talismanic, as with Paul Volcker in Wall Street and far beyond it, or Guido Carli in Italy, where the names of most past prime ministers evoke only opprobrium.

Because their own power derives largely from their supreme command of the crusade against the devil of inflation, central bankers naturally see His insidious presence everywhere. Very often, they detect 'disturbing signs of incipient inflation' or even 'alarming warnings of mounting inflationary pressure' in output, employment, and wage statistics that many respected economists view with equanimity, or find downright reassuring. Every time new statistical indicators are published, there are calls for slightly lower interest rates to achieve a bit more growth, but such outbreaks of heresy are easily squashed.

Simple, definitive proof of the doctrinal supremacy of central bankism can be found in the fact that any policy initiative that is branded as 'inflationary' is usually rejected out of hand. By contrast, the term 'deflationary' has no resonance at all. It is used as a purely technical expression, rather than a powerful condemnation of over-restrictive fiscal and monetary policies that strangle growth, and which in the

1930s brought about the Great Depression, political chaos, dictatorship and war. In the first instance it is the instrument of money that inflation hits, while deflation has an immediate impact on people, denying them the opportunity to work and earn, and to buy goods and services, which would allow others to work and earn.

It is perfectly true that real incomes and real wealth cannot be created by printing money, that inflation hurts the poor disproportionately as well as everyone who lives on a fixed income ('the cruellest tax') and wealthy rentiers who live on bond incomes. Inflation enriches all who are already rich enough to own real estate and other marketable assets, while disproportionately enriching smart speculators – but so does deflation. It is also true that, if unchecked, inflation naturally accelerates into hyper-inflation, which not only destroys currencies but also degrades economic efficiency – as people run to spend their suitcases of banknotes instead of working – and may even wreck the entire financial structure of a society. This being the worst manifestation of the devil, the ultimate Beelzebub, it is not surprising that in 1996, with inflation ultra-low at 1.5 per cent, the Bundesbank, when refusing to cut interest rates, still invokes the hyper-inflation of the early 1920s 'that led to Hitler' (it was followed by ten years of democracy, but never mind).

Inflation, then, is bad and hyper-inflation very bad indeed; but it is just as true that deflation is bad, and that hyper-deflation is disastrous. In economic theory deflation should have no consequences at all, because any upward movement in the value of money can be nullified by a compensating reduction in prices and wages. In practice, however, prices are downwardly sticky, while very few employees anywhere at any time accept wage cuts without the most bitter resistance – even in the US with its mass immigration, increasingly unfavourable labour market and weak unions. Contrary to theory, deflation starves economies, even without taking into account the purely subjective mechanism that reduces real demand, and therefore real production and real employment, when people feel poorer just because the nominal value of their houses and other assets is falling. Inflation and deflation should therefore be viewed as equally objectionable by politicians and the public; they should resound in our ears as equivalent evils, like flood and drought, or theft and robbery. It is the greatest triumph of central bankism that only inflation is viewed as sinful.

Like all religions, finally, central bankism demands sacrifices from the faithful. Catholics, Jews and Muslims have it rather easy; central bankism resembles the Aztec faith in demanding human sacrifice. None of them hesitates to impose levels of unemployment that year after year after year deprive millions of young people of the opportunity even to start a career. Moreover, the central bankers have all the moral certitude of the Aztec priests. Gathered together last August with their host, Alan Greenspan, chairman of the Federal Reserve, in Jackson, Wyoming (which instantly became the world's premier resort), the central bankers congratulated themselves at length on their success in reducing inflation by keeping real interest rates high; they did not pause to deplore miserable growth rates, but engaged instead in a sort of reverse auction. As it is, the estimated 1996 growth rates for the G7 countries (US, Canada, Britain, France, Germany, Italy and Japan) average out at 1.8 per cent, which guarantees rising unemployment, simply because the labour force and labour productivity are conjointly increasing somewhat faster. Still, in Jackson the central bankers competed with each other in calling for even lower inflation rates.

Normally it is the chief of the Bundesbank who dominates such occasions. He can preach fiscal austerity and monetary discipline to errant foreigners everywhere, because Germany was for so long the perpetual winner of the deflation Olympics (except for the Japanese, who do not count – for those idiots, employment is always the priority). But this time around, France was the surprise winner. Untroubled by an economy not merely stagnant but in rigor mortis, with a level of unemployment (above 12 per cent) unseen since the Great Depression, the French were enormously proud of their amazingly low 1.3 per cent inflation rate (as of June 1996), a full 0.2 per cent below Germany's! It was as if the defeats of 1870 and 1940 had been undone. The super-disciplined Dutch did not do quite so well with their 1.8 per cent, but that did not prevent Willem Duisenberg of the Netherlands Central Bank from sharing with confidants his fears that the Bundesbank was showing dangerous signs of laxity. After all, the German federal deficit stood at 3.6 per cent of GNP, as opposed to the winning 2.7 per cent of the Dutch (which is only 2.7 per cent away from reverting to a mediaeval gold-in, gold-out treasury, with no need of public finance at all).

The Italians, as befits real gentlemen, refrained from boasting – the Bank of Italy is the country's only élite bureaucracy – in spite of their 2.9 per cent inflation rate, a brilliant achievement indeed given all the banknotes thrown into the economy by a 6.4 per cent budget deficit. The fact that low inflation drives up the lira, making Italian exports less competitive, thus cutting growth and employment in an economy already slowing down, was not the sort of thing the central bankers bothered to discuss.

Instead, with Duisenberg in the lead, there was heady talk of ascending to the paradise of central bankism, a zero inflation rate – it would only be a matter of eliminating budget deficits by scrapping more welfare programmes, and of interest-rate discipline, easily dispensed from the magnificent heights of Jackson, Wyoming, to the vulgar crowd of Europe's 18 million unemployed. As for Alan Greenspan, he has nothing whatever to worry about, because slow growth, a 5 per cent unemployment rate and falling wages are all now accepted by Americans as perfectly normal, or even as good news. The stage has been reached at which any spurt of faster growth, any fall in unemployment, is very bad news indeed for Wall Street and all of us, because it will only lead the Federal Reserve to increase interest rates, in order to 'cool down the economy'.

In fact, nobody knows the exact rate of unemployment below which wages start rising, pushing prices upwards. For one thing, every aspect of the US economy keeps changing, while the government's budget-starved statistical bureaux can only collect the same old increasingly outdated statistical series, in the same old way. Economists continue to debate the precise level of the NAIRU (the non-accelerating inflation rate of unemployment), but the Fed takes no chances. When in doubt, Greenspan errs on the side of caution: a million people can lose their jobs because higher interest rates might, perhaps, keep inflation at one-tenth of 1 per cent below what it might have been.

How did this come about? How did the employees of one public institution among many assume a priestly status, becoming more powerful in many ways than prime ministers or presidents? One heard very little about them in the three postwar decades of rapid economic growth, sharply rising incomes and widening prosperity. Only during the 1930s, not coincidentally the years of the Great Depression, were they as prominent as they are now. A world in crisis followed with bated breath every pronouncement from the lips of the Bank of England's Montagu Norman, Germany's Hjalmar Schacht and their lesser colleagues on both sides of the Atlantic. With tragic consequences for millions of American families, and far more terrible repercussions in Europe, governments almost everywhere accepted their remedy for the Depression, which was to deflate, deflate, deflate, by cutting public spending and restricting credit. One result was that Hitler's rise to power was accelerated by mass unemployment.

We now know that the central bankers were totally wrong. The only way to refloat the sinking economies of the 1930s was to start off the chain-reaction of demand by sharply increasing government spending, and never mind a bit of inflation. Had the big boys of the world economy led the way, by inflating and importing first, to generate more demand for their own exports, everyone would have come out just fine. But only a few adventurous souls, and only one reputable economist, John Maynard Keynes, dared to contradict what seemed to be common sense, and even they were hesitant. The central bankers, by contrast, were utterly certain that they were right, just as they are now; and they gave exactly the same advice they are giving now; the only advice central bankers ever give: tighten credit, restrict spending, hold back demand. Old Sigmund had a term for that.

A simple explanation for the rise of central bankism as the prevailing wisdom of the age is institutional: while the value of money is protected with fierce determination by the central bankers, industry and labour have no such exalted defenders, only mere governments and parliaments now greatly inhibited by the caveats of central bankism. That is neatly mechanical but also circular and obviously begs the question. Perhaps there is a straightforward political explanation. In these post-socialist times, the Right everywhere is still unflinching in its allegiance to the bond-holding rentiers who oppose inflation above all things, while the Left, intellectually threadbare, is tired of complaining about unemployment, and frankly bored by the poor. In the US, the presidential election rapidly became a contest between two right-wing candidates, except that on public finance Bill Clinton managed to manoeuvre himself to the Right of Bob Dole. While Clinton tried to take the credit for the sharp cuts in all non-military public spending imposed by the Republican-dominated Congress (the Federal deficit is down to 1.7 per cent of GNP, a level unseen in two decades), it was Dole who proposed a tax cut, risking a deficit increase to stimulate growth.

In Europe, Tony Blair is only the most blatant among today's party leaders on the Left in his disdain for poor people and other losers, his overwhelming desire to sup at the table of financial success, and his contempt for the broad mass of working stiffs with small houses, big mortgages and ugly little cars. He is certainly ill-equipped to resist the plausibilities of central bankism. In France, Germany and Spain, the ex-socialist parties are not subject to the gravitational pull of fashionable society as the Labour Party is in Britain, but they can still do no more than march despairingly to electoral defeat. Such is the poverty of their ideas that they are now listening attentively to Blair's mumblings about a 'stakeholder' society – not even bothering to go to the original source, Ryuzaburo Kaku, chairman of Japan's Canon Inc.

In the absence of any intellectual counterweight to central bankism, an electoral victory of the Left can only yield right-wing policies poorly executed by ex-socialists who have no talent nor any natural affinity for commerce and finance. So it was in France under François Mitterrand, and so it is in Italy, after the victory of the ex-Communist Party, now re-labelled PDS, the Democratic Party of the Left. The PDS, as exemplified by its leading government minister, the youngish, fashionable and ever-so-modern Walter Veltroni, far more at home on Madison Avenue than in the slums of the south, is using all its power to sustain Romano Prodi's coalition government, which is entirely dedicated to central bankism. Its overriding goal is not to reduce Italy's unemployment, terribly high in much of the south, nor to refashion decaying schools and antiquated universities on modern lines, nor to endow Italy with an adequate health-care system, nor to raise the government's bureaucracy to European standards, but to bring Italy into the European Monetary Union – the apotheosis of Europe's particularly virulent form of central bankism.

The perfectly sound project of replacing Europe's confusion of currencies with the euro was born long before central bankism became today's extremist religion, and did not originally imply the acceptance of deflation and unemployment for ever and ever. Even before the Bretton Woods system of fixed exchange rates pegged to the dollar, itself tied to gold at $35 an ounce, was undermined in 1971 by Richard Nixon's decision to end the convertibility of dollars into gold, the Common Market members had proclaimed their long-term goal of establishing a single currency. But so long as exchange rates were still fixed, barring infrequent devaluations and upvaluations, the multiplicity of European currencies was only a minor inconvenience. Commerce was not disrupted by currency gyrations nor inhibited by fear of possible shifts in exchange rates – at least, not until 1973, when exchange rates were unfixed, starting the up and down floating that has been going on ever since, to the great benefit of a new and thriving industry – currency speculation – and to the detriment of all others.

The project of a single European currency remained on the horizon as the ultimate aim, but in 1979 the European Monetary System was introduced as an interim arrangement, whereby member countries agreed to keep the relative value of their currencies within narrow limits. Under EMS rules, as soon as traders push up or mark down a currency anywhere near the limits, the country in question is compelled to react, chiefly by raising or lowering interest rates to attract or repel capital inflows, as the case may be. Central banks have also attempted to calm the waters by 'open-market operations', i.e., by out-trading the traders, dumping currencies much in demand, or buying up weak currencies, sometimes acting in concert specifically to ambush speculators. The central bankers, however, have never been very good at the game. Public and politicians may believe that they are geniuses, but speculators know better: they regularly leave the table with large winnings, at the expense of the central banks, sometimes with enough to keep their great-grandchildren in the pink on the basis of one night's trading.

In any case, interest-rate jiggling and open-market operations could at best cope only with routine fluctuations. If a currency was sliding or ascending as a result of more enduring export and import trends, the only way of staying within the allowed EMS limits was to readjust the country's taxation and spending structures as a whole, in order to raise or lower overall demand in its economy. In the old Bretton Woods days, currency problems could still be dealt with by currency solutions, leaving the domestic economy out of it and instead imposing or relaxing prohibitions on the purchase of foreign currency. But such 'exchange controls' have long since been abolished in the European Union – they are of course utterly incompatible with a unified market – so that there is no barrier between currencies and economies. Although the EMS is only an approximation to fixed exchange rates, let alone the euro, it already requires the currency tail to wag the economic dog, and all that goes with it: demand, employment, taxes, social programmes. In other words, the EMS can only work if its own priorities out-rank all relevant political priorities, i.e., most of politics, and therefore most aspects of democracy. It is a foretaste of what the euro will require of its members.

Not everyone has been able to make the supreme sacrifice, as France is now heroically doing, raising its currency to majestic heights, depressing its people into a valley of despond. Having originally set the relative value of sterling much too high, Britain eventually had to withdraw from the EMS, but only after donating an immense fortune to speculators by trying and failing to out-trade them. The Germans could have saved the day by buying up the loose sterling clogging the market with their precious DMs. But that would have meant that parsimonious German savers would be paying for years of profligacy on Britain's part in importing far more than it can export. The Bundesbank of a newly unified, far more self-confident Germany naturally did nothing and it may even have dumped some of its own stock of depreciating sterling. The British response was a cascade of press and parliamentary insults – an episode worth recalling because it revealed how fragile is the ethos of European unity.

Italy, too, was forced out, though not because of any profligacy, being then as now a vigorously successful exporter. Instead the lira collapsed because of a loss of confidence in the Italian state itself, caused by the revelations of *Tangentopoli* and the resulting arrests, forced resignations and prudent withdrawals that wiped out most of the country's political class. Both foreign and domestic foreign-currency traders, and many plain Italians with much or a little money in hand, calculated – very correctly – that the lira would go down, then sold it, thus ensuring that it would indeed go down. Some feared that the mountainous public debt accumulated during decades of waste, fraud, mismanagement and some investment, would be 'monetized' by whatever new rulers emerged, that is, be at least partially repudiated by inflating the currency. At a minimum, nobody could be certain that honest new politicians, if any could be found, would be up to the fiscal acrobatics and book-keeping stratagems needed to manage a public debt one-fifth larger than GNP, not counting unfunded pension liabilities – calculators run out of zeros before that total is added up.

These episodes did not stop the onward advance towards the euro. Meeting in Hanover in June 1988, the European Union's Council of Ministers agreed on the guidelines for the specialist negotiations leading to the Maastricht Treaty signed in February 1992, which laid down the criteria for admission into the European Monetary Union, future issuer of the euro currency. With that, the advance became a forced march because 'Maastricht', complemented by a December Council meeting in Madrid and another in Verona in April 1996, set a series of rigid timetables. As early as possible in 1998, each candidate's 1997 statistics are to be examined, to determine which countries will be admitted into EMU. On 1 January 1999, the successful applicants must irrevocably adopt fixed exchange rates. In practice, that would already bring the euro into existence as Europe's money, but national banknotes and coins would continue in circulation. At that point, DMs, francs, guilders or lire – if Italy is mad enough to join – would differ only in their colour and design, being entirely interchangeable at their respective, fixed, exchange rate. Finally, by January 2002 at the latest, national currencies are to be withdrawn, ceasing to be legal tender six months later.

It is not the euro itself, however, nor the compulsory, inflexible dates of its adoption (they simply disregard the business cycle) that have transformed Maastricht from being the name of one of Europe's most pleasant minor cities into an evocation of fear, and a focus of scathing criticism from American economists, British politicians and, more to the point, European industrialists and trade unions. Currencies, after all, even the euro, can be managed in drastically different ways.

The value of sterling, for example, has often been 'defended' – i.e., forced upwards – from the 1920s onwards, to the greater glory of the British Empire, or the UK as the case may have been; to the great benefit of the City, which needed the prestige of a strong currency and/ or high interest rates to attract depositors; and to the even greater benefit of wealthy Brits who could invest more advantageously abroad – and all at the expense of British industry, whose exports were systematically overpriced, while competing imports were correspondingly underpriced. In the process, x thousand City gents were kept happily rich with scant effort, y hundreds of ultra-rich Brits cheaply accumulated many broad acres in Canada and Australia, real estate, bonds and shares in America, Europe and Japan, as well as villas on the Côte d'Azur, in Bermuda, the Bahamas, etc., while z millions of dis- or under- or never employed British industrial workers, their managers high and low, and all those foolish enough to invest in British industry paid for the fun.

That was what the 'the defence of sterling', always much applauded by an innumerate press, has amounted to, from the disastrous 1920 decision to revert to the Gold Standard through to the Thatcher government's mad-dog decision to enter the EMS at a 'prestige' level, which guaranteed trade deficits and the further decline of British industry. Of late, with equally disastrous results for French industry, the French franc has been managed in the same way, and the DM, too, is greatly overvalued, leading to the emigration of German industry both eastwards into ex-communist Europe, a new and better *Ostmark*, and westwards to the United States. Such are the fruits of central bankism – a currency that the unemployed can be proud of. The US dollar, by contrast, has mostly been allowed to float freely since fixed exchange rates were finally renounced in 1973. Far from defending the dollar, successive administrations have intervened in earnest only to push it down, nakedly exploiting their geopolitical power over the hard-currency champions, but Second World War losers, Germany and Japan, to force them to upvalue their currencies, thereby devaluing the dollar. True, US officials have often promised to complaining foreigners that they would try to raise the dollar when it was too grossly undervalued, but they never promised that they would keep their promise. In any case, a very low and still declining propensity to save has ensured chronic US trade deficits, muting currency complaints.

Amid the total indifference of the public, in spite of some highly specialized Wall Street objections, successive US governments have been gleefully happy to see the dollar fall, slide, plunge, plummet, collapse or even sink deep into the mud, for that means more exports, fewer imports, more work, more output and more profits – reckoned in dollars, and only dollars of course. At times, American tourists in Switzerland or France would be kicked out of their lodgings or denied a table by innkeepers afraid of being stuck with travellers' cheques denominated in rapidly falling dollars. Such news always caused hilarity rather than shame back in the US of A, merely prompting suggestions that the unlucky tourists should try Florida next time. Central bankism is not quite so fanatical a faith in the US, and it has never been coupled with the sheer idiocy of currency nationalism.

It is not therefore the euro itself but rather its management that counts. Will it be kept as high as possible, as sterling has been and the French franc is now, or will it be allowed to slide merrily down in between upward jumps, as with the US dollar? Two things guarantee that the euro will be valued too high for the health of Europe's already sickly economies: the specific Maastricht criteria for admission into the European Monetary Union, and the fact that from its inception its policy will be controlled exclusively by the European System of Central Banks.

The Maastricht criteria are utterly pervaded, inspissated and parboiled by the spirit of central bankism. Admission into the EMU requires that for 1997, the year of statistical 'examination', budget deficits be less than 3 per cent of GNP (even Germany's was 4.1 per cent in November 1996); that the inflation rate be within 1.5 per cent of the three least sinful entrants (even Italy can make it); that long-term interest rates (a measure of the markets' estimate of future inflation) be within 2 per cent of those of the three most virtuous entrants; that applicants be unblemished by the shame of any post-1995 devaluation; and finally, the most difficult of all criteria: that the public debt not exceed 60 per cent of the Gross Domestic Product, a condition that only France and Denmark could now satisfy. For the Netherlands at 78 per cent, or even Spain (79.8 per cent) and Portugal (70.7 per cent), let alone Germany (62.4 per cent), the permitted ratio of debt to GDP is definitely attainable by 1997 – all it takes is some stiff taxation to pay off some of the bond-holders at home or abroad. That will further depress demand, output and employment, but the newly disemployed will have plenty of company.

For Belgium at 130 per cent and Italy at 123 per cent, on the other hand, the debt to GDP ratio could only be cut to 60 per cent between late 1996 and 1997 by the most extreme measures. In theory, it need not be so. Very little of Belgium's or Italy's public debt is held by foreigners. In theory, therefore, a simple two-step operation could do the trick: first impose a huge 'patrimonial' wealth tax to extract the money, then give it back more or less to the same people, to buy back their holdings of state bonds. Already advocated as a 'simple' solution on election night 1996 by Italy's Rifondazione Comunista, the unreconstructed, pure red, hammer-and-sickle Communist Party on which Prodi's government depends for crucial parliamentary votes, the two-step would not work out quite so well in practice. In fact, it would probably wreck the country for a couple of generations.

In the first place, assessment for the patrimonial tax would unleash a tidal wave of anonymous denunciations, which would no doubt improve the country's mental health by venting all manner of long-festering animosities: Rossi has a villa under his wife's sister's maid's name; Bianchi keeps gold in his mattress; Neri has money in a Jersey bank account ... But that would only add to the crushing burden of tax assessors trying to identify and add up each household's listed and unlisted holdings of real estate, savings accounts, stocks and bonds, art works, automobiles, furniture, domestic appliances, jewellery, and perhaps clothes and toys as well. By which point, of course, all the country's liquid assets, along with very many of its entrepreneurs and the more mobile among its professionals, would long since have flown the coop to watch the proceedings from afar. That would in turn make it somewhat difficult to sell off the real estate, which cannot be wired abroad in microseconds. Shares, too, would not be easily sold in a deserted stock-market with the index near zero. Finally, any attempt to collect the tax would trigger enough appeals and law-suits to last a thousand years or so.

None of that, however, need happen. Just as the Maastricht meeting of the European Union's Council of Ministers inscribed the 60 per cent criterion into the Treaty, another meeting can take it out. In that way, Italy as well as Belgium could join the others in EMU, so long as they deflated their already deflating economy by cutting their deficit in half to the allowed 3 per cent, a perfectly achievable proposition if one does not mind a bit more unemployment. What cannot change is the governing principle of EMU: the totality of monetary policy, from interest rates to credit norms, is to be controlled exclusively by the European System of Central Banks. Appropriately enough, it is the conclave of the European Central Bank, currently in creation, with the existing central banks of each country, which is to sit at the ECB's feet to implement its every command. Its first act, as of the start of 1998, will be to conduct a statistical inquisition to determine each country's fitness for admission. By that date too, all central banks not yet deemed 'independent' are to become so; in other words, laws must be passed to ensure they are fully independent from their own governments and parliaments, as the Bundesbank and Federal Reserve, among others, already are.

No independence, however, can be as magnificent and absolute as that of the ECB itself: it is to receive no instructions either from member countries or from any institution of the European Union. Such is the sovereign status of the institution, headed by a central banker selected by other central bankers, themselves recruited and trained by their predecessors from like-minded people, which is to assume total and exclusive control over the monetary policy of all member countries from the inception of the union on 1 January 1999. Itself free of any democratic interference, the ECB will be at liberty to interfere at will in everything that has anything to do with money in all member countries.

No institution has claimed such prerogatives since the heyday of the mediaeval papacy. Beyond the enormous leverage of interest rates across the entire spectrum of economic life, beyond its control of credit in general, the ECB will be empowered to invigilate quite a few specific rules, including the three sacrosanct prohibitions: no financing of state deficits by central banks (back to gold-in, gold-out public treasuries); no loans on favourable terms to any public body or state-owned company by any private or public financial institution (*au revoir* Air France, *arrivederci* Alitalia); no guarantees by any member country of any other member country's debt, the 'no bail out' rule. To a slight degree perhaps, it will matter who heads the ECB, for while all members of the fraternity are physiologically disposed to tighten credit, restrict spending, hold back demand (old Sigmund again), some are millimetrically more latitudinarian than others. At present, the leading candidate is Willem Duisenberg of the Netherlands Central Bank, the man who has allowed it to be known that he detects signs of laxity in the Bundesbank.

Still an obscure set of initials for the time being, the letters ECB deserve to acquire all the resonance of KGB or CIA, not to add, very indelicately, SS, because the European Central Bank is all set to be the King Kong of Europe's institutional jungle. Yves-Thibault de Silguy, whose very name is redolent of the glories of absolute monarchy, a graduate of the Ecole Nationale d'Administration, of course, now the European Commissioner in charge of economic, financial and monetary affairs, and an enthusiastic advocate of the ECB, has recently raised and answered the Great Question to his own complete satisfaction: 'Some people claim that the independence of the European System of Central Banks is anti-democratic. That criticism is baseless. The ECB will be subjected to the rules of transparency and open information already imposed on central banks in most industrialized countries.' Who says that ENA graduate, French patrician Eurocrats lack a sense of humour? As I write, the *Washington Post* announces that the Federal Reserve is bringing in the FBI to investigate a leak of interest-rate recommendations. And the Fed is far more open in its dealings than any European central bank, i.e., almost as liberal with information as the North Korean Politburo.

What is much less funny is that under the ECB the euro will most certainly be managed like sterling in the 1920s rather than like the US dollar since 1974, as the very hardest of hard currencies, kept that way by the cruellest, most persistent deflation. What an outcome of all the hopes that European unity once evoked! With the economies of Western Europe stalled by a chronic lack of demand, with Russians lacking everything (except nuclear weapons), from surgical instruments in hospitals to space-heaters at home, with other ex-Soviet states even worse off, generous printings of euros sent eastwards would immediately return to employ millions in Western Europe, relaunching investment and growth, engendering bright new hopes in its despondent youth, as well as some inflation no doubt. Now *that* would be a grand project, fit for a European Union worthy of its name, and it might even avoid the mega-disaster which could so very easily ensue if two or three things go wrong in Russia. All it would take is for the ECB to be governed by a board of industrialists and trade unionists with no central bankers allowed on the premises, and headed by an accountant charged only with keeping hyper-inflation at bay by stopping the printing presses churning out the euros now and then.

As it is of course, any real help for the Other Europeans is ruled out. Instead, they, along with the US and all other exporters to the EMU countries, will be incidentally damaged by the blind charge into the valley of hard-money deflation. It might mean the loss of as much as a third of US growth. But at least the ECB should be able to save on salaries. Certainly there is no need to hire the highly paid priests of central bankism to head the ECB. So very restrictive and mechanical are its intended monetary policies, so very narrow is the scope of its decisions, that almost any clerk armed with a cheap calculator would be up to the job.

1996

FUTURE

Principles

16

Does Europe Need a Constitution?

Dieter Grimm

Expectations of a Constitution

Constitutions form the legal basis of states. Supranational institutions, by contrast, have their legal basis in international treaties. That was at any rate the position in the past. Faced with the European Union, however, this classification seems to fail. Though nobody regards it as a state, there is much talk of its constitution. Here radically differing views concur. On the one hand, the international treaties on which the Union's existence is based are increasingly referred to as its constitution. On the other hand, the treaty basis is increasingly being felt to be inadequate, and the lack of a European constitution complained of. Yet both cannot simultaneously be right. Either the constitution is already there in the form of the treaties, or else these fail to meet just those requirements that are made of a constitution. The contradictory views are therefore to be met with in different areas of discourse. The first dominates the European legal debate, and can appeal to the case law of the European Court of Justice. The second pervades the European policy debate, and most recently found expression in a constitutional initiative by the European Parliament.

However widely the views on the existence of a constitution diverge, both sides nonetheless agree on the basic assumption that the European Union, though not a state, can and should have a constitution. This assumption cannot be explained solely by the fact that the European Union is not just an inter-governmental institution of the traditional type but has sovereign rights conveyed to it by the member states that it exercises with direct effect domestically. For the Community possessed this power that goes beyond the classic dualism of states and

239

international organizations from the outset, without having a constitution therefore ascribed to or advised for it. Even ten years ago, the draft treaty on the establishment of the European Union the European Parliament put forward, while seen in professional circles as a draft constitution, met with lack of interest in political circles and got no response from the public. The international treaties were regarded as an adequate legitimizing basis for the Community's sovereign powers, while the constitution as a legal form remained reserved to states.

It was the Maastricht Treaty, which has since been concluded, that brought Europe into the public eye. The Community's specific nature is of course not changed by the Treaty. In particular, it has not turned into an entity that could itself claim statehood and squeeze the member states into a subordinate position. The Community instead remains, notwithstanding the advances in integration embodied in the Treaty, a supranational institution, and the pillars flanking the Community and together with it forming the Union, the common foreign and security policy and cooperation on justice and home affairs, still even linger at the stage of mere inter-governmental cooperation. A shift of sovereign powers, as with the Community, has not come about here. What has, though, emerged from public debate over the treaty is how far national policy is now determined by decisions by Community bodies, and how strongly domestic circumstances are marked by Community law and the case law of the European Court of Justice.[1]

This realization went hand in hand with that of the European democracy deficit, which has dominated the European debate since the Maastricht Treaty. Though member-state citizens are, as has now become generally known, greatly affected by Community decisions and are subject to its legal norms, the European Parliament they elect has only slight influence on these. Even though listed first among Community institutions, it has the least weight. European decisions, including those of a legislative nature, are determined by the executive. Even after its upgrading by the Maastricht Treaty, parliament remains confined to veto rights. Under these circumstances, European legal acts derive their democratic legitimacy overwhelmingly from the democratic legitimation of the national governments, which make up the Community's real decision-making centre, the Council. It is from this weakness in legitimation that the call for a European constitution derives, as does the response it has lately been getting from the public. The legitimation-conferring power arising in the national context from the constitution ought to be bestowed on the European Union too.

Yet there is a lot that is unclear here. The call for a constitution would be void from the outset if European legal scholars' assumption that the missing constitution already exists were right. In that case one could certainly talk about improving it, but hardly about creating it. This point therefore has to be cleared up first. That means establishing what is meant by a constitution and what constitutions are needed for. The best way to do that is to look at how constitutions came about and what problems they were supposed to solve. Yet whatever comes out of this regarding the existence of a European constitution, the differing perceptions of the constitutional question in European legal and political circles is still a fact needing elucidation of its own. If the European Union already has a constitution, the question is what European politicians none the less expect, and whether it can and should be provided. If the European Union has had no constitution hitherto, it becomes needful to go into how European lawyers err, what the treaties are short of to be a constitution, and whether it can and should be added. That is the plan this study will follow.

Constitutional Position

A Concept and Function of a Constitution

When a constitution for Europe is talked about today, what is meant is a basic legal order for the polity of the sort that arose at the end of the eighteenth century in the wake of two successful revolutions in America and in France, which has since steadily spread and now come to apply almost worldwide.[2] Constitutions in this sense had not previously existed. The word was admittedly current, but it referred to something else. Taken over from the description of nature, it denoted in the legal and political language of the time the condition of a country, as marked by the features of the territory and its inhabitants, historical development and existing power relations, legal norms and political institutions. It was therefore not a normative but an empirical concept, into which norms entered merely as elements determining the position. Where the word or its equivalent taken from another language was used normatively, it instead meant particular enactments by the ruler, but specifically not a law concerning rule itself. To the extent that individual provisions of this nature occurred, they were rather termed agreements on government or *leges fundamentales*.

Political relations were by contrast marked by the very absence of what would today be understood by a constitution. The one-time binding of all rulers and all governing functions by unalterable divine law had had its basis taken away by the split in religion. The ensuing religious civil wars enforced other structures of governance. Firstly, the prince gradually concentrated all the powers of government, previously spread spatially and by type over numerous mutually independent bearers and mostly exercised as an adjunct to land ownership, into his own hands and concentrated them into a hitherto unknown public power. Secondly, he claimed the power, equally unknown to the Middle Ages, to impose on society a secular order independent of the disputed religious truth and enforce it through the newly acquired plenitude of power. That was the birth of the modern state, which raised itself above society, now conceived of as privatized, and saw its attribute in sovereignty, understood as supreme, irresistible power over society. It was at the same time the birth of positive law, i.e., law founded on human disposition rather than divine truth and always amendable.

Two essential prerequisites for a constitution in the modern sense of the word were now present.[3] First, there now existed a differentiated system functionally specialized in political rule and equipped with the appropriate machinery, and thus eligible, by contrast with mediaeval rule, to be the object of a specialized law to regulate rule. Second, questions of order that had hitherto found their timelessly valid answer in the divine plan for the world and therefore needed not decision but discovery became eligible for regulation. Nevertheless, the step to a constitution could not come about under these conditions, since the idea of a law prior to rule and establishing and limiting its powers would have denied the monarch's right to exist as primordially legitimated ruler independent of consensus, and nullified his historical function of overcoming civil war. Conditioned by this task, the state emerged instead as absolute, and absolute rule neither needs nor is accessible to constitutional regulation. Constitutional law is here confined essentially to laying down the ruler's omnipotence and regulating the dynastic succession.

The claim to absolute rule did not, however, manage anywhere to assert itself in full. The Estates' right to a say was kept in various forms, and the still-existing feudal order continued largely to prevent direct state action at the lowest level. Again, despite the ruler's claim to absoluteness, there were legal bindings that related to his political function and could not be unilaterally terminated, and in part could even be asserted judicially. As a general rule they were based on agreements, thus pointing to the existence of powerful social groups in control of services important to rule, able to wring concessions from the prince. In accordance with their genesis, however, these legal bindings applied only between the parties to the agreement, and this did not benefit all subjects equally. They concerned only individual components of the ruling power, thought of as comprehensive; not the whole of it. They certainly had no influence on the legitimation of monarchical rule. That was instead always assumed when such agreements on government were concluded, and was limited by individual legal provisions at implementing level only. They accordingly acted only to modify rule, not to establish it.

An alternative version to underived, unbounded rule was, however, being developed with increasing precision by contemporary natural-law theory. It saw the question of the justification of political rule in a new light, after the failure of the religious model of justification viable until the split in religion. To get an answer it imagined a fictitious state of nature without rule, where all were equally free. Rights to rule could in these circumstances be based only on agreement. The question accordingly arose of the conditions on which men endowed with reason would be prepared to give up the state of nature for the state of government. The impression left by the religious civil wars made the answer seem to lie in the exchange of individual freedom for the supreme good of safety of life and limb. Yet the better the absolute state did its job of pacifying society, the less plausible did its claim to absoluteness inevitably seem. In later natural law, accordingly, the view came to prevail that the justification of rule could lie only in assuring the natural freedom and equality of each individual that was not guaranteed in a state of no rule.

However much natural law thereby anticipated the content of later constitutions, it still did not itself make any constitution. Despite its name, it was not valid law but academic theory. It was not till the revolutionary break with British parliamentary absolutism in America and with monarchical absolutism in France that the way to putting theory into practice was opened. This break differed from the numerous violent overthrows in history thitherto by not stopping at a change of ruler or form of government, but aiming instead at a new basis for rule. Political rule was henceforth to be dependent on the consent of those subject to it and be obliged to protect their freedom internally and externally, while the various functional areas of society were left autonomous, to be merely protected and coordinated by the state; which needed public power for that too. The monopoly of force aimed at by absolutism was thus now perfected, but at the same time set on a new foundation. The bearer of state authority, the sovereign, was now the people, and its exercise admissible only on their behalf and for purposes they set.

By contrast with absolute rule, rule dependent on consensus and bound by objectives needs both institution and regulation. Before persons could be called on to rule, the representatives of the sovereign had accordingly to agree on the conditions of legitimate rule. But this sort of consent of society as to the content and form of its political unity does not as such stretch beyond the historical moment and the persons involved. Only law can confer general bindingness and lastingness on it. It was therefore a matter of course for the revolutionary leaders in America and France that the model of rule had to be given legal validity. Law was, however, since the age-long process of positivization, no longer a norm valid for all time, based on divine truth, to which the holders of governmental power were subject just like all other members of society. It instead itself constituted a product of state power, subject to change. Its ground of validity lay in the national will. The possibility of return to a suprapositive law founded on unchangeable truth had gone for ever. The question was then how state power could be legally bound if law was its own product.

This is the question that found its answer in the constitution. It lay in the splitting of positive law into two groups of norms, one on the institution and exercise of state power and the other on the conduct and relations of the individual. The two were not, however, unconnected. Instead, it is the former that regulates the production and application of the latter. Law thus becomes reflexive and thereby enhances its possibilities.[4] The state's production and implementation of law are in turn subject to legal binding. This is admittedly only possible if the two types of norms are hierarchically graded and assigned to different authors. The splitting of the legal order is thus preceded by a splitting of the public power into a *pouvoir constituant*, formed by the people as sovereign, and various *pouvoirs constitués* deriving their powers from it.[5] The norms in the first group have their origin in the sovereign and bind the state power. They necessarily take primacy over the norms in the second group enacted by that power and cannot be amended by the same procedure as these. Claims to rule and acts of rule instead deserve consideration only in so far as they are in harmony with the superordinate law.

For the higher-rank group of norms deriving from the people and directed at the state power, the term 'constitution' has become established. It differs from the older legal binding of political rule because it acts not to modify rule but to establish it, not particularly but universally, not here and there, but comprehensively. The claim to comprehensive validity must certainly not be confused with the total legalization of politics. Total legalization is neither desirable nor possible.[6] The task of politics consists in the production of a just social order in changing circumstances. With complete legal binding, this task could not be carried out. That would instead confine politics to the implementation of norms and thus ultimately reduce it to administration. A society so organized would render itself incapable of adaptation or even survival. The claim to comprehensive validity means only that no extra-constitutional holders or expressions of public power will be tolerated. By contrast, the constitution can regulate neither the input to the national policy-forming process nor its outcome definitively. It is a basic order confined to laying down the goals and framework for politics, and otherwise left open to be fleshed out politically.

The constitution is not tied down to particular contents. Yet some typical features follow from its function of legalizing rule. Constitutions usually lay down the legitimizing principle for political rule and the basic legitimacy conditions of its exercise. This is done in the so-called state structure or state objectives. Then, all constitutions contain provisions as to the institution and exercise of state power: organizational and procedural rules guaranteeing the handling of public power in conformity with principles and intended to avert abuses, usually adopting the rule of law and the separation of powers for the purpose. Again, the constitution regularly sets the limits to the state's power of coercion on the one hand and to individual freedom and social autonomy on the other. This is the object of the fundamental rights. The combination of all three elements is admittedly not conceptually necessary to a constitution. But a document not showing any desire for legal bindingness or excepting major bearers of governmental functions or expressions of public power from regulatory intervention would no longer be termed a constitution, but a case of semi- or spurious constitutionalism.

Though in nature a complex of legal norms, the constitution is not exhausted in its legal validity. On the basis of its legal effect, it is instead an important factor for social integration. By fixing a society's basic consensus as to the principles of its co-existence and the settlement of its disputes, it links holders of different convictions and interests, enables them to settle their differences peacefully and facilitates the acceptance of defeats. By separating lastingly valid principles of action from decisions necessary in the short term, it gives the political process a structure that agents and the public can take as a guide, guarantees stability in change and frees politics of continual debate over goals and procedures for forming a unity that would overstrain it given the standing need for and complex objects of decision. The constitution does all this not by itself, but by drawing on social prerequisites that it can itself no longer guarantee. But for what it does there is at present no equivalent. Without a constitution, the situations it was designed to overcome would come back again.

Constitutional Nature of the Treaties

On this basis the question of a European constitution can now be given a better answer. The problem here is the possibility to disconnect the constitution from the state. Historically, the former related to the latter, and derived its significance from the legalization of state power. While the European Union consists of states, it is not itself a state. For all the uncertainty over how to characterize it and what development it ought to have in future, that remains unquestioned. Yet this statement would constitute an answer to the constitutional question only if sovereign powers lay with the state alone. For the past, this is so. States could of course enter into international obligations or join international organizations. But international obligations or decisions by international organizations took on domestic validity only on the basis of a national transformation act. The establishment of the European Community has changed this. It has been endowed by the member states with sovereign rights, which it now exercises in place of them, but with the same effect, in particular with direct domestic effect. Though not itself a state, it wields sovereign powers such as traditionally only states had.

The sovereign powers the European Community exercises within the member states are, however, not governed by their constitutional law. Though the national constitutions regulate the conditions on which the member states may transfer sovereign rights to the Community, once they are transferred their exercise by the Community bodies is no longer subject to national law. Nor could it be otherwise. A supranational organization to which member states transferred sovereign powers for common exercise would fall apart again immediately if every member could subject exercise to its own special legal system. It admittedly remains a moot point whether domestic validity of Community legal acts falls under the – nationally verifiable – reservation that it stay within the limits of the treaty powers and not clash with supreme national constitutional principles.[7] But national constitutional law cannot claim to apply to the Community bodies. Both areas of law have their own sources and their own validity conditions. This does not mean they can never conflict. But in that case it is national law that in principle must give way, not Community law.

A question then arises that before creation of that unprecedented entity, the European Community, could not have, because of the congruency of state and rule. Does the need for legalization met by the constitution refer to the form of government, namely the state, or rather to the means of government, namely sovereign power? Once the question is put that way the answer is no longer hard to find. The state is bound by law because and in so far as it exercises public power. That power bears the danger and the potential for abuse that are supposed to be restrained by the national constitution. What needs legalization once the state's monopoly of power goes and it shares its authority with non-state bearers is, then, sovereign power, irrespective of whether it lies with the state or a suprastatal entity. If the historic achievement of the constitutional state, the legalization of rule, is to be maintained, then logically we also need legal binding of the public power wielded by the European Community as the branch of the European Union empowered for sovereign action. Otherwise, what would impend in the member states where European public power intervened would be partial absolutism.

To be sure, legal binding of the public power exercised by the European Community is not lacking. The Community, for lack of a pre-existing social substrate that could give it unity, exists only as a legal community. The law it is bound by in making its legal acts is what is known as primary Community law. It has its place in the treaties the member states have concluded, to establish and advance the Community. At present the version that applies is the one resulting from the Treaty of Maastricht. This law constitutes the Community, sets its objectives, establishes its institutions, assigns their powers and orders their procedures. These are all areas dealt with at national level in the constitution. The question is whether primary Community law can on that ground itself be called a constitution, as assumed by European legal scholars, or whether the specific form of legal binding of rule contained in a constitution remains restricted to the state. That is something a comparison between treaties and constitution has to show. Here the same features can be taken as a basis as already worked out for constitutions.

The object of the legal norms contained in the treaties is, as with member states' constitutions, public power. This is transferred by the treaties to the Community at the same time as they regulate it organizationally and in content within the Community. That too is done by way of a basic order, even though it contains more in some ways and less in others than national constitutions usually do. The treaties lack a catalogue of fundamental rights bringing the relations between the Community and the natural and legal persons subject to it under the guiding principles of freedom and equality. The position is in no way changed by the newly adopted but not further fleshed out avowal of respect for human rights and fundamental freedoms.[8] By contrast, they are much more exhaustive and detailed on objectives and organizational and procedural rules than national constitutions. Neither of these points, however, deprives the treaties of their character as a basic order. Fundamental rights are a usual but not indispensable component of constitutions, and the wealth of detail in no way changes the fact that the treaties form the basis and framework for the numerous acts through which the Community produces, applies or implements secondary law.

Primary Community law also claims comprehensive validity. Who may act bindingly for the Community and what conditions have to be complied with thereby is exhaustively regulated in the treaties. There is no European public power outside the treaties, and no manifestation that cannot be traced back to them. Compared with states, however, the powers reach less far. While states claim potential omnicompetence, here the principle of limited individual empowerment applies. The treaties thus do not have constitutions' totality of content; but on the other hand the national constitutions' totality shrinks in proportion to the transfer of sovereign powers to the Community, though admittedly without this being made explicit in the text, as with federal constitutions. Primary Community law also claims primacy over the legal acts enacted by the Community – secondary Community law. It lays down the conditions for the latter to have validity. Finally, the Community institutions have no power to alter the law they are subject to. Primary Community law can be amended only by the member states to which it owes its being, by treaty.[9]

Today, constitutions are certainly no longer usually brought in or amended by treaty. But in the nineteenth century treaty-based constitutions can be found, both with mergers of states and in cases of revolutionary pressure on the monarch, without his abandoning his pre-constitutional legitimation and recognizing popular sovereignty. Even in these cases, however, amending the constitution was a matter not for treaties but for decisions, even if several agencies had to be brought to agree. On the other hand, it is inherent in a constitution in the full sense of the term that it goes back to an act taken by or at least attributed to the people, in which they attribute political capacity to themselves. There is no such source for primary Community law. It goes back not to a European people but to the individual member states, and remains dependent on them even after its entry into force. While nations give themselves a constitution, the European Union is given a constitution by third parties. It consequently does not have the disposal of its own constitution. The 'masters of the treaties', as it is sometimes put, are still the member states, who have not been, as it were, absorbed into the Union.

This comparison enables the statement that the treaties have various functions in relation to the European Union's public power that domestically go to constitutions. To the extent that constitutions are concerned with legalizing political rule, the treaties leave nothing to be desired. Fundamental requirements of modern constitutionalism are thus met in the Community. This gives the justification for the position that European legal science has taken on the constitutional question. The treaties are not however a constitution in the full sense of the term.

The difference lies in the reference back to the will of the member states rather than to the people of the Union. Many European lawyers gloss over this.[10] The European public power is not one that derives from the people, but one mediated through states. Since the treaties thus have not an internal but an external reference point, they are also not the expression of a society's self-determination as to the form and objectives of its political unity. In so far as constitutions are concerned with the legitimation of rule by those subject to it, the treaties thus fall short. This gives the justification for the position that has dominated European political discourse on the constitutional question.

This intermediate status is also reflected in the shape of the basic order. Institutionally, the European Union does not follow the state model, but has developed a pattern of its own, marked by its supra-nationality. The guiding, rule-giving body is the Council, made up of member-state government representatives. The most important Community decisions thus lie in the hands of agents who have their reference point, as far as legitimation and responsibility go, not in the Union but in the member states. The Community interest finds its organizational locus by contrast primarily in the Commission. From it comes the initiative for Council decisions; it sees to their execution and can, if need be with help from the European Court of Justice, assert Community law against the member states. Community interests are also represented by the European Parliament now that its deputies are no longer from national parliaments but directly elected by Union citizens. Yet it does not, as in member states, form the centre of democratic mediation, but remains, even after its advance from a merely consultative to a co-decisional role, essentially restricted to veto rights.

This institutional arrangement is increasingly criticized because it can no longer meet the democracy requirement of the stage of integration now reached. In fact the Community could at the beginning live well enough on the national democracies. Not only was the Council, the central decisional body, made up of representatives of member-state governments, but more, its mode of decision was unanimity and the volume of decisions comparatively slight. Today decisions have grown considerably in both number and areas. Moreover, because of the increased volume, the Council has delegated a number of deciding powers to the Commission, and for the decisions it reserves to itself it no longer as a rule requires unanimity. But this opens up a democracy gap: the democracy principle is valid for the member states, whose own capacities for decision are, however, dwindling; decisional powers are accruing to the European Community, but the principle of democracy is only weakly developed there. This leads to a growing need for democratic legitimation of its own for European policy, not derived from member-state governments.

A remedy is mostly sought in the parliament, which as an elected representative body enjoys direct democratic legitimation, but has little influence. It should be given the powers peoples' representative bodies usually have: legislation, establishing the budget, forming and checking on government. This sort of extension of powers of course affects the other institutions, especially the Council. On these conceptions it changes into a chamber of nations to the parliament, while the Commission moves up to government.[11] Here the state model is obviously the inspiration, and in that case it would certainly seem appropriate to clothe it in constitutional garb. This would do more than just take account of the demand, widespread since Maastricht, for a more transparent and comprehensible basic order for the European Union. A constitution that added the missing elements to the treaties would additionally relate the Union to the people and thus close that legitimation gap. Here, though, the European Union's capacity for democracy is mostly tacitly assumed. It is, however, thoroughly questionable whether adopting the state pattern would have the desired democratic effect. The answer to the constitutional question depends on this too.

Conditions for European Democracy

Democracies are characterized by having political rule in them legitimated not transcendentally, traditionally or through élites, but consensually. State power derives from the people and is exercised on their behalf by special agencies in turn answerable before the people for that exercise. The people are certainly not some community whose unity and will are pre-given, just needing to be given expression through the state bodies. They are instead permeated by divergences of opinion and interests, out of which negotiation or majority decision in the political process must first create unity, which can of course change. The key problem of this sort of system, in which possession and exercise of state power are separated, is mediation between people and institutions, and the biggest danger comes from the latter's tendency to become independent.[12] The constitutional solution to this problem lay in periodic election of a representative body in which the various social positions were present and strove for compromise, to be embodied in laws by which in turn the state's executive was bound. On top of this came the constitutional guarantee of free communication, without which the elections could not work.

Democracy ought not, however, to be equated with parliamentarianism. Admittedly, it is hard to conceive of democracy in large states with a continual need for decisions without a freely elected parliament. But the parliamentary process does not by itself guarantee democratic structures. On the one hand, voters' individual preferences are no longer adequately expressed in the highly generalized electoral option between vaguely defined parties. The individual is instead thrown back on additional organizations and channels of influence in order to assert his or her views and interests. On the other hand, a party-recruited parliament cannot adequately reflect and process the multiplicity of social views and interests. The parliamentary process instead builds on a social process of interest mediation and conflict control that partly eases the burden on parliamentary decision and partly patterns it. The links between the individual, social associations and the state bodies are maintained chiefly by the communications media, which create the public needed for any general opinion-forming and democratic participation at all.[13]

It is accordingly a 'statist shortcut'[14] to assume that the mediation of opinion and interests, policy formation and decision-making, stability and legitimacy-guaranteeing, that produces social cohesion is brought about by the state organs alone. These are instead dependent on the manifold mediatory structures within society which, while they relate to the state institutions, are neither guaranteed by them nor can be replaced by them. This is why the success of democratic constitutions depends not just on the intrinsic excellence of their regulations, but equally on the external conditions for their effectiveness. This also applies to the central institution of democratic states, the parliament. The democratic nature of a political system is attested not so much by the existence of elected parliaments, which is today guaranteed almost everywhere, as by the pluralism, internal representativity, freedom and capacity for compromise of the intermediate area of parties, associations, citizens' movements and communications media. Where a parliament does not rest on such a structure, which guarantees constant interaction between people and state, democratic substance is lacking even if democratic forms are present.

It is well known that the mediation process essential to democracy is not running satisfactorily even at nation-state level, partly because of the growing self-absorption of the political parties, partly because of asymmetries in interest representation, partly because of deficits in communication systems, which are often oriented more to economic imperatives than to opinion formation. At European level, though, even the prerequisites are largely lacking. Mediatory structures have hardly even been formed here yet. There is no Europeanized party system, just European groups in the Strasbourg parliament, and, apart from that, loose cooperation among programmatically related parties. This does not bring any integration of the European population, even at the moment of European elections. Nor have European associations or citizens' movements arisen, even though cooperation among national associations is further advanced than with parties. A search for European media, whether in print or broadcast, would be completely fruitless. This makes the European Union fall far short not just of ideal conceptions of a model democracy but even of the already deficient situation in member states.[15]

The prerequisites cannot simply be created. It can admittedly be expected that advancing parliamentarization of the European Union would also enhance the pressure to Europeanize the party system. A similar development could be expected with interest groups. It can certainly be assumed that there would be Europeanization at the level of leaderships and officials, while the levels of membership, because of lesser communicatory competences, would continue to be defined nationally. The distance between élite and rank and file, which in view of the professionalization of politics is already a problem for democracy nationally, would accordingly increase still further in a European context. In addition, the degree of emergent oligarchy would depend on party positions. Parties representing lower-class interests would suffer from even greater internal distance here than those tending to represent higher strata, and a similar gap could be expected between associations representing the interests of mass memberships and of anonymous enterprises. New social movements and especially ad hoc initiatives, which are taking on growing weight at national level, would by contrast be largely barred from the European level.

Prospects for Europeanization of the communications system are absolutely non-existent. A Europeanized communications system ought not to be confused with increased reporting on European topics in national media. These are directed at a national public and remain attached to national viewpoints and communication habits. They can accordingly not create any European public nor establish any European discourse. Europeanization in the communications sector would by contrast mean that there would be newspapers and periodicals, radio and television programmes, offered and demanded on a European market and thus creating a nation-transcending communicative context. But such a market would presuppose a public with language skills enabling it to utilize European media. That would be the case either if every journalist could use his own language and still be sure of being generally understood, or else – more realistically – if some European lingua franca alongside the mother tongues, like Latin of old though not confined to the educated stratum, could become established.[16] The European Union is still a very long way away from that.

Here, then, is the biggest obstacle to Europeanization of the political substructure, on which the functioning of a democratic system and the performance of a parliament depends: language.[17] Communication is bound up with language and linguistically mediated experience and interpretation of the world. Information and participation as basic conditions of democratic existence are mediated through language. In the European Union there are now eleven languages, none of which covers a majority of the population. Even English and French are each foreign languages to over 80 per cent of the Union population. Even though these two languages predominate in the Community institutions and foreign-language competence in the younger generation is increasing, this does not change the fact that the large majority of Community citizens can communicate only in their own mother tongue, and thus remain cut off from direct understanding or communication in any Europe-wide communication.[18] This is not just a private loss. They are instead 'participatively restricted' and therefore disadvantaged in the European opinion-forming and interest-mediation process, which suffers much more than any national one from remoteness from its base.

The importance of the language factor for the possibility of European democracy is often underestimated, partly because a democracy concept confined to the area of organized opinion-formation predominates, so that the language skills of the functional élites, or even a large-scale translation system, are taken as sufficient; partly because of a failure to perceive the dependency of democracy on communication opportunity.[19] Pointing to multilingual states like Switzerland, Belgium or Finland, or multinational countries of immigration like the US, does not refute this. The European countries named have between five and ten million inhabitants with two or three languages; the European Union 370 million with eleven languages. The difference is not merely quantitative. It is certainly more important that a country like Switzerland had formed a national identity well before constitutionalization and relates its multilingual political discourse to it. The US, with some 250 million inhabitants, certainly comes close to the European Union and similarly brings together people of many nationalities. By contrast with Europe, these have, however, abandoned their nation-state-based cohesion and accepted a new political homeland with a majority language and country-wide communications.

By contrast, the absence of a European communication system, due chiefly to language diversity, has the consequence that for the foreseeable future there will be neither a European public nor a European political discourse. Public discourse instead remains for the time being bound by national frontiers, while the European sphere will remain dominated by professional and interest discourses conducted remotely from the public. European decisional processes are accordingly not under public observation in the same way as national ones. The European level of politics lacks a matching public. The feedback to European officials and representatives is therefore only weakly developed, while national politicians orient themselves even in the case of Council decisions to their national publics, because effective sanctions can come only from them. These circumstances give professional and technical viewpoints, particularly of an economic nature, excessive weight in European politics, while the social consequences and side-effects remain in the dark. This shortcoming cannot be made up for even by growing national attention to European policy themes, since the European dimension is just what is lacking there.

If this is true, the conclusion may be drawn that full parliamentarization of the European Union on the model of the national constitutional state will aggravate rather than solve the problem.[20] On the one hand it would loosen the Union's ties back to the member states, since the European Parliament is by its construction not a federal organ but a central one. Strengthening it would be at the expense of the Council and therefore inevitably have centralizing effects. On the other hand, the weakened ties back to member states would not be compensated by any increased ties back to the Union population. The European Parliament does not meet with any European mediatory structure in being; still less does it constitute a European popular representative body,[21] since there is as yet no European people. This is not an argument against any expansion of parliament's powers. That might even enhance participation opportunities in the Union, provide greater transparency and create a counterweight to the dominance of technical and economic viewpoints. Its objective ought not, however, to be full parliamentarization on the national model, since political decisions would otherwise move away to where they can be only inadequately democratically accountable.

The suspicion that this assessment is a front for the idea that democracy is possible only on the basis of a homogeneous *Volksgemeinschaft* [ethnic community] is, after all that, baseless. The requirements for democracy are here developed not out of the people, but out of the society that wants to constitute itself as a political unit. It is true that this requires a collective identity, if it wants to settle its conflicts without violence, accept majority rule and practise solidarity. But this identity need by no means be rooted in ethnic origin, but may also have other bases. All that is necessary is for the society to have formed an awareness of belonging together that can support majority decisions and solidarity efforts,[22] and for it to have the capacity to communicate about its goals and problems discursively. What obstructs democracy is accordingly not the lack of cohesion of Union citizens as a people, but their weakly developed collective identity and low capacity for transnational discourse. This certainly means that the European democracy deficit is structurally determined. It can therefore not be removed by institutional reforms in any short term. The achievement of the democratic constitutional state can for the time being be adequately realized only in the national framework.

Constitutional Illusions

Converting the European Union into a federal state can in these circumstances not be an immediately desirable goal. The reason is, to be sure, not that the political form of the nation-state ought to be preserved for its own sake. The entitlement of political units to exist cannot be assessed without considering what problems they are expected to solve. In this respect the nation-state, understood as a political unit that regulates its internal affairs autonomously, is something whose time is past. A large part of the problems needing political treatment can no longer be effectively solved in the narrow state framework of the European countries. This finding creates the pressure for supranational integration. If this is none the less not to be pushed as far as a European state, that is because it could not meet the democratic requirements of the present. Its level of legitimation would be lower than a nation-state's, also lessening its capacity to solve problems, something that has not just technical but also legitimatory prerequisites. The need is instead to retain the European Union in its special nature as a supranational arrangement, and to build on this special nature; not to copy national patterns.

This also provides the answer to the constitutional question. As long as the call for a constitution has to do only with the constitutional form of the existing legal bases of the European Union, to make its goals and structures more transparent for Union citizens, then this can be accomplished by separating the treaty elements that in a nation-state are typically in the constitution from the numerous detailed regulations that have crept into the treaties alongside them. The 'core treaty' so formed would thus resemble a constitution in external form. Yet there would be no accompanying internal transformation of its character as a treaty, still less would the other treaty elements stop being part of primary Community law. Nor does anything else apply to the extent that the call for a constitution merely conceals one for institutional reforms to the Union. Institutional reforms, which might be necessary because the umpteenth enlargement of the European Union threatens to strain organizational structure and decisional procedures to the limits of their capacity, can be done by amending the treaties, without having to turn them into a constitution on the national pattern.

However, to the extent that the call 'from treaty to constitution' is aimed at adding to the treaties those elements that still separate them from a constitution in the full sense of the term, this would end up turning the European Union into a state. Not everybody who today, because of the emotional value of a constitution or in the interests of democracy, calls for a European constitution is quite clear about this. The missing elements, after all, have to do with the popular legitimation of the legal act constituting the Union, and the associated self-determination of Union citizens as to the form and content of their political unity. But this would alter the legitimating basis of the European Union. No longer would it be the member states that would determine the form and development of the Union, in the forms of democratic policy formation provided for by their own constitutions. The basic decisions would instead be taken by the people of the Union or in their name. They would be the Union's constitutional legislators. This would be true even if the member states were still involved in producing and amending the constitution. They would have their part no longer as 'masters of the treaties', but as an organ of the self-determining Union, comparable with the German Bundesrat.

That would simultaneously mean abandoning constitutive elements of the present basic order. The principle of limited individual empowerment of the Community by the member states would break down. Even if, as in the German federalist constitution, the Community were still to have only the powers explicitly conveyed to it, while the presumption of competence lay with member states, this would not change the fact that this distribution of powers would be the decision of the Union's constitutional legislators or the Union agencies empowered by them, no longer the member states. Consequently, it could be amended independently of their unanimous will. With a constitution in the full sense of the term, the Union would acquire *Kompetenzkompetenz* (the competence to decide about competences). Similarly, the primacy of Community law over national law would no longer be the consequence of the member states' order issued in the treaties, but of the constitutional precept in the Community constitution. The Community would in principle also have the power in the constitution to decide itself on its endowment with resources, including taxation, instead of being dependent on transfers from member states. These features are not those of an association of states. They typify the state.

Since this state would not, however, have the mediatory structures from which the democratic process lives, the Community would after its full constitutionalization be a largely self-supporting institution, farther from its base than ever. To be sure, there is no one-sided dependency relationship between social structures and political institutions. Institutional advances can also push social developments. But in present circumstances long periods of development have to be budgeted for. The institutional advance must on no account be over-extended. This is particularly true of the constitution. The legal foundation that fits an association of states is the treaty. It has all the features that allow legal binding of Community power, yet leaves the basic decisions about the Community with member states, where they can be democratically checked and accounted for. A European constitution would not be able to bridge the existing gap and would consequently disappoint the expectations associated with it. The legitimation it would mediate would be a fictitious one. Accordingly, when it comes down to it constitutions are still something to do with states, and anyone calling for one for Europe should be aware what movement he is thereby setting going.

1995
Translated by Iain L. Fraser

Notes

1. The European Court of Justice's importance for integration is frequently under-estimated. But it is just the times of political stagnation that have been those of most intensive judicial integration.

2. See Dieter Grimm, 'Verfassung', in *Staatslexicon*, Volume 7, 2nd edn, Frankfurt 1994, column 633, and *Die Zukunft der Verfassung*, 2nd edn, Frankfurt 1994, p. 11; also Ulrich Preuß, ed., *Zum Begriff der Verfassung*, Frankfurt 1994.

3. See D. Grimm, 'Enstehungs- und Wirkungsbedingungen des modernen Konstitutionalismus', in D. Simon, ed., *Akten des 26. Deutschen Rechtshistorikertages*, Frankfurt 1987.

4. See N. Luhmann, *Rechtssoziologie*, Volume 2, Reinbek 1972, pp. 213ff.

5. See E. Sieyès, *Qu'est-ce que le Tiers-Etat?*, ed. R. Zapperi, Geneva 1970; W. Zweig, *Die Lehre vom Pouvoir constitutant*, Tübingen 1909; K. Loewenstein, *Volk und Parlament nach der Staatstheorie der französichen Nationalversammlung von 1789*, Munich 1922; E.-W. Böckenforde, *Die Verfassungsgebende Gewalt des Volkes – ein Grenzbegriff des Verfassungsrechts*, Frankfurt 1986.

6. See N. Luhmann, *Das Recht der Gesellschaft*, Frankfurt 1993, pp. 407ff.; D. Grimm, 'Politik und Recht', in *Festschrift von Benda*, Heidelberg 1995, p. 91.

7. See the – not uncontroversial – position in the German Constitutional Court's Maastricht judgment.

8. Though the European Court of Justice has leapt into the breach and, on the basis of member-state constitutions and the European Court of Human Rights, developed a Community standard of fundamental rights against which it measures EC legal acts.

9. The institution of a European jurisdiction is therefore seen as the most striking difference between Community law and classical international law, as well as the reason why the treaties, despite their international-law origin, can act as a constitution.

10. They operate – mostly without taking account of constitutional theory – with a reduced concept of constitution. See, as an example of such nonchalant treatment of the

concept of constitution, Roland Bieber, 'Verfassungsentwicklung und Verfassungsgebung in der Europäischen Gemeinschaft', in R. Wildenmann, ed., *Staatswerdung Europas?*, Baden-Baden 1991.

11. Views taken particularly far by the European Constitution Working Group in the proposals presented under the aegis of the Bertelsmann Foundation. See European Constitution Working Group, *Die Zukunft Europas – Kultur und Verfassung des Kontinents*, Gütersloh 1991, pp. 20ff.; W. Weidenfeld, ed., *Wie Europa verfaßt sein soll – Materialien zur politischen Union*, Gütersloh 1991, pp. 11ff. Less radical is W. Weidenfeld, ed., *Europa '96. Reformprogramm für die Europäische Union*, Gütersloh 1994, pp. 32ff. Not so fixed on the state model are the draft constitutions by F. Cromme, *Verfassungsvertrag der Gemeinschaft der Vereinigten Europäischen Staaten*, Delmenhorst 1987, and the European Constitutional Group, *A Proposal for a European Constitution*, 1993, as well as – not worked out – B. Wieland, 'Verfassungspolitische Probleme der Staatswerdung Europas', in R. Wildenmann, ed., *Staatswerdung Europas?*, Baden-Baden 1991, pp. 451ff.; B. Wieland, *Ein Markt – zwölf Regierungen? Zur Organizationen der Macht in der europäischen Verfassung*, Baden-Baden 1992, pp. 175ff.

12. See D. Grimm, 'Politische Parteien', in *Handbuch des Verfassungsrechts*, 2nd edn, Berlin 1994, p. 599, paras 6ff.

13. See, for example, J. Habermas, *Faktizität und Geltung*, Frankfurt 1992 (trans. as *Between Facts and Norms: Contributions to a Discourse Theory of Law and Democracy*, Cambridge, MA 1996), esp. chapter 8.

14. M.R. Lepsius, 'Nationalstaat oder Nationalitätenstaat als Modell für Weiterentwicklung der Europäischen Gemeinschaft', in R. Wildenmann, ed., *Staatswerdung Europas?* , Baden-Baden 1991, p. 25; M.R. Lepsius, *Demokratie in Deutschland*, Göttingen 1993, p. 271.

15. This is why the suggestion that I play off idealized models against deficient realities, in the tradition of Carl Schmitt's critique of parliamentarianism, is unfounded.

16. See Ernest Gellner, 'Sprachregion, Mehrsprachigkeit, Lingua Franca, Konzepte für ein europäisches Fernsehen', *Medium*, vol. 1, 1989, p. 19.

17. See Lepsius, 'Nationalstaat oder Nationalitätenstaat', pp. 27ff., and 'Die Europäische Gemeinschaft und die Zukunft des Nationalstaats', in Lepsius, *Demokratie in Deutschland*, p. 255; F. Coulmas, ed., *A Language Policy for the European Community*, Berlin 1991; Habermas, *Faktizität und Geltung*, p. 372. Ultimately it is the 'linguistic bond' that keeps any communicative community together.

18. In a test of knowledge of English, while 28 per cent of the Dutch and 15 per cent of Danes had a good knowledge of the language, only 3 per cent of French and Spaniards and 1 per cent of Italians had. See Große Peclum, 'Gibt es den Europäischen Zuschauer', *Zeitschrift für Kulturaustauch*, vol. 40, 1990, p. 193.

19. The question has been more intensively – and very defensively – gone into recently, mostly in response to my essay 'The Lack of European Democracy', *Der Spiegel*, 19 October 1992, p. 57.

20. This assessment is shared by, among others, Lepsius, 'Europäische Gemeinschaft' and 'Nationalstaat'; F.W. Scharpf, *Optionen des Föderalismus in Deutschland und Europa*, Frankfurt 1994; P. Badura, *Der Bundesstaat Deutschland im Prozeß der europäischen Integration*, Saarbrücken 1994; J.H.H. Weiler, 'The Transformation of Europe', *Law Journal*, vol. 100, 1991, and 'Problems of Legitimacy in Post 1992 Europe', *Aussenwirtschaft (Schweizerische Zeitschrift für internationale Wirtschaftsbeziehungen)* vol. 46, 1991.

21. See P. Kirchhof, *Handbuch des Staatsrechts*, Volume 7, Heidelberg 1992, pp. 855, 880. The parliament can accordingly not be made by reforms into a 'genuine representation of the European electorate or of the people'.

22. See, among others, David Marquand, 'Integration, Disintegration and Citizenship in New Europe', in B. Schäfers, ed., *Lebensverhältnisse und soziale Konflikte im neuen Europa*, *Verhandlungen des 26. Deutschen Soziologentages*, Frankfurt 1993.

17

Reply to Grimm

Jürgen Habermas

I basically agree with Dieter Grimm's diagnosis; however, an analysis of its presuppositions leads me to a different political conclusion.

The Diagnosis

From a constitutional perspective, one may discern a contradiction in the European Union's present situation. On the one hand, the EU is a supranational organization established by international treaties and without a constitution of its own. In this respect it is not a state (in the modern sense of a constitutional state characterized by a monopoly on violence and a domestically and internationally recognized sovereignty). On the other hand, Community institutions create European law that binds the member states – thus the EU exercises a supreme authority previously claimed only by individual states. From this results the oft-bemoaned democratic deficit. Commission and Council pronouncements, as well as decisions by the European Court, are intervening ever more profoundly in the member states' internal affairs. Within the framework of the rights conferred upon the Union, the European executive may enforce its pronouncements over and against the opposition of the national governments. At the same time, as long as the European Parliament is equipped with only weak competences, these pronouncements and enactments lack direct democratic legitimation. The executive institutions of the Community derive their legitimacy from that of the member governments. They are not institutions of a state that is itself constituted by the act of will on the part of the united citizens of Europe. The European passport is not as yet associated with rights constitutive for democratic citizenship.

Political Conclusion

In contrast to the federalists, who recommend a democratic pattern for the EU, Grimm warns against any further European-law-induced eroding of national competences. The democratic deficit would not be effectively filled by a 'statist shortcut' to the problem, but rather deepened. New political institutions such as a European Parliament with the usual powers, a government formed out of the Commission, a second chamber replacing the Council, and a European Court of Justice with expanded competences, as such offer no solutions. If they are not filled with life, they will instead accelerate tendencies already apparent within the national frameworks, tendencies towards autonomization of bureaucratized politics. The real prerequisites for a Europe-wide integration of citizen will-formation have been absent up to now. Constitutional Euroscepticism thus amounts to the empirically based argument that runs as follows: as long as there is not a European people which is sufficiently 'homogenous' to form a democratic will, there should be no constitution.

The Discussion

My reflections are directed against (a) the insufficient account of alternative courses and (b) the not entirely unambiguous normative underpinnings of the functional requirements for democratic will-formation.

(a) Grimm sets before us the undesired consequences that would result from the transition of the European Community to a democratically constituted, federal state should the new institutions not take root. So long as a European networked civil society, a Europe-wide political public sphere and a common political culture are lacking, the supranational decision processes would become increasingly independent of the still nationally organized opinion- and will-formation processes. This dangerous prognosis is plausible as far as I am concerned. However what is the alternative?

Grimm's option seems to suggest that the constitutional status quo can at least freeze the extant democratic deficit. Completely independent of constitutional innovations, however, this deficit expands day by day because the economic and social dynamics even within the existing institutional framework perpetuate the erosion of national powers through European law. As Grimm himself acknowledges: 'The democracy principle is valid for the member states, whose own capacities for decision are, however, dwindling; decisional powers are accruing to the European Community, but the principle of democracy is only weakly developed there.' But if the gap is steadily widening between the European authorities' expanding scope and the inadequate legitimation of the proliferating European regulations, then decisively adhering to an exclusively nation-state mode of legitimation does not necessarily mean opting for the lesser evil. The federalists at least face the foreseeable – and perhaps avoidable – risk of the autonomization of supranational organizations as a challenge. The Euro-sceptics have, from the start, acquiesced in the supposedly irresistible erosion of democratic substance so that they do not have to leave what appears as the reliable shelter of the nation-state.

In fact the shelter is becoming less and less comfortable. The debates on national economic competitiveness and the international division of labour in which we are engaged make us aware of quite another gap – a gap between the nation-state's increasingly limited manoeuvrability, and the imperatives of modes of production interwoven worldwide. Modern revenue-states profit from their respective economies only so long as there are 'national economies' that can still be influenced by political means. With the denationalization of the economy, especially of the financial markets and of industrial production itself, national governments today are increasingly compelled to accept permanently high unemployment and the marginalization of a growing minority for the sake of international competitiveness. If there is to be at least some substantive maintaining of the welfare state and some avoiding the further segmentation of an underclass, then institutions capable of acting supranationally must be formed. Only regionally comprehensive regimes like the European Community can still affect the global system in line with a coordinated world domestic policy.

In Grimm's account, the EU appears as an institution to be *put up with*, and with whose abstractions we must live. The reasons why we should *want* it politically are not presented. I would submit that the greater danger is posed by the autonomization of globalized networks and markets which simultaneously contribute to the fragmentation of public consciousness. If these systemic pressures are not met by politically capable institutions, the crippling fatalism of the old empires will grow again in the midst of a highly mobile economic modernity. The decisive elements of this future scenario would be the post-industrial misery of the 'surplus' population produced by the surplus society – the Third World within the First – and an accompanying moral erosion of community. *This* future-present would in retrospect view itself as the future of a past illusion – the democratic illusion according to which societies could still determine their own destinies through political will and consciousness.

(b) *A propos* the second problem. Naturally any assessment of the chances for a Europe-wide democracy depends in the first place upon empirically grounded arguments. But we first have to determine the functional requirements; and for that the normative perspective in which the former are supposed to fit is crucial.

Grimm rejects a European constitution 'because there is as yet no European people'. This would on first glance seem founded upon the same premiss that informed the tenor of the German Constitutional Court's Maastricht judgment: namely, the view that the basis of the state's democratic legitimation requires a certain homogeneity of the state-constituting people. However, Grimm immediately distances himself from a Schmittian kind of definition of *völkischen* homogeneity: 'The requirements for democracy are here developed not out of the people, but out of the society that wants to constitute itself as a political unit. It is true that this requires a collective identity, if it wants to settle its conflicts without violence, accept majority rule and practise solidarity.' This formulation leaves open the question of how the called-for collective identity is to be understood. I see the nub of republicanism in the fact that the forms and procedures of the constitutional state together with the democratic mode of legitimation simultaneously forge a new level of social integration. Democratic citizenship establishes an abstract, legally mediated solidarity among strangers. This form of social integration which first emerges with the nation-state is realized in the form of a politically socializing communicative context. Indeed, it is dependent upon the satisfaction of certain important functional requirements that cannot be fulfilled by administrative means. To these belong conditions in which an ethical-political self-understanding of citizens can communicatively develop and likewise be reproduced – but in no way a collective identity that is independent of the democratic process itself and as such existing prior to that process. What unites a nation of citizens as opposed to a *Volksnation* is not some primordial substrate but rather an intersubjectively shared context of possible understanding.

It is therefore crucial in this context whether one uses the term 'people' in the juristically neutral sense of 'state-constituting people', or whether one associates the term with notions of identity of some other kind. In Grimm's view the identity of a nation of citizens 'need not' be 'rooted in ethnic origin, but may also have other bases'. I think on the contrary that it *must* have another basis if the democratic process is finally to guarantee the social integration of a differentiated – and today increasingly differentiating – society. This burden must not be shifted from the levels of political will-formation to pre-political, pre-supposed substrates because the constitutional state guarantees that it will foster necessary social integration in the legally abstract form of political participation and that it will actually secure the status of citizenship in democratic ways. The examples of culturally and ideologically pluralistic societies serve only to emphasize this normative point. The multicultural self-understanding of the nations of citizens formed in classical countries of immigration like the USA is more instructive in this respect than that derived from the assimilationist French model. If in the same democratic political community various cultural, religious and ethnic ways of life are to exist among and with each other, the majority culture must be sufficiently detached from its traditional fusion with the *political* culture shared by all citizens.

To be sure, a politically constituted context of solidarity among citizens who, despite remaining strangers to one another, are supposed to stand up for each other is a communicative context rich in prerequisites. On this point there is no dissent. The core is formed by a political public sphere which enables citizens to take positions at the same time on the same topics of the same relevance. This public sphere must not be deformed through either external or internal coercion. It must be embedded in the context of a freedom-valuing political culture and be supported by a liberal associational structure of a civil society. Socially relevant experience from still-intact private spheres must flow into such a civil society so that they may be processed there for public treatment. The political parties – not state-dependent – must remain rooted in this complex so as to mediate between the spheres of informal public communication, on the one hand, and the institutionalized deliberation and decision processes, on the other. Accordingly, from a normative perspective, there can be no European federal state worthy of the name of a democratic Europe unless a Europe-wide, integrated public sphere develops in the ambit of a common political culture: a civil society with interest associations; non-governmental organizations; citizens' movements, etc.; and naturally a party system appropriate to a European arena. In short, this entails public communication that transcends the boundaries of the until now limited national public spheres.

Certainly, the ambitious functional requirements of democratic will-formation can scarcely be fulfilled in the nation-state framework; this is all the more true for Europe. What concerns me, however, is the perspective from which these functional prerequisites are normatively justified; for this, as it were, prejudices the empirical evaluation of the present difficulties. These must, for the time being, seem insuperable if a pre-political collective identity is regarded as necessary, that is an independent cultural substrate which is articulated only in the fulfilment of the said functional requirements. But a communications–theoretical understanding of democracy, one that Grimm also seems to favour, can no longer rest upon such a concretistic understanding of 'the people'.

This notion falsely pretends homogeneity, whereas in fact something still quite heterogeneous is met.

The ethical–political self-understanding of citizens in a democratic community must not be taken as a historical–cultural *a priori* that makes democratic will-formation possible, but rather as the flowing contents of a circulatory process that is generated through the legal institutionalization of citizens' communication. This is precisely how national identities were formed in modern Europe. Therefore it is to be expected that the political institutions to be created by a European constitution would have an inducing effect. Europe has been integrating economically, socially and administratively for some time and in addition can base itself on a common cultural background and the shared historical experience of having happily overcome nationalism. Given the political will, there is no a priori reason why it cannot subsequently create the politically necessary communicative context as soon as it is constitutionally prepared to do so. Even the requirement of a common language – English as 'a second first language' – ought not be an insurmountable obstacle with the existing level of formal schooling. European identity can in any case mean nothing other than unity in national diversity; and perhaps German federalism, as it developed after Prussia was shattered and the confessional division overcome, might not be the worst model.

1995
Translated by Iain L. Fraser and John P. McCormick

18

Does Europe Need a Constitution? Reflections on Demos, Telos and Ethos in the German Maastricht Decision

J.H.H. Weiler

There is a short answer to this question: no. After all, is not Europe already part of a Constitutional Legal Order? Have we not heard (and written) endlessly about Supremacy, Direct Effect, Implied Power, Constitutional Adjudication and all other artefacts of a constitutional rather than, say, an international legal order? Has not the European Court referred to the Treaties as the 'Constitutional Charter of the Community and Union'?

And yet, if one explores beyond the repetitive description of these formal categories and searches for a theoretical and prescriptive (normative) underpinning of European constitutionalism – a justification for, say, the supremacy of Community law – one comes up with little, usually a barely concealed variant of the internationalist's *pacta sunt servanda* and the need to ensure the uniformity of Treaty obligations and rights among and within the various High Contracting Parties. But for this justification one does not have to go beyond the Vienna Convention on the Law of Treaties. This is somewhat embarrassing given the orthodoxies of European constitutionalism, a centrepiece of which is its claim to constitute a new legal order which has cut its umbilical cord from international law. More critically, given the massive transfer of competences to the Union, the unprecedented empowerment of Community institutions (and through them, indirectly, of the executive branch of the member states at the expense of, say, national parliaments) and the consequent creation of considerable democratic deficiencies in central aspects of European public life, the internationalist's construct provides a poor legitimation for this new architecture of power.

When Moses came down from Mount Sinai with his constitutional covenant and offered it to the people, they said, All that the Eternal hath spoken we will do, and hearken (Exodus XXIV:7). Very imprudent, we might think, to accept to do before you hearken. To accept a constitution without a constitutional debate. Over the last three decades or so, European public authorities – governments, legislatures, courts (!) – have, too, accepted to do (what comes out of the Union and its institutions as the supreme law of the land) with remarkably little hearkening. The condition of Europe on this reading is not, as is often implied, that of constitutionalism without a constitution, but of a constitution without constitutionalism. What Europe needs, therefore, is not a constitution but an ethos and telos to justify, if they can, the constitutionalism it has already embraced.

In this essay I wish to make a small contribution to one aspect of the constitutional debate which is finally taking place.

Let us return to the issue of supremacy. By what authority, if any – understood in the vocabulary of normative political theory – can the claim of European law to be both constitutionally superior and with immediate effect in the polity be sustained? Who is the constituent power? Why should the subjects of European law in the Union – individuals, courts, governments, et cetera – feel bound to observe the law of the Union as higher law, in the same way that their counterparts in, say, the USA are bound to and by American federal law? It is a dramatic question, since constitutionalization has formally taken place and to give a negative answer would be very subversive. This is partly why the critique of European Union constitutional democracy is often contradictory. One can, it seems, proclaim a profound democracy deficit and yet insist at the same time on the importance of accepting the supremacy of Union law. It is a dramatic question too, since it affects membership, citizenship and nationality and, thus, seems to bring European constitutionalism into direct conflict with the constitutionalism of its member states. To whom is primary allegiance owed? By whom is it owed?

I shall try and give some answers to these questions by an examination of the 'Maastricht decision' of the Bundesverfassungsgericht, the German Constitutional Court. The decision has been, naturally, the subject of extensive commentary, and is so well known as to obviate description. Despite its formal 'approval' of the Treaty, clearing the way for German ratification, and, indeed, the coming into force of Maastricht, the decision is mostly noted for the trenchant and at times defiant positions adopted by the Court *vis-à-vis* some of the hallowed constitutional precepts and doctrines articulated by the European Court of Justice, such as judicial *Kompetenz-Kompetenz*, i.e. which court has ultimate authority to pronounce on the limits to Community competences,[1] withdrawal from the Community and Union and the like. Naturally, there has been no dearth of critical comment, on these issues and others, mostly written by German constitutional scholars.

I wish to add an 'outsider's' view to this on-going critical reflection. The specific doctrinal points are of lesser interest to me. I will, instead, focus on the constitutional *Weltanschauung* of the German Constitutional Court as reflected in this decision. A decision of a court at this level on an issue of such magnitude is always more than a simple doctrinal elaboration of positive law and its application to some set of facts. It inevitably involves a construction of deeper principles and displays the constitutional ethos and sensibilities of the Court and its judges.[2] The extent to which the decision reflects broader societal attitudes in Germany cannot be established precisely. In its critical stance towards the future of the European construct the Court avoids the crass language of nationalism and the overt vocabulary of chauvinism which has characterized much political opposition to Maastricht. Instead, the positions it adopts are presented as necessary so as not to undermine the democratic nature of the polity guaranteed by the German constitution which it is the Court's duty to uphold. Thus, the Court presents itself as a guarantor of the universal values of democracy, rather than as a guarantor of German particularism.

My critique focuses on this aspect of the decision and relates to the Court's explicit and implicit assessment of the present (pre- and post-Maastricht) stage of European integration as well as its more distant future. Not to mince words, for reasons which I shall elaborate I consider the Court's decision as regards the existing Community embarrassing; as regards Europe's future evolution, I find the decision sad, even pathetic.

It is embarrassing since, while the Court presents itself as the guarantor of democracy for the future, it is forced, for political and other reasons, to accept and 'whitewash' the Community and Union of today which suffer, as I think is widely accepted, from very serious democratic deficiencies. To achieve this feat the Court is pushed to a position which implies that the Community's existing problems of democracy are and have been mediated through member-state structures and processes. But this position merely increases the embarrassment. For, on the one hand, it undermines the pressing need to increase substantially the democratization of the present Community/Union decision-making processes at both European and member-state levels – a cause consistently and laudably supported by the German government in recent years. If a constitutional court of such prestige, a court which explicitly adopts the criterion of democracy, gives the present Community a clean bill of health (despite some critical rhetoric), why tamper with its basic institutional structures and decisional processes? On the other hand, if the Bundesverfassungsgericht truly believes that state structures and processes have mediated the democratic deficiencies of the Community, this must undermine our confidence in its own democratic sensibilities and in its ability and commitment effectively to offer guarantees for the future.

It is a sad, even pathetic decision for more profound reasons. Democracy does not exist in a vacuum. It is premised on the existence of a polity with members – the demos – by whom and for whom democratic discourse with its many variants takes place. The authority and legitimacy of a majority to compel a minority exists only within political boundaries defined by a demos. Therefore, even if the surface language of the decision is democracy, its deep structure inevitably will reveal the explicit and implicit, conscious and subconscious, understanding of the Court and its judges as to the very nature of polity and the criteria of membership therein. Since the German constitution itself, like many others, does not give comprehensive answers to these issues, the Constitutional Court and its judges had to seek deeper strata, beyond the express language of the constituent document. These deeper strata are, at times, unstated, simply assumed. They appear, as language itself sometimes does, so 'natural' and 'neutral' as to explain the relatively scant attention accorded to them in the extensive German commentary on the decision. These issues of who belongs and who does not, of membership and authority, of demos and ethnos, have loomed large in the violent history of Europe this century and have shaped much political debate since the end of the Second World War. They have come centre-stage again in the period since the fall of the Berlin Wall, with the ugly rise of national and ethnic strife and 'ethnic cleansing' within the old-new states of Eastern Europe and the former Soviet empire and with the troubling rise of xenophobia, racism and anti-Semitism even in Western Europe. There is a need for intellectual and moral leadership on these issues which politicians, ever sensitive to potentially populist electorates, cannot always supply. We may expect our courts, without straying from the province of judicial propriety, to be part of that leadership. The European Community/Union offers no magic recipes to address these ills but it does, at a minimum, offer the possibility of rethinking in creative ways the concepts of polity and membership – of demos; thinking which may still preserve that which is valuable in, say, the classical European nation-state and yet guard against its excesses.

How sad, then, to observe the Bundesverfassungsgericht, faced with the need, and historical opportunity, to rethink these issues in the context of Community and member state, looking backwards, like Lot's wife, to a polity based on the tired old ideas of an ethno-culturally homogeneous *Volk* and the unholy trinity of *Volk–Staat–Staatsangehöriger* as the exclusive basis for democratic authority and legitimate rule-making. There is perhaps a merciful subtle streak of shame or, at least, unease which calls for legitimation in the Court's construct. Why else choose Hermann Heller, Socialist, anti-fascist, Jew, and critic of Carl Schmitt, as the only authority for the proposition of the homogeneity of the *Volk*? Does this not suggest a certain concern to find, shall we say, a kosher seal of approval for this late-twentieth-century version, albeit anaemic and racially neutral, of what in far away times fed the slogan of Blood (*Volk*) and Soil (*Staat*)?[3] But it is still sad for German constitution-alism if,[4] in the face of the big challenges which face Germany in dealing with its own communities of 'migrant workers', its own brand of rising xenophobia and renewed anti-Semitism and so on, and in the face of its new position of international leadership, of all the rich currents in the German national debate on polity and membership the Bundesverfassungsgericht had to pick up this one.

The decision is pathetic in the attempt of the Court to project, even impose, these problematic conceptualizations on the Community/Union itself, not simply undermining but, as will emerge, actually foreclosing the possibility of democratization at the European level and implicitly grafting on to the Community a telos which is alien to the foundational purposes of European integration.

In this essay I shall try both to spell out in greater detail the nature of my critique and also offer some alternative ways of thinking about Community/Union and the member state.

Europe: The 'No Demos' Thesis

One of the chief concerns of the German Court was the danger which the evolving process of European integration, particularly some possibilities implicit in the Maastricht Treaty, poses to the democratic character of the polity. The Court therefore had to address the potential for democratization of the European Union at the European level. The Court's position is sceptical. It is not the *per se* scepticism which is either interesting or troubling. One can and should be troubled about democracy in the European Union, and since no easy solution seems at hand scepticism about the present and caution about the future are to be lauded. What is interesting and, in my view, rather troubling is the basis on which the German Court's scepticism is founded. It is informed by what we may call the 'No Demos' thesis. This seemingly elegant thesis rests on a powerful strand – how dominant a strand it is difficult to tell – in German constitutional thinking represented in, inter alia, the writings of Paul Kirchhof, widely reputed to be the principal architect of the Maastricht decision,[5] but shared by several others.[6] In fairness to the other judges of the Court it is true that the language of the decision does not in all respects replicate the hard-core version of Kirchhof. Comparing Kirchhof's writings and the Court's ultimate decision, one gets the impression of a Court which was not altogether happy with its *rapporteur's* full-blooded views, but which did not have an alternative construct. The compromise seems a watered-down version of Kirchhof. The most generous interpretation which can be given is that there are two possible readings of the Maastricht decision. If so (I am doubtful), let this essay be a normative incentive to reject the Kirchhofian version of the judgment.

The intellectual roots of the No Demos thesis go, naturally, far further than Kirchhof. The thesis finds expression in German positive law, too, notably the law relating to citizenship – articulating the conditions of membership in the German polity. In fact, the decision constitutes a transference to the European level of the Court's understanding of the German polity.

The following is a composite version of the No Demos thesis culled from the decision of the Court itself and some of the principal exponents of the thesis. I have also spelt out in this version what I consider are some of the implications which logically follow from, or are implicit in, the thesis, even if the authors themselves shy away from stating them.

The people of a polity, the *Volk*, its demos, denote a concept which has a subjective – socio-psychological – component which is rooted in objective, organic conditions. Both the subjective and objective can be observed empirically in a way which would enable us, on the basis of observation and analysis, to determine that, for example, there is no European *Volk*.

The subjective manifestations of peoplehood, of the demos, are to be found in a sense of social cohesion, shared destiny and collective self-identity which, in turn, result in (and deserve) loyalty.[7] These manifestations have thus both a descriptive and also a normative element. They are a result of, but are also conditioned on, some, though not necessarily all, of the following objective elements: common language,[8] common history, common cultural habits and sensibilities and – this is dealt with more discreetly since the twelve years of National Socialism – common ethnic origin, common religion. All these factors do not alone capture the essence of *Volk* – one will always find allusions to some spiritual, even mystic, element as well.[9] Whereas different writers may throw different mixes of elements into the pot, an insistence on a relatively high degree of homogeneity, measured by these ethno-cultural criteria, is typically an important, indeed critical, element of the discourse. Here rests, of course, the most delicate aspect of the theory since the insistence on homogeneity is what conditions the rules for inclusion and exclusion as operational state polity. When, say, Jews were excluded from full citizenship of many European nation-states, it was often on the grounds that being a Christian was essential to the homogeneity of the people.[10] The 'organic' nature of the *Volk* is a sensitive matter. I call 'organic' those parts of the discourse which make, to a greater or lesser degree, one or more of the following claims: the *Volk* pre-dates historically, and precedes politically, the modern state. Germany was able to emerge as a modern nation-state because there was already a German *Volk*. The 'nation' is simply a modern appellation, in the context of contemporary political theory and international law, of the pre-existing *Volk* and the state is its political expression. It is on this view that the compelling case for German (re)unification rested. One could split the German state but not the German nation. Hence, there might perhaps be a unification of the states but certainly only *re*unification of the people.

Anthropologically, this understanding of, say, being German, which means being part of the German *Volk*, is 'organic' in the following sense: it has, first, an almost natural connotation. You are born German the way you are born male or female – though you can, without much difficulty, change your national identity, you will remain an 'ex-German' – and to the extent that ethnicity continues to play a role – muted to be sure – in this discourse of the *Volk*, ethnicity is even more immutable than gender: there is no operation which can change one's ethnicity. The implication of this is that one's nationality as a form of identity is almost primordial, taking precedence over other forms of consciousness and membership. I may have solidarity with fellow Christians elsewhere, fellow workers elsewhere, fellow women elsewhere, which would make me a Christian German, a Socialist German, a feminist German or even a German Christian, a German Socialist, a German feminist. But I cannot escape my *völkisch* national identity.

No one today argues that the 'organic' is absolute. One can, after all, 'naturalize', acquire membership in a new nation – though even here, doesn't the word 'naturalization' speak volumes? And one can, more as a hypothesis than a reality, imagine that should the objective conditions change sufficiently, and a measure of homogeneity in language, culture, and shared historical experience develop, a subjective consciousness might follow and a new *Volk*/nation emerge. But, realistically, these mutations are possible in a 'geological' time frame – epochal, not generational.

Volk fits into modern political theory easily enough. The German constitution may have established the postwar German state, but it did not constitute the German people, except, perhaps, in some narrow legal sense. The *Volk*, the nation, understood in this national, ethno-cultural sense, are the basis for the modern state. They are the basis, in an older, self-determination sense, of political independence in state-hood. Only nations 'may have' states.[11] The state belongs to the nation – its *Volk* and the nation (the *Volk*) 'belong' to the state.

Critically, *Volk*/nation are also the basis for the modern democratic state: the nation and its members, the *Volk*, constitute the polity for the purposes of accepting the discipline of democratic, majoritarian gover-nance. Both descriptively and prescriptively (how it is and how it ought to be) a minority will/should accept the legitimacy of a majority decision because both majority and minority are part of the same *Volk*, belong to the nation. That is an integral part of what rule by the people, democracy, means on this reading. Thus, nationality constitutes the state (hence nation-state) which in turn constitutes its political bound-ary, an idea which runs from Schmitt to Kirchhof.[12] The significance of the political boundary is not only to the older notion of political independence and territorial integrity, but also to the very democratic nature of the polity. A parliament is, on this view, an institution of democracy not only because it provides a mechanism for representation and majority voting, but because it represents the *Volk*, the nation, the demos from which derive the authority and legitimacy of its decisions.

To drive this point home, imagine an *Anschluss* between Germany and Denmark. Try and tell the Danes that they should not worry since they will have full representation in the Bundestag. Their screams of grief will be shrill not simply because they will be condemned, as Danes, to permanent minorityship (that may be true for the German Greens too), but because the way nationality, in this style of thinking, meshes with democracy is such that even majority rule is legitimate only within a demos, when Danes rule Danes. Demos, thus, is a condition of democracy. By contrast, when democrats like Alfred Verdross argued for a Greater Germany this was clearly not motivated by some proto-fascist design but by a belief that the German-speaking 'peoples' were in fact one people in terms of this very understanding of peoplehood.

Turning to Europe, it is argued as a matter of empirical observation, based on these organic cultural-national criteria, that there is no European demos[13] – not a people, not a nation. Neither the subjective element (the sense of shared collective identity and loyalty) nor the objective conditions which could produce these (the kind of homo-geneity of organic national-cultural conditions on which peoplehood depends) exist. Long-term peaceful relations, with ever closer economic and social intercourse, should not be confused with the bonds of peoplehood and nationality forged by language, history, ethnicity and all the rest.

At this point we detect two versions of the No Demos thesis. The 'soft' version of the Court itself[14] is the 'Not Yet' version: although there is no demos now the possibility for the future is not precluded a priori. If and when a European demos emerges, then, and only then, will the basic political premisses of the decision have to be reviewed. This is unlikely in the foreseeable future.[15] The 'hard' version dismisses that possibility as not only objectively unrealistic but also undesirable: it is argued (correctly, in my view) that integration is not about creating a European nation or people, but about the ever closer Union among the peoples of Europe.[16] However, what the 'soft' and 'hard' versions share is the understanding of peoplehood, its characteristics and manifestations. Soft version or hard, the consequences of the No Demos thesis for the European construct are interesting. The rigorous implication of this view would be that without a demos, there cannot, by definition, be a democracy or democratization at the European level.[17] This is not a semantic proposition. On this reading, European democracy (meaning at a minimum binding decisions by majority at the European level) without a demos is no different from the previously mentioned German–Danish *Anschluss*, except that it is on a larger scale. Giving the Danes a vote in the Bundestag is, as argued, ice-cold comfort.

Giving them a vote in the European Parliament or Council is, conceptually, no different. This would be true for each and every nation-state. European integration, on this view, may have involved a certain transfer of state functions to the Union but this has not been accompanied by a redrawing of political boundaries, which can occur only if, and can be ascertained only when, a European *Volk* can be said to exist. Since this, it is claimed, has not occurred, the Union and its institutions can have neither the authority nor the legitimacy of a demos-cratic state. Empowering the European Parliament is no solution and could – to the extent that it weakens the Council (the voice of the member states) – actually exacerbate the legitimacy problem of the Community. On this view, a parliament without a demos is conceptually impossible, practically despotic. If the European Parliament is not the representative of a people, if the territorial boundaries of the EU do not correspond to its political boundaries, then the writ of such a parliament has only slightly more legitimacy than the writ of an emperor.

European Democracy Deficit and the No Demos Thesis

That, then, constitutes the No Demos thesis, driven, it seems, by a strong concern for democratic structure and process which must, however, rest on the existence of a demos. Whether or not there is a European demos, it is hard to see how at the current stage of European integration both pre- and post-Maastricht, state structures, processes and institutions, including the German Federal Constitutional Court itself, can alone possibly provide adequate democratic guarantees for the European construct. To put this crudely and brutally: if the concern of the German Court was to safeguard the democratic character of the European construct in its future developments, and if its explicit and implicit thesis was that, in the absence of a European demos, democracy can be guaranteed only through member-state mechanisms, it is hard to see how, employing the same sensibilities, it could have given a democratic seal of approval to the already existing European Community and Union.

Whatever the original intentions of the contracting parties, the Treaties establishing the European Community and Union have become like no other international parallel, and national procedures to ensure democratic control over international treaties of the state are clearly ill suited and woefully inadequate to address the problems posited by the European Union.

This is not the place to put forward any detailed remedies for the democratic ills of the European Union. But I would submit that a realistic assessment of the problem suggests that, unless one could undo much of the existing structure and wrest back many of the existing competences of Europe, the only way to achieve a modicum of democratization would be by a combined revision of powers and processes at both the European and the member-state levels.

The No Demos Thesis: What Polity? Which Membership?

The Court could have adopted an alternative construct: highlight, embarrassing as this might have been, the democratic failings of the Community, uncured by Maastricht and in which all European and member-state institutions (including courts) connive. Since, despite these failings, the Union was formally legitimated, the Court could have, for example, approved the Treaty but insisted that the existing gap between formal legitimation and material democratic deficiency must be regarded as temporary and could not be accepted in the medium and long term. In this way the Bundesverfassungsgericht would have thrown its formidable power behind the pressure for democratization.

But this option would inevitably have to involve some acknowledgement of the need to strengthen, among other measures, the powers of, say, the European Parliament. You simply cannot be serious about democracy in Europe and believe that, given the array of powers and

competences already transferred to the Union, democratization can
take place exclusively on the national level. But this construct, I suspect,
seemed even more threatening to the German Constitutional Court.
Why so? That is one of the riddles of its decision. As I shall try to show,
for all its talk about democracy the Court, by adopting the view it has
on *Volk, Staat* and *Staatsangehörigkeit*, has boxed itself into a further
untenable situation.

Stated briefly: if the judges who subscribed to the decision truly
believe that a polity enjoying democratic authority and legitimate rule-
making power must be based on the conflation of *Volk, Staat* and
Staatsangehörigkeit, that the only way to conceive of the demos of such a
policy is in densely homogeneous organic–cultural terms, then, whether
one admits it or not, the future of European integration poses a huge
threat. The problem is not that there is not now a European demos; the
problem is that there might one day be one. And why is that a problem?
Because the emergence of a European demos in a European polity
enjoying legitimate democratic authority would signify – on this understanding of polity and demos – the replacement of the various member
state demoi, including the German *Volk*. This, I myself would agree,
would be too high a price to pay for European integration. But since on
their reading there is only a binary option – either a European state
(one European *Volk*) or a Union of states (with the preservation of all
European *Völker* including Germans) – their fear is inevitable.

I shall try to show that this view is based on one or perhaps two
profound misconceptions with unfortunate consequences both for
Germany itself (I think) and for Europe (I am sure). My challenge,
note, is not to the ethno-cultural, homogeneous concept of *Volk* as such.
It is, instead, to the view which insists that the only way to think of a
demos, bestowing legitimate rule-making and democratic authority on a
polity, is in these *völkisch* terms. I also challenge the concomitant notion
that the only way to think of a polity, enjoying legitimate rule-making
and democratic authority, is in statal terms. Finally, I challenge the
implicit view in the decision that the only way to imagine the Union is
in some statal form: *Staat, Staatenbund, Bundesstaat, Staatenverbund*.
Noteworthy is not only the 'enslavement' to the notion of state, but also,
as we shall see, the inability to contemplate an entity with a simultaneous
multiple identity. Polycentric thinking is, apparently, unacceptable.

One can argue that peoplehood and national identity have, at certain
critical moments of transition, a far higher degree of artificiality, of
social constructionism and even social engineering than the organic,
völkisch view would concede. As such they are far more fluid, potentially
unstable and capable of change. They can decidedly be constructed as
a conscious decision, not only a reflection of an already existing

consciousness. Indeed, how could one ever imagine political unification taking place if it must strictly follow the sense of peoplehood? In the creation of European states involving political unification such as, yes, Germany and Italy, the act of formal unification preceded a full and universal shift of consciousness. Although conceptually the nation is the condition for the state, historically it has often been the state which constituted the nation by imposing a language and/or prioritizing a dialect and/or privileging a certain historical narrative and/or creating symbols and myths.[18] This would, often, have to be the order in the process of unification. Think of, say, Prussia and Austria. Is it so fanciful to imagine a different historical path in which Prussia went its own way, privileging a particularist reading of its history, symbols, cultural habits and myths and developing a sense of *Volk* and nation which emphasized that which separated it from other German-speaking nations, and that Austria, in this would-be history, could have just become another part of a unified Germany?

I am, of course, taking no position here on the desirability or otherwise of European unification driven by the notion of nation and peoplehood. (As will transpire, I oppose it.) But I am arguing that to insist on the emergence of a pre-existing European demos defined in organic national–cultural terms as a precondition for constitutional unification or, more modestly, a redrawing of political boundaries, is to ensure that this will never happen. The No Demos thesis which is presented by its advocates as rooted in empirical and objective observation barely conceals a predetermined outcome.

The second objection is more central and is concerned with the notion of membership implicit in the No Demos thesis. Who, we may ask, are the members of, say, the German polity? The answer would seem obvious: the German *Volk*, those who have German nationality. They are Germany's demos. Germany is the state of the Germans defined in the familiar organic–national terms. By contrast, to say that there is no European demos is equivalent to saying that there is no European nation. I should immediately add that I agree: there is no European nation or *Volk* in the sense in which these words are understood by the German Court and the constitutionalists on which it relies.

But that is not the point. The real point is the following: is it mandated that the demos in general and the European demos in particular be understood exclusively in the organic–cultural homogeneous terms which the German Federal Constitutional Court has adopted in its own self-understanding? Can there not be other understandings of demos which might lead to different conceptualizations and potentialities for Europe? Have not German sociology and political theory themselves come up with one of the most challenging concepts in this regard, constitutional patriotism?

I have, so far, in this English-language narrative studiously avoided using the concept of citizen and citizenship. Can we not define membership of a polity in civic, non-organic–cultural terms? Can we not separate ethnos from demos? And can we not imagine a polity whose demos is defined, understood and accepted in civic, non-organic–cultural terms, and has legitimate rule-making democratic authority on that basis? To be sure, there is a German constitutional tradition from which the No Demos thesis arises which masks these possibilities since historically, at least from about the time of the Kaiserreich, there has been a strong current which insists on the unity of *Volk*–nation-state–citizenship. A German citizen is, save for a few exceptions, a German national, primarily one who belongs to the *Volk*.[19] Belonging to the *Volk* is normally the condition for citizenship. And, in turn, citizenship in this tradition can only be understood in statal terms. Here the very language reflects the conflation: the concept of state is built into the very term *Staatsangehörigkeit* (citizenship). If there is citizenship, statehood is premissed. If there is statehood, citizenship is premissed. This is not simply a matter of constitutional and political theory. It finds its reflection in positive law. That is why naturalization in Germany – other than through marriage, adoption and some other exceptions – is an act which implies not simply accepting civic obligations of citizenship and loyalty to the state but also embracing German national identity understood in this thick cultural sense, a true cultural assimilation and a demand for an obliteration of other *völkisch* loyalties and identification.[20] Thus, for example, emancipation of the Jews in Germany was premissed on a consignment of Jewishness and Judaism to the realm of religion and a refusal to accept Jewish peoplehood. To be a German citizen, under this conception, you have to be part of the *Volk*. And Germany as a state is the state of the Germans understood in the same terms. Likewise, until very recently, you could be a third-generation resident of Germany and yet be denied citizenship because you were unable or unwilling to become 'German' in a cultural and identification sense.[21] With few exceptions, the law specifically denies naturalization to residents who wish to embrace the duties of citizenship but to retain an alternative national identity. Multiple citizenship is permitted in peculiar circumstances but is frowned upon. By contrast, if you are an ethnically defined German national, even a third-generation citizen and resident of some far-flung country, you would still be a member of the *Volk* and hence have a privileged position in applying for citizenship. On this view, the legal 'passport' of membership of the polity is citizenship: citizenship is what defines you as a member of the polity with full political and civil rights and duties. But that, in turn, is conflated with nationality, with being a member of the *Volk* in the organic–cultural sense. And, since demos is defined in national terms, the only demos conceivable is one the members of which are citizens–nationals: hence the state.

I should point out that Germany is not the only state in Europe or elsewhere whose membership philosophy is so conceived. In some measure that is the philosophy of the nation-state. But it does offer a rather extreme example of the conflation of state, *Volk*/nation and citizenship.

Be that as it may, this conflation is not necessary conceptually, nor practised universally, nor, perhaps, even desirable. There are quite a few states where, for example, mere birth in the state creates actual citizenship or an entitlement to citizenship without any pretence that you thus become a national in an ethno-cultural sense. There are states where citizenship, as a commitment to the constitutional values and the civic duties of the polity, is the condition of naturalization, whereas nationality in an ethno-cultural sense is regarded, like religion, as a matter of individual preference.[22] There are states, like Germany, with a strong ethno-cultural identity, which nevertheless allow citizenship not only to individuals with other nationalities who do not belong to the majority *Volk*, but to minorities with strong, even competing, ethno-cultural identities. It is, I suppose, for the Germans to decide whether the unity of *Volk*, *Staat* and *Staatsangehörigkeit* continues to be the best way in which to conceive of their state, nation and citizenry. I shall return to this theme below.

Embedded, however, in the decision of the Bundesverfassungsgericht is an understanding not only of German polity and demos but of Europe too, notably in its 'Not Yet' formulation. When the German Court tells us that there is not yet a European demos, it implicitly invites us to think of Europe, its future and its very telos in organic–national terms. It implicitly construes Europe in some sort of 'pre-state' stage, as yet underdeveloped and hence lacking in its own legitimate rule-making and democratic authority. It is this (mis)understanding which produces the either–or – that is, zero sum – relationship between Europe and member state. If demos is *Volk* and citizenship can be conceived only as *Staatsangehörigkeit*, then European demos and citizenship can come only at the expense of the parallel German terms.

What is inconceivable in this view is a decoupling of nationality (understood its *völkisch* organic national–cultural sense) and citizenship. Also inconceivable is a demos understood in non-organic civic terms, a coming together on the basis not of shared ethnos and/or organic culture, but of shared values, a shared understanding of rights and societal duties and shared rational, intellectual culture which transcend organic–national differences. Equally inconceivable in this view is the notion of a polity enjoying rule-making and democratic authority whose demos, and hence the polity itself, is not statal in character and is understood differently from the German self-understanding.

Finally, and critically, what is also inconceivable on this view is that a member state like Germany may have its own understanding of demos for itself (for example its relatively extreme form of state= people=citizens) but be part of a broader polity with a different understanding of demos.

At the root of the No Demos thesis is ultimately a world view which is enslaved to the concepts of *Volk*, *Staat* and *Staatsangehöriger* and cannot perceive the Community or Union in anything other than those terms. This is another reason why the Union may appear so threatening, since the statal vision can construe it only in oppositional terms to the member state. But that is to impose on the Community or Union an external vision and not an attempt to understand (or define) it in its own unique terms. It is a failure to grasp the meaning and potentialities of supranationalism.

Before returning, then, to the potentialities of decoupling nationality and citizenship, it will be worth discussing the broader relationship between Union, nation and state within the European construct encapsulated in the term 'supranationalism'. It will appear that supranationalism and nationalism are not truly oppositional.

Supranationalism: Community, Nation and State

How, then, should we understand – or construe – the notion of supranationalism in this context? A word of caution is necessary here. There is no fixed meaning to the term 'supranationalism'. Indeed, from its inception there seem to have been two competing visions of its realization through the Community: a unity or statal vision – exemplified in those who favoured a United States of Europe – and a more attenuated Community vision. The two strands (which, of course, overlap) have continued to co-exist. But it is my reading of the historical map – the rejection of the European Defence Community and the European Political Community in the 1950s and the articulation of supranationalism in, especially, the Treaty of Rome and its consequences – that the Community vision prevailed in the formative years of the EC.

In trying to explain the ways in which the Community is, or has become, supranational, most discussion over the years has tended, interestingly, to focus on its relation to the 'state' rather than the 'nation'. This conflation of nation and state is not always helpful. Supranationalism relates in specific and discrete ways to nationhood and to statehood. Indeed, in my understanding and construction of supranationalism, its value system is, surprisingly, actually wrapped up with the value system of European ethno-national liberalism of the nineteenth century and, as such, can offer great comfort to those concerned to preserve the values and virtues of the nation-state.

With all the talk about *Volk* and nation, and with all our obsessions about the dangers of nationalism and chauvinism and even racism, which are often held to derive from these concepts, what can be said about them in normative terms? What values can they be said to uphold and vindicate? I will talk about nationhood but this could, in most respects, capture *Volk* and peoplehood, too.

It seems to me that, at least in its nineteenth-century liberal conception, two deep human values were thought to find expression in nationhood: belongingness and originality. (It should immediately be stated that nationhood is not the only social form in which these values find expression.)

Nationhood transcends the family and tribe, and maybe here lurks a tantalizing value: nationhood not only offers a place to the familyless, to the tribeless, but, in transcending family and tribe, calls for loyalty – the largest coin in the realm of national feeling – towards others which goes beyond the immediate 'natural' (blood) or self-interested social unit. Belongingness of this type is a two-way street. It is not only a passive value to be accepted. It is also active: to accept. Loyalty is one of those virtues which, if not abused, benefits those on both the giving and the receiving ends.

The other core value of nationhood, in some ways also an instrument for national demarcation, is a claim about originality. On this reading, the Tower of Babel was not a sin against God but a sin against human potentiality; and the dispersal that came in its aftermath was not punishment but divine blessing. The nation, with its endlessly rich specificities, co-existing alongside other nations, is, in this view, the vehicle for realizing human potentialities in original ways, which humanity as a whole would be the poorer for not cultivating.

I have spoken so far of belongingness and originality in conceptual terms – as 'values'. But these concepts also have a psycho-sociological manifestation, from which derives the incredible power with which nationhood grips human consciousness. Combined, they constitute the organizing myth around which the 'identity' of the nation is fixed. Identity has a minimalist possibility: it indicates traits, essentialist and/ or constructed, which suggest similarities among individuals – ways in which they are 'identical' with one another. But nationhood in the social sense is much more than this minimalism. It privileges these traits and understands them as a means to identify its members, and, further, calls on its members, thus constructed, to identify with one another and with the collectivity. How so and why so? Belongingness and originality combined as the organizing myth of national identity are presented as an embodiment of fate and destiny. It is one's fate to be born into a national identity and it is one's destiny to preserve that identity and to realize its potentialities. This grip on consciousness, manifested in the stunning success nationhood has had in evoking the loyalty it calls for, is, in my view, simple to understand: nationhood has responded to one of the deepest human cravings – the craving for ontological and metaphysical meaning. The element of fate – born into a nation – is a seductive answer to the question 'Who am I?' The element of destiny – preserve the nation and realize its potential – is equally seductive in responding to the question 'What am I here for?'

Speaking with approval, as I have, of nationhood as embodying the values of belongingness and originality does not mean that I accept these as even remotely adequate ontological and metaphysical responses. But one cannot but observe their power. Critically, power of such dimensions over human consciousness has huge dangers if not properly managed and contained.

It is here that one may turn from the nation to the modern state. It is worth remembering at the outset that national existence and even a vibrant national life do not in and of themselves require statehood, though statehood can offer the nation advantages, both intrinsic and extrinsic. Territoriality is, arguably, the most important intrinsic element, for it provides a most elemental bonding agent. One cannot overstate the power of autochthony in consolidating the national myth. Language, culture and history are all woven into autochthonous images. One lives from the land, one defends the land, one dies for the land, one is buried in the land. Sensuously, the national landscape, its colours, aromas and changing moods are the object of story, ballad and poems, of dreams and memories. From the dawn of history it seems as if the advantage for a coalescing nation of a Promised Land was recognized.

The extrinsic advantages of the state for the nation are those resulting from the current organization of international life which gives such huge benefits to statehood. I would argue that in the modern notion of the European organic nation-state, the state is to be seen principally as an instrument – the organizational framework within which the nation is to realize its potentialities. It is within the statal framework that governance, with its most important functions of securing welfare and security, is situated. The well-being and integrity of the state must, thus, be secured so that these functions may be attained. That is not a meagre value in itself. But to the extent that the state may claim, say, a loyalty which is more than pragmatic, it is because it is at the service of the nation with its values of belongingness and originality. (This conceptualization underscores, perhaps exaggerates, the difference from the truly radical American alternative liberal project of the non-ethno-national polity, and of a state, the republic, the organization of which, and the norms of citizenship behaviour within which, were central to its value system.)

It is evident, however, that in the European project, boundaries become a central feature of the nation-state. There are, obviously, boundaries in the legal–geographical sense of separating one nation-state from another. But there are also internal, cognitive boundaries by which society (the nation) and individuals come to think of themselves in the world.

As noted, at a societal level nationhood involves the drawing of boundaries by which the nation will be defined and separated from others. The categories of boundary-drawing are myriad: linguistic, ethnic, geographic, religious, etc. The drawing of the boundaries is exactly that: a constitutive act, which decides that certain boundaries are meaningful both for the sense of belonging and for the original contribution of the nation. This constitutive element is particularly apparent at the moment of 'nation-building' when histories are rewritten, languages revived, etc. Of course, with time, the boundaries, especially the non-geographical ones, write themselves on collective and individual consciousness with such intensity that they appear as natural – consider the virtual interchangeability of the word 'international' with 'universal' and 'global': it is hard not to think, in the social sphere, of the world as a whole without the category of nation (as in international).

Finally, at an individual level, belonging implies a boundary: you belong because others do not. As evident as the notion of boundaries is to the nation-state enterprise, so is the high potential for abuse of boundaries. The abuse may take place in relation to the three principal boundaries: the external boundary of the state, the boundary between nation and state, and the internal consciousness boundary of those making up the nation. The most egregious form of abuse of the external boundary of the state would be physical or other forms of aggression towards other states.

The abuse of the boundary between nation and state is most egregious when the state comes to be seen not as instrumental for individuals and society to realize their potentials but as an end in itself. Less egregiously but more dangerously, the state might induce a 'laziness' in the nation, banal statal symbols and instrumentalities becoming a substitute for truly original national expression. This may also have consequences for the sense of national identity whereby the state and its apparatus become a substitute for a meaningful sense of belonging and originality, with the state as an instrumentality becoming a metaphor for fate and destiny, and allegiance to the state replacing human affinity, empathy, loyalty and a sense of shared fate with the people of the state.

There can be, too, an abuse of the internal boundary which defines belongingness. The most typical abuse here is to move from a boundary which defines a sense of belonging to one which induces a sense of superiority and a concomitant sense of condescension or contempt for the other. A sense of collective national identity implies an other. It should not imply an inferior other.

The manifestations of these abuses are a living part of the history of the European nation-state which are so well known as to obviate discussion. A central plank of the project of European integration may be seen, then, as an attempt to control the excesses of the modern nation-state in Europe, especially, but not only, its propensity to violent conflict and the inability of the international system to constrain that propensity. The European Community was to be an antidote to the negative features of the state and statal intercourse; its genesis in 1951 was seen as the beginning of a process that would bring about the elimination of these excesses.

Historically there have, as mentioned above, always been two competing visions of European integration. While no one has seriously envisioned a Jacobin-type centralized Europe, it is clear that one vision, which I call the 'Unity vision', the United States of Europe vision, has really posited as its ideal type, as its aspiration, a statal Europe, albeit of a federal kind. Tomorrow's Europe in this form would indeed constitute the final demise of the member-state, nationalism placing or re-placing the hitherto warring member states within a political union of federal governance.

It is easy to see some of the faults of this vision: it would be more than ironic if a polity set up as a means to counter the excesses of statism ended up coming round full circle and transforming itself into a (super)state. It would be equally ironic if the ethos which rejected the boundary abuse of the nation-state gave birth to a polity with the same potential for abuse. The problem with this Unity vision is that its very realization entails its negation.

The alternative vision, the one that historically has prevailed, is the supranational vision, the community vision. At one level, aspirations here are both modest, compared to the Union model, and reactionary: supranationalism, the notion of community rather than unity, is about affirming the values of the liberal nation-state by policing the boundaries against abuse. Another way of saying this would be that supranationalism aspires to keep the values of the nation-state pure and uncorrupted by the abuses I have described above.

At another level, the supranational community project is far more ambitious than the Unity one and far more radical. It is more ambitious since, unlike the Unity project, which simply wishes to redraw the actual political boundaries of the polity within the existing nation-state conceptual framework, albeit a federal one, the supranational project seeks to redefine the very notion of boundaries of the state, between the nation and state, and within the nation itself. It is more radical since, as I shall seek to show, it involves more complex demands and greater constraints on the actors.

How, then, does supranationalism, expressed in the community project of European integration, affect the excesses of the nation-state, the abuse of boundaries discussed above? At the pure statal level, supranationalism replaces the 'liberal' premiss of international society with a community one. The classical model of international law is a replication at the international level of a liberal theory of the state. The state is implicitly treated as the analogue, on the international level, to the individual within a domestic situation. In this conception, international legal notions such as self-determination, sovereignty, independence and consent have their obvious analogy in theories of the individual within the state. In the supranational vision, the community as a transnational regime will not simply be a neutral arena in which states will seek to pursue the national interest and maximize their benefits but will create a tension between the state and the community of states. Crucially, the community idea is meant not to eliminate the national state but to create a regime which seeks to tame the national interest with a new discipline. The challenge is to control at societal level the uncontrolled reflexes of national interest in the international sphere.

Turning to the boundary between nation and state, supranationalism is meant to prevent abuses here, too. The supranational project recognizes that at an inter-group level nationalism is an expression of cultural (political and/or other) specificity underscoring differentiation, the uniqueness of a group as positioned vis-à-vis other groups, calling for respect and justifying the maintenance of inter-group boundaries. At an intra-group level, nationalism is an expression of cultural (political and/or other) specificity underscoring commonality, the 'sharedness' of the group vis-à-vis- itself, calling for loyalty and justifying the elimination of intra-group boundaries.

Supranationalism does not seek to negate as such the interplay of differentiation and commonality, of inclusion and exclusion and their potential value. But it is a challenge to their codified expressions in nationality, since, in the supranational construct – with its free-movement provisions, which do not allow exclusion through statal means of other national cultural influences, and with its strict prohibition on nationality/citizenship-based discrimination – national differentiation cannot rest so easily on the artificial boundaries provided by the state. At inter-group level, then, it pushes for cultural differences to express themselves in their authentic, spontaneous form, rather than the codified statal legal forms. At the intra-group level, it attempts to strip away the false consciousness which nationalism may create instead of a belongingness derived from a non-formal sense of sharedness. This, perhaps, is the first Kantian strand in this conceptualization of supra-nationalism. Kantian moral philosophy grounds moral obligation on the ability of humans not simply to follow ethical norms but, as rational creatures, to determine for themselves the laws of their own acting and to act out of internal choice according to these norms. Supranational-ism, on this view, favours national culture when, indeed, it is authentic, internalized, a true part of identity.

There is another, Enlightenment, Kantian idea in this discourse. Supranationalism, at the societal and individual rather than the statal level, embodies an ideal which diminishes the importance of the statal aspects of nationality – probably the most powerful contemporary expression of groupness – as the principal referent for transnational human intercourse. That is the value side of non-discrimination on grounds of nationality, of free movement provisions and the like. Hermann Cohen, the great neo-Kantian, in his *Religion der Vernunft aus den Quellen des Judentum*,[23] tried to explain the meaning of the Mosaic law which calls for non-oppression of the stranger. In his vision, the alien was to be protected, not because he was a member of one's family, clan, religious community or people, but because he was a human being. In the alien, therefore, man discovered the idea of humanity.

We can see through this exquisite exegesis that in the curtailment of the totalistic claim of the nation-state and the reduction of nationality as the principal referent for human intercourse, the community ideal of supranationalism is evocative of, and resonates with, Enlightenment ideas, with the privileging of the individual, with a different aspect of liberalism which has its progeny today in liberal notions of human rights. In this respect the community ideal is heir to Enlightenment liberalism. Supranationalism assumes a new, additional meaning which refers not to the relations among nations but to the ability of the individual to rise above his or her national closet.

Between State Citizenship and Union Membership

What, must now be asked, is the nature of membership in such a construct of Community and member states? Does that construct have a demos? Can it have a demos?

Note that the view that would decouple *Volk* from demos and demos from state, in whole or in part, does not require a denigration of the virtues of nationality – the belongingness, the social cohesion, the cultural and human richness which may be found in exploring and developing the national ethos.[24] It questions whether nationality in the organic sense, as a guarantor of homogeneity of the polity, must be the exclusive condition of full political and civic membership of that polity.

Let me not mince my words: to reject the possibility of a non-organic demos as impossible and/or undesirable is to adopt a world view which ultimately informs ethnic cleansing. I am not suggesting, of course, that the German Court and its judges feel anything but abhorrence for that particular solution. But their authoritative pronouncements on the German constitution cannot but be an important voice in defining the discourse and civic ethos of the public sphere.

That such an infamous practice as ethnic cleansing has an intellectual connection to the construct which makes citizenship depend on nationality and conflates both with the state is apparent from one prominent source of this construct, Carl Schmitt. The insistence on 'homogeneity' as a prerequisite for democracy may, in the urbane discourse of the Constitutional Court, seem innocuous enough. But Schmitt himself, the author of the 'Friend/Foe' concept of nationality, was able, in the climate in which he wrote, to avoid euphemisms and spell out unadorned the implications of this construct. Thus, in his *Die geistesgeschichtliche Lage des heutigen Parlamentarismus*, we find: 'Democracy thus entails firstly, of necessity, homogeneity and, secondly – if necessary – the removal or the destruction of what is heterogenous.'[25] No less. The next step followed naturally. Referring, with approval, to, *inter alia*, Turkey's expulsion of its Greek community, he noted: 'The political strength of a democracy is revealed in its ability and readiness to eliminate or keep away what is foreign and different, or a threat to homogeneity.'[26]

The final step, in which theory and praxis combine, is no surprise either. In 1936 Reichsgruppenwalters Staatsrat Schmitt convened a conference of leading figures in the legal world to discuss 'Das Judentum in der Rechtswissenschaft'. In the concluding address to the conference, Schmitt did not shy away from the implication of the theoretical construct. The cleansing began with books ('the cleansing of the libraries') but inevitably moved to demonization of their authors. 'The Jew has a parasitical, a tactical and a mercantile relation to our intellectual work.' As such, that particular heterogeneous element was defined as a 'deadly enemy'. The logic of Schmitt's final statement is unassailably pure. His concluding words speak for themselves: 'What we seek and fight for is our own unfalsified way of being, the intact purity of our German people. "By resisting the Jew," says our leader Adolf Hitler, "I am doing battle for the work of the Lord."'[27] Be all this as it may, at the level of state and nation, the conflating of *Volk* with demos and demos with state is clearly unnecessary and undesirable as a model for Europe. In fact such a model would deflect Europe from its supranational civilizing telos and ethos.

There is no reason for the European demos to be defined in terms identical to the demos of one of its member states or vice-versa. Consider the Maastricht citizenship provisions: 'Article 8: Citizenship of the Union is hereby established. Every person holding the nationality of a member state shall be a citizen of the Union'.

The Union belongs to, is composed of, citizens who by definition do not share the same nationality. The substance of membership (and thus of the demos) is in a commitment to the shared values of the Union as expressed in its constituent documents, a commitment to, *inter alia*, the duties and rights of a civic society covering discrete areas of public life, a commitment to membership in a polity which privileges exactly the opposites of nationalism – those human features which transcend the differences of organic ethno-culturalism. On this reading, the conceptualization of a European demos should not be based on real or imaginary trans-European cultural affinities or shared histories nor on the construction of a European 'national' myth of the type which constitutes the identity of the organic nation. The decoupling of nationality and citizenship opens the possibility, instead, of thinking of co-existing multiple demoi.

One view of multiple demoi may consist in what may be called the 'concentric circles' approach. On this approach one feels simultaneously that one belongs to, and is part of, say, Germany and Europe; or even Scotland, Britain and Europe. What characterizes this view is that the sense of identity and identification derives from the same sources of human attachment, albeit at different levels of intensity. Presumably the most intense (which the nation, and state, always claim to be) would and should trump any other in normative conflict.

The view of multiple demoi which I am suggesting, one of truly variable geometry, invites individuals to see themselves as belonging simultaneously to two demoi, based, critically, on different subjective factors of identification. I may be a German national in the in-reaching strong sense of organic–cultural identification and sense of belongingness. I am simultaneously a European citizen in terms of my European transnational affinities to shared values which transcend the ethno-national diversity. So much so that in a range of areas of public life I am willing to accept the legitimacy and authority of decisions adopted by my fellow European citizens in the realization that in these areas I have given preference to choices made by my outreaching demos, rather than by my inreaching demos.

On this view, the Union demos turns away from its antecedents and understanding in the European nation-state. But, equally, it should be noted that I am suggesting here something that is different from simple American republicanism transferred to Europe. First, the values one is discussing may be seen to have a special European specificity, a specificity I have explored elsewhere but one dimension of which, by simple way of example, could most certainly be that strand of mutual social responsibility embodied in the ethos of the welfare state adopted by all European societies and by all political forces. But the difference from American republicanism goes further than merely having a different menu of civic values, and here it also goes beyond Haberma-sian constitutional patriotism, despite the large intellectual debt owed to that construct. Americanism was too, after all, about nation-building, albeit on different premises. Its end state, its myth, as expressed in the famous pledge of allegiance to the American flag – 'One nation, indivisible, under God' – is not what Europe is about at all: Europe is precisely not about one nation, not about a melting pot and all the rest, for despite the unfortunate rhetoric of unity, Europe remains (or ought to remain) committed to 'an ever closer union among the peoples of Europe'. Likewise, it is not about indivisibility nor, blessedly, about God.

The co-existence of the two is another dimension of the multiple demoi. The Treaties on this reading would have to be seen not only as an agreement among states (a Union of states) but as a 'social contract' among the nationals of those states – ratified in accordance with the constitutional requirements in all member states – that they will in the areas covered by the Treaty regard themselves as associating as citizens in this civic society. We can go even further. In this polity, and to this demos, one cardinal value is precisely that there will not be a drive towards, or an acceptance of, an over-arching organic–cultural national identity displacing those of the member states. Nationals of the member states are European citizens, not the other way around. Europe is 'not yet' a demos in the organic national–cultural sense and should never become one.

Most importantly, the notion of European citizenship on this con-struct has no independent existence. It lives, symbiotically, with member states' nationalism. The two act as each other's guard, as conceptually dependent.

One should not get carried away with this construct. Note first that the Maastricht formula does not imply a full decoupling: member states are free to define their own conditions of membership and these may continue to be defined in *völkisch* terms. (But then we know that the conditions of nationality and citizenship differ quite markedly from one member state to another.) Moreover, the gateway to European citizenship passes through member-state nationality.

There is one final issue which touches, perhaps, the deepest stratum of the No Demos thesis. It is one thing to say, as does Maastricht, that nationals of member states are citizens of the Union. But are not those nationals also citizens of their member state? Even if one accepts that one can decouple citizenship and nationality and that one can imagine a demos based on citizenship rather than on nationality, can one be a citizen of both polities? Can one be a member of not just one but also a second demos? We have already noted the great aversion of one strand of German constitutionalism to multiple citizenship.

I want to address this question in two different ways. One is simply to point out the fairly widespread practice of states allowing double or even multiple citizenship with relative equanimity. For the most part, as a matter of civic duties and rights this creates few problems. This is true also in the Community. It is true that in time of, say, war the holder of multiple citizenship may be in an untenable situation. But cannot even the European Union create a construct which assumes that war among its constituent member states is not only materially impossible but unthinkable? The sentiment against multiple citizenship is not, I think, rooted in practical considerations.

It is hard to see why, other than for some mystical or truly 'blood thicker than water' rationale, say, a British citizen who thinks of herself as British (and who for ever will speak with an English accent), but who is settled in, say, Germany and wishes to assume all the duties and rights of German citizenship, could not be trusted in today's Europe loyally to do so? Moreover, we have already seen that European citizenship would have a very different meaning from German citizenship. The two identities would not be competing directly 'on the same turf'. It seems to me that the aversion to double loyalty, like the aversion to multiple citizenship itself, is not rooted primarily in practical considerations. It rests I think in a normative view which wants national self-identity – identified with the state and its organs – to rest very deep in the soul, in a place which hitherto was occupied by religion. The imagery of this position – turning to fate – is occasionally evocative of those sentiments.

The reason for this, I think, derives from the recognition of the greatest pull of nationalism. It is by evoking fate and destiny that nationalism can respond to the deepest existential yearning, that of giving to life meaning and purpose which extend beyond mere existence or selfish fulfilment. Religion, with greater legitimacy, occupies itself with these deeper recesses of the human spirit and, consequently, makes these claims for exclusivity. The mixing of state loyalty and religion risks, in my view, idolatry from a religious perspective and can be highly dangerous from a political one. Historically, it seems as if *Volk* and *Staat*, Blood and Soil, did indeed come to occupy these deepest parts of the human spirit to the point of being accepted 'über alles' with terrifying consequences. My view of the matter is not that the very idea of *Volk* and *Staat* was murderous nor even that it was evil, though, as I think is clear from this essay, my preference is for multiple loyalties, even demoi within the state. It is the primordial position which *Volk* mixed with *Staat* occupied, instilling uncritical citizenship, which allowed evil, even murderous, designs to be executed by dulling critical personal faculties, legitimating extreme positions, subduing transcendent human values and debasing one of the common strands of the three monotheistic religions: that human beings, all of them, were created in the image of God.

How then do we achieve 'critical citizenship'? The European construct I have put forward, which allows for a European civic, value-driven demos co-existing side by side with a national organic–cultural one (for those nation-states which want it), could be seen as a moderate contribution to this goal. Maybe in the realm of the political, the special virtue of contemporaneous membership in an organic national–cultural demos and in a supranational civic, value-driven demos is in the effect which such double membership may have on taming the great appeal, even craving, for belonging and destiny in this world which nationalism continues to offer but which can so easily degenerate into intolerance and xenophobia. Maybe the in-reaching national–cultural demos and the out-reaching supranational civic demos, by continuously keeping each other in check, offer a structured model of critical citizenship. They might even induce us to look for meaning and purpose not simply or primarily to statal structures at either European or state levels. Maybe we should celebrate, rather than reject with aversion, the politically fractured self and double identity which multiple membership involves, which can be seen as conditioning us not to consider any polity claiming our loyalty to be 'über alles'. Maybe it is this understanding of Europe that makes it appear so alluring to some, so threatening to others.

1995

Notes

1. The position of the European Court of Justice has been that in the interests of a coherent legal system it alone has the power to review and annul Community measures

on any grounds, including lack of competences. The Constitutional German Court, delicately but firmly, has rejected this position.

2. There are no concurring or dissenting opinions. But note that the usual remark that the decision was taken unanimously is missing.

3. I do not wish to call into question the overall good faith of the German Constitutional Court but this citation is rather strange. When it gets to the most delicate passages laying down its understanding of *Volk* and the necessity for homogeneity, the Bundesverfassungsgericht quotes Hermann Heller: 'The states need sufficiently significant areas of responsibility of their own, within which each *Staatsvolk* [the people pertaining to a state], in a political decision-making process it legitimates and controls, can develop and articulate itself, so that that which binds it – relatively homogenously – together, spiritually, socially and politically, may find legitimate expression' (cf. H. Heller, *Politische Demokratie und soziale Homogenität, Gesammelte Schriften*, Volume 2, 1971, p. 421 [427ff.]). Whether or not Heller's concept of social homogeneity really sustains the No Demos thesis (it could actually support the opposite), it would seem that the writings of other scholars would have been much more aptly quoted in support of the position of the Bundesverfassungsgericht, for example those of Josef Isensee or even Carl Schmitt himself: see *Verfassungslehre* (Munich and Leipzig 1928), p. 231. I cannot help thinking that, given Heller's biography and intellectual positions, the Bundesverfassungsgericht found it more convenient to cite him. Heller's article, which originally appeared directly after Schmitt's article 'Der Begriff des Politischen' in *Politische Wissenschaft*, Part 5: *Probleme der Demokratie* (Berlin 1928), in the very beginning refers critically to Schmitt. On Heller generally, see Christoph Müller, 'Hermann Heller', in Kritische Justiz, ed., *Streitbare Juristen: Eine andere Tradition*, Baden-Baden 1988, pp. 268–81.

4. Sad but not altogether surprising: cf. decisions of the Bundesverfassungsgericht *in re* Right to Vote on the Communal Level for Foreign Citizens.

5. Paul Kirchhof, 'Der deutsche Staat im Prozes der europäischen Integration', in Josef Isensee and Paul Kirchhof, eds, *Handbuch des Staatsrechts der Bundesrepublik Deutschland*, Volume 7, *Normativatät und Schutz der Verfassung – Internationale Beziehungen* (hereafter referred to as *HdbStR VII*), Heidelberg 1992, p. 855; Paul Kirchhof, 'Europäische Einigung und der Verfassungsstaat der Bundesrepublik Deutschland', in Josef Isensee, ed., *Europa als politische Idee und als rechtliche Form*, Berlin 1993, p. 63; Paul Kirchhof, 'Deutsches Verfassungsrecht und Europäisches Gemeinschaftsrecht', in Paul Kirchhof and Claus-Dieter Ehlermann, *Deutsches Verfassungsrecht und Europäisches Gemeinschaftsrecht*, Baden-Baden 1991, p. 11. It is remarkable how easily even semantic parallels can be detected between Paul Kirchhof's legal writings – Kirchhof was the *juge-rapporteur* in this case – and the decision of the Bundesverfassungsgericht. Criticism has also been expressed of the fact that Kirchhof published his opinion on the case at all.

6. E.g. Josef Isensee, 'Nachwort. Europa – die politische Erfindung eines Erdteils', in Isensee, *Europa als politische Idee*, p. 103; Fritz Ossenbuhl, 'Maastricht und das Grundgesetz – eine verfassungsrechtliche Wende?', *Deutsches Verwaltungsblatt*, 1993, p. 634; Udo di Fabio, 'Der neue Artikel 23 des Grundgesetzes', *Der Staat* 1993, pp. 202 ff.

7. Kirchhof, *HdbStR VII*, para. 18, expressly mentions 'critical loyalty' and at the same time criticizes tendencies to the contrary in Germany: 'In the German development – perhaps especially in its religious history – there even seems to be a consciously cultivated gesture of demonstrative scepticism and ruminative protest, which is more inclined towards resistance against state authority than towards a critical loyalty in the spirit of a common responsibility within the state.'

8. Cf. Paul Kirchhof, 'Deutsche Sprache', in Josef Isensee and Paul Kirchhof, eds, *Handbuch des Staatsrechts der Bundesrepublik Deutschland*, Volume 1, *Grundlagen von Staat und Verfassung*, Heidelberg 1987, p. 745, para. 33: 'Linguistic homogeneity is what constitutes the German *Staatsvolk*.'

9. Kirchhof, *HdbStR VII*, para. 25: 'The European states of today do not thereby screen themselves off from other states or the citizens of other states, but they do maintain their autonomy in a *Staatsvolk* internally related by birth and origin, in a space belonging to that *Staatsvolk*, and in the cultural community of language, religion, art and historical experience.' Josef Isensee, 'Abschied der Demokratie vom Demos. Ausländerwahlrecht als

Identitätsfrage für Volk, Demokratie und Verfassung', in Dieter Schwab, Dieter Giesen, Joseph Listl, and Hans-Wolfgang Stratz, *Staat, Kirche, Wissenschaft in einer pluralistischen Gesellschaft* (Berlin 1989), p. 708: 'The legitimate unity of a people has permanent viability only if it rests on a real foundation: on a minimum of effective homogeneity, a basic stock of things held in common, such as can emerge from descent, history, language, culture and interests.' Cf. also Isensee, 'Nachwort', p. 122: 'No state can exist without a certain measure of homogeneity. The will to political unity, by which a group of people may become a people (*Volk*) in the form of a nation and thereby also a potential subject of democratic self-determination, takes its cue from objective, given facts, such as geopolitical situation, economic interests, history, language, civilizational standards, ethos, culture or religion.' Similarly, relating to any 'Bund' and extensively quoting Carl Schmitt, Bardo Fasbender, 'Zur Staatlichen Ordnung Europas nach der deutschen Einigung', *Europa Archiv*, 1991, p. 401. For the mystic connotations thrown into the debate by Isensee, see 'Abschied der Demokratie vom Demos': 'The image of the *Staatsvolk* ... is the common political destiny into which the individual citizens are bound. ... Thus, in the necessarily permanent and exclusive personal inclusion in the shared destiny (*Schicksalsgemeinschaft*) of the state, there lies a guarantee for a democratic ethos of citizenship.' I am not, of course, the first to observe or criticize this 'iconography' of peoplehood: cf. Jürgen Habermas, 'Citizenship and National Identity' (1990), in Habermas, *Between Facts and Norms. Contributions to a Discourse Theory of Law and Democracy* (Cambridge, MA 1996), pp. 491–515. What is striking is the way this terminology was accepted by the Bundesverfassungsgericht.

10. It is in this delicate context that the Bundesverfassungsgericht cites Hermann Heller as its authority.

11. This idea is not really new. See Schmitt, *Verfassungslehre*: 'A democratic state which locates the preconditions for its democracy in the national sameness of its citizens conforms to the so-called nationality principle, according to which a nation constitutes a state and a state encompasses a nation. A nationally homogenous state then appears as the norm; a state which lacks such homogeneity has something abnormal about it, something which is a threat to peace' (p. 231). Only slightly weaker is Isensee, 'Abschied der Demokratie vom Demos', who perceives the nation as the optimal precondition for the state: 'A legitimate polity does not have to be based on national unity. Nor is the latter a necessary prerequisite of democracy. But it is nevertheless its best possible foundation. In terms of its conception and its self-understanding, a nation exists prior to state and constitution. It conceives of itself as a political unit and strives to organise this unit in the form of a state' (p.709).

12. Kirchhof describes the state as 'Herrschaftsorganisation', cf. *HdbStR VII*, para 31: 'The holder of the supreme state authority ensures the cohesion of the state through decision and coercion; the state distinguishes its citizens (*Staatsangehörige*) legally and effectively from foreigners (*Fremde*), claiming leadership by differentiating its own from the general, what belongs from what does not. State theory emphasizes the opposition between friend and foe so as to lend thought and action a dependable orientation.' His only footnote in this context refers to Carl Schmitt, *Der Begriff des Politischen*, Berlin 1932, pp. 13ff, esp. p. 17.

13. *HdbStR VII*, para. 12: 'The development of a cultural unity in Europe is out of the question, since nine different national languages are spoken within the community ... The linguistic image of the assenting *Staatsvolk* having a "constitution-giving authority" (*verfassungsgebende Gewalt*) cannot adequately legally encompass the emergence of a European state. It does not explain why the formation of a new state in its different constitution should bind the citizens who are not part of the electorate now but will subsequently have the right to vote. It does not justify why the emerging state – the Community of the Twelve, let us say – should be allowed to exclude other states and other citizens and thereby bring about deep changes to their European beginnings. Above all, however, it is not able to support its own premiss, namely the common ground of a European *Staatsvolk* which belongs together: a minimum of homogeneity in basic constitutional attitudes, a legal language accessible to all, economic and cultural similarities or at least some forces of approximation, the possibility of political exchange through

media which reach the whole of Europe, a leadership which is known in Europe and parties active across Europe. . . . A Europeanization without a prior European consciousness and therefore without a European people with a concrete capability and readiness for common statehood would be, in terms of the history of thought, un-European.'

14. Also some others: cf. e.g. Dieter Grimm, 'Mit einer Aufwertung des Europa-Parlaments ist es nicht getan – Das Demokratiedefizit der EG hat strukturelle Ursachen', in *Jahrbuch zur Staats- und Verwaltungswissenschaft,* Volume 6, 1992–3, p. 13.

15. Grimm, p. 16: 'It will therefore be a long time before there is a European public and a broad public discourse on a European level. A European *Staatsvolk* to which one could attribute European sovereignty is not even on the horizon.'

16. See Isensee, 'Nachwort', p. 137. He is clearly negative about this idea: 'The linguistic diversity alone presents an obstacle here to the universal, direct discourse of democracy. Everything weighs against a single state: the wealth of collective individuality, the concentration of life in crowded spaces, historical depth and cultural contrasts, the folds and wrinkles, the chasms of an old continent. Perhaps all these peculiarities of Europe will one day cease to exist, levelled by a cosmopolitan civilisation or overlaid by immigrants from other parts of the world. It might end up that Germany relates to Italy as Kansas does to Texas, that the American dream is dreamed here, too: that of a single, new society, multicultural and uninational. But if the American dream should ever be realised on the old continent, the European dream would be finished. And with it the reality of political Europe.' Similarly, Bundesverfassungsgericht Judge Hans Hugo Klein, 'Europa – Verschiedenes gemeinsam erlebt. Es gibt kein europäisches Volk, sondern die Völker Europas', *Frankfurter Allgemeine Zeitung,* 17 October 1994, p. 12.

17. Kirchhof claims in *HdbStR VII,* para. 33: 'Democracy requires a communalization (*Vergemeinschaftung*) in the *Staatsvolk.*' Referring explicitly to the European Community, the Community cannot rest upon democratic legitimation, since 'representation through the European Parliament is not founded in a European *Staatsvolk*' (ibid., para 53). Isensee, 'Nachwort', p. 133: 'There is no democracy without a demos.' Less rigorous is *BVerfGE* 89, 155/86: 'If the *Staatsvölker* convey – as they do at present – democratic legitimation via the national parliaments, then the democratic principle places restrictions on the expansion of the tasks and powers of the European Communities.'

18. This observation was also made by the same Heller whom the Court cites for its homogeneity thesis. See Hermann Heller, *Staatslehre,* Leiden 1934, p. 164: 'Neither the people nor the nation must be allowed to be regarded as the natural unity which precedes the state unity and spontaneously constitutes it. The reverse has been the case often enough, when it was the unity of the state which bred the "natural" unity of the people and of the nation.' Obviously I take issue here with Kirchhof, who claims that Germany in the nineteenth century (1866), as well as the United States in 1787, constitutes an example of economic and cultural homogeneity, common language and the existence of a people preceding that state (Kirchhof, *HdbStR VII,* para. 38). Maybe the difference in perspective is simply a reflection of the half-full, half-empty glass. Alexis de Tocqueville apparently took a view somewhat different from Paul Kirchhof as regards the USA. In a letter to Ernest de Chabrol of 9 June 1831 he writes that American society, 'formed of all the nations of the world [. . .] people having different languages, beliefs, opinions: in a word, a society without roots, without memories', could turn into one people. His answer, it seems, was that nations could be based on adherence to values – democracy, self-government, equality, etc. – like those found in the American constitution. Roger Boesche, ed., *Alexis de Tocqueville, Selected Letters on Politics and Society,* Berkeley 1985, p. 38.

19. German citizenship law is governed primarily and historically by the basic principle of *jus sanguinis,* that only descendants of German citizens obtain German citizenship. The *jus sanguinis* concept reflects a negative attitude towards immigration and an underlying concept of citizenship. It was carefully chosen in 1913 to promote and maintain the ethnic tradition of the German nation-state.

20. Naturalization in Germany requires *inter alia* a voluntary and permanent dedication to Germany ('freiwillige und dauernde Hinwendung zu Deutschland'); it is not surprising that this disposition is 'hidden' in the administrative guidelines of the naturalization bureaucracy.

21. The 'request for ethnic assimilation' has been weakened in the following way: since 1 January 1991, for foreigners aged sixteen to twenty-three who have lived continuously in Germany for eight years, citizenship is easier to attain (no more administrative discretion). Besides this, naturalization can no longer be arbitrarily refused to foreigners who have been raised and educated in Germany or who have maintained permanent residence for at least fifteen years. Even in these cases, one's former citizenship must be abandoned.

22. This, in theory, is the American constitutional design. Naturalization is understood primarily in civic terms and many proud American citizens are equally proud of their diverse ethno-national identity – African Americans, Italo-Americans, Jewish Americans, etc. Of course, in the actuation of this design there have been no shortages of pathologies such as the shameful internment of Japanese Americans during the Second World War, not to mention the ever-present burden of racism in American society.

23. Hermann Cohen, *Die Religion der Vernunft aus den Quellen des Judentums*, Leipzig 1919.

24. Therefore, attempts to redefine citizenship in a way which cuts all links between the demos and national belongingness are not strictly necessary and may go too far.

25. 2nd edn, Berlin 1926, p. 14.

26. Ibid.

27. Carl Schmitt, 'Schlusswort des Reichsgruppenwalters Staatsrat Prof. Dr. Carl Schmitt', in *Das Judentum in der Rechtswissenschaft,* Volume 1, *Die deutsche Rechtswissenschaft im Kampf gegen den judischen Geist,* Berlin 1936.

Identities

19

Deconstructing Europe

J.G.A. Pocock

History is about process and movement; yet up to now it has taken as given the perspectives furnished by relatively stable geographical communities, of whose pasts, and the processes leading to their presents, history is supposed to consist. All that may be changing, with the advent of the global village, in which no one's home is their own; with the advent, too, of a universally imposed alienation, in which one's identity is presupposed either as some other's aggression against one, or as one's own aggression against someone else, and in either case scheduled for deconstruction. Yet the owl of Minerva may continue to fly, as long as there is an ark left to fly from; and the historian, who must today move between points in time, must recollect voyages and may still recollect voyages between known points with known pasts, recalling how the pasts changed as the presents shifted.

Two voyages, then, furnished the prelude to this essay in historical reflection: one beyond what is known as 'Europe', the other within it. The former was the later, and is therefore the nearer in time; it is therefore remembered first. It was a voyage in May 1991 to New Zealand, which is this historian's home culture; he is aware that few of his readers know that there is a culture there, or can readily believe it stands at the centre of anyone's historical consciousness. It was in that month a culture very deeply in crisis and threatened with possible discontinuation: more than for most reasons because the Europeanization of Great Britain had deprived it of its economic (and, like it or not, its previous spiritual) *raison d'être*, and it has not yet found another. Not having found – wherever the fault might lie – new markets of outlet, it had resorted to policies of privatization which amounted to the forced sale of national assets in the hope of attracting new investment capital, a subjection of national sovereignty to international market forces such as the European Community – only in this case there was no community – is supposed to stand for. This had reached the point where it was being seriously proposed to sell New Zealand public schools to their own boards of trustees, and the trustees were making it known that they had no money to buy them with. In the midst of this scene of understandable demoralization, relations between the largest minority and majority ethnic groups – Maori and Pakeha, Polynesian and Anglo-European – were giving rise to a complex, serious and conceptually sophisticated debate over the legal, moral and historical foundation of the national identity.[1] The owl had taken flight, but the dusk could be felt approaching. In history nothing is as certain as night and day; but it was a measurable possibility, if not an inevitability, that the history being intelligently debated might simply be terminated because the international economy had no further need of the community whose memory and identity it was.

An effect this had upon a historian who had lived for twenty-five years in the Northern Hemisphere, while remaining a product of the Southern, was sharply to jolt his awareness of 'Europe'. The historic process he saw before his eyes in New Zealand had begun with the British entry into the European Community, and had not been alleviated by that Community's economic policies. This is to say nothing of the moral policies of some of its member nations: the sinking of the *Rainbow Warrior* has not been forgotten in New Zealand, and there is a deep conviction that the French do not care, and cannot understand that anybody else does. In New Zealand – as when resident in the United States of America – he found himself in a culture governed by 'Western' values and given shape by their historic (and imperial) expansion: yet it seemed that there was a mystique of 'Europe' which laid claim to these values while excluding others from the community which claimed to base itself upon them. And the same mystique seemed to proclaim the subjection of national sovereignty to international market forces without making more than sporadic progress towards the creation of any new kind of political community governed by its citizens, to replace that whose obsolescence it so readily proclaimed. New Zealand, only yesterday a viable social democracy with policies and a government of its own, looked like an extreme because extra-marginal case of where the post-sovereignty process might lead.

The response might be a retreat into militant and even violent local populism – the Third World, to which New Zealand was threatened with relegation, was full of examples of the kind. But New Zealanders had been and still were a non-impoverished, civilized and international people, used to travel, to join the world and its history – distant though they found them – and to look at history through looking at others' way of seeing it.

An owl departing from the South Island of New Zealand must define the region in which its flight has navigational meaning. Until half a century ago, New Zealand's national existence was situated less in the Pacific ocean than in a global area defined by British naval and imperial power, running from Britain and Flanders through the Mediterranean and India to Austrialia, Singapore and beyond. New Zealand's wars were fought along the length of this system, as late as the Malayan emergencies of the 1950s; even in 1942, New Zealand troops were not withdrawn from the Mediterranean for war against Japan, as those of Australia were, but ended the Second World War keeping Trieste from becoming part of Yugoslavia. This imperial area possessed a consciously preserved history which was less that of empire or imperialism than that of British culture, political, religious, social and historical. Of this, New Zealanders – and, subject to their own more Irish mythology, Australians – saw themselves as part; it was believed to be the history of a culture with a global capacity for creating and associating new nations. Even now, when it has survived the power that once held it together, this history is part of their perception that they inhabit 'Western civilization' though they do not inhabit 'Europe'. The accession of the United Kingdom to the European Community entailed a rejection by that kingdom's peoples of the former global capacity of their culture; it was a confession of defeat, and at the same time a rejection of the other nations of that culture, which seemed to entail a decision that there was no longer a British history in which New Zealand's past or future possessed a meaning. The South Pacific owl of Minerva, finding its environment endangered, faced the task of rewriting New Zealand's British history, while taking part in the revision of all British history in which the historians of the United Kingdom have engaged in the post-imperial and quasi-European era now going on.

An assertion by means of which the owl defined its flight path and air space was therefore the assertion that 'Western civilization' extended beyond 'Europe' into those oceanic and continental spaces irreversibly Westernized by navigation and settlement in the seventeenth through nineteenth centuries. Europeans are often anti-American enough, and the United Kingdom British hostile enough to their imperial past, to deny and wish to sever this relation to the world: but the inhabitants of the world thus created are under a necessity of keeping its history alive, and an obsessive 'Europeanness' can appear to them a device aimed at excluding them from visibility. As part of the assertion that 'the West' extends beyond 'Europe', therefore, there are owls of Minerva who define themselves as navigating in the continental spaces of North

America and Australia, or – and this is the case of the sub-species under examination – the enormous oceanic spaces of the austral Pacific ocean, which Polynesian and European navigators have lodged in their memory and tradition. Take a globe in your hands, one not mounted on a spindle which preserves the intellectual dictatorship of Gerardus Mercator; rotate it until the islands of New Zealand are at the centre of the hemisphere you face. You will be looking at one facet of the New Zealand historical imagination, and you will be able to see Australia and Antarctica, but nothing worth mentioning of Indo-Malaysia, Asia or the Americas. There is a history which has to be created in this space, and when it is not a history looking back up the lines along which culture has travelled – towards what Maori called *Hawaiki-paa-mamao*, the spirit land high up and distant – it has to be the history of small communities in an ocean of planetary size. Writing Pacific history is a challenge to the imagination: it both is and is not a history of 'the West', and it certainly is not a history of 'Europe', even when a history of 'Europeans'.

These are spaces by which the Antipodean historian defines his relation to the world, and the need to see the planet as if the Southern Hemisphere contained its centre makes him aware of others. There is the Indonesian or Indo-Malaysian space from which he is separated by the mountains of New Guinea and the deserts of Australia; there is the northern ocean defined by the 'Pacific rim' and the movements of Japanese, American and neo-Confucian capital; there are the spaces defined by the major civilizations of Asia, and west of them the extensive and at present disastrously incoherent domains of Islam. There is the enormous space of northern Eurasia, formerly co-extensive with the Soviet Union, which may be glimpsed from cruising altitude on a flight from London to Tokyo. These last two offer the imagination a post-colonial route towards Europe, and towards the memory of the second voyage by which this essay is dominated.

This is the memory of a seven-month sojourn in Europe during 1989, moving through Calabria, Sicily, Tuscany, the Alpine region, south-west Germany and the Netherlands. The revolutions of Eastern Europe were beginning, and it would have been possible to set out by *ferrovia* or *autostrada* and watch the border crumble: but there was work to be done, and in any case a lingering feeling that history is for its immediate participants and not a spectacle for tourists. One was close enough, at all events, to experience a sensation that we were witnessing the end of a European era forty years long, and of a definition of 'Europe' predicated on the partition collapsing before one's eyes. The term 'Europe' had come to be often used co-terminously with 'the European Community', an association of former imperial states having in common the experience of defeat – Germany of defeat and partition, France, Italy and the Low Countries of defeat and occupation, Britain of exhaustion following victory – and the loss of colonial empires – in all cases except the first after 1940 – which had recovered enough to form a powerful combination based on the pooling of some sovereign powers and the removal of obstacles to the movement across their frontiers of international economic forces and some of the ways of living immediately dependent on them: this is the process intended to reach a culminating point in 1992.

The formation of this Community had been accompanied by an ideology of 'Europeanness', which sometimes affirmed that the culture possessed in common by these national communities, and the history of this common culture, was of greater moral and ideological significance than their several distinct national sovereignties or than the history shaped and written – as in the classical age of European historiography it had been – by their several existences as sovereign nation-states claiming to exercise control over their several histories. Politically as well as historiographically, there had been problems attending this fecund and exciting enterprise: it was not asserted, for example, that there existed or should exist a 'European people' or a 'European state', using these terms in the singular; and consequently – following the logic of political historiography – the 'European history' which was developing was (rightly enough) a plural history of divergences and convergences, in which a cultural commonality interacted with a diversity (often a warlike and destructive diversity) of political sovereignties and national histories.

In this, European historiography continued in its classical patterns, the history of the state retaining its primacy even after giving up its claim to be a moral absolute. In partitioned Germany, and in an Italy still plagued by consequences of the forced unification of the Piedmontese and Neapolitan kingdoms in 1861, there continued to be debate whether the national state had been a historical necessity or could have taken some other path. There was less sign that the French were inclined to regard 'France' as a contingency or accident of history:[2] but even in Britain – which came to 'Europe' late, reluctantly, and with many signs of self-contempt – there was an enterprise of considering 'British history' as existing distinctly from the history of 'England' and of asking whether the extension of English sovereignty had created a 'British' nation with a history of its own.[3] The historian writing this essay and remembering these voyages could claim some role in furthering this enterprise, and since the questions which it posed could be answered in the affirmative or the negative, it might either reinforce or subvert the existence of 'British history' as a distinct and intelligible field of study.

In ways such as these, the process of 'Europeanization' stimulated the classical historiography based on the conception of the state: it became more exciting, and yielded richer information, when the state and the nation were perceived as precarious, contingent and ambivalent rather than as moral absolutes and historical necessities. At the same time, however, the experience after 1945 of Western Europe, and the planet's advanced cultures in general, was conducive to postmodernism and alienation – meaning by these overworked terms that there were many competing memberships, allegiances, values and involvements, of which none was altogether satisfactory and each might be seen as competing with the others for mastery of the individual subjectivity which they had formed among them without rendering it satisfactory to itself. This was a problem at least as old as the European Enlightenment, and long antedated the temporary settlement of 1945. Under these conditions, however, it greatly encouraged an ideology, historiography and sub-culture of alienation in which every historic formation bearing on the individual consciousness became a candidate for deconstruction and rejection by that consciousness, which was in turn forced by the logic of historicism to deconstruct and reject any self or identity it might seem to possess. Since 'Europe' was the classical locus of this kind of consciousness, the deconstructive attitude became part of the ideology of 'Europeanness' and 'Europe' was thus well placed to deconstruct its competitors, while retaining for itself an essential lack of identity, of much tactical advantage in the assertion of hegemony: the Great Boyg won by refusing to name himself.

It was of course open to anyone to give him a name. When one saw praise of *la cultura europea* in graffiti on south Italian university walls in 1989, one was given to understand that some conservative Catholic programme was using these words in a code of its own; 'Europe' meant different things to different people, and they were busy deconstructing one another's meanings. All this, however, was ideologically and historiographically normal: a 'Europe' which incessantly challenged and debated its own identity was part of the civilization to which as a 'Westerner' one belonged, and 'America' in its own way did the same thing. What left the closed or open character of 'Europe' in greater doubt was its geopolitical situation. Demarcated down to 1989 by a military, political and ideological barrier running through central Germany and Europe, the European Community could look like a neo-Carolingian construct: a regrouping of Neustria, Franconia, Burgundy and Lombardy in the area defined by the Treaty of Verdun in the ninth century, modified by one major exclusion and one inclusion of lands not so defined. The exclusion was that of eastern Germany, the inclusion that of the British islands; both areas had been historically dominated by differing forms of Protestantism.

In the latter case, standing nearer to the concerns of the owl of Minerva, the entity's insular situation had separated it in some degree from two of the major historical experiences undergone in western Eurasia. Through military weakness, it had avoided involvement in the Wars of Religion fought down to 1648 (though some argued that it was by that date caught up in a war of religion of its own insular kind); through oceanic, mercantile and industrial power, it had escaped conquest and liberation in the Wars of Revolution after 1789, and had succeeded in playing a dominant role from an external situation. From the time of their consolidation at the end of the seventeenth century, the British kingdoms had been able to exercise power in Europe while maintaining their distance from it. Only the loss of that capacity was obliging the United Kingdom to seek membership in the European Community, and however strongly the step could be justified it could not altogether lose the character of a historic defeat and an enforced separation from a past by which the British had previously known themselves. It was this step which had left the British nations of the Pacific ocean denied a role in 'European' history and in 'British' history considered as part of it: oceanically situated in the face of the economic power exerted by Japan and the Lesser Dragons, and liable to be told that as neither 'European' nor 'American' (nor 'British'?) they belonged to no 'Western' community acting together to maintain itself.

These were the circumstances in which the ideology of 'Europeanness' could appear closed, exclusive and deconstructive. It is, in fact, not the case that the European Community has developed an accredited historiography of its own; there have been tentative ventures in that direction, which down to 1989 would have led towards a neo-Carolingian synthesis addressing itself to Germans on the loss of the east, Italians on the miseries of the south and British on the loss of detachment from the adjacent continent. What took a much more visible shape was an ideology of 'Europeanness' which enjoined the rejection of previously distinct national histories without proposing a synthetic or universal history to take their place. When the British are enjoined to consider themselves 'European', it is usually with the implication that they should not consider their history as in any way distinctive; and though this injunction has not been notably effective, it has strengthened the tendency towards the kind of postmodernism in which any *Lebensform* is presupposed an act of hegemony, an imposition to be deconstructed. 'Europe' could therefore become the ideology of a post-historical

culture, in which varyingly affluent and varyingly alienated masses –
there is an alienation of the consumer as well as an alienation of the
deprived – float from one environment to another with no awareness of
moving from one past, and one commitment to it, to another. It would
be a problem in historicity to determine whether this freedom from
commitment were an illusory or a real condition; either seems possible.

The mystique of 'Europe', which has often made it possible to use
the word as an incantation with which there can be no argument, may
have been the product of a turn towards a post-historic consumer
culture, but it has also been a product of the Community's singular
success in creating a common economy, elements of a common culture,
and some institutions of a shared administrative – it seems too soon to
call it 'civic' – political structure. All these were the connotations of the
word 'Europe' as it was being used down to 1989, and as it is still used
as it looks toward 1992.

In the former of these two years, however, the collapse of the Wall,
the Curtain, and much more besides, deprived 'Europe' of its partition
along the militarized and policed frontier which had defined its identity
as opposed to the presumed alternative culture of late Leninism. It
turned out that this alternative was not merely a failure, but had for a
long time been no more than a pretence; mass action and mass
sentiment rejected it, because for many years nobody had believed in it
enough to make it work; and the liberal-democratic capitalism of the
Community was faced with the task, not of transforming a counter-
culture, but of filling a vacuum and tidying up a gigantic mess. The
collapse extended beyond the Central and Eastern Europe occupied in
1944–45, deep into the Soviet Union itself and the heartlands of
northern Eurasia, where what collapsed in 1991 was not only an
economic and political order but a system of states possessing sovereignty distributed among themselves: so that the ideological transformation of the continent instantly took on a geopolitical dimension.
'Europe', used both as a term of mystique and as a synonym for the
European Community, came face to face with a Central Europe, an
Eastern Europe, and a Eurasia extending through Siberia, which had
not been integrated into its postmodern culture and did not belong
with any simplicity to its history. The Community proved to be a
regrouping of the lands of west Latin culture, as modified by Enlightenment, revolution, and the wars of Germany with France and Britain,
uncertain in its relations with the historic consequences of Protestantism, and now obliged by the reunification of Germany to recall how far
the twentieth-century wars had been a consequence of German–Russian
encounters in the environment formed by Eastern Europe. Beyond a
Slavonic Europe of largely Catholic culture could be discerned a wide

cultural zone whose history was Orthodox and Ottoman beyond the point of belonging to the history of Latin Christianity and its secularization.

This region was ethnically diverse and politically indeterminate. Among the disturbing consequences of the liberations of 1989–91 – the tunnels at the end of the light, as someone put it – was the discovery that seventy-five to forty-five years of revolutionary totalitarianism, long credited with a capacity to wash brains and rebuild minds, had eliminated none of the ethnic and sub-national antagonisms of western Eurasia. (It did not help to add that two centuries of West European colonialism had enjoyed no better success in Africa and southern Asia.) The collapse of socialism proved to be a collapse of empire, the only if inadequate force which had attempted the subjugation of these hostile identities; and the Russian-dominated federation of the Soviet Union, the Serbian-dominated federation of Yugoslavia, began a disintegration which continued through the revolution of August 1991 and the war in Bosnia. Both European and United States policy-makers face a choice between encouraging the devolution of sovereignty as a means of creating larger market economies, and maintaining existing centralizations of sovereignty as a means of preventing endemic inter-ethnic warfare – war having become a means less of asserting the interests of states than of posing ethnic challenges to their authority. The European Community faced this problem in respect of Yugoslavia, the United States of Iraq, both of the Soviet Union; and there were uncomfortable parallels in Canadian North America. This problem has many aspects. It raises the conceptual question – now extended from west to east – whether sovereignty can be rearranged without rearranging the pasts of which sovereignty makes human communities aware, and whether sovereignty can be treated as a contingent convenience or inconvenience without history itself becoming similarly contingent and manipulable.

This is a familiar problem in Central and Eastern Europe, where the distinction between 'historic' and 'non-historic' peoples was invented as a debating device in the Austro-Hungarian Empire and turned against it – but by no means eliminated – by the policy-makers of Versailles and Trianon. A New Zealander has some reason to know what it may be like to belong to a people which thought it had a history and is now instructed by others that it has none. These are devices in the discourse of empires and the unmaking of empires. The next discovery is that 'Europe' may be at the point of becoming an empire uncertain of the frontiers of its own discourse, as it faces the question of how far to intervene in the ethnic strife of Croats and Serbs, and as differences between the policies of its major nations emerge over the admission of central and eastern states to the Community. The greatest single truth to declare itself in the wake of 1989 is that the frontiers of 'Europe' towards the east are everywhere open and indeterminate. 'Europe', it can now be seen, is not a continent – as in the ancient geographers' dream – but a sub-continent: a peninsula of the Eurasian land-mass, like India in being inhabited by a highly distinctive chain of interacting cultures, but unlike it in lacking a clearly marked geophysical frontier. Instead of Afghanistan and the Himalayas, there are vast level areas through which conventional 'Europe' shades into conventional 'Asia', and few would recognize the Ural mountains if they ever reached them. In these regions the states and cultures of Latin, Catholic–Protestant and Enlightened 'Europe' both merge and do not merge with others, of Orthodox, Islamic, Russian and Turkish provenance, as what we call 'Europe' is ambiguously continuous with what we had better learn to call 'Eurasia'.

In this perspective, to imagine 'Europe' as a cohesive entity raises questions of demarcation and definition. Are Serbians, Moldavians, Georgians and Armenians 'Europeans' because their culture is historically Christian and post-Christian? Are Albanians, Bosnians, Turks and Azeris not 'Europeans' because theirs is Islamic or post-Islamic? On what grounds could such questions be answered, and who would have the authority to decide them? In such geographical and historic circumstances, a culture which regards itself as cohesive and autonomous may find itself playing the role of empire, claiming the authority not merely to extend its frontiers but to extend or retract them at will, telling others that they are or are not 'European' as the British claim the authority to tell New Zealanders or Hong Kongers when they are or are not 'British'. In the special circumstances of western Eurasia, 'Europe' may find that it has the power to do this unshared by others, but not the authority to command the consent of the cultures affected, which alone can legitimate the inclusions or exclusions of empire. Kurds, Albanians and boat people know what it is like to be ill-informed as to whether the protection of empire is being given or refused; indeed, all *Gastarbeiter* know.

These are practical problems, which lie beyond the province of this essay, though it does seem permissible to point out that the mentality of 1992 cannot safely be any longer, but dangerously may be nevertheless, a projection of the mentality of 'Europe' as it was before 1989 and German reunification. This is an essay in and on historiography, a meditation for owls of Minerva watching history change behind them under changing global light-conditions in which it is monocentric any longer to speak of 'gathering dusk', since dusk to one culture may be dawn to another; though again, it has to be remembered that we claim to be diversifying the word's cultures precisely when, and because, we are in fact homogenizing them. The debate over multicultural education has to be read in that complex of lights and shadows. At the outset of this essay it was premissed that historiography was the study of change and memory, which is why it lies both behind and before the owls flying against the time-stream: the study of the processes of change in which we are all involved, counterpointed by the maintenance in the present of identity as members of coherent communities possessing coherent and recollectable pasts. Since it has been regularly assumed that these communities in the present are relatively autonomous political entities – it is less than a century since 'history' could be defined as 'present politics' and 'the memory of the state' – these definitions of historiography have a political dimension. They presuppose that one of the aims of the state is to exercise some control over its own history, defining its past and seeking to determine its future; that the liberal state associates individuals with it in this enterprise, that of seeking the freedom – thus history used to be defined as 'the history of freedom' – to act as citizens in the determination of their own historicized identities; that political sovereignty was so far the state's means of prescribing its historic past and future that it was doubtful whether the individual could be accounted free, in history as in politics, unless a citizen of an autonomous and sovereign political community.

There is consequently an association between sovereignty and historiography; a community writes its own history when it has the autonomous political structure needed if it is to command its own present, and typically the history it writes will be the history of that structure. Such a history need not, though it very often will, be written uncritically; it may be written in ways that reveal its existence within a historical context larger than itself, its contingency upon many historical processes which it does not command. There are other kinds of history which can and should be written, and a historian or person of historical sensibility is at liberty to decide that these kinds possess priority over political history and history of the state. A class, gender or ethnic group which has been excluded or repressed by the political community must write its own history and that of the state in terms of this experience, though whether history can be written in exclusively negative and eristic terms is another question. A national community which has existed by assimilating diverse ethnic groups to an ethnically specific culture – the United States is a major example – must decide how to measure the history of the assimilating culture against that of the cultures undergoing an assimilation which may be incomplete or false. There is nothing sacrosanct, or privileged, about the history engendered by sovereignty: and yet the history of historiography as we know it obliges us to ask whether it would exist without history of this kind, whether historiography would exist without the state. One reason for this is that sovereignty and historiography, a voice in controlling one's present and a voice in controlling one's past, have been and may still be necessary means by which a community asserts its identity and offers an identity to the individuals composing it. Certainly, it can and must be asked whether it can pursue this enterprise, and maintain the means of doing so, without making war against other communities or denying an identity, a politics and a history to subjugated communities within its hegemony. But if the abandonment and the redistribution of sovereignty are to become general practices recommended to or imposed upon states, or communities of states, which were formerly sovereign and wrote their national histories as histories of their autonomous politics, one must also ask: if the sovereignty is to disappear, what is to happen to the historiography? If the historiography is to disappear, what is to happen to the identity? If the autonomous political community is to disappear, what is to happen to the political identity and autonomy of the individual?

These questions appear to be intimately linked, and one can imagine an 'Austro-Hungarian' set of answers, in which the surrender of sovereignty to a common set of institutions is found to have privileged some communities, but not others, to claim certain kinds of hegemony as 'historic peoples', while failing to provide the governing structure itself with a history which is that of a community or provided anyone with an identity. There was in that case an 'imperial' mystique, as there is now a 'European' mystique, which claimed to have a history but on the whole failed to make good that claim; and to this it may be added that empires commonly claim to be communities and to possess histories, but often fail in a diversity of ways to satisfy the communities they incorporate that their claim is good.

At this point new sets of questions may be asked. Is the supranational community we look at in the double perspective of this essay – the European Community, since no Pacific community is in process of formation – a species of empire, in which ultimate political control belongs to some institutions rather than others, to some national communities rather than others? The problems placed before the Community by the changes taking place in Central and Eastern Europe seem to make this a reasonable question; there are said to be differing German, French and British policy preferences regarding the future of the states of Eastern Europe. If we answer the question in the affirmative, we return 'Europe' to the domain of reason of state. 'Empire' and 'confederation' are not mutually exclusive terms, but are ranged along a spectrum of meanings: it may be said, however, that if there is to be a 'Europe' commanding its political present, there must be a political structure capable of defining its own past and writing its own history. On the other hand, the 'mystique of Europe' that has taken shape does not seem to offer a political history, which as far as can be seen would have to be that of a plurality of states acting in their own history and never yet confederated or incorporated in a lasting imperial structure. This opens the way to the reply that the question has been wrongly posed, and that the community being shaped is not a political community in the sense of a redistribution of the sovereignty possessed by states, but a set of arrangements for ensuring the surrender by states of their power to control the movement of economic forces which exercise the ultimate authority in human affairs. The institutions jointly operated, and/or obeyed, by member states would then be not political institutions bringing about a redistribution of sovereignty, but administrative or entrepreneurial institutions designed to ensure that no sovereign authority can interfere with the omnipotence of a market exercising 'sovereignty' in a metaphorical because non-political sense. There would be an 'empire' of the market which would not be an empire as the term is used in the vocabulary of politics, because that vocabulary would itself have lost its hegemony.

One might emerge with an uneasy hybrid, an 'empire' of the market in which residual political authority was unequally distributed between the political entities subject to its supra-political authority; or with a more benign, at least a more familiar, scenario in which confederated nations successfully operated shared institutions designed to allow market forces that freedom of operation which it had been agreed should belong to them. The problem of empire would not have disappeared, since it would be possible to find former national communities which had been denied their sovereignty and their history, or simply abolished as viable human communities, either by inclusion within or by exclusion from supranational common markets of the sort being imagined. It will be remembered that this essay is being written in part from a New Zealand point of view. In the East European and Eurasian settings – perhaps also in the North American as regarded from Quebec – member states of hegemonic confederations are to be seen claiming an independent sovereignty, very possibly with a view to joining common markets to which sovereignty must be given up as soon as asserted; the pooling of sovereignty in some regions and the fragmentation of sovereignty in others may be two sides of the same medal; but there may be yet other regions in which market forces simply reign without bothering to exact common institutions from the communities they rule, make and unmake. There have been informal empires as well as formal.

The essay is designed to ask questions about the voice of politics and history in the conversation of mankind. What happens to the sometime citizens of a formerly autonomous community when it is enjoined to give up its political sovereignty and the capacity to write its own history; to the United Kingdom British when they are enjoined to cease claiming a history of their own and accept that they have no history except that of a Europe which has not been written yet? To the New Zealand British when they are ejected from Anglo-European history and enjoined to consider themselves part of a Pacific world which has no common history and may never acquire one? The craft of historiography suggests some responses to these predicaments. The United Kingdom British have the option of writing the history of Europe on the assumption that the history of the British peoples does indeed form part of it and radically modifies the ways in which it must be understood once this is admitted. The far more isolated and threatened New Zealanders, to whom others rather deny than extend options, may easily recognize that they are made up of voyaging peoples, Polynesian, European and latterly Asian; they may write their own history as shaped by voyaging, and voyage themselves in search of other histories to which oceanic distances connect them by the very radicalness of separation. Owls of Minerva may send back messages from other points in what is only planetary space.

But this is to presuppose that the voice of self-defining political and national historiography will survive. There have been political and social preconditions of its existence, and these may be in process of supersession. Let us imagine a state of affairs in which political communities had been effectively reduced to insignificance, and humans could identify themselves only as existing in market communities, engaged in no other self-defining activities than the manufacture, distribution and consumption of goods, images and the information (if that is the right word) relating thereto. It would in principle be possible to write the histories of such communities, and these histories might be full of unexpected and intriguing information about their conduct and the character of human life as shaped by them. The proposition that life in the non-political community is as historically informative as life in the political is as old as the New History, which has cropped up at intervals since Voltaire published the *Essai sur les moeurs*: but New Historians have usually been political actors, with political motives for de-emphasizing the political. If we imagine a dystopia or eutopia in which market communities exercised complete hegemony, we may ask whether the ruling élites of such communities would have much interest in seeing their official histories written, or whether the individual as consumer would have the same grounds as the individual as citizen, or as social actor interacting with the political, in seeing herself or himself as a critical actor modifying rule by his or her responses to it, and wishing to see the history of such modifications written.

The preconditions of historiography would not be met if the market communities had acquired an unlimited capacity of changing the produced and distributed images of what they were and what human needs they were designed to satisfy, if there were no alternative to responding to the images presented by the system that distributed them, and if the communities were incessantly and therefore uncritically engaged in this transformation of their self-images. There could then be no critical histories of images, but only images of history. To imagine this is, of course, to imagine the dystopia of *Brave New World* or *1984*, in which rulers as well as ruled are totally assimilated to the systems they operate. It may be replied that market communities do not deprive the individual of agency to the dystopian extent, while leaving open the question whether they will, under post-political conditions, contain individuals with enough sense of agency to require histories, as we know them, to be written. The problem will become more acute if we imagine market communities as lacking temporal stability, as constantly dissolved, transplanted and transformed by the market's insatiable demand for new human needs to satisfy; or if we imagine communities marginalized by the market, mere pools of unwanted labour with little or no purchasing power. Such fluctuating or frozen human masses would have little history and less need or will to write it; perhaps there are prerequisites for having a history at all. For the purposes of the present essay it is not necessary to predict the prevalence of such non-communities: but it is not mere fantasy to imagine them.

It is nearer description than imagination to say that we already have the makings of the historical or post-historical ideology which might take the place of historiography in such communities and non-communities as we have been supposing. This is the ideology of postmodernism, which – to simplify matters – may also be called the ideology of alienation, and a great deal of post-political historiography is already being written according to its specifications. It presupposes that all history is invention, and that all invention is alien and an imposition; any context in which the self might find meaning is imposed on the self by some other, or by the self acting out of a false consciousness imposed on it by some other, and any specification of the self is similarly imposed, with the consequence that the self is always false, an imposition or imposture against its own unrealizable existence. History is the study of constructs, and its aim is invariably their deconstruction. It used to be argued that this knowledge was the escape into freedom, until it was discovered that there remained no subject to be free, and it can still be argued, within limits, that it teaches a critical skill very useful to selves constantly threatened with identities imposed by others, and constantly obliged by the nature of history to be on the move between contexts in which identity must be varyingly realized and asserted. As a strategy, it is a good one for living and fighting back in the world of uncriticized market forces which incessantly impose new and non-referential images of who one is and what one wants: but as an ideology it is the instrument of that world and operates to reinforce it. The marketers of images instruct us that we have no selves other than those they choose to impose upon us; the deconstructionist intellectuals, if they are not willing to stop somewhere and make a stand, tell us exactly the same thing. In all too many cases they have become anti-humanist enough to get no nearer making a stand than casting us either as oppressed – which is not so bad – or more commonly as oppressors of some other, to whose alienated consciousness they then enjoin us to submit our own. Their motives in doing so should be scrutized and may be conjectured.

It is easy enough to see how this could become the ideology of a post-political, post-industrialist and postmodernist Europe. The affluent populations wander as tourists – which is to say consumers of images – from one former historical culture to another, delightfully free from the need to commit themselves to any, and free to criticize while determining for themselves the extent of their responsibility. How far this is a freedom to make their own history, how far a freedom from any need to make it, may be debated. Meanwhile the non-affluent form underclasses, pools of labour ebbing from one area of under-employment to another. The ideology of alienation, a luxury to the affluent, is a necessity to them, and as long as the state, feeling little need of a highly educated workforce, chooses to underpay its teachers, public education will be a means of perpetuating the underclass's pseudo-revolutionary discourse, which will double as the means of promotion into the educated bureaucracy. It will produce quite an intelligent, articulate and disenchanted populace, offered by history no means of associating themselves in politically active communities, but only in self-congratulatory yet self-accusatory sects and counter-cultures of the apparently or really alienated, capable at best of the special-issue activisms which constitute populism but not democracy. Thus the post-historical and post-political culture one can imagine taking shape in Western Europe or North America; more isolated communities might be more deeply threatened. When the historian writing this essay spoke in New Zealand and argued that neither Europeans nor Polynesians there were *tangata whenua* – people of the land – but both were *tangata waka*, peoples of the ship who could remember the voyages that had brought them,[4] it was a Maori discussant who remarked that both were threatened with becoming boat people. We were recognizing the power of market forces to uproot communities and turn them into migrant labour.

There are regions of continental and oceanic proportions beyond the common markets in which postmodernism can flourish. Early in 1991, Tatyana Tolstaya drew attention to such a region in western Eurasia not far beyond Europe: 'in the West the sense of history has weakened or completely vanished; the West does not live in history, it lives in civilization (by which I mean the self-awareness of transnational technological culture as opposed to the subconscious, unquestioned stream of history). But in Russia there is practically no civilization, and history lies in deep, untouched layers over the villages, over the small towns that have reverted to near wilderness, over the large, uncivilized cities, in those places where they try not to let foreigners in, or where foreigners themselves don't go.'[5] In using 'civilization' and 'history' as antithetical terms, Tolstaya is engaging in a dramatic departure from conventional Western language. By 'history' she means the experience and memory of the past unprocessed, in the nature of raw sewage: unmediated, uninterpreted, uncriticized and (incidentally if not centrally) unsanitized, present but not controlled, unimpeded in its capacity to drive humans to do unspeakable things. There are many areas of the settled earth (some of them in great Western cities, as the United States knows to its cost) where 'history' is like this. But when Tolstaya says that 'history' dies where there is 'civilization', she departs deliberately and for good reason from Western discourse, since there we still believe that 'civilized' societies can write and debate their history, interpret it, argue over it, succeed or fail in coming to terms with it, even regard it as 'the nightmare from which one struggles to awake', and be the more 'civilized' for this ability to criticize it and reduce it to process. Even the loss of sovereign autonomy can stimulate the owl to take flight and map the territory of the past in greater detail and new perspectives: this happened in Edinburgh and Glasgow during the Scottish Enlightenment, and has been happening in both British and New Zealand historiography in response to Europeanization.

To us it does not follow that history disappears when it is interpreted,[6] but Tolstaya may be reminding us that this state of affairs cannot be relied on to last. The privatizing state may be ending its alliance with the clerical and intellectual élites who were its accredited interpreters and critics; it would rather its universities were vocational schools – if that – than centres of inquiry; and as we look through Europe into Eurasia, where the intelligentsias have been devastated by the life and death of the Party, we may be looking into a world where the postmodern which is indifferent to history lies side by side with the pre-modern which cannot rule history and is ruled by it. Along this fault-line between tectonic plates, we wish to say, unspeakable things will continue to happen, and the historian – that spokesperson for excluded modernity – may find something useful to do: but if there is no political domain in which historical understanding seeks an opportunity to act, is there anything that can be done?

Tolstaya's very striking language reminds us of a sense in which the 'death of history', prematurely announced a little while ago, might theoretically happen. Francis Fukuyama was (perhaps) imagining that the growth of the state and the processes of revolution might cease to be effective makers of history, given the universal triumph of a global market which took no account of frontiers; that the politics culminating in state and revolution were the means by which human beings attempted to control their history; that 'history' was the name for that process when under human control; and that henceforth humans would not make their history by their own thought and action, but the forces of the market would make it for them. Tolstaya is envisaging a not wholly different state of affairs, in which 'civilization' resolves and abolishes history and only barbarism retains it. Given these premises, the post-modern historian – when not living, as many still do, in a fantasy world in which linguistic criticism secures and continues the Leninist supremacy of the inquisitorial intelligentsia – will attempt to discover 'history' in the micro- or macro-experiences of humans in the global market and its culture. Those who maintain the modernist, or at any rate the pre-postmodernist, perspective will maintain that politics does not disappear with the Bismarckian or the Stalinist state, that humans continue to set up political structures to control their own history and contest for the power which comes from the attempt to control it, and that politics and history remain among the active forces which shape human lives and give them meanings. But the new world disorder coming after 1989 calls in question the premises of this debate, by calling in question the bipolarity of Tolstaya's (to say nothing of Fukuyama's) projection. The boundaries between 'civilization' and its opposite, barbarism, between history assimilated and history uncontrolled, have been broken open, and there is a zone to which politics and history are once more relevant. Europe is again an empire concerned for the security of its *limites*, and we may cautiously recall Gibbon's projection, in which the inhabitants of the civilized provinces have 'sunk into the languid indifference of private life' and history is being made for them by the encounters of soldiers and barbarians along the frontiers – the new barbarians being those populations who do not achieve the sophistication without which the global market has little for them and less need of them.

It is time to stop projecting and fantasizing: but in late 1991 it seems apparent that 'Europe' – both with and without the North America whose addition turns it from 'Europe' into 'Western civilization' – is once again an empire in the sense of a civilized and stabilized zone which must decide whether to extend or refuse its political power over violent and unstable cultures along its borders but not yet within its system: Serbs and Croats if one chances to be Austrian, Kurds and Iraqis if Turkey is admitted to be part of 'Europe'. These are not decisions to be taken by the market, but decisions of the state; and they are revealing clearly enough that 'Europe' is still a composite of states, whose historically formed interests give them non-identical attitudes towards the problems of 'Europe' and its borderlands. Classically state-centred historiography returns to relevance, and even salience, once the crises of historic Russia and Yugoslavia present themselves before a Europe in which Germany has once again become united. There is still something for history to do – this is not put forward as a cheering prospect – whether written about the past or enacted in the present; the end is not yet. One may of course perform an act of faith, professing that these phenomena are all transitory and that sooner or later the global market will have exterminated politics and history all around the globe. When that happens, the end of history will have arrived: but to celebrate 1992 as if 'Europe' were a secure and self-regarding 'homeland', intent only on its postmodern and post-historical self, might be to look rather like the Emperor Philip the Arab, celebrating the Secular Games at one of Gibbon's great ironic moments.

This essay has been written with a certain disrespect for the post-modernist intelligentsias, whose arrogance and provincialism at the moment expose them to their share of derision. But the postmodern phenomenon itself is entitled to respect: there really are senses in which the political community is losing its place at the centre of our allegiance (and allegiance itself any centre in consequence), and the non-political structures – or alternatively, those structures which enlarge the meaning of the 'political' until it has no boundaries – surrounding our existence are acquiring histories, or non-histories, of their own. Therefore the current 'new history' or anti-history is entitled to its place. The thrust of this essay is towards suggesting that it is not entitled to more than a place, and will not be enabled to claim a monopoly or an allegiance. Politics, the state, and various kinds of war, will continue to command our attention; Tolstaya's confrontation between 'civilization' and 'history' will continue to generate a history in which both are involved; and even within, as well as outside, the global consumer culture generated by the all-conquering market, communities will continue to assert their politics in order to have a voice in determining their history. It is reasonable therefore to predict, and even to recommend, a continuing dialogue, or family quarrel, between the political and the post-political, the modern and the postmodern, the historical and the post-historical, history in older and in newer senses. It is perhaps in eastern, not western Eurasia that it will finally be seen whether 'history' has come to an 'end' or not.

'Europeans', in this prediction, would write their history in ways which both privileged and deprivileged the centrality of states, admitting that they cast long and sometimes dark shadows in a present which may transcend the past but cannot abolish it; the pretence that there can be invented some uncomplicatedly 'European' history which both includes and excludes the histories of all the nations would be given up. The 'British' would write their history into that of 'Europe', rewrite the latter's history as modified by their presence in it, and continue on occasion to write the former as seen in perspectives which are less continental than insular, archipelagic, oceanic and imperial. They would probably not be the only 'European' national society to do so. As for that culture with which this essay began – 'New Zealand', cut adrift from its 'British' history by the advent of 'Europe', and for some purposes to be renamed 'Aotearoa' – it may already have lost both political and economic control of its present and future: but if it survives at all, its historians will have learnt (as they are learning) many new perspectives. They are learning rather rapidly to write their history as that of two cultures in stubborn interaction, and this reinforces rather than diminishes their sense of its autonomy; engrossed by the processes of settlement, they are already writing micro-histories of local experience and discourse, at their own distances from the history of politics and the state. If (again) they survive, their owls of Minerva will send out messages before as well as behind them on their flight, and they will address both Pacific history – which is that of small intense communities formed, separated and connected by voyagings over oceanic distances – and the history of 'Europe', 'Britain' and other northern land-mass cultures from which they are derived and which they need to see in their own way. They will inform 'Britain' that it has a planetary history it will not be able to forget, and 'Europe' that, as there is a Eurasian world into which it shades without fixed borders, so there is an oceanic (and likewise an American) world which it created and which enlarges it into 'the West'. Barriers between empires went down in 1989, and the intercontingency of the world increased. What do they know of Europe who only Europe know?

1991

Notes

1. See Andrew Sharp, *Justice and the Maori: Maori Claims in New Zealand Political Argument in the 1980s*, Auckland 1990.

2. See Fernand Braudel, *The Identity of France*. Volume 1, *History and Environment*, London 1988.

3. J.G.A. Pocock, 'The Limits and Divisions of British History: In Search of the Unknown Subject', *American Historical Review*, vol. 87, no. 2, 1982.

4. J.G.A. Pocock, '*Tangata whenua* and Enlightenment Anthropology', *New Zealand Journal of History*, vol. 26, no. 1, 1992, pp. 28–33.

5. *New York Review of Books*, 11 April 1991.

6. See, however, J.H. Plumb's *The Death of the Past*, London 1969; and David Lowenthal's *The Past is a Foreign Country*, Cambridge 1985.

20

National Identity and the
Idea of European Unity

Anthony D. Smith

There is nothing new about the idea of European unity. It can be traced
back to Sully, Podiebrad, perhaps even Charlemagne and the Holy
Roman Empire. Nor is there anything new about national identity. Even
if not as old as nationalists would have us believe, national consciousness
can be traced back to the later Middle Ages, to the wars of the Scots,
English and French in the fourteenth century, to Joan of Arc, to Spanish
unification under the Catholic Monarchs, and certainly to the Eliza-
bethans and the age of Shakespeare; though not until the next century,
in the Puritan Netherlands and England, can one discern the first
flowerings of popular (albeit religious) *nationalism*, and not until the
American and French revolutions does nationalism appear as a fully
fledged secular ideology.[1]

So why should there be such interest now in the European idea and
its relationship to national identities? Is it simply the fact that European
unification, in whatever form, is for the first time a distinct possibility –
that we can 'make Europe' where previous generations could only
dream about it? Or is it rather that the sheer pace of social and political
change has forced us to reassess rooted structures like the nation-state,
and hallowed values like national identity?

Clearly, modern technologies and communications have led many
people to question the old certainties. They grope in some confusion
towards a new type of social order, yet are afraid to let go of the old.
They wonder whether the new structures and identities that may be
forged will answer their needs and interests as well as the habitual and
familiar ones. What exactly will a vast, over-arching 'Europe' mean for
individuals and families? Will the seat of authority become still more
impersonal and remote? Will it be less sensitive to local problems and

needs? What does growing European unification mean for the values, heritages and cultures of Europe's many ethnic communities, regions and nations?

There is a more fundamental reason for the current interest in the cultural impact of European unification. It lies in the problem of 'identity' itself, one that has played a major part in European debates over the past thirty to forty years. At issue has been the possibility and the legitimacy of a 'European identity', as opposed to the existing national identities. For nationalists, the nation is the sole criterion of legitimate government and of political community. Does this exclude the possibility of a European identity and political community? Or can, and must, a unified Europe be designated a 'super-nation'? Alternatively, should we regard a United States of Europe as a new type of 'supranational' identity and community? What exactly does that mean? These issues are central to the continuing debates between pro- and anti-Europeans, between federalists, Gaullists and today's Bruges group.

I hope to show that some of these debates are exaggerated in their assumptions and scope. It is true that at the practical level of policy the claims of these competing identities – the European and the national – may come into conflict. This appears to have been the case recently, when the states of Europe, responsive to national public opinion, were in disarray over foreign policy over the Gulf war and then over Yugoslav conflicts. A common European cultural identity, if such there be, does not yet have its counterpart on the political level; to date, each state of the European Community has placed its perceived national interests and self-images above a concerted European policy based on a single presumed European interest and self-image.

At the conceptual level, however, the contradiction between a European identity and existing national identities may be more apparent than real. It rather depends on the version of nationalist doctrine held. If we hold to a Romantic doctrine and view the nation as a seamless, organic cultural unit, then the contradiction becomes acute. If, on the other hand, we accept a more voluntaristic and pluralistic conception and regard the nation as a rational association of common laws and culture within a defined territory, then the contradiction is minimized. For in this version – which is the one generally accepted in Western countries – individuals may choose to which nation they wish to belong, and there is, as we shall see, room for competing focuses of identity. So the conflict between the claims of the nation and those of a looser European identity becomes more situational and pragmatic, even if in a political crisis it could never be eliminated. I shall return to this key question below.

First Considerations: Method

Though there have been many studies of the economic organizations and political institutions of the European Community, relatively little attention has been devoted to the cultural and psychological issues associated with European unification – to questions of meaning, value and symbolism. What research there has been in this area has suffered from a lack of theoretical sophistication and tends to be somewhat impressionistic and superficial. This is especially true of attitude studies, in which generalizations over time are derived from surveys of particular groups or strata at particular moments. In few areas is the attitude questionnaire of such doubtful utility as in the domain of cultural values and meanings.[2]

Clearly, what is needed in this field is a series of case-studies over time of changes in collective perceptions and values, as recorded in literature and the arts, in political traditions and symbolism, in national mythologies and historical memories, and as relayed in educational texts and the mass media. Such studies rarely focus on the European dimension as such. Rather, they address changes in the content of national symbolism and mythology, ethno-history and collective values and traditions, which may or many not include an opening towards a wider, European dimension, but whose central focus is the continuing process of reconstructing or re-imagining the nation.[3]

Such studies form a useful point of departure for investigations into the complex relationships between national identities and the processes of European unification in the sphere of culture and values. Here I shall concentrate specifically on the cultural domain and its links with politics, leaving on one side the processes of economic and political integration that form the main concern of European studies. I shall focus on five interrelated areas.

- The impact and uses of the pre-modern 'past' or 'pasts' of ethnic communities and nations in the continent of Europe, and the ways in which pre-modern structures and images continue to condition modern processes and outlooks.
- The origins and nature of collective, cultural identities, and more specifically of national identities, and their consequences for social and political action.
- The growth of globalizing tendencies in communications, education, the media and the arts, which transcend national and even continental boundaries, bringing a truly cosmopolitan character to society that surpasses internationalism.

- Allied to these tendencies, fundamental geopolitical and ecological changes in the world at large – often of an unpredicable nature, like the dangers of a shrinking Soviet Union or a Middle Eastern vortex, or of pollution and epidemic disease – which affect changing values.
- The processes of regional or continental unification, of which Europeanization is only the most explicit and advanced example. Here the question is not just the history of an idea or process, but the changing contents and boundaries of 'Europe' in the context of a rapidly evolving world.

Multiple Identities

A comparative method using case-studies of national identity and culture needs some kind of theoretical framework; and given the nature of our problem, a logical starting-point is the concept of collective cultural identity. This would refer not to some fixed pattern or uniformity of elements over time, but rather to a sense of shared continuity on the part of successive generations of a given unit of population, and to shared memories of earlier periods, events and personages in the history of the unit. From these two components we can derive a third: the collective belief in a common destiny of that unit and its culture. From a subjective standpoint, there can be no collective cultural identity without shared memories or a sense of continuity on the part of those who feel they belong to that collectivity. So the subjective perception and understanding of the communal past by each generation of a given cultural unit of population – the 'ethno-history' of that collectivity, as opposed to a historian's judgement of that past – is a defining element in the concept of cultural identity, and hence of more specific national and European identities.[4]

From this starting-point we might go on to characterize the cultural history of humanity as a successive differentiation (but also enlargement) of processes of identification. In the simplest and earlier societies, the number and scale of such identities were relatively limited; but as populations organized themselves into more complex agrarian societies in a variety of political formations, the number and scale of such identifications multiplied. Where once gender, age, clan and tribe had provided the chief units of identity, now there were also village communities, regions, city-states, religious communities and even empires. With the growing stratification of such societies, classes and status groups (castes, estates, ethnic communities) also took on vital roles as focuses of identification in many societies.

In the modern era of industrial capitalism and bureaucracy, the number and in particular the scale of possible cultural identities have increased yet again. Gender and age retain their vitality; class and religious loyalties continue to exercise their influence; but today, professional, civic and ethnic allegiances have proliferated, involving ever larger populations across the globe. Above all national identification has become the cultural and political norm, transcending other loyalties in scope and power.

Yet, however dominant the nation and its national identification, human beings retain a multiplicity of allegiances in the contemporary world. They have multiple identities. These identifications may reinforce national identities or cross-cut them. The gendered perceptions of the male population may reinforce their sense of national identity, whereas those of the female part of the same collectivity may detract from it. The class allegiances of upper and middle classes may subjectively fuse with their sense of national identification, whereas the class solidarities of workers may conflict with their national loyalties. Similarly, some collective religious sentiments can reinforce a sense of national identity, as we witness today in Ireland, Poland and Israel; whereas some other kinds of religious loyalty transcend and thereby diminish purely national identities, as in the case of Roman Catholicism and Islam.[5]

Under normal circumstances, most human beings can live happily with multiple identifications and enjoy moving between them as the situation requires. Sometimes, however, one or other of these identities will come under pressure from external circumstances, or come into conflict with one of the individual's or family's other identities. Conflicts between loyalty to a national state and solidarity with an ethnic community, within or outside the boundaries of that state, may lead to accusations of 'dual loyalties', and families may find themselves torn between the claims of competing communities and identities. There is in fact always the potential for such identity conflicts. That they occur less often than one might expect is the result of a certain fluidity in all processes of individual identification.

At this point it becomes important to observe the distinction between individual and collective identification. For the individual, or at any rate for most individuals, identity is usually 'situational', if not always optional. That is to say, individuals identify themselves and are identified by others in different ways according to the situations in which they find themselves; as when one goes abroad, one tends to classify oneself (and be classified by others) differently from one's categorization at home.[6]

Collective identities, however, tend to be pervasive and persistent. They are less subject to rapid changes and tend to be more intense and durable, even when quite large numbers of individuals no longer feel their power. This is especially true of religious and ethnic identities, which even in pre-modern eras often became politicized. It is particularly true of national identities today, when the power of mass political fervour reinforces the technological instruments of mass political organ- ization, so that national identities can outlast the defection or apathy of quite large numbers of individual members. So we need to bear this distinction between the collective and the individual levels of identity in mind and to exercise caution in making inferences about collective sentiments and communal identifications on the basis of individual attitudes and behaviour.[7]

National Identity: Some Bases and Legacies

This preliminary survey of the types and levels of cultural identity provides a general framework for analysing specifically national identi- ties. Here it may be useful to take together the first two areas of analysis – the impact of the pre-modern past and the nature and consequences of national identity – since in Europe at any rate it is mainly through such identities that these 'pasts' have been retained and mediated.

The concept of national identity is both complex and highly abstract. Indeed the multiplicity of cultural identities, both now and in the past, is mirrored in the multiple dimensions of our conceptions of nation- hood. To grasp this, we need only enumerate a few of these dimensions. They include:

- the territorial boundedness of separate cultural populations in their own 'homelands';
- the shared nature of myths of origin and historical memories of the community;
- the common bond of a mass, standardized culture;
- a common territorial division of labour, with mobility for all members and ownership of resources by all members in the homeland;
- the possession by all members of a unified system of common legal rights and duties under common laws and institutions.

These are some of the main assumptions and beliefs common to all nationalists everywhere. Drawing on these, we may define a nation as a named human population sharing a historical territory, common mem- ories and myths of origin, a mass, standardized public culture, a common economy and territorial mobility, and common legal rights and duties for all members of the collectivity.[8]

This definition is just one of many that have been proffered for the concept of the 'nation'. But, like most others, it reveals the highly complex and abstract nature of the concept, one which draws on dimensions of other types of cultural identity, and so permits it to become attached to many other kinds of collective identification – of class, gender, region and religion. National identifications are fundamentally multidimensional. But though they are composed of analytically separable components – ethnic, legal, territorial, economic and political – they are united by the nationalist ideology into a potent vision of human identity and community.

The ideology of nationalism which emerged in Western Europe and America in the late eighteenth century was premissed on the belief in a world of exclusive nations. The basic goals of nationalists everywhere were identical: they sought to unify the nation, to endow it with a distinctive individuality, and to make it free and autonomous. For nationalists, the nation was the supreme object of loyalty and the sole criterion of government. There was no legitimate exercise of political power which did not emanate expressly from the nation, for this was the only source of political power and individual freedom.[9]

Yet there were also important differences between nationalists in their conceptions of the nation. In fact we can usefully distinguish two main models of the nation, which emerged out of different historical contexts and which retain a certain importance even in our era. The first, or 'Western', model of the nation arose out of the Western absolutist states whose rulers inadvertently helped to create the conditions for a peculiarly territorial concept of the nation. The second, or 'Eastern', model emerged out of the situation of incorporated ethnic communities or *ethnies* (from the French), whose intelligentsias sought to liberate them from the shackles of various empires.

The Western model of the nation tended to emphasize the centrality of a national territory or homeland, a common system of laws and institutions, the legal equality of citizens in a political community, and the importance of a mass, civic culture binding the citizens together. The Eastern model, by contrast, was more preoccupied with ethnic descent and cultural ties. Apart from genealogy, it emphasized the popular or folk element, the role of vernacular mobilization, and the activation of the people through a revival of their native folk culture – their languages, customs, religions and rituals, rediscovered by urban intellectuals such as philologists, historians, folklorists, ethnographers and lexicographers.[10]

The contrast between these two concepts of the nation should not be overdrawn, as we find elements of both at various times in several nationalisms in both Eastern and Western Europe. And it is perhaps more important for our purposes to underline the distinction between the concepts of the nation and of the state. The latter is a legal and institutional concept. It refers to autonomous public institutions which are differentiated from other, social institutions by their exercise of a monopoly of coercion and extraction within a given territory.[11] The idea of the nation, by contrast, is fundamentally cultural and social. It refers to a cultural and political bond which unites in a community of prestige all those who share the same myths, memories, symbols and traditions. Despite the obvious overlap between the concepts of state and nation in terms of common territory and citizenship, the idea of the nation defines and legitimates politics in cultural terms, because the nation is a political community only in so far as it embodies a common culture and a common social will. This is why today no state possesses legitimacy which does not also claim to represent the will of the 'nation', even where there is as yet patently no nation for it to represent. Though the vast majority of contemporary states are 'plural' in character – that is, they have more than one ethnic community within their borders and so cannot claim to be true 'nation-states' in the strict sense – they aspire to become at least 'national states' with a common public culture open to all citizens. Their claim to legitimacy, in other words, is based on the aspiration of a heterogeneous population to unity in terms of public culture and political community, as well as popular sovereignty.[12]

This reiterated reference to a community of common public culture reveals the continuing influence of ethnicity and its common myths, symbols and memories in the life of modern European nations. On the one hand, these nations seek to transcend their ethnic origins, which are usually the myths and memories of the dominant ethnic community (the English, the northern French, the Castilians); on the other hand, in a world of growing interdependence, they very often feel the need to revert to them to sustain community as well as to justify their differences. The link with the distinctive pre-modern past serves to dignify the nation as well as to explain its mores and character. More important, it serves to 'remake the collective personality' of the nation in each generation. Through rituals and ceremonies, political myths and symbols, the arts and history textbooks – through these the links with a community of origin, continually reshaped as popular 'ethno-history', are reforged and disseminated.

In this respect, national identifications possess distinct advantages over the idea of a unified European identity. They are vivid, accessible, well established, long popularized, and still widely believed, in broad outline at least. In each of these respects, 'Europe' is deficient both as idea and as process. Above all, it lacks a pre-modern past – a 'prehistory' which can provide it with emotional sustenance and historical depth. In these terms it singularly fails to combine, in the words of Daniel Bell apropos ethnicity, 'affect with interest', resembling rather Shelley's bright reason, 'like the sun from a wintry sky'.[13]

Recently it has been suggested that nationalism's halcyon days are drawing to a close, and that the current spate of fissiparous ethnic nationalism runs counter to the 'major trends' of world history, which are towards ever larger economic and political units. In other words, that substance is belied by appearance – that today's ethnic nationalisms are divisive and have lost the breadth and power of the former mass democratic and civic nationalisms of Western Europe.[14]

Others take the view that the current renewal of ethnic nationalism represents the shape of the future 'post-industrial' society, one whose economy is based increasingly on the service sector and on the social and cultural needs of consumers. They argue that in such societies the means of communication and information become much more important than mass-production of commodities; that the mass media, telecommunications and computerized information spawn smaller but dense networks for those who share the same ethno-linguistic networks of language, symbols and culture. This, they argue, is the reason why we are witnessing the proliferation of ethnic nationalisms; they are intrinsic to a post-industrial 'service society'.[15]

There are in fact a number of reasons why we are witnessing an ethnic revival today, and why it is challenging the accepted frameworks of the national state. For one thing, the state itself has become immensely more powerful, both as an international actor and *vis-à-vis* society within its boundaries. Its powers, scope and capacity for intervention in every sphere of social life – and will to do so – have increased profoundly since 1945 (helped, no doubt, by the powers conferred on it by the exigencies of two world wars). Second, the spread of literacy and the mass media to the remotest hinterlands of European and other states has raised the level of consciousness and expectations of minority peoples, who witness national protests and movements in neighbouring territories almost as soon as they occur. Third, the impact of public, mass education systems, while on the face of it uniting a given national population into a single civic culture, also creates divisions along pre-existing ethnic lines. By forcing all its different peoples to employ a single civic language and by preaching allegiance to national symbols and historical myths, the state's élites may actually stir up resentment and bitterness at the neglect of minority cultures and the suppression of minority peoples' histories. The latter have not been entirely forgotten among the relevant peoples themselves; they remain embedded in separate folklore, customs, myths and symbols. State intervention, literacy and civic culture, and mass education and the mass media tend to rekindle these memories and regenerate these ancient cultures in new forms.

So recent political developments in Western as well as Eastern

Europe, not to mention the Third World, offer few grounds for hope of an early end to the proliferation of ethnic nationalisms, even if their intensity periodically diminishes. What we are currently witnessing is no more than the latest of the periodic waves of ethnic nationalism that have swept different parts of the world since the early nineteenth century, and such demotic ethnic nationalisms have always accompanied the more territorial state-based nationalisms of ethnic majorities since the first stirrings of Serb, Greek and Irish nationalisms. There is therefore little warrant for regarding recent ethnic nationalisms as inimical or irrelevant to the 'major trends' of economic development or world history, as long as most of the world's trade, production and consumption is still organized in terms of relations between sovereign (if increasingly interdependent) national states.[16]

If we disregard the evolutionary undertones of these recent interpretations of nationalism, we are left with the problems of determining the relative strength and influence of European nations, their cultures and their myths, from their ethnic pasts at the turn of the second millennium. Anthropologists have begun to explore some of the cultural aspects of the ethnic identity of such European nations as the Basque, the Breton and the Greek, but much research still needs to be conducted into the continuing impact of ethno-histories, of ethnic myths and symbols, and of the different value systems embodied in various popular traditions, ceremonies and rituals. There is also much work to be done on the recent revival of cultural heritages and political traditions in the wake of new concepts of multiculturalism, which have gained ground following demographic shifts and population migrations.

Given the multiplicity of language groups and ethnic heritages in Europe, it is reasonable to expect the persistence of strong ethnic sentiments in many parts of the continent, as well as the continuity or periodic revival of national identities, fuelled by the quest for ethnic traditions and cultural heritages of distinctive myths, memories and symbols.

A Globalizing Culture

Against these predictions must be set the 'major trends' of world history that so many have discerned and welcomed. These include:

• the rapid growth of vast transnational companies, with budgets, technologies, communications networks and skill levels far outstripping those of all but the largest and most powerful of contemporary national states;

- the rise and fall of large power blocs based on one or other military 'superpower', and forming a military–political network of client-states in an increasingly interdependent international system of states; and
- the vast increase in the scale, efficiency, density and power of the means of communication, from transport to the mass media, from telecommunications to computerized information and transmission.

What this means, in the most general terms, is an accelerating process of globalization: of trends and processes that transcend the boundaries of national states and ethnic communities, and that serve to bind together into common economic, political and cultural patterns the various populations into which the globe is at present divided.[17]

That such trends and processes can be observed is not in question. It is not difficult to point to processes that transcend national boundaries, and appear to unite different populations in those respects. This is as true of patterns of world trade, nuclear proliferation and diplomatic language as it is of styles in modern art, fashion and television serials. The question is whether there is anything new in such boundary-transcending activities and processes, and whether they serve to unite distinctive populations in more than superficial respects. Do they, in other words, portend that global cosmopolitanism of which Marx and Engels, as well as so many liberals, dream?

We should perhaps recall in this context the many imperial cultures that sought to integrate, even homogenize, ethnically different populations, from the Hellenizing policies of Alexander and his successors right up to the Russification policies of the later Romanovs. Here, too, the conscious intention to overleap local boundaries was evident, as was also the case with the 'world religions' of Buddhism, Islam and Christianity. It is true that today the English language and American cultural styles can reach an even wider audience and penetrate much more of the globe. But do they, can they, have as profound an effect? Can there be a truly cosmopolitan culture, one that is genuinely 'post-national' in form and content? The answer to such a question may have a profound bearing on the possibility of a European cultural identity.

It is undeniable that we are witnessing an immense and rapid growth of communications and information technology, spanning the globe; and with it a slower but definite, albeit uneven, increase in literacy and mass education in many countries. There is also considerable convergence in parts of each state's education system: an emphasis on technology, a concern with mathematics and science, an interest in at least one other lingua franca, and so on. In other parts of each education system, however, there is a conscious retention of national difference: in literature, in history, in the arts. In so far as the state can control and use the instruments of mass education effectively, this policy of national self-maintenance is not to be underestimated.[18]

This is not to deny the possibility that governments may actively intervene and try to change popular perceptions of their identity. One could cite here not only the recent efforts of the British government to change the content of the history curriculum to accord with its perceived 'national interests', but also the efforts of France and Germany to change earlier perceptions of each other, through the use of symbols, through massive youth exchange programmes, and by subsidizing academic studies of common history, all of which have after twenty-five years had a significant effect. (Whether the efforts of the Council of Europe to encourage changes in national histories, on both the academic and the official levels, have been effective is open to doubt.)

At the same time, there are clear limits to what governments can achieve. Thus the recent uneasy position of the German government during the Gulf war shows up clearly the constraints on governments which are at all responsive to public opinion. The same is true for other governments in such recent foreign policy crises as Yugoslavia or the Lebanese hostage situation.

There is another side to the question of cultural globalization – what will a truly cosmopolitan culture involve? Will it resemble the imperial prototype, on this occasion various versions of Americanization? Or will it be something genuinely new? The evidence to date suggests neither alternative. What a 'postmodernist' global culture is more likely to resemble is the eclectic patchwork we are witnessing in America and Western Europe today – a mixture of ethnic elements, streamlined and united by a veneer of modernism on a base of scientific and quantitative discourse and computerized technology.[19]

This is not to deny the global diffusion of some aspects of modern Euro-American culture, especially popular music, films, videos, dress and some foods. The worldwide spread of consumer commodities, of art styles in furnishing, of architecture and the visual arts, not to mention the mass media and tourism, is evidence of a global nexus of markets for similar products and the ability of consumer industries to mould shared tastes, in some degree at least. But even here, ethnic and class factors intrude. The appreciation and assimilation of Western styles and cultural products is generally adaptive: the audiences in Third World countries tend to interpret these products and experiences in ways that are specific to the perceptions and understanding of their own peoples.[20]

Side by side with this adaptive Westernization, there is also a more or less conscious rediscovery of and return to indigenous styles and values.

This process was stimulated by political nationalism or by a vaguer consciousness of and pride in the past of particular peoples and cultural areas, and has been continuing since the early nineteenth century – first in Central and Eastern Europe, then in the Middle East and India, then in the Americas, and finally in Africa and Eastern Asia. In each case, myths and memories of an ancient ethnic past (not necessarily strictly that of the revivalists themselves) have been reappropriated, often through a process of vernacular mobilization in which the peasant masses are treated as a repository of truth, wisdom and culture.

The revival of ethnic myths, memories and traditions, both within and outside a globalizing but eclectic culture, reminds us of the fundamentally memoryless nature of any cosmopolitan culture created today. Such a culture must be consciously, even artificially, constructed out of the elements of existing national cultures. But existing cultures are time-bound, particular and expressive. They are tied to specific peoples, places and periods. They are bound up with definite historical identities. Those features are essentially antithetical to the very nature of a truly cosmopolitan culture. Herein lies the paradox of any project for a global culture: it must work with materials destined for the very projects which it seeks to supersede – the national identities which are ultimately to be eradicated.

The European 'Family of Cultures'

This, then, is where the European project must be located: between national revival and global cultural aspirations. Thus expressed, it makes the old debate between pan-Europeans and anti-Europeans seem faintly antiquated.

That debate centred on the possibility and desirability of creating a unified Europe 'from above', through economic and political institutions, perhaps on the model of German unification in the nineteenth century. Pan-Europeans conceded that there would be local delays and problems, but believed that European unity was imperative to prevent a recurrence of any European 'civil war', to create a third power between East and West and to secure a prosperous future for Europe's peoples. They also argued that the route of 'state-making' from above through bureaucratic incorporation and the building of institutions was the only way forward. Just as in the past dynastic states had moulded the first nations in the West, so today the frameworks of a United States of Europe and swift political union, based firmly in the Western heartlands, would forge a European consciousness in place of the obsolete national identities.

Anti-Europeans countered by pointing to the 'unevenness' of

Europe's peoples and states, to the difficulties of deciding the boundaries of 'Europe', to the continuing strength of several European national states and to the linguistic and ethnic pluralism of Europe's mixed areas. But at the root of their opposition to pan-Europeanism, whether unitary or federal in character, was their belief in the overriding importance of existing national identities and the ethnic histories and cultures they enshrined. Behind the economic façade and the agonizing over subsidies and monetary union, the embattled camps of Brussels and Bruges agreed on the mutual incompatibility of 'Europe' and 'national' identity.[21]

But is there any warrant for this dichotomic view of cultural identities and for the battle cries on either side? We have already seen that, sociologically, human beings have multiple identities, that they can move between them according to context and situation, and that such identities may be concentric rather than conflictual. None of this is to deny the cultural reality and vivid meanings of these identities, which, transmitted through successive generations, are not exhausted by the often fickle volitions and changing perceptions of individuals. At the same time, there is plenty of historical evidence for the co-existence of concentric circles of allegiance.[22] In the ancient world it was possible to be Athenian, Ionian and Greek all at the same time; in the mediaeval world, to be Bernese, Swiss and Protestant; in the modern Third World to be Ibo, Nigerian and African simultaneously. Similarly, one could feel simultaneously Catalan, Spanish and European; even – dare one say it? – Scottish – or English, British and European.

But if the possibility of being intensely French or British *and* intensely European exists, what does it mean to feel and be European? Is 'Europe' merely the sum total of its various national identities and communities? If so, is there not something quite arbitrary about aggregating such identities simply because certain otherwise unrelated communities happen to reside in a geographical area which is conventionally designated as the continent of Europe? Which raises further questions about the eastern and southern boundaries of Europe, as well as about important internal geographical and historical divisions within that continent.

On the other hand, if 'Europe' and 'European' signify something more than the sum total of the populations and cultures that happen to inhabit a conventionally demarcated geographical space, what exactly are those characteristics and qualities that distinguish Europe from anything or anyone else? Can we find in the history and cultures of this continent some thing or things that are not replicated elsewhere, and that shaped what might be called specially 'European experiences'?

There are a number of areas in which one might seek for specifically

European characteristics, qualities and experiences. The first is linguistic. Though not all the languages of Europe belong to the Indo-European family, the vast majority do, and though there are important linguistic fault-lines between Latin, Germanic and Slav sub-families, there has been sufficient movement across these lines to speak of at least a tenuous interrelationship which is modern as well as prehistoric. At the same time, the disastrous political consequences of drawing ethnic inferences from purely linguistic relationships suggest serious limitations in this area for any support for the European idea in ethnolinguistic terms.[23]

A second area of inquiry is that of cultural geography and territorial symbolism. The recent idea of a European 'home' from the Urals to the Atlantic is supported by the lack of any serious geographical barriers (apart from the Alps and Pyrenees, and perhaps the Carpathians and the Rhine – and the Channel?), and by the protected geopolitical space between the Atlantic and the Mediterranean into which successive 'barbarian' ethnic communities poured and in which they found permanent shelter and adjacent homes. But what may be true in the north and west has no counterpart in the south and east. The Mediterranean forms a unifying internal (Roman?) lake – *mare nostrum* – rather than an impermeable boundary, while to the east the rolling plains, as the terrified populations found in the face of Hun and Mongol onslaughts and as the shifting boundaries of Poland–Lithuania and Russia–Ukraine bear witness, afford neither defence nor borderland. Besides, where is the geographical centre of the European homeland? In Burgundy or along the Rhine? In Berlin or Prague, or Budapest? In the Benelux countries, or in Provence or northern Italy? All these are historical claims, not geographical 'facts'.[24]

Third, there is the old issue of religious cleavages. Might this not provide a test of European inclusion and exclusion? There is a clear sense, going back at least to the Crusades and probably even to Charles Martel, in which Europeans see themselves as not-Muslims or as not-Jews. The history of resistance to Arab and Turkish Muslim encroachment provides potent memories, though there is the great exception of Spain and its Moorish and Jewish conduits for the enormous legacy of Arab Islam to Christian European culture.

What of the inter-Christian divides? The most potent is still that between 'Western' Christendom (Catholic and Protestant) and Eastern Orthodoxy. Hungarians, for example, emphasize their Western connections through their historic 'choice for the West' over a thousand years ago, in contrast to the Russians, for example, who chose Greek Byzantine Orthodoxy. But this brings problems of its own, not least for the position of Greece and potentially Serbia in the European Community.

If religion is a real criterion of identity, should not Poland, rather than Greece, be a member of the new Europe? And what of that other great division, between the Protestant and Catholic states of Europe? Politically, Catholic–Protestant division may have declined, but how far, again, does this extend to the vast majority of Europeans in small towns and villages? This is another aspect of the wider question of the gulf between urban élites and rural masses in Europe over perceptions of and attitudes to Europe and European unification.

Fourth, there is the more inchoate sense of the 'outsider', which has recently found expression in various European countries, directed at immigrants and guest-workers. Might not the older nationalistic exclusive attitudes to foreigners now become 'Euro-nationalist' exclusion of blacks, Asians and other non-Europeans? There is some evidence for this. But it is difficult to disentangle it from the older attitudes. If it is the case, it supports the idea that there is a continuum between collective cultural identities, as I have argued. This may well be reinforced after 1992, when common passports and European frontiers will help to 'create' an element of perceived common identity for those who travel beyond the European frontiers – and for those who seek to enter (or return to) them. The effect of such frontiers on creating an *out-group*, so vital to the formation of identity, depends of course on the degree of unity of perceptions and sentiments among the Europeans themselves, and on the degree of common political action, especially in the field of defence and foreign policy, which a more united Europe can evolve. The evidence in these fields to date has not been encouraging.

We are thrown back on history, and specifically on political and legal traditions and cultural heritages and symbolisms. Here, if anywhere, we may hope to find experiences and collective memories that differentiate the communities of Europe from other communities, and which, in some degree at least, provide common reference points for the peoples of Europe.

This is an area which, of its nature, is not amenable to rigorous positivistic criteria. We are dealing with shared memories, traditions, myths, symbols and values, which may possess subtly different meanings and significance for different communities in the area conventionally designated as Europe. The Roman heritage, for example, penetrated certain areas more than others, and some not at all. Christianity embraced most of the continent eventually, but it did so unevenly and split early into separate cultural and ethnic traditions. The various attempts to recreate the Roman Empire foundered, but they left their imprint on some areas of Europe more than others. Even such 'event-processes' as the Crusades, the Renaissance, the Reformation and the

Enlightenment affected some areas, peoples and states more than others, and a few hardly at all.

So what is common to all Europeans? What can they be said to share and in what respects can they be said to differ from non-Europeans? To these kinds of questions there can never be satisfactory answers. Europeans differ among themselves as much as from non-Europeans in respect of language (Basques, Finns, Hungarians), territory (Russians, Greeks, Armenians), law (Roman, Germanic), religion (Catholic, Orthodox, Protestant) and economic and political system (democracy, communism, unitary state, federalism, etc.) – *as well as* in terms of ethnicity and culture.

On the other hand, there *are* shared traditions, legal and political, and shared heritages, religious and cultural. Not all Europeans share in all of them; some share in particular traditions and heritages only minimally. But at one time or another all Europe's communities have participated in at least *some* of these traditions and heritages, in some degree.

What are these partially shared traditions and heritages? They include traditions like Roman law, political democracy, parliamentary institutions, and Judaeo-Christian ethics, and cultural heritages like Renaissance humanism, rationalism and empiricism, and romanticism and classicism. Together they constitute not a 'unity in diversity' – the official European cultural formula – but a 'family of cultures' made up of a syndrome of partially shared historical traditions and cultural heritages.

The idea of a 'family of cultures' resembles Wittgenstein's concepts of 'family resemblances' and of the 'language game', which features several elements, not all of which figure in each particular example of the game. What we have instead is a 'family' of elements which overlap and figure in a number of (but not all) examples. So, for example, the Italian Renaissance and its humanism found its way into many, but not all, parts of Europe, as did the spirit and methods of the French Enlightenment. 'Europe' here represents a field favourable to diffusion and cross-fertilization of cultural traditions, but one of uneven receptivity. Specific European states or communities may reveal only certain of the above traditions or heritages, or only to a limited extent. But the sum total of all Europe's states and communities has historically revealed a gamut of overlapping and boundary-transcending political traditions and cultural heritages, which together make up what we may call the European experience and the European family of cultures.

There has always been such cultural cross-fertilization in various parts of Europe. What now needs to be established is how far those shared traditions and heritages have become part of each of Europe's national identities, how far each national tradition has embraced and assimilated these 'trans-European' cultural heritages; how far romanticism, Roman law or parliamentary democracy has taken on a peculiar national form, or conversely the extent to which French, or German, classicism and humanism partake of some shared trans-European tradition.

It is important here to distinguish between families of culture and political or economic unions. The latter are usually deliberate creations; they are consciously willed unities, rationally constructed sets of institutions, the kind of frameworks that some European states are trying to hasten and others to delay. Families of culture, like a lingua franca, tend to come into being over long time-spans and are the product of particular historical circumstances, often unanticipated and unintentional. Such cultural realities are no less potent for being so often inchoate and uninstitutionalized. Thus the sentiments and identities that underpin the Islamic *umma* or community of Muslims are no less significant than any official Islamic social and political institutions.[25]

But this very lack of institutionalization poses severe difficulties for the researcher. One of them is the problem of interpreting recent trends and developments as, in some sense, European manifestations. Can the growth of mass tourism, for example, be interpreted as a contribution to a more European identity? The fact that many more Europeans can and do travel abroad is open to several interpretations. When the British working classes took package holidays to Spanish beaches, were they even exposed to Spanish, let alone European, culture? Has the long-standing German love affair with Italy made any difference to the intensity of German nationalism, in this or the last century? Or shall we rather agree with Karl Kautsky that the railways are the greatest breeder of national hatreds (and by implication the most potent force for anti-Europeanism)?[26]

Or take the astonishing growth of large-scale 'European' music festivals and travelling art exhibitions. Do these great events testify to a new 'European spirit'? Can they not equally be seen as expressions of local pride, be it in Edinburgh or Spoleto, Moscow or Leeds, in the Royal Academy or the Louvre or the Prado? By their nature such artistic events are all-inclusive; great artistic events are as likely to be shown in America or Japan and include contributions from all parts of the world. Europe may well have become a 'great museum' for the heritage industry, but only its greater openness and capitalist spirit have given it the edge over other tourist centres and 'great museums' in the Middle East or Asia.[27]

Given these problems, where may we look for signs of a possible European identification – and among whom? It is one thing for élites in Brussels, Strasbourg and some European capitals to identify with and work for a united Europe, quite another to attribute such sentiments and beliefs to the great mass of the middle and working classes, let alone the surviving peasantries of Southern and Eastern Europe. Whence will *they* derive a sense of European identity?

One answer often given suggests the mass, standardized, public education system. The problem here is that there is no pan-European system, only national systems; and what they teach, or omit to teach, is determined by national, not European, priorities. In other words, education systems are run by and for national states. Until there is a single, centralized, unitary European state, we cannot expect too much from the national education systems of each European state. This can be confirmed by a glance at schoolroom texts in history, civics and literature. Even when they include positive reference to contemporary Europe, the bulk of such texts are national in content and intent. The recent study of French school history textbooks by Suzanne Citron is a striking case in point.[28]

What about the mass media? Are they equally tied to purely national criteria of choice and content? Here there is clearly more variety between different European national states. Yet even here, national priorities are very much in evidence: news stories tend to be relayed or at least interpreted from a national standpoint, drama, comedy shows, children's tales, even the weather reports, accord the national state and its literature and outlook first place. Given the linguistic and historical barriers and the national frameworks of most mass media institutions, this is only to be expected.

Some changes are occurring in these areas, and, given the political will of the élites, more rapid changes may soon take place. But the question still remains: how will the new European message be received? Will it be reinterpreted by audiences and pupils in ethnic and national terms, as with so many cultural products? For until the great majority of Europeans, the great mass of the middle and lower classes, are ready to imbibe these European messages in a similar manner and to feel inspired by them to common action and community, the edifice of 'Europe' at the political level will remain shaky. This is all too clear today in respect of foreign policy and defence, where we are witnessing the need for European governments to respond to their national public opinion and the failure of Europeans to agree on a common policy. Once again, the usual divisions of public opinion between European states have been exposed, and with them the tortuous and divided actions of Europe's governments. Once again, too, the division between Britain and the Continent has become plain, and with it the crucial relationship of all European states to American political leadership. The 'European failure' only underlines the distance between the European ideal and its rootedness in the popular consciousness of Europe's

national populations – and hence the distance between European
unification at the political and cultural levels and the realities of
divergent national identities, perceptions and interests within Europe.

Clearly these are areas for detailed and intensive research, which
would focus not on ephemeral attitudes but on what is taught and
portrayed and how it is received by the majority of Europe's populations.
In more concrete terms, this means examining the ways in which news
and documentaries are purveyed; how far a European dimension is
added to, and received in, matters of art, music and literature; how far
education systems are harmonized and teachers and taught acculturated
to the different values, goals and forms of education and training, and
how far history textbooks are rewritten to accommodate a European
standpoint.[29]

If this were not problematic enough, there is the deeper question of
popular myths and symbols, and historical memories and traditions.
Here we are placed firmly back in the pre-modern past of each national
state. There is no European analogue to Bastille or Armistice Day, no
European ceremony for the fallen in battle, no European shrine of
kings or saints. When it comes to the ritual and ceremony of collective
identification, there is no European equivalent of national or religious
community. Any research into the question of forging, or even discovering, a possible European identity cannot afford to overlook these
central issues.[30]

We encounter similar problems when it comes to the question of a
genuinely European political mythology. The founding fathers of the
European movements, such as Coudenhove-Kalergi, recognized the
problem. They tended to look back to the imperial myths of the
Carolingian and Ottonian Holy Roman Empire and to the medieval
urban civilization centred on the Rhine as their models of a 'golden
age' of European Christendom. But as a modern political *mythomoteur*,
these models are deeply flawed. Secularism has made deep inroads into
the political consciousness of most classes in several European states,
too deep for any genuine religious revival to be less than divisive.
Besides, the imperial format of such myths is profoundly inimical to the
spirit of democracy which the West espouses and Eastern Europe so
ardently seeks. There is also the persistent unease over locating one's
guiding myth in a particular part of Europe at the expense of the rest.
Once again, these models assert the primacy of 'the West' as the home
of innovation and progress, traceable to that early spirit of capitalism in
the free cities of late medieval Europe.[31]

It is clear that such historical *mythomoteurs* are inappropriate for the
modern European project. But where else can one look for the
necessary political mythology? Is it possible for the new Europe to arise

without 'myth' and 'memory'? Have we not seen that these are indispensable elements in the construction of any durable and resonant collective cultural identity?

Here lies the new Europe's true dilemma: a choice between unacceptable, historical myths and memories on the one hand, on the other a patchwork, memoryless scientific 'culture' held together solely by the political will and economic interest that are so often subject to change. In between, there lies the hope of discovering that 'family of cultures' briefly outlined above, through which over several generations some loose, over-arching political identity and community might gradually be forged.

Europe in a Wider World

At present the tide is running for the idea of European unification as it has never done before. This is probably the result of dramatic geopolitical and geocultural changes, which remind us that the future of 'Europe', as indeed of every national state today, will be largely determined by wider regional, or global, currents and trends. The most immediate of these, of course, has been the dramatic shift in world power resulting from the adoption of perestroika in the Soviet Union and the liberation of the states of Eastern Europe and the republics of the former Soviet Union to determine their own political future. But this same current may serve simultaneously as a model and a warning: what may flow so suddenly and vigorously in one direction may equally swiftly change course, for reasons that have nothing to do with intra-European developments, and in so doing reverse the climate that seemed so conducive to the project of European unification.

There are many other currents and trends affecting the chances of fulfilling a European project. We may cite several:

- dramatic regional developments, like the vortex of conflict in the Middle East, into which European states may be drawn, severally or together;
- the dangers of ethnic conflict, separatism and large-scale wars in other parts of the world such as the Indian sub-continent or Africa, which may again involve one or more European states and so divide the interests of those states and even threaten, by example, their stability and cohesion;
- the impact of waves of migrants and guest-workers on the economies and societies of European states, which may differentially affect their attitudes and priorities;

- larger problems of environmental pollution and ecological disaster, as well as epidemic disease, which may require both individual action by each European state and wider, perhaps global, responses which may pre-empt the integration of Europe; and
- problems of large-scale crime and terrorism, which may again call for immediate action by individual states, or by bodies larger and more powerful than any European organization.

The point of this list, which could be extended, is simply to underline the dramatic pace and scope of change within which the project of European unification must locate itself. Unification is in fact one of several possible responses to wider changes; but these trends do not all work in the same direction, and they may be reversed. Hence the importance of basing any European project on firm and deep cultural and social foundations that are to some extent independent of economic and political fluctuations, even of the much vaunted trends of mass democracy and popular capitalism.

There is another and equally important issue raised by the project of European unification and its relationship with nations and nationalism. Identities are forged out of shared experiences, memories and myths, in relation to those of other collective identities. They are in fact often forged through opposition to the identities of significant others, as the history of paired conflict so often demonstrates. Who or what, then, are Europe's significant others? Until now, the obvious answers were the protagonists of the ideological Cold War. In this context Europe was often seen as a third force *between* the respective superpower blocs, though there was always something unreal about such a posture. Now, however, the problem of relationship to other identities has become more perplexing. To whom shall Europe be likened? Against whom shall it measure itself? Today's geopolitical uncertainty makes a direct comparison and relationship with the United States ambiguous; Europe is increasingly wholeheartedly a part of the 'capitalist' and 'democratic' camp of which the United States is likely to remain the military leader. Shall Europe look to Japan as its *alter ego*? But Japan is an ethnically almost homogeneous society, it poses no military or political threat, and its economic rivalry is still mainly directed at the United States.

There is another. a less pleasing, possibility: the relationship of a unifying Europe to a disaggregated Third World. There is the prospect of an increasingly affluent, stable, conservative but democratic European federation, facing, and protecting itself from, the demands and needs of groups of states in Africa, Asia and Latin America. To some extent this prospect is still mitigated by the remaining ex-colonial ties between certain European and certain African or Asian states. But were the European project to achieve its political goals, it would entail not just economic exclusion but also cultural differentiation and with it the possibility of cultural and racial exclusion. The forging of a deep continental cultural identity to support political unification may well require an ideology of European cultural exclusiveness.

These dangers are well known in respect of the maintenance of national identities by individual European states. In many respects, it is European institutions that are leading the struggle against racial discrimination, ethnic antagonism and anti-Semitism, though with mixed success. The deeper question remains. Is not the logic of cultural exclusion built into the process of pan-European identity formation? Will not a unified Europe magnify the virtues and the defects of each of Europe's national identities, precisely because it has been built in their images? And might a European 'super-nation' resemble, in its external as well as its internal policies and relations, this national model?[32]

This is a fear that has been often expressed. It is one that still haunts the European political arena, as each of Europe's national states seeks to influence the future shape of a European union along the lines of its own self-image. In its relations with minorities inside Europe, as well as with states and peoples outside the continent, these images have not been appealing ones. Here too lies an agenda for policy-oriented research, one beset by sensitive issues and thorny problems.

Facing and understanding these problems is a precondition for forging a pan-European identity that will eschew these undesirable and self-defeating images and features. Shaping a cultural identity that will be both distinctive and inclusive, differentiating yet assimilative, may yet constitute the supreme challenge for a Europe that seeks to create itself out of its ancient family of ethnic cultures.

1992

Notes

1. On the forerunners of the idea of European unity, see Denis de Rougemont, *The Meaning of Europe*, London 1965.

2. Studies of European economic and political integration go back to Karl Deutsch *et al.*, *Political Community and the North Atlantic Area*, Princeton 1957, and Ernest B. Haas, *Beyond the National State*, Stanford 1964. Cf. William Wallace, *The Transformation of Western Europe*, London 1990, chapter 4.

3. See, for example, the essays in Eric Hobsbawm and Terence Ranger, eds, *The Invention of Tradition*, Cambridge 1983, and also in Elizabeth Tonkin, Maryon McDonald and Malcolm Chapman, eds, *History and Ethnicity*, London 1989.

4. For studies of ethnic identity, see George de Vos and Lola Romanucci-Rossie, eds, *Ethnic Identity: Cultural Continuities and Change*, Chicago 1975, and A. L. Epstein, *Ethos and Identity*, London 1978.

5. On the relationships between religion and nationalism, see Donald E. Smith, ed., *Religion and Political Modernisation*, New Haven 1974, and Pedro Ramet, ed., *Religion and Nationalism in Soviet and East European Politics*, Durham, NC 1989. For some case-studies of

the relationships between gender and nationality, see Floya Anthias and Nira Yuval-Davis, eds, *Woman Nation State*, London 1989.

6. For the concept of 'situational ethnicity' see J. Y. Okamura, 'Situational Ethnicity', *Ethnic and Racial Studies*, vol. 4, no. 4, 1981, pp. 452–65.

7. On the 'individualist fallacy' see E.K. Scheuch, 'Cross-national Comparisons with Aggregate Data', in Richard L. Merritt and Stein Rokkan, eds, *Comparing Nationals: The Use of Quantitative Data in Cross-national Research*, New Haven 1956.

8. This definition summarizes long and complex discussions of the many definitions of 'nation'. See, *inter alia*, Karl Deutsch, *Nationalism and Social Communication*, 2nd edn, New York 1966, ch. 1; and Walker Connor, 'A Nation is a Nation, is a State, is an Ethnic Group, is . . .', *Ethnic and Racial Studies*, vol. 1, no. 4, 1978, pp. 377–400.

9. For fuller discussions of nationalist ideologies, see Elie Kedourie, *Nationalism*, London 1960; Elie Kedourie, ed., *Nationalism in Asia and Africa*, London 1971; and A.D. Smith, *Theories of Nationalism*, 2nd edn, London 1983. On the multi-dimensionality of national identity, see A.D. Smith, *National Identity*, London 1991, chapter 1.

10. On the distinction between these types of nationalism, see Hans Kohn, *The Idea of Nationalism*, 2nd edn, New York 1967, and A.D. Smith, *The Ethnic Origins of Nations*, Oxford 1986, chapter 6.

11. I have adapted the definitions given in the introductions to Charles Tilly, ed., *The Formation of National States in Western Europe*, Princeton 1975, and Leonard Tivey, ed., *The Nation-state*, Oxford 1980.

12. See Walker Connnor's seminal article, 'Nation-building or Nation-destroying?', *World Politics*, vol. 24, 1972, pp. 319–55; and Ernest Gellner, *Nations and Nationalism*, Oxford 1983.

13. See Daniel Bell, 'Ethnicity and Social Change', in Nathan Glazer and Daniel P. Moynihan, eds, *Ethnicity: Theory and Experience*, Cambridge, MA 1975.

14. This argument is presented in the last chapter of Eric Hobsbawm, *Nations and Nationalism since 1780*, Cambridge 1990.

15. This argument is presented with force and clarity by Anthony Richmond in 'Ethnic Nationalism and Post-industrialism', *Ethnic and Racial Studies*, vol. 7, no. 1, 1984, pp. 4–18; it is also implicit in Benedict Anderson, *Imagined Communities: Reflections on the Origin and Spread of Nationalism*, London 1983.

16. The ethnic revivals in the West in the 1970s suggests the difficulty of 'reading' any 'major trends' of world history. Regions and ethnic communities are being revitalized *alongside* a strengthened national state and an over-arching European Community. On ethnic nationalism in the West see Milton Esman, ed., *Ethnic Conflict in the Western World*, Ithaca, NY 1977, and A.D. Smith, *The Ethnic Revival in the Modern World*, Cambridge 1981.

17. For a discussion of globalization, see Mike Featherstone, ed., *Global Culture: Nationalism, Globalisation and Modernity*, London 1990.

18. For a searching analysis of the role of mass, public education systems in shaping national identities, see Gellner, *Nations and Nationalism*.

19. The argument is presented fully in A.D. Smith, 'Towards a global culture?', *Theory, Culture and Society*, vol. 7, 1990, pp. 171–91.

20. This point is documented in Philip Schlesinger, 'On national identity: some conceptions and misconceptions criticised', *Social Science Information*, vol. 26, no. 2, 1987, pp. 219–64.

21. For the early debates between pan-Europeans and anti-Europeans, see Miriam Camps, *What Kind of Europe? The Community since de Gaulle's Veto*, London 1965, and Wallace, *The Transformation of Western Europe*, chapter 4.

22. On the idea of concentric circles of allegiance see James Coleman, *Nigeria: Background to Nationalism*, Berkeley 1958, appendix.

23. On Europe's linguistic divisions, see Andrew Orridge, 'Separatist and autonomist nationalism: the structure of regional loyalties in the modern state', in C. Williams, ed., *National Separatism*, Cardiff 1982, and John Armstrong, *Nationals before Nationalism*, Chapel Hill 1982, chapter 8.

24. On Europe's protected geopolitical position, see Introduction, Tilly, *The Formation of National States*; for Europe's problematic eastern boundaries, see Raymond Pearson,

National Minorities in Eastern Europe, 1848–1945, London 1983, and Roger Portal, *The Slavs*, London 1969.

25. On the Islamic *umma* and the Muslim states, see Erwin Rosenthal, *Islam in the Modern National State*, Cambridge 1965. Pan-Europeans have sometimes tried to construct culture areas through the deliberate manufacture of myths, symbols and traditions: see Lord Gladwyn, *The European Idea*, London 1967.

26. On Karl Kautsky's argument, see Horace Davis, *Nationalism and Socialism: Marxist and Labor Theories of Nationalism*, London and New York 1967. There is evidence that mass tourism among the younger generations of Western Europe, which grew up in an era of peace, has confirmed their lack of national antagonisms.

27. European élites, going back to the feudal nobility and clergy, have always been more cosmopolitan and open to outside influences than the middle and lower classes: see Armstrong, *Nations before Nationalism*, chapter 3, and Smith, *The Ethnic Origins of Nations*, chapter 4.

28. Suzanne Citron, *Le Mythe national*, Paris 1988, analyses the strongly nationalistic content and framework of French school history textbooks, based on Lavisse, which came into use during the late nineteenth century under the Third Republic. The continuing debate in Britain over the place of British, even English, history, as opposed to European and world history, illustrates the same issues; see Raphael Samuel, ed., *Patriotism: The Making and Unmaking of British National Identity*, London 1989, Volume 1, and Juliet Gardiner, ed., *The History Debate*, London 1990.

29. Even this does not take us to the heart of the problem. We need also to explore people's attachments to national landscapes, or myths thereof; to certain events and heroes from the national past; to certain kinds of social institutions and mores, food, family life and village community; and how far all these are felt to override, conflict with or deny a more over-arching European identity that is inevitably more abstract, intellectual and political.

30. The centrality of such rites and ceremonies for creating and maintaining collective cultural identities is only now receiving the attention it deserves. See, e.g., John Breuilly, *Nationalism and the State*, Manchester 1982, chapter 16; Hobsbawm and Ranger, *The Invention of Tradition*.

31. The primacy of Western Europe as a 'core' to the northern, southern and especially eastern 'peripheries' (which in mediaeval times were sparsely inhabited) was seized on by the myth-makers of the European idea; see Gladwyn, *The European Idea*, and de Rougemont, *The Meaning of Europe*.

32. A fear summed up in Johan Galtung, *The European Community: A Superpower in the Making*, London 1973, but with recent events taking on a new meaning: namely, the fear that Germany's economic domination might influence the political shape of a future Europe, and the chances of greater cultural and racial exclusiveness, at the expense mainly of Third World migrants but stirring all too vivid memories of the Nazi past. Fears, like memories, are no less real for being intangible and difficult to research.

Trajectories

21

A Continental Architecture
Jacques Attali

In a play called *Redevelopment,* written in 1987, Vaclav Havel portrays a
team of architects, living in a grand house on top of a hill, who are
planning the reconstruction of the town that lies at its foot. From time
to time inhabitants arrive to petition them, insisting that they like their
town the way it is and objecting to any proposed changes. They are
invariably arrested by the secret police, also installed in the house, who
terrorize the architects as well as the locals. The police constantly harass
the architects with impossible orders, one day even urging them to
'think freely and work out new methods of urban planning'.

The same task faces Europe(s): to think freely about a continental
architecture, without repeating earlier blueprints or fearing the absence
of orders from East or West. Balance between integration and diversity
is not (as in America or Asia) a simple matter of economic efficiency
or market shares, but also involves political and military stability. And
given that these two other spaces are developing their structures, it is a
matter of some urgency to adopt a plan, at least for the next forty-nine
years.

At a moment when the world is made up of blocs, of integration
networks, when history is becoming geography, Europe has to know
what it is; and to know how, and with whom, it can construct a future.

At present – and perhaps for a few short years more – the initiative
in answering these questions and devising a continental architecture
belongs to the member countries of the European Union, and more
particularly the Franco-German couple. Later on, other countries –
starting with Russia – will make the game more difficult by ceasing to
accept what the West tries to impose.

The Twelve have not yet made their choice, indeed they have not yet really discussed it. Their plan remains a mixture of contradictory ambitions: to apply the Maastricht Treaty; to admit the northern countries; to give aid to the Central European countries; to make peace in the Balkans; not to isolate Russia; not to cut links with America; to be more open to the South; to launch an employment programme; to create a democracy on the European scale; to maintain the diversity of the nations. This is all well and good. But unfortunately these objectives – all desirable – are not compatible with one another (or rather, need to be hierarchized, organized and synchronized).

As in all the great periods of history, however, the essential choice concerns alliances. Modes of living and social projects will all flow from that. At a time when fashion in Europe favours the local, the everyday, the micro-social, I am aware that in advancing these ideas I may seem to be swimming against the tide; except to people who understand that thinking small condemns one to stay small.

A European Federal Union

The first choice available to the West Europeans, and the simplest to imagine – at least in theory – would be to apply the Maastricht Treaty without enlarging the Union before making it irreversible. This would mean that the Twelve were progressively setting up a genuine federal Union with a common currency, a common defence system and a common foreign policy. It would be an integrated political space governed by a constitution; the experimental terrain of a society of multiple allegiance, in which the European would no longer be the citizen of one state, but several: the one in which he was born, the one in which he lives, the one in which he works. It would be a 'democracy without frontiers'.

To succeed, this arrangement should be irreversibly under way before the end of the century, before the pressure of new candidates for membership has become irresistible.

For a start, this implies the establishment of a single currency whose creation can only be decided at a stroke, without warning, once the lowering of short-term interest rates has been initiated. After that, helped by the reduction of interest rates and social levies, a genuine employment programme could be launched; while at the same time housing, urban renewal, transnational communications and telecom-munications schemes could be started on a continental scale, costing around 5 per cent of Community GNP. This programme – whose details were worked out two years ago by the Commission, the EIB and the EBRD – would make it possible to rethink the basic essentials of economic policy. It would be the way to invent a reduction in labour costs without adopting either the Asian solution (low wages) or the American one (weak social protection).

Meanwhile the federal character of the political union would be strengthened. The Council of Europe would become a collective head of state whose presidency would fall for two years at a time – not six months as at present – to a single large country or group of small countries. The Commission – whose president would be elected by the parliament and answerable to it – would become the Union's government; there would be only ten Commissioners (in place of the present seventeen).

Legislative power would be exercised by two chambers, the European Parliament and the Union Council (that is, the Council of Ministers – regarded as an upper house and no longer as a government – sitting in a semicircle rather than round a table). Voting rights in the Union Council would be proportional to the populations of the representatives' different countries, and a dissenting minority would have to include at least two large countries and one small one. Where possible, decisions would be referred to national parliaments in application of the principle of subsidiarity.

Defence would be coordinated, in the name of the Union Council, by the Western European Union, the European pillar of the Atlantic alliance, which would acquire the means – by expanding the Eurocorps – to ensure respect for peace and human rights throughout the continent. In particular, Europe would be responsible for all action by the Twelve in Bosnia. Nuclear weapons, on the other hand, would remain national.

The federal Union could also answer the needs of the East, supplying it with technical assistance and above all promoting an open system of trade, establishing conditions favouring the development of the private sector and boosting direct foreign investment.

When – and only when – these reforms have been accomplished, the Union might expand to include other countries.

The governments of the member states would have to organize and manage the resulting mutations of society, and would be responsible for social law, education and health, all domains in which national specificities should be preserved. They would train the young accordingly, with reference to the demands of each national identity. They would finance a minimum income intended for the young and the elderly – those below and above working age – who are the main consumers of portable objects.

This is the most seductive scenario, and one that still had meaning when the Soviet bloc existed. But it no longer really seems to represent a possible option. Inside the Union, everyone would prefer expansion to precede the move towards federalism. And outside, while candidates for membership are jostling at the door, Russia and the United States will both oppose the creation of this federal union, which would be a new political superpower. So this figure should doubtless be shelved with other dead ideas; unless the violence which is again looming in the East reminds the Westerners of their former ambitions.

A Confederal European Space

The next scenario seems better suited to the climate of the times: the European Union would extend to cover its close neighbours, but without reforming itself first. It would restrict itself to constructing an enlarged market and concluding security arrangements between the European Council and its closest neighbours.

In a first phase, the Union would expand to admit the northern European countries, if they still wanted to join (which is not certain), and if the southern countries did not reject them (which they might do). The Union would then 'weigh' 380 million people, 30 per cent of world production (more than NAFTA and twice as much as Japan), 46 per cent of world trade and 30 per cent of service transactions. It would be impossible to ignore as a commercial power, despite the weakness represented by the absence of a common currency.

Later, the Union would accept applications from the Baltic countries, Poland, the Czech Republic, Slovakia, Hungary, Bulgaria, Romania, Slovenia and Ukraine. Current association agreements with the EEC would first be renegotiated so that countries wishing to join could be treated as members-in-waiting, rather than as competitors.

Only after 'digesting' these new arrivals would the Union set out to apply any remaining relevant parts of the Maastricht Treaty. These would not amount to much.

At the end of the century this 'European space', a somewhat shapeless confederal zone of twenty or twenty-two members, would decide whether Russia and Turkey should be associates or full members. Eventually, it would constitute a market of more than five hundred million people that would help democracy to take root in the East (as happened earlier with Greece, Portugal and Spain) and provide a counterweight to US influence. The East would tempt investors with its skilled and relatively cheap manpower. The accumulation of export earnings and the influx of foreign capital would raise the real exchange rates in the East and, in consequence, the incomes of the inhabitants, who would then have fewer reasons to emigrate. Eastern citizens would gradually become solvent consumers, actors in the European game and creators of employment in the West.

But the establishment of this European space does imply the abandonment of many of the ambitions embodied in the Maastricht Treaty: with twenty or twenty-two members, it would be impossible to move towards the single currency or establish common economic, social, judicial and foreign policies. The European space would be only a vast free trade zone, not even a single market (owing to the constant fluctuation of exchange rates). Competition for jobs between the member countries would also lead to the progressive dismantling of social security systems.

Under this system, if the present Community rules were adhered to, the common institutions would be weakened, dissenting minorities would want to apply exceptional measures in increasing numbers of cases, and power would tilt in the direction of the small countries: eight countries representing a tenth of the total population would be able to defy all the others . . .

A European space along these lines would be dominated by Germany. In the absence of a single currency, the Deutschmark would become the common currency. Three-quarters of EEC internal trade already takes place in marks, and 40 per cent of the Community's production is German. Germany would insist that the effects of the inevitable revaluation of the mark on the incomes of its farmers should be subsidized by Brussels, and reject all attempts to put a ceiling on its grain output; it would make its own bilateral arrangements with the United States on any subject it liked, as it has already done. It would impose its own financial policy on the other members of the Union, and then its economic, social and defence policies; eventually it could even acquire nuclear weapons, and form an alliance with northern Europe and the Ukraine against the southern countries. It is even conceivable that a smaller European federal union might then be constituted by Germany and its nearest neighbours.

Perhaps at the moment these hypotheses seem a little far-fetched: a Germany weakened by the imperatives of reunification and overtly rooted in the Community is hardly ready at the moment for adventures of that sort. Reasonable Germans are perfectly well aware that neither Russia, nor France, nor Britain would accept German domination of Europe. They know, too, that managing the European space would cost them an enormous amount: the Community would have to triple its regional funds from a total of about 25 billion Ecus a year to more than 60 billion, and Germany would have to pay the largest share of the increase, at a time when, for many years yet, it will also have to finance the reconstruction of the eastern Länder and try to restore the foundations of its own competitive edge. If its competitiveness remains inferior to that of France, a European space with two centres and two strong currencies might also take shape. One cannot help wondering what direction Germany will take after Helmut Kohl. Will he turn out to have been (as he once told me he was) the last German leader to favour a federal Europe? A good deal depends on the personality of the next chancellor; it is in the best interests of France, and of world peace, for the line embodied in the present holder of that post to be followed for as long as possible.

Unfortunately this is not the most likely eventuality. The reasons that drove Germany to participate in the construction of a united Europe disappeared in 1989. As a country it will speak increasingly loudly in support of its own interests.

This conforms to the logic of the development of the main relations of political force: it obeys market logic, and has the support of the élites in Germany, eastern Europe and the English-speaking countries, all of whom see it as meaning the end of French ideological domination of the European project.

For the Anglo-Saxons, though, it would only be an intermediate stage in the process leading towards a third scenario: the Euro-Atlantic Union.

A Euro-Atlantic Union

The third scheme, which has the avowed support of the Anglo-Saxons, would see the European Union integrating progressively with North America in a common economic, cultural and political space. A new economic institution – a vague trade agreement somewhat in the image of the agreement between the countries bordering the Pacific – would group the member countries of the Atlantic Alliance.

The essential political institution of the Euro-Atlantic Union would be NATO, which would extend its activities to the economy (as, incidentally, the initial NATO treaty had stipulated) and its zone of membership to Poland, the Czech Republic, Hungary and other eastern countries.

There would be no need for institutions to promote cultural convergence; that would be taken care of by market forces.

The creation of a Euro-Atlantic space would be in the mainstream of history. To begin with, it would be a natural completion of the destiny of peoples which, so often over the centuries, have given their lives for each other. Next, as we have seen, the dismantling of the Berlin Wall has weakened Community institutions and strengthened Euro-Atlantic ones. Indeed new ones have appeared, like the EBRD, whose breadth is increased still further by Japan's membership; other institutions, like the CSCE, have been given new justification and found new activity in the role of Euro-Atlantic forums.

This Euro-Atlantic union was to have been one of the explicit projects of George Bush's second mandate (had he been returned by the
electorate). Bush intended to encourage the Twelve to set up a
transatlantic economic alliance of the same type as NAFTA to prevent
an American protectionist landslide. When General Scowcroft spoke to
me about it, in September 1992, my response was interested: why not, if
it really was going to be an alliance between equal partners? A trade
agreement with the United States – or with NAFTA – would be no bad
thing for the Community, if it meant the institution of fair and explicit
rules.

Under this new order, an élite of expatriate citizens, of economic
nomads, would travel and communicate across frontiers and time zones.
Moving capital, goods and information, they would circulate through
the world economy in the same way that sailors and explorers once
navigated the same ocean. These privileged beings would live in a space
without frontiers, without government or laws, governed in fact by a
planetary utopia devoid of political rules: a utopia of the abstract
market, of 'Western democracy'. Control of images – their distribution
as well as their content – would be its means of influence on the rest of
the world, where most of the population lives.

In this Euro-Atlantic space, the Community's institutions would be
integrated with those of NATO and would be subject to G7 and thus to
the United States (as happened with the EBRD).

Politically, Euro-Atlantism serves as camouflage for US domination of
Europe; economically, it could become a reality; culturally, it is almost
one already. Militarily, it is an empty concept: if the central European
countries try to join NATO to protect themselves against Russia, Russia
will try to prevent them; and the West might then turn them down,
fearing the prospect of automatic involvement in central European
conflicts. Either East Europe is excluded from NATO, and NATO no
longer has any role; or it is admitted, turning NATO into an alliance
against Russia, Japan and the South, or into an instrument for internal
policing in the Balkans, something nobody wants.

This scenario is opposed by a number of forces. Partisans of the
European Union would resist its implicit vassalization, along with the
Germans who prefer the Deutschmark to the dollar. Part of European
industry will also be against it, fearing a decline of its own influence: in
a capitalism which is thoroughly globalized, Europe(s) will simply
become a zone where production costs are too high. Its internal market,
if it is not protected, will be dismembered by currency fluctuations, and
employment will flag as a result. Instead of improving productivity in
the service industries, liberal governments will try to reduce labour costs
in the worst possible way – by cutting real wages – and this will have the

effect of delaying still further the automation of manufacturing industry. A vicious circle of decline... If this happens, perhaps a third of Europe(s) will be condemned to the high levels of long-term unemployment already present in several regions. The élites will desert the continent, which will lose its place in the world economy and become a mere geographical outline without vision, morality, ethics or rules. This is hardly the sort of outcome European leaders would pursue as an explicit project.

Nor would Russia agree to such a process, which would lead it into isolation; if it were faced with a Euro-Atlantic bloc, nobody could stop it from sliding into claustrophobia. We should not forget the lessons of the eighteenth century, when France supported Poland against the Tsar and Prussia, while Britain supported anyone who could damage France... Euro-Atlantism would recreate East–West tension in a radically new context.

And finally, the United States itself stands to gain little from a transatlantic integration of this sort. On the contrary, the US – increasingly focused on the Pacific – would like to see Europe taking East Europe and Russia in hand, and sharing other burdens with America ... the South, the environment, the drugs problem and so on. It is in the interests of the United States to have the support of a strong Europe. It is thus likely to favour the establishment of a continental Union, an economic and political grouping of all the countries in the continent.

A Continental Union

Churchill, who was often prophetic, wrote in 1947 that 'the security of the world demands a unity in Europe from which no nation should be excluded'.

The fourth possible scenario proceeds from this intuition. It would involve equipping the whole continent, no nation excluded, with confederal institutions; but without dissolving the European Union, which would become a member country of the new grouping. In a nutshell, this scenario would make the East Europeans and the single market compatible, and thus associate them immediately with its advantages; but without preventing the European Union from consolidating.

The first element of the continental Union would be a continental common market extending as far to the East as democracy and market structures. This framework – totally distinct from a premature widening of the European Union – would have the advantage of linking continental development immediately with a global political vision, making it possible to manage social dumping and create conditions for a long-term transition, but without hampering the development of the European Union.

Conceived along the lines of the NAFTA model, it would have a common external tariff and continental preference in public purchasing – for protection against low-cost Asian industries – and would also authorize the free movement of labour between all member countries. It would control movements of capital and goods across its frontiers, prevent the disorder in the East from leading to nuclear catastrophes and huge movements of population, and launch some great projects to unite its inhabitants and bring their standards of living closer together.

A continental common market of this sort would be a factor of growth, with three hundred million consumers becoming progressively better off. According to first estimates, German exports would increase by 25 per cent, France's by 20 per cent and the United Kingdom's by 15 per cent, with imports growing at the same rate. That would justify the development of big transport, telecommunications and energy networks linking the two parts of Europe, huge projects that could be financed by the EIB and the EBRD. Modernization of the oil and gas industries in the former USSR would then become possible, something that would change the face of the continental economy. Like the railway in nineteenth-century America, like communications technology in today's Japan, exploitation of the East's vast energy reserves by a continental economy will be Europe's big chance over the coming century.

At the same time, the Continental Union would acquire the instruments of a continental agricultural policy and a continental ECSC (European Coal and Steel Community). The European Union would pursue its destiny by joining it as a member. It could be the site of new social achievement and bold new forms of work organization.

The Council of Europe would be the Union's parliament, the political forum for settling conflicts and the instrument of common policies. A Security Council made up of some of the continent's countries would be its executive body.

The Continental Union would then forge a continental defence identity to take over responsibility for stabilizing the armed forces of the former USSR, policing the continent (stopping war, barbarism and violations of human rights) and finding mechanisms for settling conflicts, on the basis of principles formulated by the CSCE: respect for democracy, human rights, minorities and the inviolability of frontiers; observance of disarmament agreements; and negotiated settlement of any conflicts over succession on state or regional levels. A Continental

Union would not imply the withdrawal of the Americans from European institutions of which they are founder members, like the EBRD and CSCE. The bank would act as spokesman for the East's interests, as a forum for the expression of their hopes and as the instrument for financing the East's public and private infrastructures.

Overall, the Continental Union would not represent a factor of uniformization but would facilitate the mixing and crossing of cultures and languages, giving birth to new differences which would be richer than the old ones.

A priori, the creation of such a union looks impossible. Some of us have been trying to interest the powers that be in the idea for a good two years now, but without success; only a strong and coherent political will could triumph over the prevailing passivity, myopia, fear of the great outdoors and drawbridge psychology. European firms could get there before the politicians: I look forward to the day when Russian, Polish and Ukrainian companies are buying from French, German and British firms; for continental links will then be irreversible, and the Continental Union will be a realistic possibility. If by some chance the project gains ground politically, it would be useful to appoint a group of wise men to prepare a report – as in 1956 the Messina conference asked the Spaak group to write the report which opened the way to the Treaty of Rome – setting a timetable for the removal of trade restrictions and settling the problems in agriculture and services, balances of payments, training, investment funds and movements of capital and labour. The Continental Union could establish all its institutions in fifteen years: the same timetable as the one fixed by the Spaak Report for the Common Market (created, in the event, in only eleven years).

It would then be time for Europe(s) to stop regarding itself as a Christian club, and became a space without frontiers stretching from Ireland to Turkey, Portugal to Russia, Albania to Sweden; culturally, it would have to favour the nomad over the sedentary, generosity over withdrawal into the self, tolerance over assertion of identity; in short, multiple belonging over exclusion. Recent debates on the right to humanitarian intervention, voting rights for foreigners, citizenship and the right to asylum, open the way towards these mutations.

The Continental Union, of which the European Union would be, with Russia, one of the essential motors, could become a pole of stability in the world, providing a counterweight to the American empire and taking Africa – its own backyard – in hand. Eventually the European Union, after becoming federal, could expand until its territory co-incided with that of the Continental Union.

Personally, I am convinced that this is where the future of Europe(s) lies, that this is the answer to the problems that undermine it at present, employment and growth in particular.

The Anglo-Saxons and East Europeans are attached to Euro-Atlantism; the Germans dream of a European space; and France still believes in a federal Union. In this context a Continental Union offers a better guarantee of everyone's interests than any other solution: it would protect the achievements of the European Union and give it a bigger market, without enabling anyone to become predominant.

But we have to cope with the world as it is. And we must be ready for the possibility that neither a federal European Union nor a Continental Union will be feasible, in the absence of leaders capable of inspiring peoples with ambitions on that scale.

In that case it would be a good idea, anyway in France, to invert radically the order of priorities set during the 1950s. Before we can find a project, an ambition, a stance appropriate to great adventures, we will have to change our outlook. Instead of uniting with northern Europe before aiding the South, we could ally ourselves with the South to balance northern Europe. A Mediterranean union grouping three southern European countries (France, Spain and Italy) with three Maghreb countries (Morocco, Algeria and Tunisia) might be an alternative or even complementary strategy. In the medium term that union would possess almost as many inhabitants as the European Union itself, and it would certainly help establish political stability in a zone which is vital to France. It could be constituted initially as a common market, then evolve in the direction of cultural and political unity; in any case, such a grouping would be closer to the French spirit than any Euro-Atlantic space.

Obviously these southern markets will not replace the European ones, or anyway not for a very long time. But a successful Mediterranean union would pave the way for the subsequent opening of large African markets. A common market between Europe(s) and Africa will be the target for the next century.

This scenario has a surprising side. But it, too, is in the mainstream of history; France may be Christian, Atlantic and European, but it is also Muslim, Mediterranean and African. And its future – like that of every great power – resides in the multiplicity of its connections, in the resolute acceptance of its ambiguities.

Of course the reality will not conform exactly to any of these models, but will result from a mixture of the pure forms described here; and there are numerous possible events, especially in Russia, that could alter the context of the continent so profoundly that wholly unforeseen emergencies could arise. Here, people may decide to keep themselves to themselves; there, they may conjure up some dictator who will impose his own law on history.

Despite all that, these blueprints should be considered for their own sake. Politicians who really want to think about the world, and make their mark on it, would gain by having a clear position on them.

1994

Translated by John Howe

22

Europe in the Twenty-first Century: The World's Scandinavia?

Göran Therborn

Looking Out from the World Bank

An instructive way of looking at the world of today and tomorrow is to follow the gaze of one of the globe's most important institutions. The World Bank's maps use the Peters projection, which shows Europe as a small far-northern periphery of peninsulae and islands, out on the western fringe of the huge Asian land-mass, separated by the narrow Mediterranean waterway from the big central continent of Africa, and by the wide Atlantic ocean from the impressive semi-continent of North America. Any Eurocentric view of the world is likely to be disturbed by a look in this mirror. The World Bank, after all, is harder to dismiss than, say, any Third World nationalist, Muslim zealot, or East Asian business politician. Though centred in Washington DC and heavily impregnated with North American values and perspectives, the World Bank is no doubt regarded by many Europeans as a fellow 'Western' institution.

Europe in the Peters projection of the globe looks very much like the Nordic countries on a standard European map – a small northern periphery – except that Scandinavia normally looks larger on the maps of Europe. This writer, of Swedish origin and nationality, is obviously suspect of bias if he predicts a probable future of Europe in the world as a Scandinavia, or Norden,[1] writ large, and, to be sure, other futures are also possible. But, to take this argument a little further, I would say that a Scandinavian scenario is in the long run one of the most attractive futures left to an irreversibly ex-imperial continent.

However, before jumping to any conclusions, let us take a sober look at Europe's standing and visible challenges at the turn of the third Christian millennium.

357

The future standing of Europe in the world will depend on three complex variables: the relative weight, the relative specificity, and the relative unity of Europe.

Still Heavyweight, but . . .

Western Europe has long since abdicated from claims to rule the world, although the Dutch, the French and the Portuguese had to be ousted from their colonies by force. The bungled Anglo-French-Israeli attack on Egypt in 1956 was the last attempt to play the role of world power. The recent war of the Yugoslav succession has demonstrated Europe's weakness, even as a regional power. German diplomacy may have contributed to raising the temperature of the conflict but, once the small-scale wars broke out, Germany and the EU contributed significantly neither to the military outcome nor to the (still provisional) settlement. It was the Americans who paid and trained the Croatian army, it was the US Air Force that turned the balance in Bosnia, and the settlement is mainly dependent on American troops. A long distance has been travelled from Berlin 1878 to Dayton, Ohio, 1995. France, the major post-First World War patron of Balkan states and model of Balkan high culture, also remained on the military sidelines, in spite of the intense anti-Serbian agitation among Parisian intellectuals, and instead flexed its nuclear muscles in the peaceful waters of Mururoa.

In so far as the Soviet Union was a European power, its collapse entails a further weakening of Europe in the global theatre of power.

Commemorations are scaled down to correspond with lowered aspirations. The start of Western Europe's outward expansion was remembered in 1992 by a world trade exhibition in Seville, organized as an ecologically conscious theme park for tourists, without any of the imperial glory and nation-state braggadocio of the pre-Second World War exhibitions. And the arrival of European modernity in 1789 was two centuries later turned into a pure media spectacle, while politically correct opinion held that the French Revolution was both vicious and unnecessary.

Production and Prosperity

Economically, Europeans are, of course, still among the primary league players. In absolute terms, five of the world's ten largest economies are European. After the USA, China and Japan, Germany is number four, France number five, Italy sixth, the UK eighth, and Russia tenth. The other big teams are India and Brazil. But the five European major players added up do not match the US or the two East Asian powers combined.[2] With the addition of its three latest members, the joint EU GDP (just) overtook that of the United States, while being about two and half times as large as that of the Japanese.[3] But to what extent is the EU a single economic power?

In terms of prosperity Europeans still fare well. Of the World Bank's twenty-four 'high-income countries', fourteen are European. If Iceland and Luxembourg were included, the result would be sixteen out of twenty-six. All sixteen are Western European, and only two countries of Western Europe, Greece and Portugal, are in division two in the prosperity leagues.

Furthermore, the status of some of the non-European high-income earners is dubious. One, Hong Kong, is bound to disappear in 1997, and two are small desert sheikhdoms of windfall profits, Kuwait and the United Arab Emirates. And half the non-European prosperous societies are ex-European historical off-shoots, the USA, Canada, Australia, Israel and New Zealand. While the economic achievements of Hong Kong are genuinely Chinese, the fact that Hong Kong for a short period passes as a high-income country is due to its position as a European colonial enclave. In other words, only Japan and Singapore so far represent the achievement of completely non-European highest-rank prosperity.[4] By the year 2000 South Korea is likely to knock on the door of the rich men's club, and the beautiful little island of Mauritius may try in only a couple of years.[5]

How significant average GDP per capita and its growth are among rich countries is far from obvious, unless median incomes, the overall distribution, and the quality of life are taken into account. But, anyway, the distance of Western Europe from the United States and Japan in those respects should not be forgotten. If the per capita GDP of the EU Fifteen in 1994 was 100, the US figure would be 143 and the Japanese 116.[6] The gap is widening, not only between Japan and Europe, but also between the latter and the USA. The somewhat higher annual per capita growth of (West) Germany in 1980–93, at 2.1 per cent compared to the USA's 1.7 per cent, is not enough to compensate for the absolute difference in the per capita size of the economy, which is growing.[7]

On the other hand, Western Europeans are increasing their distance from the world as a whole, except for North America and East Asia. In 1980–93 all Western Europe, except its richest Swiss part, increased its already high GNP per capita percentage-wise more than the world as a whole, from an absolute base four times higher than the world average. The World Bank has estimated global growth per capita for the period mentioned at 1.2 per cent annually, while Spain grew by 2.7 per cent, the UK by 2.3 per cent, Germany and Italy by 2.1 per cent, and France by 1.6 per cent per year.[8]

In summary, Western Europe is a rich corner of the world, and it is growing relatively more prosperous. But it is not the world's economic motor.

I am not an aficionado of business consultancy, so I see little reason for entering into predictions or warnings about future competitiveness – and, indeed, I would not be competent to do so. A scholarly contribution to this literature concluded in 1993 that 'well positioned for the twenty-first century' were 'most likely ... Japan, Korea, and certain other East Asian trading states, Germany, Switzerland, some of the Scandinavian states, and *perhaps* the EC as a whole'.[9] Without entering the fray of competitive ranking and forecasting, there seems to be at least one caveat that needs to be added to the usual triangular disputes about the relative standing or potential of the US, Japan and Western Europe.

In order to obtain some purchase on the question of which is the leading among the world's big and rich economies we must be attentive to patterns of post-industrial international exchange. The OECD has recently released a compilation of international exchanges of services, from financial services or property rights usage to tourism. The USA emerges as very different from the other rich economies in this respect.

Table 1. International Services Transfers in
1992 for the World's Leading Economies
(net value in millions of US dollars)

USA	42,193
Japan	−42,194
Germany	−33,004
France	19,972
UK	6,383
Italy	−1,403
Canada	−9,293

Source: OECD, *Services. Statistics on International Transactions* 1995, table A1.

This pattern seems to indicate the special, central position of the US. It is further underlined by the balances for specified services. In management services, for instance, the US net balance is $7.019 billion, the British $1.622, the French $0.843 whereas the Japanese deficit is $0.529 and the German $0.946. In financial services the City of London leads, yielding a net UK balance of $2.975 billion, as against $1.966 for the

US, $0.744 for Germany, and a French deficit of $444 million. From computer-related services the US reaped a net surplus of $2.388 billion, whereas Germany ran a deficit of $188 million.[10]

For more than a century the New Worlds of immigration, the Americas and Oceania, have been generating more employment than the Old World of Europe. That difference long predates the rise of right-wing neo-liberalism and its tirades against 'Eurosclerosis'.[11] The trend is continuing, and, in spite of slow labour force growth, New World jobs are still growing faster than in Europe.

For 1960–90 the labour force of OECD Europe grew by 0.7 per cent annually, while the growth of employment stayed at 0.5 per cent. In the US the corresponding figures were 1.9 per cent and 1.9 per cent, in Japan 1.1 per cent and 1.1 per cent.[12] The gap has widened further in the 1990s. Between 1990 and the third quarter of 1995, total employment declined by 3.1 per cent in the EU, while increasing by 4.4 per cent in Japan and by 6.8 per cent in the USA. Extra-European figures are not out of reach of Europeans. In the 1990s, for instance, Norway has matched Japan, and Austria the USA, but the major Western European economies have manifested a certain rigidity on their slow path of employment.[13] Since the mid-1970s seemingly permanent high unemployment has become a significant characteristic of Western European economies. For every business cycle, the peak and the trough rates of unemployment have risen.

By way of conclusion, Europe is hardly the centre of the world economy, but Europe is still reproducing itself as a small semi-arctic outpost of prosperity, out of reach (and increasingly so) of the bulk of the world's population. Statistically, however, average prosperity is to some extent being undermined by a tendential rise in unemployment.

Population

In sheer numbers Europe is becoming steadily lighter in the world.

Table 2. Europe's Proportion of the World's Population 1950–2025
(per cent)

1950	1993	2025 (estimate)
22	13	9

Note: Europe includes Russia and the non-Caucasian and non-Central Asian republics of the former USSR.
Sources: United Nations, *Statistical Yearbook*. 40th series, 1995, p. 12; World Bank, *World Development Report 1995*, pp. 210–11, 228.

The population projection reflects the fact that Europe, together with Japan, is close to a static natural population equilibrium. Birth and death rates are almost cancelling each other out.

Table 3. Crude Birth and Death Rates in the World 1993 (per thousand)

	Birth rate	Death rate
Europe	12	11
Japan	10	8
USA	16	9
South America	26	7
Africa	42	14
China	19	8
India	29	10
South East Asia	27	8
World	25	9

Sources: United Nations, *Statistical Yearbook*, 40th series, 1995, p. 12; World Bank, *World Development Report 1995*, pp. 212–13.

The outcome of this demography is already visible in the age structure. In 1990 14.5 per cent of the population of Western Europe was over sixty-five years old, 12.3 per cent of the US, 11.9 per cent of the Japanese, but 4.8 per cent of the other Central, East and South Asian population, 3.6 per cent of the West Asian cum North African population, and 4.6 per cent of the Latin Americans. Extrapolations into the future indicate that, in the 2020s, about a third of the Western European population will be more than sixty years old.[14] Death rates are now exceeding birth rates in Germany, Italy and Switzerland.[15] Since the end of the Soviet Union, a dramatic excess of deaths over births has arisen in Russia, Ukraine, Belarus and the Baltic republics.[16] Part of Europe is dying out.

Whereas population biology is tending towards a static state, migratory flows are keeping up a certain momentum, although not (yet) enough to stop estimates of a slight population decline in the first decades of the next century. Europe has gone from almost half a millennium of net emigration to the status of an immigration continent in the first half of the 1960s. But it is only since the mid-1980s that the pace of migration into (Western) Europe has quickened. Between 1985–87 and 1992, the number of immigrants into Western Europe almost trebled.[17] In the 1990s, migration has constituted the bulk of the population growth in the EU Fifteen. Net migration into Germany in the 1990s has been more than twice that into the US, 6.7 and 3.3 per thousand population per annum, respectively.[18]

Europe, Africa and North America are the main destinations of cross-national migration in the world. In relation to the native population, the ratio of non-national migrants is highest in North America, about 6 per cent in 1993, as against 5 per cent in Europe (exclusive of former USSR and Yugoslavia), and about 3 per cent of the African population. Africa and Europe (including the former multinational socialist states) are currently the largest producers of refugees in the world.[19]

Peripheries are normally not attractors of population. Europe's increasing attractiveness as a continent of immigration is an expression of outsiders' recognition of the unabated centrality of Europe, at least in the provision of life-chances, if not in the wielding of power. The recent migratory turn also highlights the absurdly privileged global position of Europe in the nineteenth century and the first half of the twentieth. The powers of the continent were directly ruling major parts of the non-European world, and extracting wealth from most, while at the same time exporting large parts of its poor population to the rest of the world. The almost unique economic dynamism of the whole continent after the Second World War, and in particular of its poorer southern and eastern parts, made possible a relatively successful adaptation to novel circumstances.[20] In this abstractly cold historical light, the recent rise of xenophobia in Western Europe, for all its personal venom and viciousness, should rather be seen as a secondary reaction.

Pulling all these elements together, with the decline of the big-power military strengths of Europe, its remaining political divisions, its stably founded but clearly not predominant economic capacity, the great and visibly secure prosperity of its citizens, and its ageing and tendentially shrinking native population, it seems that Europe has little, if anything, to gain from entering a race for world championship. Further, the world view of the global business consultants, with their vision of an inexorable struggle for world competitive ranking, seems no more founded on what matters to most people than was the 1930s ideology of the inescapable struggle for *Lebensraum*. On the other hand, there is no evidence of European marginalization, either pending or current.

In sum, Western Europe is still a heavyweight, but its punch is not as hard as it used to be. Some of its weight is fat rather than muscle, and it is getting slower. But it also looks unscathed, exuding good training and experience.

Specificity under Pressure – Imitation

The specificities of European societies derive from the historical trajectory of Europe, ancient and modern. This writer would tend to give more weight to the European route to modernity than to its ancient traditions in accounting for contemporary European sociology,[21] but the point will not be argued here. What seems to be called for, however, is some assessment of the life expectancy of the peculiarities of the Europeans.

Synoptically summarized, there are then two kinds of significant European specificities. One refers to the aggregate of European societies and their common characteristics in comparison with the rest of the world. The other is 'Europe' as a supranational, supra-state collective or social mega-network.

Both kinds are subject to three sorts of challenge. One is the possibility of the characteristics being eroded, by internal processes and/or under external pressure. Alternatively, the specific traits of Europe may recede into the background, as marginal or irrelevant in relation to broader and stronger global processes. Thirdly, Europe's special features may become increasingly difficult to discern, because they are taken up elsewhere, by imitation or by parallel developments.

European Modernity: Class and Welfare State

Of the many particularities of European social relations as aggregates, this essay will touch upon only two, the special significance in Europe of industrial class relations and of a socially interventionist 'welfare' state. The two are, of course, historically related, the latter pretty much an outcome of the former.

Modernity in Europe was an endogenous development of the continent taken as a whole. This meant that the bitter and violent conflicts for and against modernity all took on the character of civil war. This endogeneity had at least three important implications.

First, the European route to modernity pitted socio-economic classes against each other more clearly than elsewhere. That was inherent in the nature of the process, as classes are internal social divisions, but it was strongly reinforced by the unique importance of industrialization to European societies. Only in Europe did industrial employment become at least relatively dominant (in a trisectoral employment structure).[22] The polarized industrial division of labour gave a further impulse to class consciousness, class mobilization and class organization in Europe. The West European political party system derives from clear-cut class cleavages, typically with one major party descending from specific working-class representation, and the other from a core of bourgeois and middle-class representation, representing non-working-class politics, either by claiming transcendence of class by nation or religion (Christian Democracy) or by expressing agrarian or middle-class interests.

Secondly, the internal conflict path meant that established religion was always clearly on the side of anti-modernity. When modernity finally won, this meant a serious defeat of established Christianity. Today, Europe is by far the most secularized part of the world once governed by what Max Weber called the world religions.[23] (The Confucian area is not quite comparable to the rest of the religious world.)

Thirdly, the protracted internal struggles for and against modernity gave rise to a large set of elaborate doctrines and principled ideological systems. Europe was the womb of almost all the major isms of the nineteenth and twentieth centuries, from legitimism, monarchism and republicanism, to liberalism, conservatism, traditionalism, radicalism, socialism, Marxism, fascism and anti-fascism. Only fundamentalism is of non-European origin; the word was coined in the US in the 1920s to designate anti-modern Christian Protestantism.

With a party system historically based on class division, relatively high levels of class voting – striking in comparison with, say, Brazil, in spite of the rise in that country of a major Workers' Party, with a charismatic, genuinely working-class leader[24] – still characterize Western Europe. Trade unions carry more weight in Europe than elsewhere, especially in German-speaking Europe. The weakening of the trade-union movement in the 1980s and 1990s has not transformed West European unions into mere clones of their American or Japanese cousins.[25]

In terms of ideological doctrines, Europe is still the world's major producer, although the successful export drive has passed from the Soviet Union and the Socialist International to neo-Tory Britain. The major item of ideological export is no longer 'socialism' but 'privatization' and (free-market) 'economic reform'.[26] The relatively meagre ideological output – outside Christian fundamentalism – of the US Right, of the Reagan presidency and of the Gingrich Congress is noteworthy.

On the other hand, de-industrialization and its concomitant sociopolitical re-alignments have injured Europe. The industrial class basis of European politics is being undercut, although it retains a relative advantage.

Table 4. The Proportion of Industrial Employment 1960–90
(Percentage of Total Employment)

	1960	1974	1980	1990
OECD Europe	37.4	38.1	35.8	30.9
USA	35.3	32.5	30.5	26.2
Japan	28.5	37.0	35.3	34.1

Source: OECD, *Historical Statistics 1960–1990*, p. 40.

The unique European preponderance of industrial over agricultural and services employment – the former much larger than in the US and the latter much smaller than in USA, and clearly smaller than in Japan – has been lost since 1980. Europe has even become less industrial than Japan, although the distance from the US has been, by and large, maintained.

Sociological experience teaches us that institutions do not usually disappear simply because they are undermined. The institutions of industrial class society are still in place in Europe, and they are not likely to evaporate in the foreseeable future. But they are less significant as rallying-points of collective identity and behaviour, from class voting to May Day marching or attending meetings. The efforts of the political parties to distance themselves from the unions and their more direct class allegiances are palpable all across Europe in the 1990s, from Scandinavia to the Iberian peninsula, via the British Isles.

There are no signs of any accelerating decline of class relations and class politics in Europe. Even the basis for predicting a continuous linear erosion is flimsy. Electoral politics in Western Europe is still moving, up and down, Right or Left, within the classical social para-meters. At the time of writing, seven of the fifteen EU states – all small, true – have a prime minister with some claim to represent the labour movement. The current British and Spanish, and, more obliquely, the French and the German, right-wing governments emerged victorious out of rather clear-cut Right–Left divisions anchored in the social structure. In Italy, the Left–Right social division of electoral politics seems to have become clearer in recent years, after the corrupt centrist politicians were forced by the courts to step down.

Also, with regard to non-electoral social conflicts, the current pattern of tendencies is complicated. Against, for instance, the resigned accept-ance of permanent mass unemployment one should also notice the occasional flare-up of still potent class-based social protest. Two major examples of the latter recently have been the Italian trade union mobilization in autumn 1994 against pension cuts, which led to both a new pension reform and a new government, and the French protests in December 1995 against government proposals for major reductions of social entitlements. In that case, too, the most controversial proposals were withdrawn.

The welfare state has come under siege, from global financial markets – generally manned by highly paid young males, to whom social issues are as alien as the other side of the moon – and from the bulk of economists, while internal support is increasingly withheld by an upper middle class, increasing both in assertiveness and in selfishness. The notions of more options for the prosperous and more concentration on the basic minimum for the 'really needy' are in the ascendant, while social rights, solidarity and social integration are being correspondingly demoted. But how far has this new ideological discourse eaten into actually existing institutions of public social rights?

Table 5. Social Security Transfers and Total Current Public Disbursements 1960–93 (Percentage of GDP)

	1960		1974		1985		1993	
	Transfer	*Total*	*Transfer*	*Total*	*Transfer*	*Total*	*Transfer*	*Total*
Europe	9.5	31.4	13.3	40.0	17.7	49.5	19.4	52.3
USA	5.0	27.2	9.5	36.4	10.9	37.0	13.2	37.3
Japan	3.8	17.5	6.2	32.9	10.9	32.3	12.1	34.9

Note: Europe = OECD Europe.
Source: OECD, *Historical Statistics 1960–1994*, tables 6.3 and 6.5.

On the whole, the specificity of the European state has maintained itself well so far.[27] The pressure on it is likely to be kept up, and may well even mount further. But attacks on the welfare state are intensifying even more in the US, and there are so far no visible signs of any slashing of a Western European state to American or Japanese proportions. In terms of the amount of social security transfers, if not in the overall size of the state, the UK was in 1960 much closer to the US than to, say, West Germany, and to the richer part of OECD Europe as a whole. By 1980 this British position was reversed. One and half decades of militant right-wing government have succeeded only in bringing back the UK to a social location half-way between the US and Europe, according to the OECD, while EU statistics put the UK still squarely within the EU Twelve mainstream.[28]

The two major characteristics of modern European societies, their industrial class pattern of social relations and conflicts and their sizeable social state, are not the currently proud focuses of European collective identities. Both are being undercut by powerful forces, internal as well as international. However, like all traditions and institutions, they also show a strong resilience, and de facto they continue to shape the continent in characteristic ways.

Beyond the Nation-State: Bloc or Model?

An intricate inter-state, or, at the beginning, inter-monarchical, system has characterized Western Europe since the Middle Ages. From the mid-nineteenth to the mid-twentieth century that state system gave rise to a series of devastating wars, each even more destructive than the last. Finally, these experiences generated a specific set of suprastate institutions.

This is not the place to analyse the process of European unification, or even to summarize it. What needs to be underlined, though, is its global specificity, and thereby its great relevance to the standing of Europe in the world, of today and of tomorrow.

The actually ongoing building of 'Europe', which started after the Second World War, is a process of system integration, of building a loosely coupled, open system. As such, 'Europe' is a set of supranational, suprastate institutions, a social mega-network.

The European Union is the most concrete and tangible of this set, with a highly visible political apparatus and a substantial budgetary underpinning. The EU operates not only as a 'common market' – its impact on trade has been uneven and unsystematic – but, more characteristically, as a pool of economic resources and initiatives, and as a normative area, governed by an extensive body of rules, vigilantly and strongly protected by a European judiciary, to which even nation-states are held liable.

The Council of Europe, with the European Convention on Human Rights, its Commission and its Court of Human Rights, and its European Social Charter have made Europe into an arena of human rights, more specific and more compelling than in any other area of the world. The rulings of the European Court of Human Rights are accepted as binding by the states which have ratified its jurisdiction.

A third major institution of normative Europe is the Organization for Security and Cooperation in Europe, officially constituted in 1992 and 1994 (when the name changed from 'Conference' to 'Organization'), but dating back to the institutionalized thaw of the Cold War, the Helsinki Agreement of 1975. The seventh section of the latter listed a set of fundamental freedoms and rights to act and provided for a review process. The now-permanent OSCE has a special monitoring and dialogue-initiating office on democratic institutions and human rights, located in Warsaw.

The global specificity of the current sociology of Europe resides most visibly in suprastate 'Europe'. Not that the continental drawing together of the Western part of Europe is unique, or even pioneering. Pan-American efforts in this direction clearly antedate the European ones, starting with more or less regular pan-American state congresses in 1889, leading to a loose prewar pan-American Union and a set of hemispheric professional recurrent conferences and institutions, like the Inter-American Child Institute in Montevideo, and in 1948 to the Organization of American States (OAS). Ex-colonial Africa has created its Organization of African Unity (OAU), and particularly in West Africa, a number of regional organizations, one of which intervened in the civil wars in Liberia to certainly no less effect than the EU in ex-Yugoslavia.

However, in contrast to the OAS and the OAU, the EU, and, for those countries that have ratified its human rights jurisdiction, the Council of Europe, are suprastate, not just legally binding on member states. That this is also functioning in practice is shown by the rulings of the European Court of Justice and Court of Human Rights, and their de facto acceptance by member states. The European Commission represents a union, not just a set of sovereign member states. A rare combination of a relatively balanced internal composition of power, intensive socio-economic internal exchange and large-scale economic strength on the global stage has resulted in 'Europe' (i.e., the EU) being widely perceived in the world as one 'bloc'.

It was as such a bloc that the East Asian countries encountered Europe at the Bangkok summit in March 1996. And it is as such a bloc that 'Europe' has inspired looser economic groupings in the Americas in the 1990s – NAFTA, Mercosur – and, most recently, the agreement on an Andean Community. The European Commission and Court of Human Rights have provided models for the recently established American equivalents.[29] 'Europe' as a bloc of prosperity attracts a growing queue of applications for membership, from long (and probably hopelessly) waiting Morocco and Turkey to the ex-communist East–Central strip of Europe, from Estonia to Bulgaria.

Europe's future standing in the world will depend largely on the future of its suprastate organizations and institutions. Their problem is one not of erosion and decline, but rather of over-extension and emulation. What will happen to Europe as a normative area if the Council of Europe accommodates continuous violent suppression of minorities, in Turkey, Croatia and Macedonia or Russia? Will a European Union of twenty-five or thirty members become more like the proposed All-American Free Trade Area than a European Community? Will the OSCE achieve anything, or fail in its virtually impossible missions to postwar Bosnia, Chechnya and the Caucasus? In an ideal world the Council of Europe would decrease in significance and specificity, in favour of a strong UN system of human rights flanked by many regional institutions. However, implosion by virtue of internal disunity is another risk, which is dealt with below.

As a unit, Europe may appear in the world, and to the world, as a power bloc, as a normative or institutional model, or, thirdly, as a nullity without significance. This last is not possible in the forseeable future, but it cannot be ruled out for ever.

European modernity once provided the world with a political model which was a mixed blessing, the nation-state. Our own disastrous experiences of what the nation-state might lead to generated a set of economic and normative suprastate institutions. The latter represent the specific dynamic of Europe on the threshold of the twenty-first century. What chances do these institutions have of maintaining, or even increasing, the centrality of Europe and its power in the world, or of providing a new model of economic organization and/or of citizenship and human rights? In the conclusion below I shall return to this question. But, first, we should look briefly at two other issues impinging upon Europe's future relations with the world.

Clouds over Unity

The position of Europe in the world will be significantly affected by tendencies of global unification, or 'globalization', and by its own capacity to unite. Both processes are likely to be revealed as more complicated than is commonly believed.

The Limits of Globalization

Tendencies of globalization have attracted much attention in the last couple of decades. The transnational corporations flattening the earth into one giant chessboard of competitive locations; the financial markets interconnected across all the time-zones of the globe and with a gambling turnover exceeding the annual GDP of any state on the planet; a worldwide mass culture encircling the earth through satellite transmissions, audible in the remotest corners, visible in the ubiquity of the same trainers and jeans, and digestible as global fast food; these factors are all real and well known. On a more modest scale some steps have been taken towards a normative globalization, with the big UN conferences on human rights, on population, on the environment and on poverty, with ensuing declarations and conventions, and sometimes monitoring, reporting systems, and evaluation committees. Increasingly powerful and ambitious international economic organizations like the IMF and the World Bank are forcing neo-liberal economic and social policies, largely inspired by US orthodoxy, on to all poor and/or indebted states of the world.[30]

All this delimits Europe both as an economic power and as an institutional model. But there is little reason to assume that globalization trends are reducing Europe to any other interchangeable chunk of the world.

The existence of a global economic system is not a novelty. It dates back at least 150 years to the time when Britain's Royal Navy opened up China to the international drugs trade ('the Opium War'). Far from being extinguished, the persistence of different 'corporate cultures' has been discovered recently by students of and consultants to the management of large corporations.[31]

Given that, the fact that Europe is well represented among the big corporate players is more than statistically interesting. In 1990, 45 of the world's 100 largest industrial corporations and 199 of the 500 biggest service corporations were European.[32] Though trading goes on round the clock, financial institutions are not spread randomly across the continents. In the gigantic area of foreign currency trading, London has recently reinforced its standing as *the* centre of the world.[33]

The activation of regional economic arrangements in the last decade, in South-East Asia, in the Pacific and in the Americas in particular, testify to the continuing importance of economic geography. Moreover, empirical economists have pointed to the increased importance of micro-regions to 'post-Fordist' production.[34] Rather than regionalization and globalization competing against each other, with the latter overtaking the former, the two appear rather to be off-shoots from the same tree, that of supranational opening and transcendence.

Finance apart, the world market is not outgrowing national economies, submitting them to intensified global competition. In 1956, world exports constituted 9.4 per cent of world GDP, according to the IMF. This figure was almost unchanged till 1973–74, standing at 10.9 per cent in 1972. The OPEC oil crisis raised the share to 16.1 per cent in 1974, and world exports have hovered around that value ever since, going to up 17–18 per cent around 1980–81, then slightly declining, to about 15 per cent by the end of the 1980s.[35] Figures for the OECD, which accounted for three-quarters of world trade prior to 1973 and two-thirds ever since,[36] show a similar pattern of international dependence on trade: stabilility up to 1973–74, then a hitch followed by basic stability, with a slight downward turn in the late 1980s and early 1990s, picking up again in 1994.[37]

The notion of 'intensified global competition' includes a strong element of rhetoric. With regard to trade in goods, both the EU Twelve and Japan exhibit a slight trend towards diminishing world market dependence since 1980, whereas the USA is oscillating around the same trend line.[38] The increase in the market shares of the Asian 'tiger economies' has been at the expense of other 'developing' countries, whose slice of the pie has shrunk. The former have not cut at all into the overall exports of the OECD world, as noted above.

Global mass culture is mainly American or American-cum-British. The US and the UK, in that order, dominate both the music and the audiovisual markets. Among the OECD countries, only the USA, with $2,031 million in 1992, and the UK, with $25 million, run a surplus on film and TV rights.[39] But culture is effective largely within institutional structures, and the latter are still strongly shaped by states and by situated ethnicities. Therefore, the global cultural radiation is received largely in the form of hybridization or creolization.

The 1990s have also seen one important turn towards de-globalization. The collapse of the USSR and the end of the Cold War meant the end of four decades of global cleavage and alignments. The Gulf war and the protection of the Kuwaiti oilfields proved to be a brief episode and not the beginning of a global Pax Americana. In international power politics, regional powers and regional divisions are currently increasing in significance, at the expense of globalism.

The main forces of globalization no longer derive from Europe, and have not done so since Europeans launched the Second World War. True, the global Cold War was acted out from a script drafted on the basis of the rival ideologies of European modernity, and its centre-stage was the heart of Europe. But, of the two main actors, one was a European expatriate and the other a cousin from the Eastern country-side. However, there are so far no signs of global power driving continental (or smaller) regions out of business. And in the global economic games being played European players are well represented, although perhaps at risk of being off-side. Globalization is cutting into European cultural specificity, including European political and corporate culture, and in the longer run this will leave new institutional imprints. But we are not witnessing the disappearance of historical geography.

In other words, Europe will continue to have its own standing in the world, whatever that standing may be.

Difficulties of Europeanization

It is not just the world that has problems with unification. So too has Europe. However, from a worldwide perspective on the future, the problems of the latter look somewhat different from those that dominated European public debates prior to the 1996 EU Inter-governmental Conference. Since Europe is unlikely to become a first-rank global political and military power in the twenty-first century, concerns about a unified foreign and security policy have little more than a parochial interest. Nor is European monetary union likely to have any crucial impact upon Europe's relative economic position in the world. The idea of EMU is mainly a peculiar conception of a political union.

Economically, its overriding concern is stability, not competitiveness or growth.

Only to the extent that future world markets are carved up between protectionist blocs will European unity be very important to the relative economic position of European corporations, trading sites and states. That is *not* the direction in which regionalization in the world is currently heading. On the contrary, the major thrust is in the sphere of opening markets, albeit the regional before the borderless. European economic power will depend not directly on the unit of 'Europe' as one organization or collectivity, but on the dynamism and luck of the major European players. But it is true that social disintegration in Europe might well negatively affect the dynamism of European actors.

Unemployment and Ethnic Multiculturality

The major social problems that the unity of Europe faces are twofold. One is the mounting socio-economic segmentation and polarization within the nations of Western Europe, a product of rapid ethnic diversification in the big cities and sluggish labour markets, with unemployment steadily rising from one business cycle to the next for twenty years. The other is the discrepancy between, on one hand, an institutional-cum-cultural adaptation of Eastern Europe to Western models and, on the other, the drastic widening of already large divides in terms of resources and life-chances for the bulk of the East European population, as the cost of breaking up the previous institutional structures.

Neither problem is likely to lead to acute social disintegration in the foreseeable future (with the possible exceptions of Russia, Ukraine and some Balkan countries). Both seem, for the time being, to be containable within the existing institutions of Western cities and nation-states and of the extensive forms of East–West cooperation. But unless they are tackled seriously, and in a concerted and sustained way – which appears unlikely at the moment – internal Western divisions and the East–West divide are more likely to be exacerbated than to recede. They will then have heavy negative consequences for the quality of life of the whole European population. Virtually everybody is likely to have to pay a price for social exclusion, marginalization, poverty and despair, a price paid in the currency of fear, crime and occasional but recurrent violence. Even the rich may weep, to paraphrase the title of a Mexican soap opera very popular in post-communist Russia.[40] Deep socio-cultural and economic divisions will also undermine the norms and institutions of 'Europe' and of individual European societies, even though a minimum of democracy may not be threatened, at least not outside the former Soviet Union, the former Yugoslavia and Albania.

Table 6. Standardized Open Unemployment Rates in the EC/EU 1961–95

1964–73	1974–79	1980–89	1990–95
2.7	4.7	9.3	9.6

Sources: OECD, *Historical Statistics 1960–1994*, table 2.20; Eurostat, *Statistics in Focus. Population and Social Conditions, no.3*, table 1, for unemployment in 1995.

The employment problem consists not only in the unemployment rate, but also in the dropouts, from the labour force as well as from school, early retirement, and unemployability disguised as disability. The self-imposed fiscal constraints of Maastricht are increasing the attempts to shuffle the problem around, raising the statutorily 'normal' retirement age, tightening the disability criteria. How is the labour market going to bear that? Well, not by any particularly expansionary economic policies characteristic of Keynesianism, now held to be obsolete by economically correct opinion. The only recipe with any popularity is the creation of a more dualistic labour market. Alongside the normal European labour market, there is to be one with much lower wages, few – if any – social rights, and with no security. The extent to which this deliberate division of labour into two lanes will be carried out remains to be seen. But if it should succeed, we have some knowledge of what it will look like: something like the South Bronx or South Central Los Angeles.

The traditionally rather mono-ethnic cities of Western Europe have in recent decades acquired a considerable amount of multicultural diversity. In some ways this is an echo of the rich multiculturality characteristic of Eastern European cities, from Constantinople/Istanbul to Helsingfors/Helsinki, before the waves of national assimilation and ethnic cleansing.

The change has been enormous because of its concentration in certain cities, mainly capitals or other central towns. In Oslo, for instance, the children of immigrants constitute a quarter of the city's primary school children, in spite of Norway's restrictive immigration policies. In Amsterdam about half of all schoolchildren have immigrant backgrounds, and in Paris in 1990 a third of all youths aged under seventeen lived in immigrant families. Uniquely in Europe, Britain produces racial statistics, so we know that in the early 1990s 'non-whites' made up nearly a fifth of the Greater London population. In Frankfurt and Brussels a good quarter of the resident population are 'foreigners'. On a national level, one in five children aged under eighteen in Sweden has at least one immigrant parent.[41]

Even if one considers multiculturality as an asset, as does this author, sociology and history teach us that it is not unproblematic. What 'Europe' will mean to the West Indians or Bangladeshis in Inner London, to the Maghrébins in the suburbs around Paris, to the Turks and Kurds in Berlin and Frankfurt is far from self-evident. And if there is little or no proper space for them on the labour market, or for their cultures among the cultures of Europe, the ensuing society will not be the normative area promised by the Council of Europe with its recognition of the rights of diversity.

The prospects for a rich, peaceful and stimulating multiculturality, as against those for ghettoization, crime and ethnic strife, are difficult to assess. Evidence available so far precludes any straightforward extrapolation in either direction. Unemployment hits proportionately more immigrants and immigrants' children than natives. The immigrant population tends to have a higher crime rate than the native. Ethnic violence has become part of social life all over Europe. Xenophobic and racist parties and politicians have gained widespread support in several countries, notably Austria, Belgium, France and Switzerland. Protest riots against racism and discrimination have occurred in Britain, France and Germany.

On the other hand, there are also a large number of positive interethnic contacts, including marriages. Public policy and public opinion are strongly in favour of multicultural integration. Immigrants, for their part, are not reducible to passive objects of discrimination. As migrants they tend to represent the more vigorous and active part of their original population. Therefore it is not surprising that many of them, or their children, do very well at school. The raw school records do not take class into account, which gives a distorted picture of school performance and migration. Swedish data show that in Sweden immigrant children did better at school than native ones, if the socioeconomic background was allowed for. How far these results, which cover a period from the late 1970s to the early 1990s, can be generalized is uncertain. A Norwegian study found no educational disadvantage linked with immigrant origin. In Britain and France the picture seems to be one of differentiation. Indian children in Britain and East Asian children in both countries do extremely well, whereas West Indian and North African boys, in particular, do worse than the native children.[42] In all countries there is a considerable new ethnic entrepreneurship, and also, in the areas of high concentration, new ethnic politics.

So far, there is a general consensus among comparative students of the matter that Europe has not yet produced anything equivalent to the American ghettos. And I can see no strong reason for believing that it is likely to do so. But migration pressures are likely to persist, from North and sub-Saharan Africa, from South Asia and the Caribbean – where the 'cultures of migration' and networks already exist – and possibly also from the Middle East, unless there is a peace settlement and some prospect of development. Immigration from Eastern Europe has up till now been less than many had predicted, except from former Yugoslavia. The overwhelming majority of migrants from the rest of Eastern Europe have been people claiming an ethnic connection. People claiming German descent have left Russia, Poland or Romania for Germany, people from the former USSR claiming Jewish origin have gone to Israel, and people in Bulgaria of Turkish background have moved to Turkey. But a build-up of westward migration pressure from Russia and Ukraine cannot be ruled out.

To conclude, even if disaster scenarios are unlikely, West European societies of the future are likely to be less cohesive than in the past, harbouring more mechanisms of exclusion than in the 1960s and 1970s. And, certainly, there will be less unity or social integration than in pre-modern European culture and identity. Even the memory of the fatal national wars will disappear as a centripetal force – indeed, this could occur in only a few years, when Helmut Kohl's generation leaves the political centre-stage. However, there are as yet no tendencies to socio-economic and/or cultural polarization or segmentation in sight of a scale sufficient to break up the institutional inertia either of 'Europe' or of the West European nation-states.

The East–West Divide

The adoption of capitalist democracy in Eastern Europe has not turned out to be a 'quick fix' route to Northwest European prosperity. But estimates of the costs of systemic change are controversial, and how long they will have to be paid is uncertain. To analyse this comprehensively is outside the scope of this essay, but, in order at least to hint at the magnitude of the difficulties in formation of one Europe, a couple of indicators are needed.

Among the wealth of material currently produced, two data sets will be used. One is a body of vital statistics brought together by the UN Children's Fund.[43] The other is a comparative cross-national survey undertaken in early 1995 in the Višegrad countries and eastern Germany by an international research team directed by Professor Zsuzsa Ferge in Budapest.[44]

The Unicef data show a clear difference between, on one hand, the countries of the former Soviet Union and the Balkans and, on the other, Poland, the Czech Republic, Slovakia, Slovenia and, with qualification, Hungary. The latter group maintained their late-communist mortality rates during the early 1990s and have already started to improve, although not yet at the rate of improvement during the 1980s. The successor states of the USSR and the Balkans (the countries outside former Yugoslavia), on the other hand, have experienced a dramatic rise in mortality rates, which were considerably higher than those in Western Europe even before 1989–91.[45]

The table below summarizes the picture.

Table 7. Changes in Life Expectancy at Birth 1989–94 (years)

	Males	*Females*
Czech Republic	0.8a	1.2a
Hungary	−0.6	0.4
Poland	0.6a	0.5a
Slovakia	1.4	1.1
Slovenia	0.6a	0.6a
Belarus	−3.3	−2.3
Bulgaria	−1.4	−0.3
Estonia	−4.7	−0.8
Latvia	−4.3	−1.2
Lithuania	−4.0	−1.0
Moldova	−1.2a	−1.2a
Russia	−6.0	−3.1
Ukraine	−3.0a	−2.0a

Note: a = 1989–93.
Source: Unicef, *Poverty, Children and Policy: Responses for a Brighter Future*, p. 27.

The preliminary report of the survey of the luckier East Central European countries indicates considerable hardship there as well. About a third of the respondents talk of deficient nutrition, for instance.[46] Poland shows a uniquely dramatic increase in relative poverty. In 1989 the poorest 5 per cent earned 45 per cent of median net income; in 1994 they got 22 per cent. The poorest 10 per cent had their proportion of the median lowered from 55 to 33 per cent. The new Polish income distribution pattern is taking the form of a so-called Pareto curve, characteristic of early modern or pre-modern societies, with the bulk of the population in the lowest income groups and a long right tail showing the small number of the prosperous.[47]

By the turn of 1995–96 only Poland was about back at its GDP of 1989, which because of the 1979–82 crisis was little above the GDP of 1978.[48] Eastern Europe (except the Commonwealth of Independent States) as a whole was about 12 per cent below its level of 1989, and the

CIS had had its GDP almost halved.[49] By early 1995, Czech and Hungarian real wages were 82–83 per cent of those in 1989, Polish 72 per cent and Russian 47 per cent.[50]

The costs of systemic change mean that the economic gap between Eastern and Western Europe has widened since 1989, specifically with regard to the standard of living of the median inhabitant. If the GDP gap between the EU and Eastern Europe (including the Baltics but excluding the CIS) in 1989 was 100, it was 125 by the turn of 1995–96. If the divide between the most prosperous Eastern European country and the least prosperous EU country, the Czech Republic and Greece respectively, was 100 in 1989, it had widened to 123 by the end of 1995.[51]

Of course, far from everybody has lost from the turn to capitalism. Rudolf Andorka has calculated that (up to 1995) about 70 per cent of the Hungarian population were losers in the transition, in relative as well as in absolute terms, as their share of a declining sum of personal income decreased.[52] In absolute terms, according to Andorka's data, only the most prosperous 10 per cent of the population gained economically between 1989 and 1995.[53] In Bulgaria and, above all, in Russia, the differentiation between winners and losers is much starker.[54]

Another indicator of the problems ahead for any eventual EU enlargement is the conversion of national income levels into international currency. Currency rates do not adequately reflect the local purchasing capacity of each currency, so they are not to be taken literally as measures of comparative standards of living. However, the pattern does hint at the gap an enlarged EU will have to grapple with.

Table 8. Income Distribution in East Central Europe in Terms of the Pooled Income of the Region, 1994
(Percentage of each nation's population located in the different quintiles of the region's income-earners)

Quintiles	Czech Republic	East Germany	Hungary	Poland	Slovakia
1st (lowest)	11.7	0	20.3	48.5	31.2
2nd	17.9	0	26.5	19.8	32.6
4th	41.0	6.4	25.0	12.7	16.3
5th	1.1	93.5	1.6	0.8	0.2

Source: Z. Ferge *et al.*, *Social Costs of Transition*, p. 90.

Most eastern Germans, whose incomes are somewhat lower than those of their western German compatriots, have incomes higher than those of almost all Czechs, Hungarians, Poles or Slovaks. Poland, by far the most populous of the EU applicants, has by far the largest number of very poor people.

From the survey data it comes as no surprise that, in all four EU applicants, the 1980s was regarded as the time when the household did best in social terms (in comparison with the Second World War, the 1950s and 1994). In Poland and Hungary a plurality regarded 1994 as the worst period, whereas in Czechoslovakia the prewar period was somewhat more often held as the worst. (The eastern Germans were evenly divided over whether the 1980s and 1994 was their best time.[55]) But these popular opinions are at odds with the policies and perceptions of the politicians and the intellectuals of East Central Europe, and with those of their coaches and advisers in the West.

It is also noteworthy that the social policy recommendations with which the World Bank is bombarding Eastern Europe spell out the message, 'Forget Western Europe. Look to Latin America or South-East Asia (Singapore). In particular, look to the Chilean private pension funds.'[56]

Whatever the (il)legitimacy and the (in)stability of popular opinion, and whatever the reception of American counselling, the enlargement of 'Europe' will not be an easy task. But the future standing of Europe in the world will certainly not be unaffected by how that task is tackled and solved.

The East–West divide and the internal polarization in the East will interact with the economic and ethnic segmentation and tensions in the West, and with the political efforts at wider continental integration. This will probably involve an upper-middle-class continental rapprochement – already palpable; a tendency to aggravate the frustrations both of the working and of the unemployed classes both East and West, without bringing them closer together; and the growth of complex continental networks of crime and illicit business.

Conclusion: A Second West Germany or Scandinavia Enlarged?

The future of Europe in the world will be a function of its weight, its specificity and its unity. Western Europe is still a global heavyweight, but it has lost some force and speed. The institutional specificity of European societies as a whole remains, but is subject to erosion both from inside and from the external environment. Globalization is not trumping European-type regionalization. But the most dynamic specific aspect of Europe, the effort at building a suprastate 'Europe', alongside the continental system of nation-states, is facing difficult tasks of unification, both within the increasingly segmented Western European societies and also in terms of bridging the recently much widened gap in life-chances for the bulk of the population in Eastern and Western Europe.

Table 9 summarizes a set of important possible future positions in the world.

Table 9. Kinds of Standing in the World

	Relative Performance	*Model*	*Power*
Political	+/−	+/−	+/−
Economic	+/−	+/−	+/−

A plus sign in the columns of either political or economic relative performance (in comparison to the average of the world according to prevailing criteria − which may be political efficiency and stability or armed might, and economic growth or level of wealth) is a prerequisite for influence or power. A negative sign in both means underdevelopment or marginalization. In order to distinguish sharply between power and influence, I have here called the holder of the latter a 'model'. A model is taken as influential only to the extent that other people choose to regard it as such. Lack of plus signs under both influence (model capacity) and power means insignificance, irrelevance. It is also possible to have plus signs in all cells, that is, exercise both economic and political influence as well as power.

Europe is not going to underdevelop or be marginalized in the foreseeable future, either politically or economically. In the next century it will not become equivalent to the East Africa or Central America of the twentieth century. But will it remain a significant, major player in the world? And, if so, will it be an institutional or policy model or a power bloc?

'Europe' as a global role model might take two forms, not necessarily incompatible with each other. It might be an economic model, of market unification and suprastate economic organization, or possibly, though much less likely, of economic institutions in general. 'Europe' might also be taken as a normative model, of human rights, citizenship, gender and generation relations, of supranational norms and institutions.

As a power bloc 'Europe' is most unlikely to manifest itself in any form other than an economic one, as a continental 'trading state' of the sort that the West Germans and the Japanese created so successfully after their military defeat. Even a successful EU agreement on a common foreign and security policy is unlikely to yield any globally impressive military power. And without the backing of force and a willingness to use it, 'Europe' is unlikely to become a normative power, telling other parts of the world what political, economic and social institutions they should have.

In the final analysis, Europe is likely to keep a significant position in the world of the next century. But not all places in the sun are available. A position as a major politico-military power of global reach seems to be ruled out for Europe, as far into the future as any eye can see, *pace* the proud descendants of La Grande Armée. Acceptance of Europe as a significant economic-institutional model appears very unlikely, for the time being. Lacking the American backing of military muscle, mass culture and prestigious economics education, Europe as an economic role model would have to rely – at least to begin with – almost exclusively on demonstrably superior economic performance, once the inspiration to other regional market arrangements has faded. There have been few signs of this in the past twenty years, and it is unlikely that ageing Europe will provide the world with any new economic achievements to compare with those of, for example, East Asia.

This leaves us with two possible options, which are not necessarily mutually exclusive, but could very well mix in various combinations. One would be the position of a major, purely economic, power, the other that of a socio-political institutional model of some significance and influence, even if not generally accepted as such. In the former case Europe would become a sort of postwar West Germany or Japan of the next century, i.e., an economically prominent 'trading state'. In the latter, it would be a Scandinavia writ large.

Both variants are European and therefore have a common background and certain common preconditions of relative success. Both represent a break with a military past which was, ultimately, disastrous – although the major Scandinavian defeats occurred in the century from 1709 to 1809. Instead, both concentrate on internal socio-economic construction, although in neither case economically inward-looking or protectionist, but rather open to, and reaching out for, world markets. Both the Federal Republic of Germany and the Scandinavian countries became eminently prosperous in this manner.

They differ in two basic respects: most obviously, of course, in their size and significance in the world, but also in their interest in social experimentation and in universalistic social norms. 'No experiments' was once a winning electoral slogan in postwar West Germany, whereas 'social reform' has been a persistent aim of successful Scandinavian politics. Scandinavians have also been outstandingly active in extending universalistic and suprastate norms, in the Council of Europe, in the United Nations and UN conferences and conventions, in the Palme and Brundtland Commissions and in the most recent Commission on Global Governance. German foreign policy has had a strong suprastate component in its commitment to European unification, but has not shown any notable universalistic interests.

Both variants are built on strong, if differently organized, forms of social integration, and both require a well-managed prosperous economy. But there is one major difference in the economic prerequisites. The German model of economic power-play requires the constant sharpening of a competitive edge on a long economic blade. A Scandinavian model needs only the capacity for competitive sharpness in certain niche fields and the maintenance of a certain amount of relative prosperity.

Both a German- and a Scandinavian-model Europe would require some positive solutions to the two major problems of European unity, the economic–cultural divisions within Western Europe and the gaps between Eastern and Western Europe. A European 'Scandinavia' would demand the maintenance of a characteristically European world. A European 'Germany' would have to generate yet more feats of large-scale international competitiveness.

Which ideal-typical option to choose is a matter of preference. But I would hazard that, at least by the second half of the twenty-first century, the best Europeans can hope for is to constitute a nice, decent periphery of the world, with little power but some good ideas.

1996

Notes

1. Norden is the more adequate term, covering the five sovereign states of Denmark, Finland, Iceland, Norway and Sweden, as well as the autonomous Åland islands, Faroes and Greenland. But Scandinavia, which in native parlance included only Denmark, Norway and Sweden, is the only designation that has made it into the big world.

2. Commission on Global Governance, *Our Global Neighbourhood*, Oxford 1995, p. 148.

3. OECD, *Historical Statistics 1960–1990*, Paris 1992, table C.

4. World Bank, *World Development Report 1995*, 40th series, New York 1995, pp. 163, 228.

5. Ibid., p. 221.

6. OECD, *National Accounts 1960–1993*, Volume 1, Paris 1995, pp. 193ff.

7. Ibid., pp. 193ff, World Bank, *World Development Report 1995*, pp. 163, 221.

8. World Bank, *World Development Report 1995*, p. 163.

9. Paul Kennedy, *Preparing for the Twenty-First Century*, London 1993, p. 334.

10. OECD, *Services. Statistics on International Transactions*, Paris 1995, tables A 14–18.

11. For empirical time series, see also A. Maddison, *Phases of Capitalist Development*, Oxford 1982; G. Therborn, 'Tar arbetet slut? och post-fordismens problem', in U. Björnberg and I. Hellberg, eds, *Sociologer ser på arbete*, Stockholm 1987.

12. OECD *Historical Statistics 1900–1990*, tables 1.3 and 1.6

13. OECD, *Main Economic Indicators, December 1995*, Paris 1995, p. 23.

14. World Bank, *Averting the Old Age Crisis*, Oxford and New York 1994, tables A1, A2.

15. Eurostat, *Statistics in Focus. Population and Social Conditions. no. 6*, Luxembourg 1996, table 1.

16. Unicef, *Poverty, Children and Policy: Responses for a Brighter Future*. 'Economies in Transition' Series. Regional Monitoring Report no. 3, Florence 1995, tables A1–2.

17. G. Therborn, *European Modernity and Beyond. The Trajectory of European Societies 1945–2000*, London 1995, pp. 41ff., 50.

18. Eurostat, *Statistics in Focus*, fig. 1, table a2.

19. Commission on Global Governance, *Our Global Neighbourhood*, pp. 206–7; United Nations, *Statistical Yearbook*, 1995, p. 12; World Bank, *World Development Report 1995*, pp. 52–3.

20. Therborn, *European Modernity and Beyond*, pp. 133ff.

21. G. Therborn, 'Routes to/through Modernity', in M. Featherstone, R. Robertson and S. Lash, eds, *Global Modernities*, London 1995.

22. Therborn, *European Modernity and Beyond*, pp. 68ff.

23. Ibid., p. 275.

24. This assertion is based on Brazilian state (i.e., province) polls collected in 1993–95, the exact reference to which is not available to me where I am writing. On European–US comparisons, cf. Therborn, *European Modernity and Beyond*, p. 287.

25. Ibid., pp. 309–10.

26. An interesting symptomatic reading of this new ideological export is provided by A. Galal and M. Shirley, eds, *Does Privatization Deliver?*, Washington DC 1994, a publication oozing the zeal of true believers. Justly, the editors recognize Lady Thatcher's United Kingdom as the 'pacesetting privatizer' (p. 6).

27. ILO, *World Labour Report*, Geneva 1995, pp. 120–2.

28. OECD, *New Orientations for Social Policy*, Paris 1994, tables 1b and 1c; OECD, *Historical Statistics 1960–1994*, Paris 1996, table 6.3; Eurostat, *Eurostat Yearbook 1995*, Luxembourg 1995, graph 2.

29. The issue of human rights is, of course, much more serious and difficult in the Americas than in Western Europe, but, according to Chilean human rights activists interviewed in Santiago in January 1996, the new American institutions are doing a good job.

30. A good example is the World Bank's country report on Hungary: 'International comparison shows that Hungary spends a far larger share [about the same as that of Austria or Italy] of its resources on welfare than other market economies at similar stages of devleopment. . . . if Hungary is to join the ranks of high-income countries, reforming its welfare system is a *sine qua non*' (World Bank, *Hungary, Structural Reforms for Sustainable Growth*, Washington DC 1995, p. 25). The report then goes on to make it clear that, unless you cut pension rights severely and abolish general family allowances, you will never join the club of the rich.

31. See, e.g., C. Hampden-Turner and A. Trompenaars, *The Seven Cultures of Capitalism*, New York 1993, and, as a testimony from within the corporate world, M. Albert, *Capitalisme contre capitalisme*, Paris 1991.

32. *Fortune*, 29 July and 26 August 1991.

33. *Financial Times*, 28 March 1996.

34. M. Piore and C. Sabel, *The Second Industrial Divide*, New York 1984. Cf. also, more generally, P. Drugman, *Economics and Geography*, New York 1992.

35. IMF, *International Financial Statistics, Supplement on Trade Statistics*, Washington DC 1988, pp. 50–51.

36. 68 per cent in 1974, 68.7 per cent in 1994: IMF, *International Financial Statistics Yearbook 1995*, Washington DC 1996, pp. 124–5.

37. OECD, *Historical Statistics 1960–1994*, table 6.12.

38. Eurostat, *Eurostat Yearbook 1995*, pp. 260ff.

39. OECD, *Services. Statistics on International Transactions*, Paris 1995, table A21.

40. The original title is *También los ricos lloran* [The Rich also Weep].

41. For sources, the reader is referred to Therborn, *European Modernity and Beyond*, pp. 49–50, to the latest Swedish official population statistics, *Befolkningsstatistik*, and, for Oslo, to an unpublished paper by Jon Langlo of the University of Trondheim, July 1996.

42. R. Eriksson and J. Jonsson, *Ursprung och utbildning*, Stockholm 1993; Langlo, 'Skolesprestasjoner'; National Statistical Office, *Social Focus on Ethnic Minorities*, London 1996; J. Costa-Lascoux, 'Immigration: de l'exil à l'exclusion?', in S. Paugaam, ed., *L'Exclusion. L'état des savoirs*, Paris 1996.

43. Unicef, *Poverty, Children and Policy*.

44. Ferge, E. Sik, P. Róbert and A. Fruszina, *Social Costs of Transition. International Report*, Draft, Vienna 1995.

45. Unicef, *Poverty, Children and Policy*, pp. 24ff, 143.

46. Ferge *et al.*, *Social Costs of Transitions*, p. 114.

47. Ibid., pp. 74, 86.

48. P. Marer *et al.*, *Historically Planned Economics. A Guide to the Data*, Washington DC 1992, p. 257; World Bank, *Hungary*, Washington DC 1995, pp. 1–3; World Bank, *From Plan to Market. World Development Report 1996*, Oxford and New York 1996, p. 26, European Bank for Reconstruction and Development, *Economics of Transition*, vol. 4, no. 1, 1996.

49. EBRD, *Economics of Transition*, Vol. 4, no. 1, 1996, p. 282.

50. Unicef, *Poverty, Children and Policy*, p. 130.

51. Calculated from EBRD, *Economics of Transition*, vol. 4, no. 1, 1996, p. 282, and OECD, *Historical Statistics 1960–1994*, A4.

52. Rudolf Andorka, 'The Development of Poverty During the Transition Process', unpublished manuscript, Budapest University of Economic Sciences 1995, p. 8.

53. Ibid., and supplementary data communicated orally in Budapest, 23 May 1996.

54. World Bank, *From Plan to Market*, p. 70.

55. Ferge *et. al.*, *Social Costs of Transition*, pp. 51–2.

56. A polite and discreet formulation may be found in print: World Bank, *Hungary*, pp. 31ff. Sterner and more assertive versions circulate as 'policy papers' and oral coaching, which I had some opportunity to observe in Budapest in spring 1996, as the incumbent of the European Chair of Social Policy.

Notes on Contributors

Sam Aaronovitch
Professor of Applied Economics at South Bank University. Author of, among other works, *The Insurance Industry in the Countries of the EEC* (1985), and editor of the quarterly journal *Local Economy*.

Perry Anderson
Professor of History at UCLA. His publications include *Lineages of the Absolutist State* (1974) and *A Zone of Engagement* (1992).

Timothy Garton Ash
Fellow of St Antony's College, Oxford. His publications include *The Uses of Adversity: Essays on the Fate of Central Europe* (1989), *In Europe's Name: Germany and the Divided Continent* (1994) and *The File: A Personal History*, forthcoming in summer of 1997.

Jacques Attali
First President of the European Bank for Reconstruction and Development; from 1981 to 1991 Special Adviser to François Mitterrand; now Conseiller d'Etat. His publications include *Millennium: Winners and Losers in the Coming World Order* (1992) and the three-volume *Verbatim* (1993, 1995).

Wynne Godley
Fellow of King's College, Cambridge, and former Director of the Applied Economics Department at Cambridge; member of the econ-

omic advisory panel to the Treasury. Co-author of *Macroeconomics* (1983).

Peter Gowan
Principal Lecturer in European Politics at the University of North London; founder-editor of *Labour Focus on Eastern Europe* and a member of the Editorial Board of *New Left Review*.

John Grahl
Senior Lecturer in Economics at Queen Mary and Westfield College, University of London; has published widely on issues of European integration. His latest book, *After Maastricht*, a study of monetary union, will be published in 1997.

Dieter Grimm
Justice in the German Constitutional Court and Professor of Public Law at the University of Bielefeld. His publications include *Recht und Staat der bürgerlichen Gesellschaft* (1987), *Die Zukunft der Verfassung* (1994) and *Deutsches Verfassungsgeschichte, 1776–1886* (1995).

Jürgen Habermas
Emeritus Professor of Philosophy at the University of Frankfurt. His books include *The Philosophical Discourse of Modernity* (1987), *Postmetaphysical Thinking: Philosophical Thinking* (1992) and *Between Facts and Norms: Contributions to a Discourse Theory of Law and Democracy* (1996).

John Keegan
Defence Editor of the *Daily Telegraph*, and former Senior Lecturer at the Royal Military Academy, Sandhurst. His publications include *The Mask of Command* (1987), *A History of Warfare* (1993) and *The Face of Battle* (1995).

Karl Lamers
Deputy of the Bundestag since 1980, and spokesperson on foreign policy for the CDU. Author of *Suche nach Deutschland: nationale Identität und die Deutschlandpolitik* (1983).

Edward Luttwak
Burke Professor of Strategy at the Center for Strategic and International Studies, Washington DC, and former consultant to the Defense Department, State Department and National Security Council under President Reagan. His publications include *The Grand Strategy of the Roman Empire* (1976) and *The Endangered American Dream* (1993).

Alan S. Milward
Professor of History at the European University Institute, Florence. His publications include *The Reconstruction of Western Europe, 1945–'51* (1987), *The European Rescue of the Nation-State* (1993, with G. Brennan and F. Romero), and *The Frontier of National Sovereignty: History and Thought, 1945–1992* (1995, with R. Ranieri, F. Lynch and F. Romero).

Conor Cruise O'Brien
Pro-Chancellor of the University of Dublin; former Albert Schweitzer Professor at New York University, and Minister of Posts and Telegraph in the Irish Republic. Currently Visiting Fellow Professor at the Fordham Law School in New York. His recent books include *The Great Melody: A Thematic Biography of Edmund Burke (1992), Ancestral Voices: Religion and Nationalism in Ireland* (1994) and *The Long Affair: Thomas Jefferson and the French Revolution* (1996).

Tommaso Padoa-Schioppa
Deputy Director of the Bank of Italy. His publications include *Europe After 1992: Three Essays* (1991) and *The Road to Monetary Union: The Emperor, The Kings, and the Genies* (1994).

J.G.A. Pocock
Emeritus Professor at Johns Hopkins University. His publications include *The Machiavellian Moment: Florentine Political Thought* (1975), *Politics, Language and Time: Essays on Political Thought and History* (1975) and *Virtue, Commerce and History: Essays on Political Thought and History* (1985).

Anthony D. Smith
Professor of Studies in Nationalism at the European Institute, London School of Economics. His publications include *The Ethnic Origins of Nations* (1988), *National Identity* (1993) and *Nations and Nationalism in a Global Era* (1995).

Guy Standing
Director of the ILO's technical programme in Eastern Europe in 1992–94, and its labour market division in 1994–96; adviser to the South African government on labour market reform. He is currently working on a book on the challenge of global labour market flexibility. His most recent publication is *Enterprise Restructuring and Russian Unemployment: Reviving Dead Souls* (1996).

Göran Therborn
Director of the Swedish Collegium for Advanced Study in the Social

Sciences in Uppsala, Sweden, and Professor of Sociology at the University of Göteborg. His publications include *Science, Class and Society* (1976), *Why Some People are More Unemployed than Others* (1986) and *European Modernity and Beyond: the Trajectory of European Societies, 1945–2000* (1995).

William Wallace
Reader in International Relations at the London School of Economics, Professor of International Studies at the Central European University, and Liberal Democrat peer in the House of Lords. His publications include *The Dynamics of European Integration* (1990), *Regional Integration: The West European Experience* (1994) and *Policy-Making in the European Union* (1996, with Helen Wallace *et al.*).

J.H.H. Weiler
Manley Hudson Professor of Law and Jean Monnet Chair at Harvard University. A collection of his essays, entitled *The Constitution of Europe: Do the New Clothes Have an Emperor?*, will appear in autumn 1997.

Abbreviations

CAP	Common Agricultural Policy
CDU	Christian Democratic Union [of Germany]
CGT	Confédération Générale du Travail
CJTF	combined joint task force(s)
Coreper	Committee of Permanent Representatives of Member States
CSCE	Conference on Security and Cooperation in Europe
CSU	Christian Social Union [of Germany]
DM	Deutschmark
EBRD	European Bank for Reconstruction and Development
EC	European Community
ECB	European Central Bank
ECOFIN	Economic and Financial Affairs Committee
ECSC	European Coal and Steel Community
EDC	European Defence Community
EEA	European Economic Area
EEC	European Economic Community
EFTA	European Free Trade Association
EIB	European Investment Bank
EMI	European Monetary Institute
EMS	European Monetary System
EMU	European Monetary Union
ERM	Exchange-Rate Mechanism
ESRC	Economic and Social Research Council
EU	European Union
FAST	Forecasting and Assessment in Science and Technology
FCO	Foreign and Commonwealth Office [of the UK]

FRG	Federal Republic of Germany
GATT	General Agreement of Tariffs and Trade
GDR	German Democratic Republic
IGC	inter-governmental conference
IMF	International Monetary Fund
INF	intermediate-range nuclear forces
JESSI	Joint European Submicron Silicon Initiative
Mercosur	Mercado del sur
MRP	Mouvement Républicain Populaire
NAFTA	North American Free Trade Association
NAIRU	non-accelerating inflation rate of unemployment
OAS	Organization of American States
OAU	Organization of African Unity
OECD	Organization for Economic Cooperation and Development
OEEC	Organization of European Economic Cooperation
OPEC	Organization of the Petroleum Exporting Countries
OSCE	Organization for Security and Cooperation in Europe
SFIO	Section Française de l'Internationale Ouvrière
WEU	Western European Union

Acknowledgements

'The Springs of Integration', by Alan S. Milward, was first published as 'Allegiance. The Past and the Future', in the *Journal of European Integration History*, vol. 1, no. 1, 1995.

'Rescue or Retreat? The Nation-State in Western Europe, 1945–93', by William Wallace, was first published in *Political Studies* 42, 1994 with permission from Blackwell Publishers, Oxford and Cambridge, MA on behalf of the Political Studies Association.

'Under the Sign of the Interim', by Perry Anderson, was first published in the *London Review of Books* on 4 January 1996.

'Pursuing a Chimera', by Conor Cruise O'Brien, was first published in the *Times Literary Supplement* on 13 March 1992, as part of a Special Survey, 'The Frontiers of Europe'.

'From Albert Speer to Jacques Delors', by John Keegan, was first published in the *Spectator* on 15 August 1992.

'Strengthening the Hard Core', by Karl Lamers, was first published as 'Reflections on European Policy' by the CDU/CSU parliamentary group in the Bundestag on 7 September 1994; 'Europe/Documents, no 1896/96', © Agence Europe.

'Catching the Wrong Bus?', by Timothy Garton Ash, was first published in the *Times Literary Supplement* on 5 May 1995.

'The Europe to Come', by Perry Anderson, was first published in the *London Review of Books* on 26 January 1996.

'The Social Bases of Monetary Union?', by Alan S. Milward, was published as 'Approaching Reality: Euro-money and the Left', in *New Left Review* 216, March/April 1996.

'Engineering the Single Currency, by Tommaso Padoa-Schioppa, was first published as the 'Introduction' to *L'Europea verso l'unione monetaria*, Einaudi, Turin 1992.

'The Hole in the Treaty', by Wynne Godley, was first published as 'Maastricht and All That' in the *London Review of Books* on 8 October 1992.

'Building on Maastricht', by Sam Aaronovitch and John Grahl, of the South Bank University and Queen Mary College, University of London, was originally given as a paper at a workshop on 'Alternative Economic Policy in Europe', held in Brussels on 27–29 September 1996.

'Central Bankism', by Edward Luttwak, was first published in the *London Review of Books* on 14 November 1996.

'Does Europe Need a Constitution?', by Dieter Grimm, was first published in the *European Law Journal*, vol. 1, no. 3, November 1995; © Blackwell Publishers Ltd, Oxford and Cambridge, MA.

'Reply to Grimm', by Jürgen Habermas, was first published as 'Remarks on Dieter Grimm's "Does Europe Need a Constitution?"', in the *European Law Journal*, vol. 1, no. 3, November 1995; © Blackwell Publishers Ltd, Oxford and Cambridge, MA.

'Demos, Telos, Ethos and the Maastricht Decision', by J.H.H. Weiler, was first published as 'Does Europe Need a Constitution? Reflections on Demos, Telos and Ethos in the German Maastricht Decision', in the *European Law Journal*, vol. 1, no. 3, November 1995; © Blackwell Publishers Ltd, Oxford and Cambridge, MA.

'Deconstructing Europe', by J.G.A. Pocock, was first published in the *London Review of Books* on 19 December 1991.

'National Identity and the Idea of European Unity', by Anthony D. Smith, was prepared for a seminar series on 'Europe in the 1990s: Forces for Change', held at the Royal Institute of International Affairs, London, in 1991. It was first published as 'National Identity and the Idea of European Unity' in *International Affairs*, vol. 68, no. 1, 1992.

'A Continental Architecture', by Jacques Attali, was first published in *Europe(s)*, Fayard, Paris 1994.

Index